rld.

plete

es.

THE APOCALYPSE.

A SERIES OF SPECIAL LECTURES

ON THE

REVELATION OF JESUS CHRIST.

WITH

REVISED TEXT.

BY J. A. SEISS, D.D.,

AUTHOR OF "LAST TIMES," "LECTURES ON THE GOSPELS," "VOICES FROM
BABYLON," "A MIRACLE IN STONE," ETC., ETC.

VOL. III.

TENTH EDITION.
(CONSISTING OF 5000 SETS.)

CHARLES C. COOK,
150 NASSAU STREET,
NEW YORK, N. Y.
1909.

PREFACE TO VOL. III.

PORTIONS of this course of Lectures have been so long before the public, and the character of the work has thereby become so familiar to those interested in it, that there can hardly be need for further prefatory explanations in sending forth this concluding volume, particularly after what has been said in the prefaces to the preceding volumes, and in the Lectures themselves. It might be of interest to tell how the author was led to see and embrace the view of the Apocalypse which he holds; but as that is so personal, and is not likely to contribute to any better understanding of what he has written, the omission may readily be excused. Suffice it to say, that so heavy an undertaking, and the travelling of a road so laborious and long, has not been without very strong convictions very impressively and unexpectedly begotten, and that the work was begun and has been pursued under a somewhat peculiar stress. By the goodness of that God from whose providence that urgency came, and in despite of all discouragements, hindrances, interruptions, and delays, the original purpose has been carried through to completion. And if what has now been produced shall serve to clear and edify the minds of

others to the extent that these studies have served to instruct and satisfy the writer on a profoundly important
but much-abused and much-misunderstood subject, ample
will be the reason to thank God that the labor was begun,
and that strength was given to finish it.

Request has been made that this concluding volume
be accompanied with a chart, or table, to exhibit to the
eye, in one view, the several parts of these Apocalyptic
presentations, and their relations to each other in the order
of events as they are to occur. Something of such a
chart has therefore been placed at the beginning of this
volume. Though full justice can hardly be done to the
subject in that way, a brief statement of the periods
and events in their general outlines, as they are contemplated in this wonderful prophecy, is thus furnished,
and may help the reader to a clearer conception of the
matter, as it lies in the apprehension of the author, and
is elaborated in these Lectures.

First of all is *the present Church Period,* stretching
from the days of the Apostle to the beginning of the great
Judgment time. To this Period belongs the first vision,
including the judgments or sentences of the Lord Jesus
upon the Churches, which are contained in the Seven
Epistles. This Period ends with that impending incipient
stage of Christ's coming, invisible to the world at large,
for the taking of those of his saints who are waiting and
ready, according to Luke 17 : 34–37. When that coming will take place no man knoweth, and for it, as liable
to occur at any moment, and as the very next prophetic

event in the order of time, all Christians are now and continually to be in waiting expectation and readiness. It is this particular event that marks the ending of the present dispensation, and the beginning of the great Judgment Period; for "judgment must begin at the house of God." (1 Pet. 4 : 17.) The occurrence of it is indicated in the Apocalypse in the beginning of the fourth chapter, where the Seer beholds a door opened in the heaven, and hears the trumpet voice calling him up thither.

Then comes *the great Judgment Period*, extending from this stealthy ereption of the ready and waiting saints to the forthcoming of the Sitter on the white horse, with all the glorified saint-armies, for the destruction of the powers confederated against the Lamb in the battle of the great Day. This Period embraces all the events connected with the breaking of the seven Seals, the sounding of the seven Trumpets, and the pouring out of the seven Bowls of wrath, as described from the fourth to the end of the nineteenth chapters. The length of time covered by this Period is at least forty years, most likely seventy years, if not more. It involves a material change or modification in the dispensation. The Throne set in the heaven, with which the Living Ones and the Elders are connected, as described in chapters four and five, presents the peculiar arrangement or organization of the celestial economy by which the administrations during this Period are to be conducted. The events embraced are largely extraordinary, miraculous, varied, and complex. They

are partly punitive, and partly gracious, for in wrath
God remembers mercy. The termination or consummation of this Period is the visible manifestation of Christ,
with the completed body of his glorified saints, for the
destruction of Antichrist and his armies, and the binding
and confinement of Satan.

Then comes *the great Millennial Period*, the thousand
years during which Satan is bound. It dates from the
destruction of the Antichrist and his enemies. It involves a still further change or modification of the dispensation. Its special marks are: the absence of Satan's
deceits and machinations, the supplanting of all human
governments by the direct heavenly rule and dominion
of Christ and his glorified saints, and that new order
called the shepherdizing of the nations with a rod of iron,
or the irresistible enforcement of the principles of righteousness in all things, by which the whole living world
shall then be reduced to order and obedience to truth
and right. It is the following up of the victory of the
battle of the great Day, resulting in the enthronement
of all the glorified saints with their Lord in the invincible rulership of the world, which rule never terminates,
but finally opens out into an eternal reign over the redeemed and renewed earth. That which more particularly marks the termination of this Period is, the loosing
of Satan for a brief space, his leading astray of certain
remote peoples who think to throw off the dominion
of Christ and his glorified saints, the quick destruction
of these rebels by fire from heaven, the consignment of

Satan to his final perdition, the recall of all the unsanctified dead before the great white throne for their final sentence, and the complete and everlasting erasure of all sin, all death, and all curse from the face of the earth.

Then comes *the Eternal State*, in immediate succession to the thousand years. It begins with the completion of the new heavens and earth, the coming of the heavenly Jerusalem into its place, and the final establishment of Christ and his glorified ones in their everlasting dominion over the redeemed world and its populations. Thenceforward everything proceeds in undisturbed and everaugmenting blessedness, world without end.

Such, in brief, is the Course of Time, and the progress and outcome of the great administrations of our God, as set forth in his Word, mapped out in the foreshowings beheld and recorded by the aged Apostle John,—the outline sketch of God's revealed Plan of Grace, Judgment, and Redemption, sought to be traced and exhibited in detail in these Lectures.

And now, earnestly praying the Divine Blessing upon what has been written, and upon all who read the same, the author devoutly commits the results of his labors to the care and direction of that good and wise Providence which has enabled him to complete the work, and to the serious attention of all who take pleasure in learning about what must shortly come to pass.

PHILADELPHIA, May, 1880.

CONTENTS OF VOL. III.

(ix)

LECTURE FORTY-NINTH.

CHAP. 21 : 9–27.

LECTURE FIFTIETH.

CHAP. 22 : 1–5.

LECTURE FIFTY-FIRST.

CHAP. 22 : 6–15.

LECTURE FIFTY-SECOND.

CHAP. 22 : 16–21.

LECTURE THIRTY-FOURTH.

THE 144,000—THOSE WHO MAINTAIN THE CONFESSION OF CHRIST
OVER AGAINST THE WORSHIPPERS OF THE BEAST—THE SAME
SEALED ONES OF CHAPTER SEVEN—THEIR CHIEF CHARAC-
TERISTICS—THEIR PECULIAR REWARD—THE FOUR ANGEL-
MESSAGES.

REV. 14 : 1-13. (Revised Text.) And I saw, and behold, the Lamb
standing on the mount Sion, and with Him an 144,000, having His
name and His Father's name written on their foreheads.

And I heard a sound out of the heaven as a sound of many waters,
and as a sound of great thunder : and the sound which I heard
[was] as of harp-singers harping with their harps. And they sung a
new song in the presence of the throne, and in the presence of the four
Living Ones and the Elders : and no one was able to learn the song but
the 144,000 who have been redeemed from the earth.   These are they
who were not defiled with women, for they are virgins; these [are] they
who follow the Lamb whithersoever He goeth; these were redeemed
from men, a first-fruit to God and to the Lamb; and in their mouth
was not found what is false ; they are blameless.

And I saw another angel flying in mid-heaven, having a Gospel
everlasting to preach to [*upon* or *over*] those who dwell upon the earth
and to [*upon* or *over*] every nation, and tribe, and tongue, and people,
saying with a great voice, Fear God and give to Him glory, because
the hour of His judgment is come : and worship Him who made the
heaven, and the earth, and the sea and fountains of waters.

And there followed another, a second angel, saying, Fallen, fallen,
the great Babylon, which hath made all the nations drink from the
wine of the wrath of her fornication.

And there followed them another angel, a third, saying with a great
voice, If any one worship the beast and his image, and receive [the]
mark on his forehead, or on his hand, even he shall drink of the wine
of the wrath of God, which is mingled without dilution in the cup of
His anger, and shall be tormented with fire and brimstone in the pres-

ence of the angels and in the presence of the Lamb : and the smoke of
their torment goeth up to the ages of ages ; and they have no rest day
or night, who worship the beast and his image, and whosoever re-
ceiveth the mark of his name.

Here is the patience of the saints who keep the commandments of
God and the faith of Jesus. And I heard a voice out of the heaven
saying, Write, Blessed are the dead who die in the Lord from henceforth : Yea, saith the Spirit, that they [may, in that they] shall rest
out of their labors ; for their works follow with them.

THE blackest storms often give place to the
loveliest sunsets. The winds and thunders
exhaust themselves. The clouds empty and break.
And from the calm heavens behind them comes a
golden light, girthing the remaining fragments of
gloom with chains of brightness, and overarching
with the bow of promise the path along which the
terrible tempest has just passed. Like this evening glory after the summer's gust, is the chapter
on which we now enter. We have seen the coming of the Antichrist in all the frowning blackness
of Satan's angry malice, and have shuddered at the
awful shadow, distress, and darkness which he casts
upon the world. We have seen what havoc he
makes with human peace, and the base humiliation
he brings upon the proud oaks and lofty cedars of
the mountains of human conceit and self-will. We
have felt the sickening shock of horror at the contemplation of his hellish power, his blasphemies,
and his unparalleled tyranny. We have gazed
upon the progress of the most disastrous storm
hell's malignant wisdom can devise, or that is ever
allowed to afflict our race. We have watched the
thickening blackness of darkness amid which the

indignation of God is poured upon the intoxicated nations which will not have Christ to rule over them. But now the scene begins to change. The reign of terror cannot last. God's merciful goodness cannot allow it long. The earth would dissolve under it if those days were not shortened, but for the elect's sake they are shortened. Three and a half years is the fulness of their duration. In heaven's count the tempest holds but for an "hour." And here already we begin to see the light breaking in from behind the clouds and darkness. Further details of what is to befall these terrible Beasts, their systems and their followers, remain to be looked at; but the golden rays begin to show themselves. Where perdition has been holding grand jubilee of destruction, appear the symptoms of a better order. The still lingering gloom begins to show some gilding of its edges. And over the pathway of "the abomination of desolation" are seen the forming outlines of the arch of beauty, hope, and peace. In place of the horrid Beasts, the Lamb comes into view. In place of the blaspheming herd, the redeemed appear, with the name of the Father and the Son upon their shining brows. Voices from heaven, intoned with mighty joy, and attuned to golden harps, are heard in song,—"new song," fit to be sung before the throne and all the celestial company. A first-fruit of a new beginning is waved before God. Successive angels cleave the air on outspread wing proclaiming messages of hope and patience to the faithful sufferers, and telling of the nearing deliv-

erance. And the whole picture begins to look to
the effectual and everlasting sweeping away of the
horrible nightmare of a distressed and helpless
world. The Holy Spirit of the Father and the
Son assist us to a right understanding of what it
all means!

I. *Who are these* 144,000? Some answer, they
are representatively the true people of God of all
ages—the symbol of the whole body of the sanctified and saved. Others say, they are the choice
spirits of the congregation of the glorified, selected
and honored above all common Christians because
of their pre-eminent qualities and abstinences on
earth. Others tell us, they are the company of
those who have remained true in faith under the
errors and falsities of the Papacy. And still others
say, they are none else than the assembly of the
noble spirits who achieved the Reformation of the
sixteenth century, and that their harp-notes and
new song is "the harmony of the Reformed Confessions!" I see not how it is possible for either
of these interpretations to stand. Without entering upon the many points in which they severally
fail to conform to the record, I may say, they all
do violence to the consecutiveness and self-con-
sistency of this Book, and defy all legitimate dealing with the particulars of the sacred description.
We must find a better meaning, or give in that it
is impossible to do anything more than *guess* at
what the Lord intended to show us, whilst one
guess is just as good and reliable as another. But

God's Word is truth; and therefore there must be truth in this presentation,—truth which will hold together with the rest of the Book, with the dignity of a divine prophecy so solemnly given, and with the grammatical sense of the words in which the account is presented. Nor do I know why candid and earnest men, but for their arbitrary and stilted theories, should be at a loss for an interpretation answering to the requirements. Let us look at the matter carefully, and see.

A considerate glance at the particulars of this vision will at once discover a direct and strong contrast having special relation to what went before in the preceding chapter. The account of the 144,000 is really only another side of what is related of the Beasts, the counterpart of the same history. Over against the wild and savage monster is a gentle and loving Lamb. Over against the confessors and worshippers of the Beast, having his mark, is the company of the Lamb's followers, having their mark, even the name of the Father and the Son written in their foreheads. Over against the Beast's moral system, which is nothing but harlotry, spiritual and literal, the worship of idols and the trampling under foot of all God's institutes, here is an opposing style of life and conformity—a virgin purity which refuses to be debauched by the prevailing fornication. Over against the slavery of those who sell themselves to the powers of perdition which then have command of the world, here is redemption from

the earth and from man, a ransom out of the
thraldom which holds others. Over against the
new order of things set up by the Antichrist, these
sing "a new song,"—a victory and glory never
shared by any but them. Over against the going
of the Beasts and their dupes into perdition, there
is here a going whithersoever the Lamb goeth.
Over against the doings in the presence of the
Beast, under his patronage and authority, the
doings here are in the presence of the Throne,
and in the presence of the Living Ones and Elders, under the approval and counsels of Heaven.
Everything in the mouth of the Beasts and all
theirs, is *pseudos*, false, a lie; the special characteristic of these is, that nothing *pseudos*, false, or a
lie is found in their mouth. The Beast's number,
and that by which he marks and numbers all his,
is six sixes, the bad number intensified; the number and numbering here is by twelves, the sacred
number of completeness. And in every item there
is distinct allusion to things under the Beast, by
way of contrast and opposition, proving that the
account of these 144,000 is a counter-part of the
same history, which can properly apply to none
but persons who live contemporaneous with the
Beast, and maintain themselves by divine grace in
a course of life and profession over against him.

But this is not the first time we hear of this
144,000. Chapter seven told us of a body of
people consisting of this precise number, of which
we can hardly suppose two, unless specially instructed to that effect. The fact urged by some

that the company here is not introduced as "*the* 144,000," presents no grammatical reason for considering them distinct from the 144,000 there, as the best of Greek scholars agree. The insertion of the article is needless where the identification is otherwise so clear, and would only tend to fix the emphasis at the wrong place. Nor could the article, if inserted, make the indications of identity any stronger than they are. This company is not so important as to call for the same sort of designation as when reference is made to "The Lamb," "The Living Ones," "The Elders," etc. The number in Chapter VII is the same with the number here, — a number so remarkable and unique, that we must have very clear reasons for supposing that it does not refer to the same parties in both instances; but no such reasons appear. There the 144,000 are presented as a select and special class of God's servants, chosen, marked, and set apart as none else, sealed by an angel with the seal of the living God. So with the 144,000 here there is a special and peculiar isolation from all other classes of the saved. They are distinct from the Living Ones, from the Elders, and from the multitude which no man can number; and they are so unique and separate in their history, experience, and reward, that no one is able to learn or sing the song which they sing. Those in Chapter VII were marked in their forehead with the seal of the living God; these have that mark, even "the Lamb's name and His Father's name written on their foreheads." Those were all He-

brews, chosen from the several tribes of undivided
Israel; and so it would seem to be with these.
They have on their foreheads the name of *the
Father*, which is the Jewish mark. They also
have their place *on Mount Zion*, which though it
may not mean the earthly hill, still connects with
the seat of the palace and throne of David, Solomon, and all the Jewish kings. Those sealed
ones were to be supernaturally protected and preserved amid the plagues that followed; and these
appear as persons marvellously kept and sustained
under the consummation of those plagues, the
Antichrist. The history of the 144,000 in Chapter
VII is incomplete taken by itself. No object or
outcome of that sealing is anywhere stated, if not
to be found in the passage before us. The position
these sealed ones were to hold, the relations they
were to occupy as the specially chosen of their
time, are all left untold if not told in this chapter.
Neither can we find adequate reason for the mention at all of that special sealing without some
such continuation of the history as given here. I
accordingly conclude with entire confidence, that
the 144,000 on Mount Zion are the identical
144,000 sealed ones spoken of in Chapter VII,
with only this difference, that there we see them
in their earthly relations and peculiar consecration; and here we see them with their earthly
career finished, and in the enjoyment of the heavenly award for their faithfulness.

And this fixes what must condition the whole
interpretation of this Book, to wit, that from the

opening of the sixth seal until after the sounding of the seventh trumpet, the third woe, and the revelation of the Man of sin, no more time elapses than the ordinary length of a human life; for those who are already mature men, and capable of a sacred setting apart as witnesses for God when the sixth seal is broken, are still living and active under the reign of the Antichrist. Alas, what a world of learned labor thus falls to the ground!

II. *What are the chief marks or characteristics of these* 144,000? The first and foremost is that of a true and conspicuous confession. They have the name of the Lamb and the name of His Father written on their foreheads. This is their public mark as against the mark of the worshippers of the Beast. There is nothing more honorable in God's sight than truth and faithfulness of confession. " With the mouth confession is made unto salvation." (Rom. 10 : 10.) The confession of these people is in opposition to the unbelieving Jew, who rejects and repudiates the Son; and in opposition to the Antichrist, who denies both the Father and the Son. As children of Abraham, they have embraced Christianity; and as Christians, they take issue with the Beast, and persist in testifying against his blasphemous usurpations of the place of God and the only Saviour.

Another particular is their unworldliness. Whilst most people in their day " dwell upon the earth," sit down upon it as their rest and choice, derive their chief comfort from it, these are " redeemed

from the earth,"—withdrawn from it, bought away
by the heavenly promises and the divine grace to
live above it, independent of it, as no longer a
part of it.   Also is it said that they are "redeemed
from men,"—segregated entirely from the common course of the world, and removed from the
ordinary fellowship of men.   Less than this the
language concerning them can scarcely mean.
They are quite severed from the world in heart
and life.

A third point is their pureness.   We are not to
suppose with some that these 144,000 are all males
who have never been married; for there is no
more impurity in marriage than in abstinence
from marriage.   Celibacy is not the subject or
virtue in this description, but *purity*, freedom from
contamination by the corruptions which prevail in
their time.   The reign of the Antichrist is the
reign of harlotry, both literal and spiritual.   It is
a time when chaste marriage is no more regarded
than the worship of the true God.   But from all
such defilements these people have kept themselves unspotted.   "They are virgins," in that
they have lived chaste lives, both as to their faithfulness to God in their religion, and as to their
pureness from all bodily lewdness.   The kingdom
of heaven is likened to "ten virgins."   The object
of Paul's ministry to the Corinthians was, that he
might present them "as a chaste virgin to Christ."
And this is the sort of virginity attained and maintained by these people.

A further quality is their truthfulness.   "In

their mouth was not found what is false." There is a peculiar depth in John's conception of truth and its opposite falsehood. Any one who fails to confess Christ in all the length and breadth of His nature and offices, any one who fails to live his profession or to show by his works what he speaks with his lips, is to him a liar. The meaning here has the same deep significance. It is a great thing for people to be careful about their conversation, always conforming their words to the reality of things. To speak falsehood, to exercise a deceitful and untrustworthy tongue, is a devilish thing; for Satan is a liar and the father of lies. These people were truthful in these respects, but had also a higher and profounder truthfulness. The times in which they live are the times of hell's worst lies,—times when the whole world has gone mad over lies,—times when the entire order of society is a lie,—times when men's religion is a lie,—times when their very god is a lie,—times when everything is pryed away from the foundation of truth by the dreadful leverage which perdition then possesses. And it is over against all this that nothing false is found in their mouth. They have the true faith; they hold to it with a true heart; they exemplify it by a true manner of life. They are the children of truth in the midst of a world of untruth.

III. *What, then, is their Reward?* Taking the last particular first, they stand approved, justified, and accepted before God. " They are blameless."

The added words, " before the throne of God," are
not in the best manuscripts, and are dropped now
by common consent as no part of the original.
They make no difference in the sense, for the
blamelessness of these people must needs be a
blamelessness before the throne; but if the phrase
be emphasized it might suggest a connection with
the throne which does not here exist. It is to be
observed that these 144,000 are by no means the
highest class of saints, as some have erroneously
supposed. They do not come into the congregation of the saved until after the highest orders of
the saints have been caught up to God and to His
throne. The Living Ones are saints from the
earth, for they sing the song of redemption by the
blood of Christ. So also are the Elders. But
these are already in their heavenly glory wearing
the crowns which Christ will give at that day,
even before these people are sealed. These 144,000
sing their song *in the presence of* the Living Ones
and the gold-crowned Elders; this expresses a
lesser dignity. Neither is there a word said about
crowns for them. They sing in the presence of
the throne, but they are not connected with it, as
the Living Ones, nor seated on associated thrones,
as the Elders. They are not therefore of the highest orders of the saved and glorified. There are
many mansions in the Father's house, many degrees in glory, and many ranks of saints as well
as of angels. There is such a thing as being saved
with loss, such a thing as missing our crowns even
though we may get to heaven. There are also

many "*virgins*," real virgins, who go and buy, and come at length with deficiencies repaired, but are in readiness too late to be admitted to the place and honor of the queen. These 144,000 are virgins; they come to glorious honor through their confession, purity, and devotion; but they come in at a period when the Bride is already made up, and cannot be of the first and highest order of the glorified. But still, they are approved and justified before God, which is in itself a great, high, and glorious attainment. To stand before God approved and blameless from the midst of a condemned world,—a world given over to the powers of perdition by reason of its unbelief and sins,—a world which has become the theatre of all the consummated wickedness of the ages,—a world in which it is death to wear any badge or adhere to any profession contrary to the mark of the Antichrist, is an achievement of grace and faithfulness in which there may well be mighty exultation.

In the next place, they have a song which is peculiarly and exclusively their own. Though not connected with the throne, as the Living Ones, nor crowned and seated as the Elders, they have a ground and subject of joy and praise which neither the Living Ones nor the Elders have; nor is any one able to enter into that song except the 144,000. None others ever fulfil just such a mission, as none others are ever sealed with the seal of the living God in the same way in which they were sealed. None others ever have just such an experience, in such a world as that through which they come to glory. None others share with them in that particular administration of God which brings them away from the earth and men to their place on Mount Zion. Therefore, as angels cannot sing the song of the redeemed, never having been the subjects of redemption, so no other saints can sing the peculiar song of this 144,000. They have a distinction and glory, a joy and blessedness, after all, in which none but themselves can ever share.

They stand with the Lamb on Mount Zion. To be *with the Lamb*, as over against being with the Beast, is a perfection of blessing which no language can describe. It is redemption. It is victory. It is eternal security and glory. To be with the Lamb *on Mount Zion* is a more special position and relation. It respects Jerusalem and the throne of David. It will not meet the case to take Mount Zion here as simply "the heavenly Jerusalem;" for that is not so distinctively the standing-place or point of occupation of these 144,000. It must take in some new and exalted order touching the earthly Jerusalem, the Jewish nationality, and that throne and Kingdom of David everywhere promised to be rebuilt and restored, never to fail any more. The scene thus looks over into the new earth, to that time when "the ransomed of the Lord shall return, and come to Zion with songs and everlasting joy upon their heads, and shall obtain joy and gladness, and sorrow and sighing shall flee away" (Is. 35 : 10),—to that time when "they shall call Jerusalem the throne of the Lord, and all the nations shall be gathered unto it, to the name of the Lord, to Jerusalem" (Jer. 3:17),—to that time when "the

Lord of Hosts shall reign in Mount Zion, and in Jerusalem, and before His ancients gloriously" (Is. 24: 23). Glorious things are spoken of Jerusalem which have never yet been fulfilled. On His holy hill of Zion God hath said that He will set up His King, even His Son, who shall rule all the nations (Ps. 2). The Lamb is yet to take possession of the city where He was crucified, there to fulfil what was written in Hebrew, Greek, and Latin over His head when He died. And when that once comes to pass, these 144,000 are with Him, His near and particular associates in that particular relation and administration.

They are " a first-fruit to God and to the Lamb," not the first-fruit of all the saved, for the Living Ones and the Elders are in heavenly place and glory above and before them; but a first-fruit of another and particular harvest; the first-fruit from the Jewish field, in that new beginning with the Israelitish people for their fathers' sakes, which is to follow the ending of the present "times of the Gentiles." What the Living Ones and Elders are to the Church universal, these 144,000 are to the recovered, restored and redeemed children of Abraham, in that new order which is to come when the times of the Gentiles are fulfilled. They are all Jews. They are brought to the confession of Christ, and sealed in their foreheads with the name of both the Father and the Son, during the time that the rest of their blood-kin are covenanting with and honoring the Antichrist as Messiah. They are the particular witnesses for the Father and the Son during those darkest days of Jacob's trouble. And they take the first rank with Christ in His special relations and administrations in the final redemption of the Hebrew race. For this they were extraordinarily sealed, and this is the reward of their faithfulness as against the lies and infamies of the Beast. Hence, also, it pertains to their honor and blessedness to attend the Lamb whithersoever He goeth. They are His heavenly suite and train in all His reign on Mount Zion.

IV. *What, now, of the Angel-Messages?* When Christ made His last entry into Jerusalem, and fault was found with the loud proclamations which were ringing to His praise as the Messiah-King, He answered: "If these should hold their peace, *the stones* would immediately cry out." The truth of God and His claims *must* be spoken. If men are silent, other things must become vocal to testify for Jehovah. And when Antichrist succeeds in hushing up, or burying away in caves, mountains, and wildernesses all testimony for the Eternal One whom he seeks to abolish, the heavens speak, and the angels whom he cannot touch or slay become the preachers. Mid-heaven is their pulpit, and all nations, tribes, tongues, and peoples are their auditors. Hell may slay, imprison, and silence every human witness for God, but cannot chain the proclamation of His truth. God's word cannot be bound. It liveth and abideth forever. It must be heard.

The First Message.—That an Angel is the preacher
here, is proof positive that the present dispensation is then past and changed. Of old, Angels
were employed for the giving of the Law, and in
the Judgment time they are everywhere represented as again taking very conspicuous part in
the divine administrations with regard to our
world; but in the dispensation under which we
now are, the charge of preaching and witnessing
for God and the declaring of His Word, is the peculiar office of the Church. It is a calling and
office committed to men, to the chosen of our
human race. Angels are ministers to the heirs
of salvation, but not in the sense of being the
appointed public proclaimers and preachers of the
Gospel. That is man's work, and man's peculiar
honor, as things now are constituted. But here
Angels are the preachers, with three or four distinct messages: one "having a Gospel everlasting;" one proclaiming the doom of Babylon; and
one denouncing eternal damnation upon every
worshipper of the Beast, or wearer of his mark.
Of course, then, we have here another dispensation, a different order of things from that which
now obtains. The same is also intimated in the
features of the Word preached. It is no longer
the meek and entreating voice, beseeching men to
be reconciled to God, but a great thunder from
the sky, demanding of the nations to Fear *the God*,
as over against the false god whom they were
adoring,—to Give glory to *Him*, instead of the infamous Beast whom they were glorifying,—to

Worship *the Maker* of all things, as against the worship of him who can do no more than play his hellish tricks with the things that are made; and all this *on the instant*, for the reason that "the hour of judgment *is come*."

Paul once said, if an angel from heaven preach unto you any other Gospel than that ye have received, let him be accursed. And when he so said, he spoke the very truth of God; but it is the truth with special reference to the present dispensation, till the Church-period has come to its end in the day of judgment; for here, when "the judgment *is come*," an angel from heaven preaches, and what he preaches is not "*the* everlasting Gospel" as the English version is, but "*a* Gospel everlasting." It is not indeed "another Gospel," for it is in inner substance the same old and everlasting Gospel, but now in the dress and features of a new order of things—the Gospel as its contents shape themselves in its address to the nations when "the hour of judgment is come," and the great final administrations are in hand.

Luther once said that he did not like this Book, because its spirit did not agree with his feelings as to the Gospel. He was right as to the fact. His great soul, permeated through and through with the very life and spirit of reconciliation in Christ Jesus as now preached to men, felt that here is something different, just as the Christian heart is disturbed by the imprecatory Psalms. But when we locate the matter rightly, and learn that here the Church-period has given place to

the presence and ongoing of the day and hour of
judgment, the whole matter clears up. Mercy
towards the poor infatuated world still lingers in
the very hour of wrath. In the heat and height
of his indignation God still remembers it. Hence
still something of a Gospel message sounds. And
when there is no more voice on earth to speak it,
an angel from heaven, uttering himself from the
sky, proclaims to the guilty nations where they
are, what has come, and what immediate revolution is needed, if they would not sink at once to
everlasting destruction. It is *Gospel*, but it is the
Gospel in the form it takes when the hour of judgment has set in. It is one of the very last calls
of grace to an apostate world.

The Second Message.—With the hour of judgment comes the work of judgment. A colossal
system of harlotry and corruption holds dominion
over the nations. There is no country, no people,
but is won to it, and intoxicated by it, and induced
to cast off all the bonds of sacredness for the infamous delusions of the Antichrist and his false
prophet. God has allowed it for the punishment
of those who would not have Christ for their
Lord, but now He will not allow it longer. Therefore another Angel comes with the proclamation:
" *Fallen, fallen, the great Babylon, which hath made
all the nations drink from the wine of the wrath of her
fornication.*" The announcement is by anticipation as on the very eve of accomplishment, and as
surely now to be fulfilled. The particulars are

given in the seventeenth and eighteenth chapters. There also the explanation of the object of this announcement is given. It is mercy still struggling in the toils of judgment, if that by any means some may yet be snatched from the opening jaws of hell; for there the further word is, "Come out of her, my people, that ye may have no fellowship with her sins, and that ye receive not of her plagues."

The Third Message. — And for the still more potent enforcement of this call a third Angel appears, preaching and crying with a great voice, that whosoever is found worshipping the Beast and his image, or has the Beast's mark on his forehead or on his hand, even he shall drink of the wine of the wrath of God which is mingled without dilution in the cup of His anger, and shall be tormented with fire and brimstone in the presence of the angels and in the presence of the Lamb, and the smoke of their torment ascends to the ages of ages, and they have no rest day and night! It is an awful commination; but these are times of awful guilt, infatuation, and wickedness. And when men are in such dangers, marching direct into the mouth of such a terrible perdition, it is a great mercy in God to make proclamation of it with all the force of an Angel's eloquence. The same is also for the wronged and suffering ones who feel the power of these terrible oppressors. It tells them how their awful griefs shall be avenged on their hellish persecutors. So, therefore, with mighty energy the Angel proclaims the eternal doom of the abettors of the Antichrist.

There be those who mock and jeer at the idea of an eternal hell for the wicked. Many are the jests they perpetrate at the expense of these preachers of fire and brimstone. But here a great and mighty Angel from heaven is the preacher, and his sermon from beginning to end is nothing but fire and brimstone, even everlasting burning and torment for all who take the mark of Antichrist! Shall we believe our modern sentimental philosophers, or abide by the word of our God and of his holy angels? Alas, alas, for the infatuated people who comfort themselves with the belief that perdition is a myth—the bugbear of antiquated superstition!

The Fourth Message.—There is no suffering for any class of God's people in any age, like the sufferings of those who remain faithful to God during the reign of the Antichrist. Here, at this particular time and juncture, is the patience or endurance of them that keep the commandments of God and the faith of Jesus. To come out of Babylon, and to stand aloof from its horrible harlotries, is a costly thing. It is equivalent to a voluntary coming forward to the state-block to have their heads chopped off. Therefore there is another proclamation from heaven for their special strengthening and consolation. Whether this word is also from an Angel we are not told; but it is a message from glory and from God. And it is a sweet and blessed message. It is a message which John is specially commanded to write, that it may be in the minds and hearts of God's people of every age, and take away all fear from those who in this evil time are called to lay down their lives because they will not worship Antichrist. That message is : " *Blessed are the dead who die in the Lord from henceforth : Yea, saith the Spirit, that they may, in that they shall, rest out of their labors, for their works follow with them.*" This is true of all the saints of all ages, but it is pre-eminently and specially true of those who at this time lose their lives for their faithful obedience. It may look like calamity, but in comparison with the miseries of a life of faith under such a hellish despot, it is a blessedness. Death to a good man at any time is a greater beatitude than a disaster; and when a life of truth and honor becomes so great a sorrow as at this time, it is a blessedness to have it ended. The implication is, that from this point on till death itself is vanquished, there is no more peace or comfort for a good man on earth, and therefore that no better thing can happen him than to die. When there is no more peace for us but in death, why should we wish to live? When all hope for earth has faded out, why should we desire to remain in it? When to open our mouths for Christ, or to bow the knee or speak a prayer to the God that made us, exposes to indignity and torture, why not welcome death, and account it good fortune to have the chance for such a release ? *Rest* —*Rest!* What would not those dupes of Antichrist finally give for *Rest!* But what they can never have, they that die in the Lord get through death. Like the worn mariner wearied out with his long and painful endurance of the tempests, dangers, and hardships of the sea, enters the calm port for which he steered so hard;—like the soldier, scarred, mutilated, and sick of the miseries of deadly conflict, comes back from the field of blood to repose in the peace and security of his happy home;—so do they rest out of their labors. And their works follow with them. The very hardships past make the peace the sweeter. Not a word of faithful testimony, not a tear of sympathy, not a sigh of prayer, not a gift of a cup of water in a disciple's name, shall fail in its contribution to the blessedness. Therefore it is written: "Blessed are the dead who die in the Lord from henceforth." And when violence, cruelty, and slaughter are the consequence of a life of truth and purity, the sooner it is over the greater the beatitude.

Here, then, is the comfort of the saints. Whatever they suffer, their peace is sure. Unable to live, death is their blessedness. Heaven speaks it. The Spirit confirms it. The apostles of God have written it. And from it springs a consolation—

> Which monarchs cannot grant, nor all the powers
> Of earth and hell confederate take away;—
> A liberty which persecution, fraud,
> Oppression, prisons, have no power to bind.

LECTURE THIRTY-FIFTH.

Rev. 14 : 14–16. (Revised Text.) And I saw and behold a white
cloud, and upon the cloud is seated one like a son of man, having on
his head a crown of gold, and in his hand a sharp sickle. And another
angel came out of the temple, crying with a great voice to him that sat
on the cloud, Send thy sickle, and reap; because the time to reap is
come, because the harvest of the earth is dried [dead ripe].

And he that sat on the cloud cast his sickle on the earth, and the
earth was reaped.

And another angel came out of the temple which is in the heaven, he
also having a sharp sickle. And another angel came out of the altar,
he who hath power over the fire ; and he cried with a great cry to him
who had the sharp sickle, saying, Send thy sharp sickle, and gather
the clusters of the vine of the earth, because her grapes are fully ripe.

And the angel cast his sickle into the earth and gathered the vine
of the earth, and cast [what he gathered] into the great wine-press of
the wrath of God. And the wine-press was trodden outside of the city,
and blood came forth out of the wine-press up to the bits of the horses,
for a distance of a thousand six hundred stadia.

PROCLAMATION having gone forth that the
hour of judgment is come, that great Babylon
is on the brink of her fall, and that the damnation
of every worshipper of the Beast is at hand, we

find ourselves face to face with the last great administrations of divine wrath. And the nature and machinery of those administrations is the matter which now comes before us. The more specific details are given in the succeeding chapters, but a general summation is first presented in two visions, the Harvest and the Vintage, which, for awful brevity of narration and expressiveness of imagery, are perhaps the most wonderful in all this wonderful Book. God help us to consider them with reverent and believing hearts!

I. THE VISION OF THE HARVEST.

Some worthy expositors take this as a foreshowing of the final gathering home of the people of God. That the Scriptures often speak of such a harvest of the good seed of the Saviour's sowing there can be no question. John the Baptizer spoke of a time of threshing, when the Lord "will gather the wheat into His garner." (Luke 3 : 17.) The Saviour commenced His heavenly instructions with an account of His sowing and husbandry, the harvest of which he said would be "the end of the age," when He "will say to the reapers, Gather the wheat into my barn." (Matt. 13.) He also said, "So is the kingdom of God, as if a man should cast seed into the ground, and should sleep and rise night and day, and the seed should spring and grow up, he knoweth not how; for the earth bringeth forth fruit of herself; first the blade, then the ear, after that the full corn in the ear. But when the fruit is brought forth, immediately he putteth in the sickle, because *the harvest* is come." (Mark 4 : 26–29.) But that this is the harvest foreshown in the text seems to me very improbable, if not entirely out of the question. According to the record up to this point, the great harvest of the good seed has already been reaped. The Living Ones, the Elders, the innumerable multitude, the Man-child, and the 144,000, all of whom are of the good seed, are in heaven before this reaping comes. This reaping is also immediately preceded by the gathering of a great company to glory, which is very unaccountably separated from the harvest of saints directly to follow, if so we are to understand it. Ordinarily, indeed, we would think of harvest as a thing of gladness and blessing. The Scriptures also speak of harvest as a great joy. But it is the same with respect to the vintage, which all accept as here applying exclusively to the punishment of the wicked. Any argument of that character bears as strongly against taking the vintage in the sense of a destruction as the taking of the harvest in that sense.

It must be remembered that evil has its harvest as well as good. There is a harvest of misery and woe,—a harvest for the gathering, binding, and burning of the tares,—as well as for the gathering of the wheat into the garner of heaven. And this harvest of punishment has quite as prominent a place in the Scriptures as the harvest of the gathering home of the saints. " Thus saith the Lord

of hosts, the God of Israel; the daughter of Babylon is like a threshing floor, it is time to thresh
her; yet a little while and the time of her *harvest*
shall come." (Jer. 51: 33.) Here is a harvest of
judgment,—a harvest of woe to Babylon, and the
harvest of the text follows as the direct consequence of the proclamation of great Babylon's fall.
Is it not, therefore, most naturally to be taken as
the same in both cases? So again in Joel (3: 11–
16), looking to the very time and events with
which we are here concerned, the word is: "Assemble yourselves, and come, all ye heathen, and
gather yourselves together round about; thither
cause thy mighty ones to come down, O Lord.
Let the heathen be awakened, and come up to the
valley of Jehoshaphat: for there will I sit to judge
all the heathen round about. Put ye in the sickle,
for *the harvest* is ripe : come, get you down, for
the press is full, the vats overflow; for their wickedness is great. Multitudes, multitudes in the valley
of decision : for the day of the Lord is near in the
valley of decision. The sun and the moon shall
be darkened, and the stars shall withdraw their
shining. The Lord also shall roar out of Zion,
and utter his voice from Jerusalem, and the
heavens and the earth shall shake." Here is both
a harvest and a vintage; the one like and part of
the other, and both exclusively applicable to the
destruction of the wicked. This harvest and this
vintage are unquestionably the same described in
the text. They belong to the same period of time,
they are called for after the same manner, and for

the same activities; and they respect the same parties, whether as to the bearer of the sickle, the reapers, or the persons whom the reaping touches. It seems to me impossible, therefore, rightfully to take this harvest as anything else than the final cutting off of the hosts of the wicked, the visitation upon them of the fruits of their sowing. That harvest of which the 144,000 are a first-fruit is a very different matter from this. That is a harvest of gathering to the Lamb on Mount Zion; this is a gathering to the Valley of Jehoshaphat for destruction. Verse 15 is a literal allusion to Isaiah 27: 11, which refers to a scene of breaking and burning, and final withdrawal of all mercy. The express mention of the sharpness of the sickle also shows that we have to do with a scene of judgment. The mention of the cloud likewise points to a work of judgment, for wherever Christ appears on a cloud, the work immediately in hand is always a judgment. The name of the Son of man also points in the same direction; for it is as the Son of man that all judgment has been committed to Christ. (Jno. 5: 27.) And such a contrast as would make only the vintage expressive of wrath and punishment, and the harvest one of a purely gracious character, has not a single trait or item of the account to support it.* The harvest is simply

---

* Mede, Bishop Newton, Lowman, Doddridge, Bengel, Hengsten-berg, Faber, Stuart, W. Robinson, William Jones, etc., agree that the *harvest* as well as the *vintage* here denotes a harvest of wrath. Mede well observes, "that the idea of harvest includes three things : the reaping of the corn, the gathering of it in, and the threshing of it ;

one phase of a great final visitation upon the apostate world, of which the vintage is another phase.— Let us look at it, then, a little more particularly.

" *I saw, and behold a white cloud.*"   From this we may be quite sure of what is coming.   That cloud is the signal of the second advent of the Lord Jesus.   When He ascended, "a cloud received him out of their sight;" and at the same time it was told from heaven, "This same Jesus, which is taken up from you into heaven, shall so come in like manner as ye have seen him go into heaven." (Acts 1.)   The cloud took Him, and the cloud shall bring Him.   "They shall see the Son of man coming *in a cloud* with power and great glory." (Luke 21: 27.)   And what was thus predicted, the Apocalyptic seer here beholds fulfilling. That cloud is "*white*," like fire at its intensest heat, like the lightning itself, portending the purest as well as the hottest wrath towards the powers which have usurped the dominion of the earth.

" *On the cloud is seated one like a Son of man.*"   No one else is here to be thought of but our blessed Lord Jesus.   In John's first vision he saw, in the midst of the golden candlesticks, "One like to a Son of man;" and that One said, "I am the First and the Last, and the Living One; and I became dead, and behold I am living for the ages of the

---

whence it is made a type in Scripture of two direct opposites; of *destruction*, when the reaping and the threshing are considered; of *restitution and salvation* when the ingathering is considered." It is here *the reaping* only.

ages ; and I have the keys of death and of hell."
(Rev. 1: 17.) It was the glorified Son of Mary
there, and it is the same here. As the Destroyer
of the works of the Devil, and as the Judge of the
quick and the dead, it belongs to Christ to reap
the earth and to clear it of the hellish seed of the
great enemy. The man of sin is to be destroyed
only by the manifestation of the Saviour's presence.
(2 Thess. 2 : 8.)

" *Having on his head a crown of gold.*" Daniel
"saw in the night visions, and behold one like the
Son of man came with the clouds of heaven, and
came to the ancient of days, and there was given
Him dominion, and glory, and a kingdom." (Dan.
7 : 13, 14.) It was the same Son of man, in the
same cloud, settled in all the regal prerogatives of
the same supreme dominion, and manifested for
the same purpose of dispossessing and destroying
the Beast. The sitting of Christ on the throne of
His glory is for the judgment of the nations (Matt.
25 : 31, 32), and the taking to Him of His great
power as the King is to destroy them that corrupt the earth, that He may set up in their place
His own glorious dominion. (Rev. 11 : 17, 19 ; 19 :
16.)

And to this end, this heaven-crowned King
holds " *in his hand a sharp sickle.*" There is nowhere such a description or holding forth of the
instrument in any harvest scene referring to the
gracious home-bringing of the good. The earth
is to be cleared of its *ill* products now, therefore
only a cutting implement is in hand, and so con-

spicuously displayed. The work is one of vengeance and sore judgment, therefore it is " sharp."

Thus seated in regal majesty, with His terrible
instrument in hand for His appointed judicial
work as the Son of man, there goes up to Him a
mighty cry to send forth His sickle and reap,
claiming that the time of the reaping has come,
and that "the harvest of *the earth*" (not *the Church*)
is dried to dead ripeness. This cry is from an
angel, called " *another* angel," in allusion to those
mentioned in verses 6, 8, 9. Some take it as the
commission of the Father for Christ to proceed;
but that commission the great Harvester must
already have had in order to take the position and
equipment in which He here appears. It is not
so much a commission as a *prayer*, a plea, an urgency. It does not come from the Father, but
from the quarter of the afflictions and abominations calling for vengeance. This angel comes
" *out of the temple ;*"—not " the temple which is in
heaven," as in verse 17, or it would be so stated,
but " the temple " as distinguished from " the
temple which is in heaven;" hence the temple on
earth, referring either to the material temple rebuilt and reconsecrated, or the spiritual temple as
made up of those who keep the commandments
of God and the faith of Jesus, or both ; that is,
from the very point and place where the Antichrist
has enacted his greatest enormities of wickedness.
Abel's blood cried unto God from the ground.
(Gen. 4 : 10.) The cry of Sodom's wickedness
came up unto Jehovah. (Gen. 28 : 20, 21.) In like

manner great Babylon's sins came up into heaven.
(Rev. 18 : 5.) And this cry to the sitter on the
cloud comes out of the earthly temple as the cry
of righteous indignation at the abominations that
are being done against that temple and its God,
attesting the over-ripeness of the transgressors,
and claiming the due judgment upon them, as the
time has come.

The interests of God on earth are all more or
less under the guardianship of angels. An angel
had charge of the healing in Bethesda's pool, and
angels have charge of God's temple too. The
Archangel Michael presides over the affairs of the
children of Daniel's people, and in the time of the
Antichrist it is prophesied that he shall stand up
for them. (Dan. 12 : 1.) And this angel-cry from
the temple to the crowned, seated, and armed
King of Judgment, to send His sickle and reap,
is plainly connected with the administrations of
these angel-helpers against oppression and oppressors. It shows us that when the time of
judgment comes to the full, everything will be in
a condition of one grand outcry for speedy vengeance. Iniquity will then have come to the full,
to a thorough drying out of every modifying particle of immaturity, giving mighty argument for
the loud outcry of every holy being for judgment
to strike.

And as the cry is, the answer comes. " *He that
sat on the cloud cast his sickle* (ἐπὶ) *on, or against, the
earth,* AND THE EARTH WAS REAPED." Tremendous
words ! What an experience for the race of man

is bound up in their awful brevity ! What plagues
descend with that sharp sickle ! What a crash
comes with its alighting upon a world now dead
ripe for final judgment ! What powers and systems fall before it ! What sores and agonies it
brings to them that bear the mark of the Beast
and worship his image ! What pestilential putres-
cences it strikes into the sea whence that Beast
rises, and into the rivers and fountains whence his
subjects drink ! What new blazes of consuming
heat it gives to the sun ! What torment it inflicts
upon the throne of the Beast, and darkness and
anguish upon his kingdom ! What cries, and
thunders, and lightnings, and earthquakes, and
hailstorms, and trembling of nations, and anxie-
ties of men, it arouses into activity ! How does
every upas growth give way before the sharp edge
of that terrible sickle ! Just how much of this
great Harvest pertains to the reaping, as distinguished from the vintage, we are not fully informed;
but it cuts from their foundations all the main
sinews of the Antichrist. It includes all the disasters that come from the pouring out of the great
bowls of wrath. It brings down great Babylon
with a crash that fills the world with lamentations
and horror. It strips the great Adulteress of all
her pride and queenliness, and fills her with torment, and sorrow, and burning. It sinks all the
riches and glories of a godless world into one
common ruin, never to be brought up again. And
of the two phases of those ministrations of the
wrath of God which are to clear this planet of the

products and representatives of rebellion against His Throne, this is one, and perhaps the most general and far-reaching of the two. When the seer says "*the earth was reaped*," he tells of an amount of cutting down, divesture, and sorrowful sweeping away forever which the Scriptures describe as the termination of the whole present order of things; for " the Harvest is the end of the world." (Matt. 13 : 39.) But it is nevertheless only one phase of the destruction which shall then be wrought. After the grain-harvest comes the grape-harvest. Accordingly we have

II. THE VISION OF THE VINTAGE.

"Another angel" appears. He is "another " as a comer forth from the temple, and he is an " angel " with reference to his *mission*, not with reference to his nature; for this angel is really the same as the Sitter on the white cloud. As to office, Christ is often represented as an angel, both in this Book and elsewhere. His very name, *Christ*, or *Messiah*, implies as much. He is the One sent and appointed of the Father. In the Old Testament He is continually spoken of as the Jehovah—angel. In chapters 10 and 20 He appears as an angel. And in the very nature of the case we must here understand the Lord Himself, though in the character of an angel. The two images of the Harvest and the Vintage are too closely inter-connected for us to assign one to Christ and the other to a created angel. The

sharp sickle in the one is the same as in the other.
The work is so great, and belongs so essentially to
the mission and prerogatives of Christ, that it
would trench upon the honor and appointment of
Him to whom the Father hath committed all judgment, to refer it to a single ordinary angel.   The
destruction wrought is unquestionably the same
which is more particularly described in the latter
part of chapter 19; but there it is specifically assigned to the Lord Jesus himself.   And so in
Isaiah 63, the treader of the wine-press, corresponding to the picture here given, is none other
than Christ.   We would therefore involve ourselves in too many difficulties, not to admit that
this *another messenger* is the same as the Sitter on
the cloud.

He comes " *out of the temple which is in heaven ;*"
the temple which is in heaven, as distinguished
from the temple which is on earth.   "The holy
places made with hands are the figures of the true,"
fashioned after " the patterns of things in the heavens." (Heb. 10 : 23, 24.) It is in the heavenly
temple that Christ now is, there appearing in the
presence of God for us, as our great High Priest;
and out from thence He is to come when He comes
the second time. (Heb. 10 : 24–28.) We have
here reached the time appointed for the destroying
of them that corrupt the earth.   Hence the great
commissioned One appears.   He leaves His place
in the temple which is in heaven, and stands ready,
with sharp sickle in hand, for the work assigned.

Where he stands is not said; but the silence naturally carries us back to the white cloud.

Appearing with the sharp sickle, a great cry goes up to Him: "*Send thy sharp sickle and gather the clusters of the vine of the earth, because her grapes are fully ripe.*" He who makes this cry is an angel who comes "*out of the altar*," of course the earthly altar, or it would be otherwise stated, as in the preceding verse. This angel is "he who hath power over the fire." The altar-fire is the fire of divine justice; the fire which ever burns against sin and sinners; the fire which spares no victim however innocent when in the place and stead of transgressors; the fire which ever cries out with mighty voice for the burning up of all rebels against God's righteous authority. There is a living spirit in charge of it; and that spirit calls for vengeance against the Antichrist. The grapes in this case are the grapes of Sodom, "sour grapes," the clusters of wickedness ripened to the full. Such iniquities, blasphemies, tyrannies and systematic abominations, as the Antichrist develops, have no parallel on earth. In these all the depravities head up to their maturity. In these appears the consummation or final ripeness of the whole earth-growth and mystery of evil. The angel of the altar-fires is never so outraged as by this perfected vintage of earth's wickedness. Hence the loud and clamorous outcry for vengeance upon these clusters. The "grapes of gall" are "ripe." The time for cutting them has come. The Messenger with the sharp instrument is pres-

ent. And the spirit of the justice-fires cries for
the sickle to come in all its whetted sharpness.
From under that altar had gone forth the plaint
of murdered saints : " Until when, Thou Master,
holy and true, dost Thou not judge and avenge
our blood from them that dwell on the earth."
(Rev. 6 : 10.) But now the very angel of the altar
adds his mighty voice, and there can be no more
delay.

" *And the Angel cast His sickle into the earth, and
gathered the vine of the earth.*" The vine of the earth
is that which stands over against " the vine of
heaven." The true vine is Christ, and Christians
are the branches. " The vine of the earth " is Antichrist, and its branches are his adherents and followers. The saints are not of the earth, but born
from above ; these are of the earth, born from the
wisdom that is from below—the seed of the Devil's
sowing—the children of the wicked one. The
grapes of this vine of the earth are the matured
children of wickedness, and " their wine is the poison of dragons and the cruel venom of asps."
(Deut. 32 : 32, 33.) They have by this time gone
as far as, in the nature of things, they can go.
They are "*fully ripe.*" Hence the sharp sickle of
the great judgment strikes, and the vine of the
earth is cut, and its clusters gathered into the great
wine-press of the wrath of God.

A more particular description of this gathering
of the hosts of Antichrist into the wine-press, and
the treading of it by the King of kings, and Lord
of lords, is given in the latter part of chapters 16

and 19. It is in reality a war scene, the gathering
of armies, the bringing together of the kings of the
earth and of the whole world to the battle of the
great day of God Almighty. It is for military purposes that they come, seduced, drawn, and impelled
by unclean spirits that issue out of the mouth of
the Dragon, out of the mouth of the Beast, and out
of the mouth of the False Prophet. The region
of their assemblage is the Holy Land. The various
names denotive of the locality all circle around
Jerusalem. "*Armageddon*" is the place named in
the Apocalypse, which is the mount or city of
Megiddo, or the great Esdraelon plain, "the Valley of Megiddo." That has ever been one of God's
great battle-grounds for the judging of the armies
of the wicked. There Jabin's hosts, with their
900 chariots of iron, were utterly overwhelmed by
Jehovah's special interference. There the Midian-
ites, and Amalekites, and children of the East
were routed before Gideon's 300 men with pitchers
and lamps. There Samson triumphed with his
crude instrument over the might of the Philistines.
There the ruddy son of Jesse met and slew the
great Goliath, and opened a breach of destruction
upon those who defied Israel's God. And it is but
fitting that here should be the seat of the wine-
press for the final crushing out of the mightier
Jabin and Goliath of the last evil days. "*The Valley of Jehosaphat*" is named by Joel as the place
which, geographically taken, denotes the immediate vicinity of Jerusalem, or else that part of Idumea where, by the special aid of heaven, Jehosa-

phat put down the rebellion of the Edomites. "*Bozrah*" is named by Isaiah as the place where the mighty Saviour treads the wine-press alone, and stains all His raiment with the blood of His foes. (Is. 34 : 6–8 ; 63 : 1–6.) The probabilities are that all these particular localities are included, and that a line of encamped forces shall extend from Bozrah, on the southeast, to Megiddo, on the northwest. And, singularly enough, this would measure exactly 1600 *stadia*, the distance named in the text as that over which the blood from this great wine-press of Jehovah's anger flows. The same would also best realize Habakkuk's vision of the same scene, where he beheld, and " God came *from Teman*, and the Holy One *from Mount Paran*. His glory covered the heavens, and the earth was full of His praise. His brightness was as the light ; He had horns coming out of his hand ; and there was the hiding of His power. Before him went the pestilence, and burning coals went forth at his feet. He stood and measured the earth : He beheld, and drove asunder the nations ; and the everlasting mountains were scattered, the perpetual hills did bow. Thou didst march through the land in indignation ; thou didst thresh the heathen in anger. Thou wentest forth for the salvation of thy people, even for salvation with thine anointed ; Thou woundest the head out of the house of the wicked, by discovering the foundation unto the neck." (Hab. 3 : 3–16.)

The march of the terrific indignation of God on this occasion would, therefore, seem to be from the Sinaitic hills, crashing through Idumea, thundering by the walls of the holy city, and thence on to the great field of Esdraelon, where the chief stress of the awful pressure falls. Along this line will the main bodies of these assembled nations lie, eager, determined, and confident in the schemes that occupy them, not knowing that they are already in the great wine-press of the wrath of God. "Multitudes, multitudes," armies on armies, hosts on hosts, are there. The Beast is there; the False Prophet is there; and the kings, captains, mighty men, and drilled legions of all the nations in league with Antichrist are there; all gathered into one great pen of slaughter.

"*And the wine-press was trodden.*" What strength have grapes against the weight and power of a man when he comes to set his feet upon them? And the riper they are, the more helpless. They must needs be crushed, their existence destroyed, their life-blood poured out. And so with these "fully ripe" clusters, now gathered into the great wine-press of the wrath of God. No weapon they can raise, no resistance they can make, can avail them. The beast was hailed as the Invincible; but his invincibility is nothing now. The False Prophet could make fire come down from heaven in the presence of men, but he can command no fires to withstand the lightnings of the angry and inexorable Judge. The heel of Omnipotence is upon them, and they can only break and sink beneath it.

Long ago had Jehovah spoken of this time and

said: "Let the earth hear, and all that is therein; the world, and all things that come forth of it. For the indignation of the Lord is upon all nations, and His fury upon all their armies; He hath utterly destroyed them, He hath delivered them to the slaughter. Their slain also shall be cast out, and their stink shall come up out of their carcases, and the mountains shall be melted with their blood. And all the host of heaven shall be loosed, and the heavens shall be rolled together as a scroll; and all their host shall fall down, as the leaf falleth off from the vine, and as a fallen fig from the fig-tree. For my sword shall be bathed in heaven: behold, it shall come down upon Idumea, and upon the people of my curse to judgment. For it is the day of the Lord's vengeance, and the year of recompenses for the controversy of Zion." (Is. 34 : 1-8.) But men would not hear, neither believe; therefore, the sword of the Lord is filled with their blood. He cometh from Edom, with dyed garments from Bozrah, treading the wine-press alone, treading them down in His anger, trampling them in His fury, and staining all His raiment with their blood. "When they say, Peace and safety, then sudden destruction cometh upon them, and they cannot escape."

It is "*outside of the city*" that this treading of the wine-press takes place. "The city," mentioned thus absolutely, with no other note of identification, can be none other than "*the holy city*," the city of Jerusalem. The fact that this great judgment does not come within its gates, is evidence of its being "the holy city," the place owned of God, the memorial of His salvation in the time of His fierce anger. Amid all the consuming wrath, the judgment stays outside the walls of Jerusalem. Within its holy inclosure is safety. And by some gracious interposition of Heaven, none of the doomed hosts of Antichrist are at this time inside of it. Has it become the possession of the 144,000 whom we saw on Mount Zion? Has the Lamb by this time cleansed it with judgment as in Ezekiel's vision (chapter 9)? Hath He already consecrated and appropriated it as the intended metropolis of the new kingdom? Has His wonder-working power come forth in such force in connection with the glorification of the 144,000, as then already to have started there an administration expelling the dominion of the Beast? Joel says, Jehovah shall then utter His voice with power from Jerusalem. (Joel 3:17.) Has it not then already become the seat of His throne? If so, this would explain why all these armies of the nations are there. Even apart from this, the implication is clear that these forces are gathered for war against the holy city, and against the Lamb. In the ordinary course of things there would be nothing in Jerusalem requiring or occasioning such a tremendous gathering of the kings and armies of the world. If, however, some visible presence of the heavenly kingdom about to take possession of the earth has there begun to display and assert itself; if divine majesty, miracle and power have by this time taken hold, introducing a new rule and order, exhibiting the presence of the eternal reign of the Son of man, and manifesting the potencies of the world to come; there is ample call and occasion for this mustering of all the powers of earth and hell. Determined to crush it out, "the kings of the earth set themselves, and the rulers take counsel together, against the Lord, and against His anointed." (Ps. 2 : 2.) A power which could thus cleanse and clear the temple and city of everything contrary to God, and hold at bay all attempts of the unsanctified to enter, would be a thing wholly intolerable to Antichrist. He who claims to be the only rightful object of human adoration, could not endure the presence of such temerity against his majesty. If strength in earth and hell exists to subdue and crush it, that strength must be called forth. And thus these kings and nations, with their armies, are convened. It is meant to make sure of success. They fill the land with their collected forces. They mass themselves in line from Bozrah to Megiddo. They compass about the holy city. But into it they dare not enter. And when the wine-press of their destruction is trodden, it is " trodden *outside of the city.*" Before they are able to strike a blow, "the Lion of the tribe of Judah" is upon them in all the terribleness of His great exterminating judgment.

"*And blood came forth out of the wine-press up to the bits of the horses for a distance of* 1600 *stadia!*" A river of human blood 160 miles in length, and up to the bridles of the horses in depth, tells an

awful story. When the Romans destroyed Jerusalem so great was the bloodshed that Josephus
says the whole city ran down with the blood to
such a degree that the fires of many of the houses
were quenched by it. When Sylla took Athens,
Plutarch says the blood that was shed in the
market-place alone covered all the ceramicus as
far as Dipylus, and some testify that it ran through
the gates and overflowed the suburbs. Nor are
we to think of any exaggeration or hyperbole
in the very definite description of what John here
saw as the consequence of the treading of this
wine-press. It is " *the great wine-press of the wrath
of God.*" It is the last great consummate act of
destruction which is to end this present world.
The masses on whom it is executed are "the
kings of the earth and of the whole world, and
their armies" (Rev. 16 : 14; 19 : 19), stationed in
a line from Bozrah in Edom to Esdraelon in
Galilee. They are to be utterly consumed, so as
to "leave them neither root nor branch." (Mal.
4 : 1.) It is "the great and dreadful day of the
Lord" about which all the prophets of all the
ages have prophesied. It is the result of the re-
sentment and anger of Him who is Faithful and
True, who in righteousness doth judge and make
war, whose eyes are as fire, on whose head are the
many crowns, whom all the armies of Heaven follow upon white horses, out of whose mouth goeth
a sharp sword, and who " treadeth the wine-press
of the fierceness and wrath of Almighty God."
And it must needs be all that John here states, a

belt of blood from Bozrah to Esdraelon up to the
horses' bridles in depth ! Isaiah says : " The land
shall be drunk with blood, and its dust made fat
with fatness, for it is the day of Jehovah's vengeance, the year of recompenses for the controversy against Zion." (Is. 34 : 7, 8.)

Ah, yes ; men in their unbelief may laugh at
the Almighty's threatenings. Because sentence
against an evil work is not executed speedily,
their hearts may be fully set in them to do evil.
And the proud rationalism of many may persuade
them that God is too good and merciful ever to
fulfil in any literal sense these sanguinary commi-
nations. But it will be no laughing matter then,
no mystic fancy, no meaningless orientalism of the
age of extravagant speech. God hath set His own
eternal seal to it, and said : " Seek ye out of the
Book of the Lord, and read : no one of these
things shall fail." (Is. 34 : 16.) And yet people
make light of it, and turn away to their sins and
follies as if it were all nothing !

Child of Adam, hear, and be admonished now
while salvation is so freely offered. Be not deceived, for God is not mocked. Those impieties
of thine, those guilty sports and gayeties, will yet
have to be confronted before the judgment seat.
Those gatherings in the gaming-hells and drink-
shops of Satan, those sneers and witty jests at
sacred things, those fiery lusts burning on the
altars of carnal pleasure, are all written down in
the account-books of eternity to be brought forth
in the great day. That wicked profanation of thy

Maker's name, that broken pledge, that unfulfilled
vow to God and man, that scene of riot, that hidden going to the haunts of the profligate, all are
noted for future settlement. The blood of
wronged and murdered innocence will not always
cry in vain. The wail of trampled helplessness
will not be unheard forever. The mother who
destroyed her babe, the clerk who dipped too deep
in his employer's till, the enemy who set fire to
his neighbor's goods or sought to blacken his good
name, the boy who cursed his parents in secret,
the spiteful slanderer and persecutor of God's
ministers and people, and every despiser and
neglecter of the great salvation, must each answer
at the tribunal of eternal justice. And if clean
repentance out of these and all such sins be not
speedy and complete, there is no hope or mercy
more. Before us stands the Angel with the sharp
sickle for all the enemies of God, and beside Him
is the great wine-press of destruction. Think, O
man, O woman, how would you fare were He this
night to strike! If not *in the city*, in reconciliation
with the King, outside is only death and damnation, and nothing can make it different.

LECTURE THIRTY-SIXTH.

THE SIGN OF THE SEVEN LAST PLAGUES — THE VISION OF THE
SEA OF GLASS MINGLED WITH FIRE — THE HARP-SINGERS
STANDING BY IT—THE SEVEN PRIEST-ANGELS—THE GOLDEN
BOWLS—NOT THE FRENCH REVOLUTION—THE PLAGUE OF
SORES—THE PLAGUE OF THE BLOODY SEA—THE PLAGUE OF
THE BLOODY RIVERS AND WATER-SPRINGS—THE PLAGUE OF
SUN-HEAT — THE PLAGUE OF DARKNESS — NO PENITENCE
FROM THESE JUDGMENTS.

REV. 15 : 1-8. (Revised Text.) And I saw another sign in the heaven great and marvellous, seven angels having seven plagues, the last, because in them, the wrath of God was completed.

And I saw like to a sea of glass mingled with fire, and those who conquer from the beast, and from his image, and from the number of his name, standing on [*over* or *by*] the sea of glass, having harps of God. And they sing the song of Moses, servant of God, and the song of the Lamb, saying, Great and marvellous thy works, O Lord God, the Almighty, just and true thy ways, Thou the King of the nations : who shall not fear, O Lord, and glorify thy name ? because alone holy, because all the nations shall come and worship in thy presence, because thy judgments [righteous doings] have been made manifest.

And after these things I saw, and there was opened the temple of the tabernacle of the testimony in the heaven ; and there came forth the seven angels who had the seven plagues out of the temple, clothed in pure bright linen, and girdled about their breasts with golden girdles. And one from among the four Living Ones gave to the seven angels seven golden bowls full of the wrath of God, who liveth to the ages of the ages. And the temple was filled with the smoke from the glory of God, and from his power ; and no one could enter into the temple until the seven plagues of the seven angels were completed.

Rev. 16 : 1-11. (Revised Text.) And I heard a great voice saying to the seven angels, Go and pour out the seven bowls of the wrath of God into the earth.

And the first went forth, and poured out his bowl into the earth; and there became a noisome and grievous sore upon the men who had the mark of the beast, and those who worshipped his image.

And the second poured out his bowl into the sea; and it became blood as of one dead, and the things in the sea, and every soul of life, died.

And the third poured out his bowl into the rivers and the fountains of waters; and they became blood. And I heard the angels of the waters saying, Righteous art thou, who art, and who wast, holy One, because thou hast judged thus: because they have shed blood of saints and prophets, and thou hast given them blood to drink; deserving are they. And I heard the altar saying, Yea, Lord God the Almighty, true and just are thy judgments.

And the fourth poured out his bowl on [or *over*] the sun; and it was given to it to scorch men with fire. And the men were scorched with great scorching, and they blasphemed the name of the God, he who hath authority over these plagues; and they repented not to give glory to him.

And the fifth poured out his bowl on [or *over*] the throne of the beast; and his kingdom became darkened, and they bit their tongues from the pain, and they blasphemed the God of the heaven from their pain, and from their sores, and repented not out of their deeds.

THE accomplishment of the Harvest and the Vintage brings to the end of this present world. The next in succession would be the setting up of the eternal Kingdom, and the evolution of the new heavens and earth. But the Harvest and the Vintage do not adequately set forth all that we need to know about these closing scenes. Further particulars included in this momentous period require to be shown in order to complete the picture. The fate of the infernal Trinity,—the Dragon, the Beast, and the False Prophet,—and of what pertains to them, is to be more fully described before we come to the Millennium, the descent of the New Jerusalem, and the planting of God's Tabernacle with men:

Hence the same ground covered by the visions of the Harvest and Vintage is traversed again and again with reference to particular objects and administrations. As we have four distinct Gospels to give us a full and accurate portraiture of the one glorious Saviour, so we have these several presentations with reference to one and the same momentous period of the end. Each vision, however, has its own particular office, scope, and features, giving some special aspect or phase in the general sum of events. It is not mere repetition of the same thing, but the separate presentation of particular administrations or occurrences of which the whole is made up.

Chapters 15 and 16 belong together. They form one whole, touching one important subject, to wit: the third or last *woe*. The contents bear a close analogy to the conclusion of chapter 11, if they be not indeed the continuation and amplification of what was there summarily introduced; for all these visions are very intimately related, both in general subject and time. There the temple in heaven was opened, and lightnings, voices, thunders, earthquake, and great hail followed. Here the same temple is opened, and out of it issue seven angels, with the seven last plagues, who empty their bowls of the wrath of God in calamities upon the wicked world, culminating in the very things named as the result of the opening there. There the Elders said that the nations were enraged, that God's wrath had come, and that the time to destroy them that corrupt the earth had been reached. Here we are shown the pouring out of that wrath, its particular instruments, subjects, operations, and results.

John begins by telling of "another *sign* in the heaven." In chapter 12 he told of two signs: the sign of the sun-clad Woman, and the sign of the great Red Dragon. It is with reference to them that he calls this "*another* sign." Three signs were given to Moses, Gideon, Saul, and Elijah. Three signs are mentioned in Matthew 24 as heralding the Lord's coming,—the sign of the Son of man in heaven, the putting forth of leaves by the withered fig-tree, and the lapse of the world into the condition in which it was at the time of the flood. And so we have here three signs. The signs of the Woman and the Dragon, answer to the first and second chapters of Exodus; the sign now before us, answers to the judgments which followed, through the ministry of Moses and Aaron.

This sign is "great and marvellous." It is great, as involving so much more in range and intensity than anything of the kind that has ever been; and it is marvellous, with reference to the unparalleled character of what it foretells. What it describes is altogether extraordinary, and on an astounding scale. It is the consummation of marvels in this present world. The sign itself is, "Seven Angels having seven plagues, the last ones, because in them the wrath of God was completed." Signs of healing accompanied the preaching of the Gospel; signs of death attend the end of the world. Much of the Apocalypse treats of plagues —" the plagues that are written in this book." Those here signified are " *the last*," with reference to what happened to Egypt, or with reference to the judgments under the Seals and Trumpets, or simply with reference to the particular end of things which they are to work. They are visitations upon the living world—upon men in the flesh. They have been named " the opening artillery of God, ere the shock of battle comes." The seven Angels who bear them have been likened to priests of heaven, pouring out the drink-offerings of wine over the sacrifice ere it is slain and consumed.

But before proceeding to give the particulars of this great and marvellous " sign," the Seer interjects another vision, of a more gracious order, though connected with these outpourings of the plagues. When the wicked are cut off, the righteous shall see it; and when these plagues fall upon Antichrist and his hosts, those who through suffering and death keep clear of his worship and mark, are on high, singing, and harping, and giving glory to God and the Lamb, as stroke upon stroke from the heavenly temple smites their oppressors. John writes: " *I saw like to a sea of glass mingled with fire, and those who conquer out from the Beast, and from his image, and from the number of his name, standing on, over, or by the sea of glass, having harps of God.*"

This likeness to a sea of glass reminds of that " glassy sea " which spread out before the throne in chapter 4.* If it is the same, it has become ominously commingled now; for there it was "like unto crystal" in clearness, but here it is "mingled with fire." There it seemed to be a part of the economy and pavement of the heaven; here it appears rather as a mighty reservoir of just judgments about to be precipitated upon the world below. There it looked like a sort of base on which the whole celestial establishment rested, representing perhaps the purity, vastness, and strength of God's counsels, on which all things depend; here it does not seem to be the support of anything, though the victors named may be over, by, or even on it. It is probably meant to symbolize the vastness, purity, justice and severity of the divine counsels in those retributions about to fall upon the wicked. It is best taken as a sea of just judgments which are poured forth in the seven final plagues, whilst in that regard at the same time a sea of blessed vindication and joy to those faithful ones whom the Beast persecuted unto death.

The picture of these victorious ones standing on the shore of this sea, holding harps of God, and singing the song of Moses, directly recalls the rescued and victorious children of Israel on the further side of the Red Sea, beholding the discomfiture of their foes, and singing and rejoicing in the mighty accomplishments of the wonder-working Jehovah. "Then sang Moses and the children of Israel this song unto the Lord, and

---

* Volume I, pp. 247, 248.

spake, saying, I will sing unto the Lord, for He
hath triumphed gloriously; the horse and his rider
hath He thrown into the sea. Who is like unto
Thee, O Lord, among the gods, who is like Thee,
glorious in holiness, fearful in praises, doing
wonders?" (Ex. 15 : 1-11.) And here the victors
sing the song of Moses over again, looking out
upon another sea of judgment as its fiery waves
dash upon their oppressors. Here, however, the
song goes beyond that of Moses, and takes in that
of the Lamb as well, which is the song of victory
over sin and death, the song of justification and
eternal life through the blood and triumph of
Jesus, whose dominion and right as the Lord of
the nations are attested by these mighty judgments. Of old it was prophesied, that, when "the
king" for whom Tophet is ordained and prepared
is smitten, the victory over him shall be celebrated
" with tabrets and harps" (Is. 30 : 32, 33); and
here John beholds the fulfilment. They stand by
the sea of glass mingled with fire, having harps
of God, and they sing, saying, " Great and marvellous are Thy works, O Lord God, the Almighty,
just and true are Thy ways, Thou, the King of the
nations! Who shall not fear, O Lord, and glorify
Thy name, alone holy? because all the nations
shall come and worship in Thy presence, because
Thy judgments have been made manifest!" When
consuming wrath falls on the servants of the false
god, the true God's worshippers are beyond the fiery
sea, singing their adoration to their Deliverer. Having felt the Dragon's wrath, they are joyously free

and secure from the great wrath of God. And their outlook is one of abiding blessedness. Verily, there is nothing like being firm and true to what is right. Whatever it may cost for the time, it will be amply recompensed in the great day.

With this statement concerning those whom the Beast and False Prophet cannot conquer, the holy Apostle proceeds with what he began to tell about as " another sign in the heaven "— the seven last plagues. He first describes the heavenly economy of them, and then the execution of them, together with their several effects. Let us follow him reverently.

He saw " *the temple of the tabernacle of the testimony in heaven opened.*" This was the innermost part of the temple, the Temple of the temple, the Holy of holies, the deepest centre of the dwelling-place and throne of God.

The tables of stone, inscribed with the precepts of the Law, which God gave to Moses, are called the "tables of testimony." These were commanded to be put into the holy Ark, which thence was called " the Ark of the testimony." This Ark had its place in the innermost and holiest department of the Tabernacle, which thus became the particular tent or " tabernacle of the testimony." And this innermost shrine of the temple in heaven, John saw open, revealing, as stated, in chapter 11 : 19, the very ark itself, and indicating that all the hidden powers of eternity were now about to show themselves in active earthward administrations.

From the depth of this holiness issued *seven angels*. They are priest-angels, for they are clothed in pure bright linen, and girded about their breasts with golden girdles, which is the priest's dress. They appear as priests, because they come for the sacrificing of a great sacrifice to the offended holiness and justice of God. The girdle of the Jewish high priest was a mixture of blue, and purple, and scarlet, and fine-twined linen, along with the "gold" (Lev. 16:4); the girdles here are pure gold; for the temple is higher, and the administration holier; and the officiators belong to heaven, not earth.

"*And one from among the four Living Ones gave to the seven angels seven golden bowls full of the wrath of God.*" This is not the first time we hear of these Living Ones taking part in the actual administration of judgment. They are indeed glorified men;* but "do ye not know that the saints shall judge the world?" (1 Cor. 6:2, 3.) When the horsemen of chapter 6 were sent forth, " one from among the four Living Ones " gave the command, as with a voice of thunder. Here a corresponding part of the same judgment work is to be executed, and the vessels containing the wrath of God are handed out by one of the same Living Ones. The vessels themselves were not *bottles*, as our English version would intimate, but shallow, pan-like, golden bowls, or censers, such as were used in the temple to hold the fire when incense was

* See vol. i, pp. 254-262.

burned. They are priestly censers, as in chapter 8 : 5. That which gives vitality to the prayers of saints and sustains the Jehovah worship, at the same time carries the burning coals of judgment upon the wicked. That which seethes and smokes in these holy censers is God's punishment upon transgression, the consuming intolerance of His holiness toward sin and sinners. Seven of these bowls, full to the brim with the wrath of Him who liveth for the ages of the ages, are thus handed to the seven priest-angels to be poured upon the sacrifice preparatory to its final consumption. And terrible is the smoke of their burning.

When the first tabernacle was dedicated, a cloud filled it, and Moses was not able to enter into it because of the cloud of the glory of the Lord. (Ex. 40 : 34, 35.) When Solomon's temple was dedicated the cloud of the divine glory so filled the house that the priests could not stand to minister because of it. (1 Kings 8 : 10, 11.) It was *a cloud* then, veiling the insufferable brightness of that Jehovah-presence which it indicated; but here is the day of the fierceness of divine wrath, and in place of the shadowing cloud is the lurid fiery smoke;—the same which Iasiah saw (6 : 1–4) in his vision of the enthroned Jehovah. It fills the temple in heaven; and so intense is the manifestation of the divine glory and power that no one, even of the sons of God, is able to enter until the filled censers have been quite emptied out upon the doomed world. And from the midst of these awful signs a great voice sounds, like the trumpet sounding from the smoke and fire on Mount Sinai, saying to the seven angels, " *Go, and pour out the seven bowls of the wrath of God into the earth.*"

Glancing now for a moment at some of the current interpretations of these seven last plagues, we cannot but wonder that any should consider all this tremendous and unparelleled ado in heaven to be for nothing more than a few petit events in the ordinary course of human history. Yet some gravely tell us that the first bowl is the French Revolution; the second bowl, the naval wars of that Revolution; the third bowl, the battles of Napoleon in Italy; the fourth bowl, the tyranny and military oppression of Napoleon; the fifth bowl, the calamities which befell the city of Rome and the Pope in consequence of the French Revolution; the sixth bowl, the wane of the Turkish power, the return of the Jews to Palestine, and the subtle influences of infidelity, Popery and Puseyism; and the seventh, some further war with Romanism and disaster to the city of Rome. But can it be possible that God Almighty from His everlasting seat, the temple in heaven, all angels and holy ones on high, should thus be in new and unexampled commotion, with the mightiest of all celestial demonstrations, over nothing but a few occurrences in a small part of the smallest section of the globe, and those occurrences far less in meaning or moment than many others in other ages ! According to such interpretation mankind have been living for the last 100 years amid the extreme terrors of " the great and terrible day of the Lord " without ever knowing it! yea, dreaming the while that we are happily gliding into the era of universal liberty and peace! Are France and Italy *the earth!* Are half a dozen naval battles, scattered over a dozen years, and touching here and there a speck of sea hardly to be pointed out on a terrestrial globe, to be taken as the turning of the whole ocean to blood, by which everything that lives in the sea dies! If Napoleon's artillery was the sunscorch of blasphemers, was not the blasphemy of the scorchers by far worse than the blasphemy of the scorched! Alas for the worth of Revelation if this is the proper way of reading it!

The greatest plagues of judgment of which we read in the past were those poured out upon ancient Egypt. They were literal plagues, which happened according to the terms in which they are recorded. These seven last plagues are the consummation of God's judgment plagues, including in them all that have gone before, and rendering in final and intensest perfection what was previously rehearsed on a smaller scale, preliminary to the great performance. What the preparatory rehearsal was, that must the final rendering be. The last plagues must therefore be literal too. In what sense or degree, however, was the French Revolution, or the doings of Napoleon Bonaparte, a consummation of the plagues of Egypt? Read, and ponder.

The first priest-angel "*poured out his bowl into the earth, and there became a grievous sore upon the men who had the mark of the Beast, and those who*

worship his image." Did none but Romanists suffer
from the French Revolution and the military des-
potism which it evolved? If so, this plague does
not refer to that event; for it touches only such
as have the mark of the Beast. The sores of Lazarus at the rich man's gate were not Romish
errors, nor French infidelity; but the sore of this
angel's outpouring is denoted by the same word
which described the ailment of Lazarus. It is the
Egyptian plague of ulcers intensified. Burnt earth
was there scattered, "and it became a boil, breaking forth with blains, upon man and upon beast;"
and it was "upon the magicians, and upon all the
Egyptians." (Ex. 19 : 8–12.) When Moses afterwards pronounced the curses of heaven upon those
who disown God and throw off allegiance to Him,
he said: "The Lord will smite thee with the botch
of Egypt, and with the emerods, and with the
scab, and with the itch, whereof thou canst not
be healed. The Lord shall smite thee in the
knees, and in the legs, with a sore botch that cannot
be healed, from the sole of thy foot unto the top of
thy head." (Deut. 28 : 15, 27, 35.) This has never
yet been fulfilled; but John here sees it fulfilled
upon those who have cast off the worship of Jehovah for the worship and mark of the Antichrist.

"*And the second poured out his bowl into the sea;
and it became blood, as of one dead, and the things in
the sea, every soul of life, died.*" So far as the naval
battles of the French Revolution affected the sea,
they killed nothing of the living things therein, but
fattened them, and scarcely stained a single wave;

so far were they from turning all the ocean's waters into bloody clots. One of the plagues of Egypt was, that God "turned their waters into blood, and slew their fish." (Is. 105 : 30.) Under the second trumpet (chapter 8 : 8) the sea was affected, and the third of it was turned into blood. But here the whole sea is affected, and a change is wrought which makes all its waters like to the blood of one dead,—clotted, putrescent, and utterly destructive of the life of what lives in the sea. Hengstenberg and others say that we are here to think of "the shedding of blood in war;" but there is not a word said about war; and if living things in the sea mean human beings, peoples, nations, tribes, and tongues, this plague sweeps them all out of existence; for every living thing in the sea dies of this blood. If it refers to war, it is a very anomalous war, for it leaves neither conquered nor conquerors, and the plagues which follow have no subjects on which to operate. Stuart holds that "a literal fulfilment is not to be sought after;" but if it is not literal, then were not the plagues of Egypt literal, nor is any other sort of fulfilment possible; and thus the tremendous record is rendered meaningless. I take it as it reads; and if any dissent, on them is the burden of proving some other sense, and of reducing to agreement their mutually destructive notions as to what it does mean. Take it as God has caused it to be written, and there can be no disagreement; take it in any other way, and the uncertainty is endless.

"*And the third poured out his bowl into the rivers*

and the fountains of waters; and they became blood."
When Moses stretched out his hand upon the
waters of Egypt, upon their streams, upon their
rivers, and upon all their pools of water, " all the
waters that were in the river were turned to blood;
and the fish that were in the river died; and the
river stank, and the Egyptians could not drink of
the water of the river; and there was blood throughout all the land of Egypt." (Ex. 7 : 19–21.) And
what thus happened with *one* river and *one* country,
now occurs in all waters in all countries.   Under
the third trumpet (chap. 8 : 10, 11), a third of the
rivers and water-springs became nauseous and nox-
ious with bitterness; but this plague touches them
all, and turns them into blood, so that the hosts
of Antichrist can find nothing to drink but blood.
A more dreadful plague can hardly be imagined;
but it is just.   " The angel of the waters," he who
has the administration of this plague, is amazed
at the greatness of the infliction, but breaks forth
in celebration of the righteousness of Him who
was, and is [now no longer *to come*, because
already come], and praises Him for having thus
judged.   The punishment is full of horror; but
it is deserved.   They shed the blood of saints and
prophets, and it is due that now their only drink
is blood.   " Yea, Lord God the Almighty,"
answers the altar, " true and just are Thy judgments!"   When God once comes with His terrible awards upon the wicked, the righteousness of
them will be so conspicuous, and the justice
and truth of His administrations will be so

clear and manifest, that it will not be in the power of any holy being to find a flaw, to raise a question, or to withhold the profoundest Amen. And when the earth refuses to yield any drink but blood to its apostate population, angels, and altar, and all heaven must confess and answer that it is just; they deserve it.

"*And the fourth poured out his bowl* [here the preposition changes from εἰς to ἐπί] *on or over the sun; and it was given to it* [*the sun*] *to scorch men* [*mankind*] *with fire. And the men were scorched with great scorching.*" This belongs to the predicted "signs in the sun." Under the fourth trumpet (chap. 8 : 12), the heavenly bodies were affected; but in a different way from this. There the sun was one-third darkened; here its power and heat are increased, till its rays become like flames. The sun exists and shines by God's command; and He can make it scorch and torture, as well as cheer and warm. Moses and Malachi have spoken of that day as one that shall " *burn as an oven,*" when men shall be " devoured with burning heat." (Deut. 32 : 24; Mal. 4 : 1.) Here also belongs the fulfilment of Isaiah's words : " The earth mourneth and fadeth away, the world languisheth and fadeth away, the haughty people of the earth do languish; because they have transgressed the laws, changed the ordinances, broken down the everlasting covenant, therefore hath the curse devoured the earth, and they that dwell therein are desolate; therefore *the inhabitants of the earth are burned, and few men left.*" (Is. 24 : 4–13.) Some say, " It is not of the natural scorching of the sun's rays, and of the injurious effects flowing from it, such as excessive heats, drought, and famine, that we are here to think;" but of what else can we think? It is the sun that is smitten; that smiting causes the emission of rays that scorch and burn to a degree that John says they are *fire;* and to think of anything but scorching and consuming heat from the sun is simply to browbeat the words of inspiration. Men are scorched by an extraordinary power of the sun, oppressed, burned, killed by its fiery rays, smitten with sunstroke, overwhelmed with siroccos, suffocated with solar heat; and yet we are not to think of the sun, or of any injurious effects from its burning rays! O the havoc which men make of God's word to fit it to their faulty theories! Here is one of the last plagues of "the great and terrible day of the Lord;" and it is nothing less than God's glorious sunshine, intensified with fiery heat, so that it burns and scorches earth and man, decimating the inhabitants of city and country alike. Disastrous plague!

We would think that such a succession of ills would bring the most infatuated to their senses, and that there would come forth from all the world one loud repentant cry to God for mercy. We would think it impossible for people with souls in them to hold out against such exhibitions of angry Almightiness. But no; they only blaspheme the name of the God having command of these plagues, and repent not to give glory to Him.

They have all sold themselves to hell and received the sacrament and seal of it upon their bodies, and they only dare and sin on to their inevitable damnation.

Many are waiting for times of affliction and death to bring them to repentance and salvation; but those who wilfully sin away their good days count in vain on something softening and remedial from the judgments of their despised and incensed Maker. The sun may scorch, and extort still further blasphemies, but it cannot change the stubborn heart, or burn into it the saving fear and love of God. Sin is a cancer, which, if left to run too long, can never more be cured. Another judgment-plague descends, but with no better effect.

"*The fifth Angel poured out his bowl on or over the throne of the Beast; and his kingdom became darkened, and they bit their tongues from the pain, and they blasphemed the God of the heaven from their pain, and from their sores, and repented not out of their deeds.*" The effects of these judgments overlap each other. The sores of the first plague are still felt during the second and third, and even here under the fifth. This proves that these plagues all fall upon the people of one and the same generation, and hence dare not be extended through centuries. The Antichrist has but 3½ years, and all seven of these last plagues fall upon him and his followers. Here his very throne is assailed, and his entire dominion is filled with darkness. The last but one of the Egyptian plagues was a plague of darkness. The Book of Wisdom (17:21) says: " Over them was spread a heavy night, an image of that darkness which should afterward receive them; but yet were they unto themselves more grievous than the darkness." Here is a corresponding darkness, coextensive with the world-wide empire of this Beast. From the centre of his kingdom, even to its utmost limits, everything is darkened. Isaiah prophesied of this when he said, " Behold, *the darkness shall cover the earth, and gross darkness the people.*" (Is. 60 : 2.) Joel prophesied of it when he said: "The day of the Lord cometh, *a day of darkness and of gloominess, a day of clouds and thick darkness.*" "The sun shall be turned into darkness, and the moon into blood." (Joel 2 : 1, 2, 31.) Nahum prophesied of it when he said that the fierceness of God's anger shall be poured out like fire, and "*darkness* shall pursue His enemies." (Nah. 1 : 6, 8.) Our blessed Saviour prophesied of it when He declared: "In those days, after that tribulation, *the sun shall be darkened, and the moon shall not give her light, and the stars of heaven shall fall,*" failing in all their offices of light-givers. (Mark 13 : 24, 25.) And great are the miseries of that darkness; for it causes those who feel it to bite their tongues by reason of the distress which it adds to all the rest of their torments. And is it nothing but the suppression of the monasteries and Romish clergy in France in 1789, and Napoleon's levies upon the revenues and siezure of the properties and person of a helpless old Pope? Have all the prophets been thus stirred up by the Holy Ghost to tell the world of those few, limited, and temporary calamities incident to ordinary human ambition and war, that all men of all ages might stand in awe and fear God lest they should come under Napoleon's dealings with the papacy? Would it not seem as if some shadows of this coming darkness were already upon the understandings of some of Christ's professed ministers? God help them to the light, that they may repent out of their sad mistreatments of these great revelations, and give to Him the glory by doing just honor to His Holy Word!

The darkness which thus comes over the kingdom of the Beast must be literal, as that of Egypt was; for that was the prelibation of this,—the pre-rehearsal of what is to come. If not literal, it is impossible for any man to tell us what it is. People may guess and reason, but that cannot fix the meaning of God's word. And to carry the theory of a mere "figurative representation" into all the sacred predictions which refer to it, can only spread this darkness upon some of the most momentous portions of divine revelation. It is at all events vastly better to risk mistake by clinging fast to the plain sense of what God has caused to be written for our learning, than to go floundering through a world of fancies, ever learning, but never able to come to the knowledge of the truth. And if in the great day of fulfilment, when God shall turn these prophecies into living realities, things should not turn out according to the terms used by the Holy Ghost, we shall be the more excusable for having clung to the record as it stands. In any event, our simple faith will be our best apology.

This darkening of the Beast's kingdom, added to the earlier inflictions, brings terrible distress. The description indicates the intensest writhings of anguish, the very madness of vexation and pain. The people who suffer these plagues bite their tongues, chew them, gnaw them, as their best diversion from their misery. Their tongues have spoken blasphemies, and they themselves thus punish them. Earth has become like hell for wickedness, and so it becomes like hell for darkness and torment,—nay, still further like hell, because there is no repentance in its inhabitants. Instead of cursing themselves for their impieties, they curse God as the offender, for thus interfering with their preferences and their peace. To the ulcers, the bloody waters, the sun-scorches, now comes this horrible darkness; and a God of such administrations they disdain to honor, even under all their miseries. They will gnaw their tongues with pain and rage rather than speak a prayer of penitence to Him. Nothing but cursing and horrid denunciations will they utter. When they saw the two slain Witnesses come to life again and ascend to heaven, they were willing to own that the God of heaven is God, and to give Him something of His glory. But it was only a temporary reverence, which soon faded away. Here they are again compelled to acknowledge Him as "the God of heaven," but it is only to heap new blasphemies on His name.

Some talk of conversion in hell, and of an ultimate restoration of the wicked. Does this presentation look as if such a thing were possible? If hell-torments can cure men of their wickedness, why are not these people subdued to penitence? These are the outpourings of that very divine wrath which makes hell; but where is the remedial impression, the turning from sin, the seeking for reconciliation? And while sin lasts, hell must last. These people have rebelled until the very spirit of perdition has settled in upon their souls, and henceforth there is no more hope for them. Another bowl of wrath is poured out; but its effect is the opening of the ways for the gathering of them together to the scene of slaughter; and then follows the last, which lets loose upon them all the long-chained thunders of angered Omnipotence, overwhelming their works and lives in a sea of blood!

Many, my friends, are the pictures of God's judgments upon those who reject His Gospel, and refuse to have Him rule over them. A dreadful catalogue we have had before us to-night. But with how poor and feeble an interest do many regard these momentous revelations! There is perhaps nothing which a sinner, or neglecter of God and his soul, so little expects, as the punishment of his sins. Of ungodliness in general, its sinfulness, its danger, and the certain judgment of God upon it, he can discourse with fluency and confidence. He has no doubt that God is a holy God, and will by no means spare those who fail to make their peace with Him. But when it comes to his own sins, negligence and disobedience, what thought or feeling has he of that awful account-ability which in the abstract he so readily admits? To what extent does he realize that *his* sins will find him out, or that *he* is the one in danger? He listens; he assents; he hears with pleasure the array of reasoning about righteousness, temper-ance, and judgment to come; he even admires the vivid and faithful preaching of the sure and ter-rible wrath of God upon transgressors; and yet he goes on in his sins and disobedience, betimes a little disturbed, but soon recomposed in his impeni-tence, unconverted from his old ways, till the end comes, and he dies as he lived, unreconciled to God, unsanctified, and unsaved.

Have I thus hit upon the case of any one now listening to me? Then let this subject be to you an effectual warning. Here is the laying open to your view of what must come upon the unbeliev-ing world. Here is the sacred foreshowing of the end which awaits them that know not God, and obey not the Gospel of His Son. There is an in-dissoluble ligament which binds together impeni-tence in sin and inevitable damnation. Even the incense bowls of the holy altar are full of the wrath of God for all despisers and neglecters of the great salvation. Angels of the heavenly tem-ple stand girt in gold, prepared and ready to pour them out. And we need only listen with an atten-tive ear to hear the rustle and mutter of the dread-ful thunder of those cataracts of God's indignation upon them that turn not from their sins. Have you never felt the sting and rankling poison in your soul, if not in your very bones, of some past transgressions of which you have made yourself guilty? Has your conscience never smitten you, and made your sleep uneasy, and tinged your thinking with bitterness, for the sort of life you have been leading? Is there not some conscious shame and sense of wretchedness going along with the indulgence even of those darling lusts and dislike of sacred things which you allow to have place in your heart? And what is all this but the premonitory drops of that wrath of God which must presently come in great deluging showers? O child of man, give heed, and turn, and fly, before the threatening avalanche of the Almighty's judgments comes! And now, whilst this little feeling of anxiety and disturbance is upon you, let it not pass without a thorough change in all your ways; lest the next time the feeling of compunction comes, it may find you amid the hopeless torments of eternal death.

LECTURE THIRTY-SEVENTH.

Rev. 16 : 12-21. (Revised Text.) And the sixth poured out his bowl
on [or *over*] the great river, the Euphrates; and the water of it was
dried up, that the way of the kings, they from the sunrising, might be
prepared. And I saw out of the mouth of the dragon, out of the mouth
of the beast, and out of the mouth of the false prophet three unclean
spirits, like frogs; for they are the spirits of demons, working miracles,
which go forth on [or *over*] the kings of the whole habitable world, to
gather them to the battle of the great day of God the Almighty. (Behold, I come as a thief; blessed he that watcheth, and keepeth his garments, that he walk not naked, and they see his shame.) And they
gathered them together to the place which is called in Hebrew Harmageddon.

And the seventh poured out his bowl on [or *over*] the air; and there
came forth a voice out of the temple from the throne, saying, *It is
done.* And there became lightnings, and voices, and thunderings; and
there became a great earthquake, such as became not since there became a man on the earth, such an earthquake, so great. And the great
city became into three parts, and the cities of the nations fell, and
Babylon the great was remembered in the presence of God, to give to
her the cup of the wine of the fierceness of his anger. And every island
fled, and mountains were not found, and a great hail, like as a talent [in
weight], fell out of the heaven on the men; and the men blasphemed
God on account of the plague of the hail, because the plague thereof is
exceedingly great.

THE vision of the seven last plagues presents a distinct series of events, giving details of the last great afflictions which fall upon the world, then quite given over into the Devil's hands. Thus far we have briefly considered five of these disastrous outpourings from the golden bowls. Two more remain to engage our present attention. Let us not forget to look devoutly to God our Father to help us understand them.

"*And the sixth angel poured out his bowl on or over the great river Euphrates; and the water of it was dried up, that the way of the kings, they from the sunrising, might be prepared.*" This must mean the literal river. The ulcers are literal; the sea, streams, and watersprings, turned to a condition resembling blood are literal; the heat and scorching from the sun are literal; the darkness which covers the dominion of the Beast is literal; and this must necessarily be literal too, whatever mysteriousness may be involved. The opening of a dry passage through the Red Sea, and through the Jordan, when Israel came out of Egypt and entered Canaan, were literal matters of fact; and they were openings for judgments upon the wicked, as well as of help and favor to the Lord's chosen. The drying up of the tongue of the Egyptian sea prepared the way for the great and final destruction of the oppressive powers that sought Israel's ruin. The rolling back of Jordan's waters was likewise the preparation and opening for the fall of Jericho, and the overthrow of the Canaanitic confederations. And this drying up

of the great river Euphrates is a corresponding
event, to prepare the way for the more wonderful
destruction to which the kings of the earth and
their armies are gathered in the great day of God
Almighty.   Isaiah (11 : 15) refers to it where he
says : " With His mighty wind shall he shake his
hand over the river [evidently the Euphrates], and
shall smite it in the seven streams, and make
men go over dryshod."   A recovery of certain
remnants of the Jewish people is there connected
with this miracle, " as it was to Israel in the day
that he came up out of Egypt;" but here, as there,
one of the most marked things is the opening for
and leading of the doomed powers to their destruction.   Zechariah refers to this, along with
some of the preceding plagues, where he says :
" He shall pass through the sea with affliction, and
shall smite the waves in the sea, *and all the deeps
in the river shall dry up*, and the pride of Assyria
shall be brought down." (Zech. 10 : 11; see also
Jer. 51 : 36.)   At the sounding of the sixth trumpet, the same great river was referred to as a bond
or boundary to certain destructive powers, which
were then let loose in dreadful inflictions upon the
wicked populations of the earth.*   So here it is
referred to as a barrier in the way of movements
which terminate in fearful disaster to those who
for unholy purposes avail themselves of its removal.

From time immemorial the Euphrates, with its

---

* Rev. 9: 13-21.   See Vol. II, pp. 109-122.

tributaries, has been a great and formidable boundary between the peoples east of it and those west of it. It runs a distance of 1800 miles, and is scarcely fordable anywhere or at any time. It is from three to twelve hundred yards wide, and from ten to thirty feet in depth; and most of the time it is still deeper and wider. It was the boundary of the dominion of Solomon, and is repeatedly spoken of as the northeast limit of the lands promised to Israel. (Gen. 15 : 18; Deut. 11 : 24; Josh. 1 : 4.) Some think that Abraham is called a *Hebrew*, and all his descendants *Hebrews*, because he crossed this river, migrating from the further side of it to this. History frequently refers to the great hindrance the Euphrates has been to military movements; and it has always been a line of separation between the peoples living east of it and those living west of it. But in the time of the pouring out of the sixth bowl of judgment this river is to be mysteriously smitten and dried up, that the kings from the sunrising may have an easy passage for their armies in coming to join the great infernal crusade against the Lamb. It looks like a gracious event, and a gracious aspect it has in some of the prophecies respecting it, for it also facilitates the return of certain remnants of the Israelitish people; but as God's opening through the Red Sea proved a trap of destruction to the persecuting Egyptians, so will it be in this case to the kings from the sunrising. Availing themselves of the easy passage thus afforded to come forth, they come to a scene of slaughter from which they never return. It is the outpouring of a bowl of wrath which opens their way. It is a judgment, though it seems for the time to be a favor.

But the mere drying up of the river would not so much harm them were not other agencies at work, to induce them to make use of the facilities thus afforded. The kings and armies of the world would not come together into Palestine were there not a very extraordinary influence to bring about the marvellous congregation. Accordingly the rapt seer tells of a mysterious infernal ministry in the matter. Not only does this sixth bowl of wrath dry up the Euphrates. It likewise evokes spirits of hell to incite, deceive, and persuade the nations to their ruin. John says: "*I saw out of the mouth of the Dragon, and out of the mouth of the Beast, and out of the mouth of the False Prophet, three unclean spirits, like frogs; for they are the spirits of demons, working miracles, which go forth on or over the kings of the whole habitable world, to gather them to the battle of the great day of God, the Almighty.*"

When the unexampled wickedness of Ahab was come to the full, and it was determined in heaven that an end should be made of him, "The Lord said: Who shall persuade Ahab, that he may go up and fall at Ramoth-Gilead? And one said on this manner, and another said on that manner. And there came forth a spirit, and stood before the Lord, and said: I will persuade him. And the Lord said unto him, Wherewith? And he

said: I will go forth, and I will be a lying spirit
in the mouth of all his prophets. And He said:
Thou shalt persuade him, and prevail also; go forth
and do so." So the Lord put a lying spirit in the
mouth of all Ahab's prophets; and he went up to
Ramoth-Gilead, and was wounded between the
joints of his harness, and was brought back a dead
man, and the dogs licked up his blood. (1 Kings
22 : 19–38.) A spirit of hell was allowed to go
forth to inflame and deceive him to his ruin.
And so it is in this case, only on a vastly greater
scale, and with mightier demonstrations, to persuade and deceive all the kings and governments
of the earth to join in an expedition which proves
the most terribly disastrous of all the expeditions
ever undertaken by man. In Ahab's case there
was but one evil spirit; here are *three*, if indeed
this definite number does not mean an indefinite
multitude. It is something of the plague of frogs
repeated; and then the number was infinite. By
these demon spirits the cause of the Dragon, the
Beast, and the False Prophet, is furnished with a
universal ministry. They are sent out by this infernal Trinity, issue from it, do its bidding, act for
it and in its interest. They have the power of
working miracles, Satanic miracles, by which they
offset everything divinely supernatural, and persuade by their preaching, oracles, and lying wonders, stirring up all the powers that be to unite in
one universal movement to suppress and extermi-
nate the incoming kingdom and power of the Lamb.

To tell exactly who and what these seducing

devils are, and exactly how they manage their infernal mission, may not be in our power. It is not
necessary that we should have definite knowledge
of that sort. But this is not the only place where
their agency and successes are mentioned. Paul
tells us that the Spirit speaketh expressly, that in the
latter times seducing spirits shall manifest themselves, even teaching demons, deceiving men with
their lies. (1 Tim. 4 : 1, 2.) They are spirits; they
are "unclean spirits;" they are "demon spirits;"
they are sent forth into activity by the Dragon
Trinity; they are the elect agents to awaken the
world to the attempt to abolish God from the
earth; and they are frog-like in that they come
forth out of the pestiferous quagmires of the universe, do their work amid the world's evening
shadows, and creep, and croak, and defile, and
fill the ears of the nations with their noisy demonstrations, till they set all the kings and armies of
the whole earth in enthusiastic commotion for the
final crushing out of the Lamb and all His powers.
As in chapter 9, the seven Spirits of God and of
Christ went forth into all the earth to make up
and gather together into one holy fellowship the
great congregation of the sanctified; so these
spirits of hell go forth upon the kings and potentates of the world, to make up and gather together
the grand army of the Devil's worshippers.

Nor need we wonder at their success. Those
who will not hear and obey the voice of God, are
sure to be led captive by the Devil and his emissaries. How great was the stir, and how intense

the enthusiasm, awakened throughout Europe by the crusader craze set on foot by Peter the Hermit! How were the nations aroused and set on fire to recover the holy places from the dominion of the Moslem! What myriads rushed to arms, took the mark of the red cross on their shoulders, and went forth as one man, never once calculating by what means they should live, much less reach the expected victory! And what thus happened throughout Europe in reference to a campaign professedly *for* Christ, may readily happen throughout the whole habitable world, when the question of the sovereignty of the earth hangs upon the success or failure of one last, grand, and universal engagement of battle. It is in sacred irony of the universal enthusiasm stirred up by these spirits, that Jehovah says by the mouth of Joel (3 : 9–11): "Proclaim ye this among the Gentiles; prepare war; wake up the mighty men; let all the men of war draw near; let them come up. Beat your ploughshares into swords, and your pruning hooks into spears; let the weak say, I am strong. Assemble yourselves together round about!" The divine taunt thus expressed reflects the character of the proceedings which it scorns. The heathen are on fire with rage. The kings of the earth set themselves. The rulers take counsel together against the Lord, and against His Anointed. The cry is, Let us break their bands asunder, and cast away their cords from us! But He that sitteth in the heavens laughs, and the Lord hath them in derision. (Ps. 2 : 1–4.)

Just here, however, there breaks in a singular note of warning. Whilst the unclean spirits are successfully stirring up the kings of the whole habitable world and gathering them for the battle of the great day, John hears a voice, which says, " *Behold I come as a thief; blessed he that watcheth, and keepeth his garments, that he walk not naked, and they see his shame.*" What means this strange announcement here? It is plainly the voice of Jesus, and the word is like to that so often given to the Church with reference to His coming again; but how does it apply here, after so many classes, including the great body of the saved, are already in heaven, with all their anxious watching past? By referring to the vision interjected at the opening of this account of the seven last plagues, we may perhaps come upon the true explanation. There is a gathering of saints under these plagues, as well as a gathering of the armies of the apostate world. Those who live at the time of the Antichrist do not all worship him or his image. Some hold out to the last against the acknowledgment of Antichrist as God, and will not be marked with his number or his name. Most of them die martyrs to their faith, but they conquer all the blandishments and bloody persecutions of the Beast, unstained by his hellish abominations. In the preceding chapter we were furnished with an anticipative vision of their heavenly reward for their faithfulness. They ultimately stand by the sea of glass, having harps of God, and singing the song of Moses and the Lamb. John sees them there in glory and immortality. Their great characteristic is, that, having lived under the Beast, they conquered in all the terrible trials and temptations endured from him. Having thus reached their heavenly glory, there must have been a coming of Christ for them, a resurrection and translation for them, as there had been a resurrection and translation for other classes and companies at other periods and stages of these judgment administrations. The occurrence of the vision of their blessedness in connection with these last plagues indicates that it must be in among these outpourings that Jesus comes for them. When once the kings of the earth and their armies begin to gather for the great battle, the last act is close at hand, and the last of the Gospel age is reached. Somewhere about this time, then, Christ comes for this last band of the children of the resurrection, whether dead or yet living. Of course, it is a coming of the same kind and character as his coming for those saints who were taken earlier; for it is the completion of that one coming for his people which is everywhere set forth. Here also, as in all other cases, nothing but a state of watchful readiness when the call comes can secure a share in the blessing. Though these people may have fought valiantly, if at the time they be not found steadfast and faithful at their posts, they must lose their reward. And failing in readiness at this last act of Christ's coming for His saints there would necessarily be entailed upon them a peculiar and irremediable nakedness. Whatever

might be left for them on earth, it would strip
them forever of all opportunity to share in any
privileges or honors of the children of the resurrection. Hence this particular admonition interjected at this particular place. It is a note of
indication that now at any moment Christ is about
to call for such of His people as yet may be on
earth. It is a note of instruction and direction to
keep themselves in strictest readiness by watchful
expectation and careful severance from the defiling abominations around them. And it is a note
of warning that if found unready their nakedness
and shame will be beyond remedy, as then the
whole matter will be over, and the door of admission into the peculiar kingdom of the elect will be
closed forever. There is a blessedness for them
even down amid these last extremities of the judgment time; but it can only be secured, as in every
other case, by constant watchfulness, prayer, and
readiness for the summons when it comes.

But, with this admonitory note from the Saviour, the narrative proceeds as if nothing had occurred. So few will be the number of saints remaining in those days, so obscure their condition,
and so indifferent the world to what happens to
them, that their sudden ereption to glory causes
no interruption to the wild doings of the nations,
and produces not even a ripple in the current of
their movements. The mission of the unclean
spirits effects its purpose. The whole world is in
a furor of enthusiasm to conquer and dethrone
the Lamb, and to crush out of the earth every

vestige of His authority and power. From one end of the world to the other, everything is alive and bristling with this thought. The spirits of demons have so taught the nations, and they proceed accordingly. East, west, north, and south the call to battle sounds; and kings, nations and armies are on the march—on the march to the scene of conflict—" *to the place which is called in Hebrew Harmageddon.*"

Where, then, is Harmageddon? Some say it is the great Valley of the Mississippi. A few years ago some said it was Sebastopol, or the Crimea. Others think it is France. Whilst many take it as a mere ideal place, for an ideal assemblage, having no existence in fact. To such wild, contradictory, and mutually destructive notions are men driven when they once depart from the letter of what is written. *Harmageddon* means the Mount of Megiddo, which has also given its name to the great plain of Jezreel, which belts across the middle of the Holy Land, from the Mediterranean to the Jordan. The name is from a Hebrew root which means *to cut off, to slay;* and a place of slaughter has Megiddo ever been. It is the great battlefield of the Old Testament between the Theocracy and its various enemies. In Deborah and Barak's time, " the kings came and fought, then fought the kings of Canaan in Taanach, *by the waters of Megiddo.*" (Judges 5 : 19.) When the good king Josiah fell before the archers of Pharaoh Necho, " he came to fight *in the valley of Megiddo.*" (2 Chron. 35 : 22–24.) And where God's king, in mortal flesh, thus fell a victim to the power of the heathen, there God's King, in resurrection glory, shall revenge himself on His enemies. Whether we take it as the mount or the valley, it makes no difference, for the mount and valley are counted as one, each belonging to the other. It was the valley in Josiah's fall, it is the mount in Messiah's victory. But with this gathering of the kings of the earth and their armies to this place this sixth bowl ends. It breaks off abruptly because it simply brings things into readiness for the final catastrophe, which only the seventh and final bowl brings forth.

"*And the seventh angel poured out his bowl on or over the air; and there came forth a voice out of the temple from the throne, saying,* IT IS DONE." This tells us direct from the Judgment-seat itself that here the end is reached, and that with this outpouring the whole contents of the wrath of God upon this present world are exhausted. When Christ yielded up His life on the cross, He said: "IT IS FINISHED!" The great sacrifice was complete. It was the ending up of all judgment upon them that believe, leaving nothing more of divine condemnation to come upon them. Here a similar word is given; for it is the completion of another sacrifice, the ending up of all judgment on them that believe not, but leaving nothing more of probation, help, or hope for them.

The particular consequences of this seventh outpouring are more fully described in the chapters which follow; but the commotions and disasters which it brings upon the earth are here stated in general, and they are without a parallel in the history of man.

" *And there became lightnings, and voices, and thunders.*" These are aerial convulsions. The contents of this bowl are poured upon the air, and the first impressions are in the air. The whole earth is to be affected, therefore the pouring is upon the most universal and all-inclosing element. There have been many atmospheric commotions during the progress of these judgment scenes, but here they reach their climax and consummation, fulfilling what so many of the prophets have spoken touching the changing and folding up of the heavens (Ps. 102 : 25, 26; Is. 51 : 6), the shaking of their powers (Matt. 24 : 29; Heb. 12 : 25), the passing of them with a great noise, and the dissolving of them with fire (2 Peter 3 : 10, 12). Speaking of this very time, when "the multitude of all the nations fight against Ariel," Isaiah says : " The Lord of hosts shall visit with thunder, and with earthquake, and great noise, with storm and tempest, and the flame of devouring fire." (Is. 29 : 6.) Of the same did Asaph sing : " Our God shall come, and shall not keep silence, a fire shall devour before Him, and it shall be very tempestuous round about Him. He shall call to the heavens from above, and to the earth, that He may judge his people." (Ps. 50 : 3, 4.) A world is to be finally ended, and these are the signs and attendants from above. But below they are correspondingly terrible.

" *And there became a great earthquake, such as became not since there became a man on earth, such an earthquake, so great.*" Here is the fulfilment of what Isaiah prophesied concerning the arising of the Lord " to shake terribly the earth " (chapter 2 : 19, 21). Here is what Haggai wrote about, when he recorded the saying of the Lord of hosts : " Yet once, and I will shake the heavens, and the earth, and the sea, and the dry land ; and I will shake all nations " (chapter 2 : 3, 4). The full force of this earthquake, unprecedented in time for its extent and violence, is indicated in its effects. By reason of it, John says :

" *The great city became into three parts, and the cities of the nations fell.*" The great city here is Jerusalem, for it is specially distinguished from the cities of the Gentiles, which are entirely ruined. It is only partially destroyed, because now in part possessed and appropriated as the Lord's. (Rev. 11 : 1, 2.) At the resurrection and ascension of the Two Witnesses, there was a great earthquake, when the tenth of the city fell (chapter 11 : 12, 13). Here there is a greater earthquake, and a much vaster effect. This is the time when the Mount of Olives is to cleave in two from east to west, " and half of the mountain shall remove toward the north, and half of it toward the south," leaving a very great valley between the two parts. (Zech. 14 : 4.) Such an occurrence must necessarily affect the foundation and topography of the city itself. The earthquake rends it into three parts. The implication is, that great chasms divide it, and that great damage occurs to it. Zechariah tells of a trichotomy of the land at that time, in which two parts shall be cut off and die, and one part shall be left. (Zech. 13 : 8, 9.) If the same applies to the city, then this dividing of it into three parts effects the destruction of two parts, while only one part remains standing. Three miraculous Witnesses appear there in those last years; first Enoch and Elijah, and then at last Christ himself. Enoch and Elijah are put to death, but Christ is living forever. So the death of the two miraculous Witnesses is avenged on two-thirds of the city, and the one-third, which Christ has taken for His, remains standing, as His power and dominion stand. Multitudes of the population doubtless perish amid these terrible commotions; but there is a refuge provided for those who acknowledge the Lord and call upon His name. (Zech. 13 : 9; 14 : 5.)

But the calamity to Jerusalem is not so great as the effect of this unprecedented earthquake upon the cities of the Gentiles. The great city is rent into fractions, but it does not utterly fall; "the cities of the nations" are universally ruined. The whole earth is shaken terribly by this bowl of the wrath of God, and we are told of no city in all the world that escapes. Rome falls, and Paris falls, and London falls; and wherever there are cities of the Gentiles they fall, shaken down, overwhelmed, or burnt up, under the terrible visitations of this great day of God Almighty. O the death and ruin which shall then be wrought! It

is the end of this present world, and this is the
way it comes.

"*And Babylon the great was remembered in the
presence of God to give to her the cup of the wine of
the fierceness of His anger.*" The description and
fate of great Babylon forms the subject of the
next chapters. There are peculiarities of detail
with reference to her which need to be more particularly set forth; but here is the time and place
in which all that befalls her occurs. There is a
grade in the progress of this woe. Jerusalem is
smitten, but only partially destroyed, because
something of the sacred is there. Then the Gentile cities, which stand a remove deeper down in
moral character, are entirely destroyed, for they
all belong to the Beast. And then Great Babylon,
standing at the base in the scale of guilt, is made
to drink the bitterest draught of all, because she
is the source and centre of the prevailing abominations.

And interlinked with the rest of the effects
wrought by these convulsions of an ending world,
the configuration of the earth is changed. John
beheld : "*And every island fled, and mountains were
not found.*" He does not say that islands ceased
to be, or no mountains are to remain or exist afterwards; but that there is to be a sudden recession
of the islands from their present places, and that
some mountains that now are shall entirely disappear. In other words, great portions of the earth
as it now stands will be quite altered in their po-
sitions and relations. The globe itself is not to

be annihilated. The matter of which it is composed is not to pass out of existence. But some of its elevations shall be depressed, and the present lines between sea and land shall be greatly altered, making ready for another climate, and for a better heavens and earth. What mountains shall sink, what shores be changed, and in what directions or to what extent the islands shall be moved we are not told. The facts alone are stated. There was something of this change under the sixth seal, as the effect of the great earthquake there beheld; but that was little more than the mere loosing of the mountains and islands from their places. (Rev. 6 : 14.) Here there is an entire disappearance of some mountains, and a *fleeing, or running away from* their old places, on the part of the islands. That was the beginning of the change; this is the consummation of it. Desolation comes to all that now is, and chaotic confusion to the whole face of the world. Looking down to this very period, and to these very occurrences, Jeremiah says (3 : 23–26) : " I beheld the earth, and lo, it was without form and void. I beheld the mountains, and lo, they trembled, and all the hills moved lightly,"—leaping and gliding from their places. " I beheld, and lo, the fruitful place was a wilderness, and all the cities thereof were broken down at the presence of the Lord, and by His fierce anger." And along with all the rest of these terrific and destructive convulsions comes also a most disastrous precipitation from the sky. John says : " *A great hail, like as a talent* [*in weight*], *fell out of the heaven on the men* [*or man-kind*].'' The Jewish talent for silver-weight was about 115 pounds, and that for weighing other things was about 135 pounds. The Egyptian talent was about 86 pounds, as also the Greek. Some make the Attic talent about 56 pounds, and a talent was used at Antioch which weighed about 390 pounds. Just which of these is meant we cannot say; but taking the mean of all, or even the lightest, we have a weight equal to as much as a strong man can conveniently lift. Hail of a pound in weight is terribly destructive; but this would give us hailstones as large as the blocks of ice which commerce wagons about our streets. Such masses falling upon houses would crush in the strongest of them, batter down walls, stave ships, and leave but few retreats of safety for human life on the surface of the world.*

---

* Few persons can form a conception of the terrible character of a great hailstorm. Here is an account of one which occurred at Constantinople in the month of October, 1831, written by one who witnessed it:

"After an uncommonly sultry night, threatening clouds arose about six in the morning, and a noise, between thunder and tempest, and yet not to be compared to either, increased every moment, and the inhabitants of the capital, roused from their sleep, awaited with anxious expectation the issue of this threatening phenomenon. Their uncertainty was not of long duration; lumps of ice as large as a man's foot, falling singly, and then like a thick shower of stones, which *destroyed every-thing with which they came in contact*. The oldest persons do not remember ever to have seen such hailstones. Some were picked up half an hour afterwards which weighed above a pound. This dreadful storm passed over Constantinople and

The stones thrown by the Roman catapults against Jerusalem, Josephus says, were of the weight of a talent; but these rugged ice masses, concreted in the troubled atmosphere on high, would necessarily come with more violence than Roman catapults could cast the same weight. When the plague of hail fell upon Egypt, only such lives suffered as were exposed in the open fields and highways (Ex. 9 : 19). But it will be infinitely worse when this great hail falls. Think of the earthquake which lays men's abodes in ruins, driving them to the open plains, and then this terrific hail coming upon them where no shelter is! What can they do? How must they be cut down by this dreadful artillery of the heavens!

> Day of anger! Day of wonder!
> When the earth shall rend asunder,
> Smote with hail, and fire, and thunder!

But what is the moral effect? Do the people bend, and own their sins, and sue for Heaven's pity and forgiveness? Alas for those in whom the spirit of hell has once taken firm root! No one having the brand of Antichrist ever repents. John

---

along the Bosphorus, over Therapia, Bojukden, and Belgrade; and the fairest, nay, the only hope of this beautiful and fertile tract, the vintage, just commenced, was destroyed in a day! Animals of all kinds, and even some persons, were *killed, an innumerable number are wounded, and the damage done to the houses is incalculable.* The force of the falling masses of ice was so great that they broke to atoms all the tiles on the roofs, and, like musket-balls, shattered planks.''

What would it have been if the ice masses had been fifty or one hundred times larger ?

beheld: "*And the men blasphemed God on account of the plague of the hail, because the plague thereof is exceedingly great.*" Such obstinacy in sin and guilt was unknown when the world was younger. When the hailstorm was heavy upon Egypt there was something of relenting. Pharaoh confessed his sin, and asked Moses to intercede for him. For the moment, at least, he agreed to let Israel go. But here transgressors have come to the full. They are dead-ripe for final judgment. Antichrist has taught them to curse God and die; and so they curse and blaspheme to the last, unsoftened and unchanged by all the terribleness of an oncoming perdition. It is by these plagues that their earthly existence ends, with the whole economy of things to which they cling; but their last words are curses, and their last breath is blasphemy.

Friends and brethren, I am at a loss at which to wonder most: whether at the severity of Almighty God upon the finally impenitent, or at the unconcern, neglect, and hardihood of men, who, with all this dreadful outcome before their eyes, still march calmly on in the very path which can have no other termination. O how dreadful! Retreat to the Lazar-house to refresh one's self with the groans and miseries of the wretched, a dance in the chamber of death, the singing of glees around the coffin of a beloved and honored friend, the making of merry jests over the fresh grave of one's own dear mother, would not be half so unseemly, so unfeeling, and so insane, as to go on in a life of indifference and impenitence, with eyes open and ears informed of all the horrible consequences which must come of it! There is but one explanation,—people do not half believe. They profess to receive and honor the Bible, but they do not credit what it so plainly says. They would feel indignant and resentful were we to call them infidels, and yet they are infidels. They may not speak the infidel's creed, but they live it every day, and think well of themselves whilst they do it. The inner temper of their souls—their spiritual tone—is infidel. The practical spirit which influences and controls them is the infidel spirit, and accords with the infidel reasoning. Either they do not think at all, and so reduce themselves to the level of the irrational brute; or their thinking is secretly, if not confessedly, tinged with the suspicion that these mighty revelations are nothing but unsubstantial speculation or doubtful theory. They have a deep persuasion of the certainty, regularity, and permanence of what they call natural laws, and have schooled themselves into such a trust and confidence and worship of Nature, that they see no need, or likelihood, or possibility of any other divinity or divine administrations. Thunder, lightning, tempests, plagues, pestilences, famines, earthquakes, eclipses, comets, at which mankind once trembled as signs of God's angry interference with human affairs, they find so largely explainable on natural principles that they are slow to admit that God has anything to do with these things, or that He is able to use them as His weapons of judgment. They talk of God, but to them He is an impotent God. Consciously or unconsciously, their souls are thus in a condition of skepticism, which empties the Divine Word of all reality to them. They hear it, and see what it says, but have a lingering feeling that it cannot be true just as it reads, and so pass it by as a dead letter.

O ye people of earthly wisdom, be not deceived! Where there are such effective laws as you speak of, there must needs be an Almighty Lawgiver who made them and put them into force; and He who could make them can also unmake them, and modify them as He pleases. Is efficient government any less the administration of sovereign power because it acts through great, settled, and well-known laws? Is His majesty disabled by having shown itself so great? What is more irrational than rationalism? Is God helpless to fulfil His word because He in Nature proves himself Almighty? Hath He made the blunder of binding His hands with His own Omnipotence? Such would seem to be the essence of some men's reasoning.

Be admonished then, dear hearer, and be not deluded to your ruin by the impertinent indifference and unwisdom of these evil times. Be sure that God is God, and that His Word must stand, though worlds dissolve. Now is your golden opportunity. You see what is the end that cometh. You see with what forbearance and mercy the threatened thunderstrokes of death are still held back, that men may hear and fear, and turn to Him

and live.   There is eternal security, if, with a true
and honest heart, you will only believe what is
written, and set your soul to obey and trust as He
counsels and directs.   It may cost you some sharp
trials now, but it will bring you safety and salvation when the skeptical and blaspheming world
goes down under the fierceness of His just anger.
Overwhelmingly dreadful as the foreshowing is,
there is no cause for despair if you will but take
warning now.   Only fix your trust in Jesus, and
follow and obey Him in sincerity and in truth,
and when His judgment strikes, it shall not harm
you.

> Though mountains from their seats be hurled
>   Down to the deep, and buried there,
> Convulsions shake the solid world,
>   Our faith shall never yield to fear.

LECTURE THIRTY-EIGHTH.

Rev. 17 : 1–17. (Revised Text.) And there came one of the seven angels who had the seven bowls, and talked with me, saying, Hither, I will show thee the judgment of the great harlot that sitteth upon many waters, with whom the kings of the earth committed fornication, and the inhabitants of the earth were made drunk from the wine of her fornication.

And he bore me away in spirit into a wilderness, and I saw a woman sitting upon a scarlet beast, full of names of blasphemy, having seven heads and ten horns. And the woman was clothed in purple and scarlet, decked with gold and precious stone and pearls, having a cup of gold in her hand full of abominations and the unclean things of her and of the earth's fornication, and upon her forehead a name written, *Mystery, Babylon the great, the mother of the harlots and of the abominations of the earth.*

And I saw the woman drunken from the blood of the saints, and from the blood of martyrs [witnesses] of Jesus : and I wondered great wonder when I saw her.

And the angel said to me, Wherefore wonderest thou? I will tell to thee the mystery of the woman, and of the beast that carrieth her, having the seven heads and ten horns.

The beast which thou sawest. was and is not, and is to ascend out of the abyss, and goeth into perdition : and they shall wonder who dwell upon the earth, whose names are not written upon the book of life from the foundation of the world, when they behold the beast, because he was, and is not, and shall once more be here [or *come again*].

(107)

Here [is] the mind that hath wisdom: the seven heads are seven mountains where the woman sitteth upon them, and are seven kings; the five are fallen, the one is, the other is not yet come, and when he shall come, he must continue a little time. And the beast that was and is not, even he is the eighth, and is out of the seven, and goeth into perdition.

And the ten horns which thou sawest are ten kings which have not yet received kingdom; but they receive power as kings one hour with the beast. These have one mind, and give their power and authority to the beast. These shall make war with the Lamb, and the Lamb shall conquer them, because he is Lord of lords and King of kings, and they who are with him, called and chosen and faithful.

And he saith to me, The waters which thou sawest, where the harlot sitteth, are peoples and multitudes and nations and tongues. And the ten horns which thou sawest, and the beast, these shall hate the harlot, and shall make her desolate and naked, and shall eat her flesh, and shall burn her with fire. For God gave into their hearts to do his mind, and to make one mind, and to give their kingdom to the beast, until the words of God shall be fulfilled.

WE have already twice heard of Great Babylon, and calamity to her; once in chapter 14 : 8, by anticipation; and once in chapter 16 : 19, where her sins were said to have come into remembrance, and the cup of the fierceness of the wrath of God to have been administered to her. The particulars of that visitation, as well as the whole character and relations of this mystic personage, are given in the chapters upon which we now enter. As the first reference was somewhat anticipative, so these further accounts are somewhat retrogessive, and go back to exhibit in all its length and breadth what in the previous chapter was only synoptically stated.

The subject itself is one of great prominence in the Apocalypse, as in all the prophecies; but it has proven about as difficult as it is conspicuous.

On none of the current methods of treating this Book is it possible to come to any clear, consistent, and satisfying conclusions with regard to it. The body of preterist expositors have found themselves necessitated to take Great Babylon as meaning the city, the church, or the ecclesiastical system of Rome, not so much because the features of the record call for it, or really admit of it, when fairly dealt with, but because unable on their theory to do any better. That Rome and the Romish system are involved, may readily be admitted; but that this is all, and that the sudden fall of Great Babylon is simply the fall of Romanism, or the utter destruction of the city of Rome, must be emphatically denied, if the inspired portraiture is to stand as it is written. If we cannot find more solid ground than that on which the Rome theory rests we must needs consign the whole subject to the department of doubt and uncertainty, and let all these tremendous foreshowings pass for nothing. Unite with me, then, dear friends, in praying God to open our understandings, that we may not fail to take in what He really intends that His people should see in these sacred visions.

The first thing which strikes me in the study of this subject, is one which I have nowhere seen duly noticed, namely: the evident correlation and contrast between the Woman here pictured and another Woman described in the twelfth chapter. There, "a great sign was seen in the heaven, *a Woman;*" here, it is remarked, "he bore me away in spirit into a wilderness, and I saw *a Woman.*"

Both these Women are mothers; the first
"brought forth a son, a male [*neuter*, embracing
either sex], who is to rule all the nations;" the
second "is the mother of harlots and of the abominations of the earth." Both are splendidly
dressed; the first is "clothed with the sun." Her
raiment is light from heaven. The second is
"clothed in purple, and scarlet, decked with gold,
and precious stone, and pearls." All her ornaments are from below, made up of things out of
the earth and the sea. Both are very influential
in their position; the first has "the moon," the
empress of night, the powers of darkness, "under
her feet;" the second "hath rule, or kingdom,
upon the kings of the earth." Both are sufferers;
against the first is the Dragon, who stands watching to devour her child, and persecutes and pur-
sues her, and drives her into the wilderness, and
sends out a river to overwhelm her, and is at war
with all her seed that he can find; against the
second are the ten kings, who ultimately hate her,
and make her desolate and naked, and eat her
flesh, and burn her with fire, whilst God in His
strength judgeth her, and visits her with plague,
death, and utter destruction. Both are very conspicuous, and fill a large space in the history of
the world, and in all the administrations of divine
providence and judgment. That they are counterparts of each other there can hardly be a reasonable doubt. The one is a pure woman, the
other is a harlot. The first is hated by the powers
on earth, the second is loved, flattered, and caressed

by them. Where the one has sway, things are heavenly; where the other lives, it is "wilderness." The one produces masculine nobility, which is ultimately caught away to God and to His throne; the other produces effeminate impurity, which calls down the fierceness of the divine wrath. The one is sustained and helped by celestial wings; the other is supported and carried by the Dragon power,—the Beast with the seven heads and ten horns. The one has a crown of twelve stars, wearing the patriarchs and apostles as her royal diadem ; the other has upon her forehead the name of the greatest destroyer and oppressor of the holy people, and is drunken with "the blood of prophets and of saints, and of all that have been slain upon the earth." The one finally comes out in a heavenly city, the New Jerusalem, made up of imperishable jewels, and arrayed in all the glory of God and the Lamb; the other finally comes out in a city of this world's superlative admiration, which suddenly goes down forever under the intense wrath of Heaven, and becomes the habitation of demons, and a hold of every unclean spirit.

These two Women, thus related, and set over one against the other as opposites and rivals, must necessarily be interpreted in the same way. As Antichrist corresponds to Christ as a rival and antagonist of Christ, so Great Babylon corresponds to the Woman that bears the Man-child, as *her* rival and antagonist.

By recalling, therefore, who and what is meant

by the first Woman, we will be in position to un-derstand who and what is meant by the second.

Beyond question, the sun-clad Woman is God's great symbol of the visible Church,—the Lamb's Wife,—the bone of His bone, and flesh of His flesh, fashioned out of His rifted side as the Second Adam, who fell into the deep sleep of death for that purpose. As Methodius taught, "The woman seen in heaven, clothed with the sun, and adorned with a crown of twelve stars, is, in the highest and strictest sense, our Mother. The prophets, considering what is spoken of her, call her Jeru-salem, at other times The Bride, the Mount Sion, the Temple and Tabernacle of God." She is not the church of any one period or dispensation, but the entire Universal Church of all time, as Victo-rinus, the earliest commentator on this Book, held and affirmed, saying: "The Woman clothed with the sun, having the moon under her feet, is the Church of the Patriarchs, and of the Prophets, and of the holy Apostles"—that is, the Church from the days of Adam and Eve on to the last victory over the worship, name, and mark, of the final Antichrist. What then can this rival Woman be but the organized Antichurch, the pseudo-church, the Bride made out of Satan, the univer-sal body and congregation of false-believers and false-worshippers? As Christ has had a visible Church in all time, embodying the wisdom and spirit of heaven, and maintaining the confession of His truth and worship, so has the Devil had a corresponding following in all time, embodying

the sensual and devilish wisdom and spirit, and
maintaining the profession and teaching of Satan's
lies. And as the first Woman denotes the one, so
the second Woman denotes the other. The proofs
of this will appear as we consider the particulars
of the case.

1. One of the most characteristic features of this
Woman is her *harlotry*. The Angel calls her " The
Great Harlot," and she wears on her forehead as
her name, "The mother of the harlots, and of the
abominations of the earth." Harlotry is the standing symbol in the word of God for a debauched
worship, idolatry, and false devotion. When people
worship for God what is not God, or give their
hearts to idols, or institute systems, doctrines, rites,
or administrations, to take the place of what God
has revealed and appointed, the Scriptures call it
whoredom, adultery, fornication. (Jer. 3 : 6, 8, 9;
Ez. 16 : 32; Hosea 1 and 2; Rev. 2 : 22.) The reasons are obvious. The breaking down of the divine
laws and ordinances necessarily carries with it the
dishonor of the marriage institution, and hence
all supports of godly chastity and pureness. Accordingly all false religions are ever attended with
lewdness, even in connection with their most honored rites. The sacredness of marriage has no
place in them. Besides, the very essence of the
divine law is, that we love God our Lord with all
the heart, mind, soul, and strength. This is Jehovah's due and requirement of all that live.
Hence the bestowal of worshipful affection on any
other object, or the putting of anything whatever

in the place of the true God, is, in the very nature
of the case, a great spiritual harlotry; for it is the
turning of the soul from the only legitimate object of its adoration, to take into its embrace what
has no right to such room and place.   And as this
Woman is a *harlot,* " the great Harlot," and " the
mother of the harlots and the abominations of the
earth," she must needs be the great embodiment,
source, and representative of all idolatry, false
worship, and perversion of the word and institutes
of God.   This helps to determine her character as
the rival and antagonist of the Woman clothed
with the sun, and makes her the symbol of the
universal body of the faithless, just as the sun-
clad Woman is the symbol of the universal body
and congregation of believers.   She can by no
means be Rome alone, whether Pagan or Papal,
any more than the sun-clad Woman is the early
Church alone, or Protestants alone.   There were
believers and saints in the 4000 years before the
Christian era, and so there were idolaters and per-
verters of the institutes of God in plentiful abundance before there were Popes or Roman emperors.   And as the pure Woman is made up of the
whole congregation of the faith*ful* from the beginning, so must this great Harlot be made up of all
the faith*less* from the beginning.

2. This conclusion is rendered the more necessary by the name which this Woman has written
upon her forehead. How could she be " the mother
of the harlots and of the abominations of the earth"
if her existence does not date back to, and above

all include, the great harlotries and abominations
which preceded both the Popes and the Roman
emperors? Besides, we have here the motherhood of various harlots, or systems and economies
of harlotry and abominations of the earth. If
Pagan Rome is to be understood, that was but one
individual system. If *Papal* Rome is to be understood, that again is but one individual system.
The implication would thus be that the earth had
no systems of harlotry or abominations but the
one found in Pagan or Papal Rome, and this
mother of the harlots would thus have no children
to show! The record is that she is herself the
great original of all harlotries and abominations
of the earth, that many others have sprung from
her, and that all the harlotries of time have her
for their primal representative and mother. The
imagery, therefore, goes back to the beginnings,
out of which all false systems, and false worships,
and abominations of the earth have come.

3. Accordingly, also, we have in the very front
of this Woman's name a designation which carries
us back to the commencement of the whole ill-
condition of things in this present world. Rome
never was "Babylon" in the sense of being "the
mother of the harlots and the abominations of the
earth." Her place in the chart of time renders
that impossible; just as impossible as that some
Sarah of to-day should be the mother of the patri-
arch Isaac, and so of the Jewish race. Neither
was the Babylon of Nebuchadnezzar's day "the
mother of the harlots and the abominations of the

earth," and for the same reason. It comes too late. We must go further back, and much nearer to the landing of the Ark on Ararat, for such a beginning and motherhood. But when we search for it we find it, and find it under the very name which this mother of all harlots and abominations of the earth bears written on her forehead. The tenth and eleventh chapters of Genesis tell the story.

Turning to these chapters of national origins, we learn that *the beginning of the kingdom of Nimrod*, the grandson of Ham, *was Bab-el*, or BABYLON, in the land of Shinar, whither the then inhabitants of the earth, who were as yet of one language and one speech, journeyed together from the East. The implication is, that they came thither under the leadership of Nimrod, whose name means *a rebellious panther*, and that under him began that first great work of rebellion against God which brought the confusion of tongues, and inaugurated the original of all the subsequent harlotries and abominations of mankind. Against the command and known intent of the Almighty, it was there undertaken to "build a city and a tower whose top might reach unto heaven," and to make themselves a name that they might not be scattered abroad upon the face of the earth. It appears, also, that from the hunting and slaying of wild beasts, and with the armed forces grouped around him in that business, Nimrod betook himself to the subjugation and enslavement of men, compelling them into his service and daring schemes.

Thus he " began to be a mighty one in the earth," the organizer of an arbitrary imperialism over against the patriarchal order and the divine institutes. The Arab records tell us that he was the first king, and thus the beginner of all kingcraft and tyranny which have since so much oppressed the world. It is said of him that he professed to have seen a golden crown in the sky, that he had one made like it, and that he put it on his own head, and thus claimed to rule in the name and as the earthly impersonation of the powers of the sky, either as Orion or the Sun.

The Bible says that it was further arranged for the people to make for themselves " *a name*,"—*a Sem*, token, sign, banner, ensign, or mark of confederation, fellowship, and organized unity, as an undivided people, lest they should become dispersed over the earth into separate societies. (Compare Jer. 13 : 11; 33 : 9; Ezek. 39 : 13; Zeph. 3 : 20.) Against God they had determined to hold together, and they wished to have a badge, standard, something by which they could be known, and in which they could all glory and rejoice as the centre and crown of their unity. That *Sem*, or *Sema*, was to be a mark of consolidated greatness, a loftiness and pride to them ; that is, in the language of the time, a *Sema-Rama*. Thus we have the name of the mythic *Semiramis*, the Dove-Goddess, which was the ensign of all the Assyrian princes, and which figures so largely as Ashtaroth, Astarte, the heavenly Aphrodite, and Venus. Semiramis is said to have been the wife of Nim-

rod; so that the *Sem*, or token, of the Nimrodic
confederation was probably the image of his wife,
with a dove upon her head, with wings spread
like the horns of the new moon. This, in the
language of the time, would be called *Sema-Rama*,
because the great *Sem*, name, or token, of the
combination against being scattered abroad. The
symbol of such a name or confederation would
naturally and almost necessarily take the place of
a god, and become the holy mother, the great
heavenly protectress, the giver of greatness and
prosperity to those rallying under it.

So again, Nimrod called his first and capital
city *Bab-el*, which, in the language of the time,
means *The Gate of God;* of course not the God of
Noah and Shem, for the whole proceeding was in
known and intended antagonism to the true God
and His will and commands. Hebraistically, and
by way of accommodation to the judgment which
Jehovah there inflicted, *Babel* is made significant
of *confusion* (Gen. 11 : 9), but in the original application of the name it means *The Gate of God.*
Thus, in the very name of the place, we have the
intimation and proof that these Nimrodic proceedings were not only the organization of a new and
oppressive style of government, but with it, as an
essential part of it, the inauguration of a new and
idolatrous religion, the parent apostasy of the
post-diluvian world.

The Bible says that Nimrod was *a mighty hunter
before the Lord.* The Targum of Jonathan inter-
prets this to mean that he was *a mighty rebel before*

the Lord, the mightiest rebel before the Lord that ever was in the earth. The Jerusalem Targum reads it that he was *mighty in sin* before the Lord, a hunter of the sons of men, exhorting them to leave the judgments of Shem and adhere to the judgments of Nimrod. Hence it was the proverb concerning every notorious adventurer in wickedness and oppression, As the mighty Nimrod in rebellion and sin before God. Jarchi accordingly understands the record to be, that Nimrod was a most brazen offender, who did not fear or hesitate to withstand God to his very face. And every intimation concerning him shows that he was the Heaven-defying founder of a new system of rule and worship, instituting a government by brute force and earthly wisdom and policy, and a religion which quite abolished the true God, and set men to the adoration of the sun, moon, and stars, impersonated in himself, wife, relatives, and chief consociates, and represented in the idol standards of his kingdom.

It is a mistake to suppose that idolatry was the gradual growth of well-disposed but unenlightened human thinking. Its rise was sudden. It was conceived in intentional rebellion. It was the invention of a proud and tyrannous ambition at war with Jehovah's commands. It was brought into being to counteract the will and worship of the true and known God. It was the creature and handmaid of power for the deification of " the lust of the flesh, the lust of the eyes, and the pride of life" in the place of the Creator. And it originated with old Babylon, and Babylon's first king, the great rebel Nimrod, that very *Bar-Chus* (son of Cush), or *Bacchus*, who figures among the Greek and Roman gods as the great overflowing, enlivening, healing, and directing power. It is also a fact that all the Pagan mythologies and idolatrous devotions the world over, whatever their diversities, show a oneness of character, and an underlying likeness which proves that they are from one original source, and but modifications of one and the same primal invention, traceable to old Babylon and the Nimrodic plan to defeat the purposes of the God of Noah. The original design was thwarted by the confusion of tongues. Contrary to their oaths to the Dove-goddess of their standards, the people were obliged to disperse and leave off the building of their tower. But the charming novelties which Nimrod taught them were not lost. The seeds of the fascinating invention went with the dispersion, planting themselves in every new settlement, and growing ever fresh crops as the streams of humanity ran on amid the centuries, but ever reproducing the likeness of the original mother. Whatever changes or additions came, it still was old Babylon, which ever abides, potent through all the ages, and known to the judgment angels as " *Babylon the great, the mother of the harlots and of the abominations of the earth.*"

4. It is further said of this Woman that " the inhabitants of the earth were made drunk from the wine of her fornication." This is not true of Rome, Pagan or Papal; for before and beyond

either, the earth had a hundredfold more inhabitants untouched and uninfluenced by one or the other
than ever were under the tutorage of both of them
together. To talk of " the *Roman* earth" in such
a description is worse than impertinence. "The
inhabitants of the earth" are *the inhabitants of the
earth*, and the people of the generations before
Rome, and where Rome has never reached, as
well as under Rome. The wine of old Babylon's
fornication was a debauching system of idol worship and carnal self-exaltation, over against the
revelations and institutes of Jehovah. It was
already bottled and labelled before the first dispersion. It went with that dispersion into every
country and nation under heaven. As a matter of
fact, we find it to this day among all the nations
of the earth, affecting if not controlling their
thinking, their policies, their faith, and their worship. Not less than two-thirds of the population
of the earth at this hour are Pagan idolaters,
drivelling under the same old intoxication which
came forth from Nimrod and Babylon; whilst the
great body of the other third is either Mohammedan, Catholic, Jewish, infidel, or adherents of
some tainted and antichristian faith and worship.
Nor is there a kingdom or government on the
face of the whole earth at this hour which does
not embody and exhibit more of the spirit and
rebellion of Nimrod than of the spirit, commandments, and inculcations of God. All the kings of
the earth and all the governments under heaven
have more or less joined in the uncleanness and

fornication of that same old Babylonian Harlot, who has defiled every spot and nook of the whole inhabited world, notwithstanding that God from the beginning set the seal of His wrath upon it. The Jewish whoredoms, and the Papal whoredoms, and the Mohammedan whoredoms, and the whoredoms of all perverted Christian religionists, though not entirely letting go the confession of the one only God, are still in essence the same old harlotry which first found place and embodiment on the banks of the Euphrates. It is the same old Babylon, and her harlot daughters, bearing rule or kingdom upon the dominions of the earth, and intoxicating the inhabitants thereof out of the wine of her fornication.

The cup held out is *golden*. To the sensual and carnal heart and imagination the world's religion and progress is something bright and glorious, the glittering fulness of good and blessing. But in that shining cup is only abomination and uncleanness—spiritual prostitution—nothing but spiritual prostitution.

The cup is *one;* and in all the varied systems of false faith and false worship which taint our world there is held out and received but one and the same essence, and that essence is the harlotry of old Babylon. It is most direct in Paganism ; but it is in Mohammedanism, in Papism, in the degenerate Catholicism of the Eastern churches, and in all the heretical isms, infidelities, and mere goodishnesses which afflict our Protestant Christianity as well. So true is it that Great Babylon, the mother of the harlots and of the abominations of the earth, hath made the inhabitants of the earth drunk with the wine of her fornication.

5. This Woman is also herself drunken — "drunken from the blood of the saints, and from the blood of the martyrs or witnesses of Jesus." "In her was found the blood of prophets, and of saints, and of all that have been slain [as martyrs] upon the earth." This is proof positive that the Great Harlot is not Papal Rome only, for all *the prophets* were dead hundreds of years before the rise of the Papacy; and myriads on myriads of God's true people died as martyrs to the faith ere ever there was a Pope or a Papal hierarchy. The same is proof positive that she is not Pagan Rome alone; for the old prophets were dead or gone before either Cæsar lived, or ever Romulus was born; and great hosts of martyrs suffered before Rome was at all. Drunken as the Romish power made itself upon the blood of the witnesses of Jesus, Roman government is not chargeable with the shedding of *all* the martyr blood that has flowed upon the earth. It is, however, very certain, and beyond dispute, that all the persecution and slaying of saints, and prophets, and witnesses for God that have ever occurred upon earth, past or present, ancient or modern, stand charged against the mystic kingdom of idolaters, false religionists, and such as accepted fellowship with spiritual harlotry. Persecution of God's prophets or people is itself a mark and evidence of spiritual whoredom. It shows alienation from God and His true

worship. And wherever such presentation finds place, or saints are sacrificed for their faith, there this great Harlot is in living and visible force and presence, whether among Pagans or Jews, Mohammedans or Christians, Catholics or Protestants. It is the old Nimrod over again, tyrannously enforcing his murderous will against the will and commands of God.

6. Again, this mystic Woman sits upon many waters, which waters the angel says "are peoples, and multitudes, and nations, and tongues." There is a vastness and universality in these terms, and in the extent of these symbolic waters, which ill accords with the extent of the Papal dominion. Though extending over many peoples, multitudes, nations, and tongues, there are many, many more peoples, and far greater multitudes, and numbers of nations, and tongues, over which the hierarchy of Rome has no control, whose interest and sympathy she does not possess, and on whom she cannot lean for support. So with regard to Pagan Rome, there were peoples, and multitudes, and nations, and tongues, never within the territory of the Cæsars, and many indeed of whom the Cæsars had no knowledge. Giving the words the latitude which properly belongs to such a description as this, the masses of the earth's population, not only of one period, but of all periods since nations came into being, would seem to be the conception. And it is only when we understand this mystic Harlot as the whole body of organized alienation from God, as in heathenism, false re-

ligion, and spiritual prostitution, that we find an object coextensive in time and territory with the "peoples, and multitudes, and nations, and tongues," which make up the seat, dependence, and support of this great Harlot. At one period or another she has been found sitting on every people, and nation, and tongue, since the tongues or multitudes of men have been sundered.

7. John further saw this Woman sitting upon a scarlet Beast, full of names of blasphemy, having seven heads and ten horns. This Beast is the same described in chapter 13. He is referred to here, not so much to make us better acquainted with him, as to give us a full understanding of the Great Harlot and her relationships. The "wisdom" or inner sense and meaning of the presentation is, that "the seven heads are seven mountains, where the Woman sitteth upon them, and are seven kings." These are the words which are supposed to fix the application of the picture to the city of Rome, as Rome is called a city of seven hills. But a flimsier basis for such a controlling and all-conditioning conclusion is perhaps nowhere to be found. The seven *hills* of the city of Rome, to begin with, are not *mountains*, as every one who has been there can testify; and if they were, they are not more characteristic of the situation of Rome than the seven hills are characteristic of Jerusalem. But the taking of them as literal hills or mountains at all is founded upon a total misreading of the angel's words.

A *mountain*, or prominent elevation on the surface of the earth, is one of the common scriptural images, symbols, or representatives of a kingdom, regal dominion, empire, or established authority. So David, speaking of the vicissitudes which he experienced as the king of Israel, says: "Lord, by Thy favor Thou didst make *my mountain* to stand strong"—*margin*, "settled strength for *my mountain;*" meaning his kingdom and dominion. (Ps. 30 : 7.) So the Lord in His threat against the throne and power of Babylon said: "I am against thee, O destroying *mountain*, which destroyest all the earth; and I will stretch out mine hand upon thee, and will roll thee down from the rocks, and will make thee a burnt *mountain.*" (Jer. 51 : 25.) So the kingdom of the Messiah is likened to "a stone, which became a great *mountain*, and filled the whole earth." (Dan. 2 : 35.) And this is exactly the sense in which the angel uses the word here, as he himself tells us. He does not say "the seven heads are seven mountains, where the Woman sitteth upon them," and there leave off; but he adds immediately, "*and they are seven kings,*" or *personified kingdoms*. The mountains, then, are not piles of material rocks and earth at all, but royal or imperial powers, declared to be such by the angel himself. The description, therefore, so far from fixing the application to the Papacy, or to the city of Rome, decisively settles that it cannot possibly apply to either, for neither has seven such mountains. The late Albert Barnes has written in his *Notes* that "all respectable interpreters agree that it refers to Rome; either Pagan,

Christian, or Papal." Of course he is one of the
"respectable interpreters," but then he should be
able to tell which of the objects he names it is, for
it cannot be all three. Most people assign Dr. E.
W. Hengstenberg, the great Berlin professor,
a place among "respectable interpreters," but
Hengstenberg says Rome cannot possibly be
meant by these seven heads. The angel says they
are seven regal mountains, seven kings, seven
great ruling powers. Rome Papal cannot be
meant, for Rome Papal has no such count of seven
regal powers. Rome Christian cannot be meant,
for Rome Christian, as distinguished from Rome
Papal, never supported and carried the great Harlot in any possible sense, and could not without
ceasing to be Christian. Rome Pagan cannot be
meant, for Rome Pagan ceased with the conversion of the throne, and no count of emperors or
kings can be found in it to " respectably " fill out
the angel's description. The succession of the
forms of administration, enumerated as *Kings,*
Consuls, Dictators, Decemvirs, Military Tribunes, and
Emperors, were not seven kings or regal mountains. Prior to the empire most of these administrations were less than anthills in the history of
the world, and furnished rather slender ponies for
the great purple-clad and pearl-decked mother of
harlots to ride on in her majesty. Rome surely
comes into the count of these seven mountains of
empire ; but to make Rome the whole seven, including also the eighth, requires a good deal more
"respectability" of interpretation in that line

than has thus far appeared. Barnes is sure the
whole thing applies to Rome because this Woman
"hath rule or kingdom upon the kings of the
earth, and there was no other empire on the earth
to which this could be properly applied." But
this assumes that the Woman is an empire, for
which there is not a particle of evidence. The
Woman is *not* an empire any more than the Church
of Christ is an empire. She rides upon empires,
kings, and powers of the world, and inspires, leads,
and controls them; but she herself is not one of
them, and is above all of them, so that they court
her, and are bewitched and governed by her—
governed, not with the reins of empire, but with
the lure of her fornication. This Woman is longer-
lived than any one empire. We have seen that
she began with Nimrod, bears the name of Babylon, and is not destroyed until the day of judgment. The seven imperial mountains on which
she rides must therefore fill up the whole interval;
or there was a time, and the most of her history,
when she did not ride at all, which is not the fact.
Seven is itself the number of fulness, which includes the whole of its kind. The reference here
is to kings, to mountains of temporal dominion,
to empires. It must therefore take in all of them.
And when men once get over their "respectability," and rise to the height and range of the in-
terpreting angel's view of things, they will have
no difficulty in identifying the mountains, or the
times to which they belong.

Of these seven regal mountains, John was told

"*the five are fallen*," dead, passed away, their day
over; "*the one is*," that is, was standing, at that
moment, was then in sway and power; "*the other
is not yet come, and when he shall come, he must continue a little time.*" What regal mountain, then, was
in power at the time John wrote? There can
be no question on that point; it was the Roman
empire. Thus, then, we ascertain and identify the
sixth in the list, which shows what sort of *kings*
the angel meant. Of the same class with this, and
belonging to the same category, there are five
others—five which had then already run their
course and passed away. But what five imperial
mountains like Rome had been and gone, up to
that time? Is history so obscure as not to tell us
with unmistakable certainty? Preceding Rome
the world had but five great names or nationalities
answering to imperial Rome, and those scarce a
schoolboy ought to miss. They are Greece, Persia,
Babylon, Assyria, and Egypt; no more, and no
less. And these all were imperial powers like
Rome. Here, then, are six of these regal mountains; the seventh is not yet come. When
it comes it is to endure but a short time. This
implies that each of the others continues a
long time; and so, again, could not mean the dictators, decemvirs, and military tribunes of the
early history of Rome, for some of them lasted but
a year or two. Thus, then, by the clearest, most
direct, and most natural signification of the words
of the record, we are brought to the identification
of these seven mountain kings as the seven great
world-powers, which stretch from the beginning

of our present world to the end of it. Daniel
makes the number less; but he started with his
own times, and looked only down the stream.
Here the account looks backward as well as forward. That which is first in Daniel is the third
here, and that which is the sixth here is the fourth
in Daniel. Only in the commencing point is there
any difference. The visions of Daniel and the
visions of John are from the same Divine Mind,
and they perfectly harmonize, only that the latest
are the amplest.

By these seven great powers then, filling up the
whole interval of this world's history, this great
Harlot is said to be carried. On these she rides,
according to the vision. It is not upon one alone,
nor upon any particular number of them, but upon
all of them, the whole seven-headed Beast, that
she sits. Those seven powers, each and all, support the Woman as their joy and pride; and she
accepts and uses them, and sways their administrations, and rides in glory by means of them.
They are her devotees, lovers, and most humble
servants; and she is their patronizing and most
noble lady, with a mutuality of favors and inter-
communion belonging to her designation. This
is the picture as explained by the angel. But, to
say that the Romish Papacy was thus carried,
nurtured, and sustained by the ancient empires of
Greece, Persia, Babylon, Assyria, and Egypt,
would be a great lie on history. It was not so. In
the nature of things it could not be so. By no
means then can this Harlot be the Papacy alone,
as maintained by all "*respectable* interpreters."

Furthermore, it is a matter of fact, that as surely
as Rome in John's day, and Greece, Persia, Babylon, Assyria, and Egypt, before Rome, existed
and bore sway on earth as regal mountains, so
surely and conspicuously were they each and all
ridden by this great Harlot.   They were each and
all the lovers, supporters, and defenders of organized falsehood in religion, the patrons of idolatry,
the foster friends of all manner of spiritual harlotry.   Nimrod, the hunter of the sons of men
and author of despotic government, established
his idolatrous inventions as the crown and glory
of his empire, and intertwined the worship of
idols with the standards of his power.   It was the
same with Egypt, whose colossal remains, unfading paintings, and mummy scrolls confirm the
Scripture portraitures of her disgusting devotions,
and tell how the priests of these abominations
were honored by the throne, of which they were
the chief advisers.   It was so with Assyria, as the
recent exhumations of Nineveh abundantly attest.
It was so with the Babylon of Nebuchadnezzar,
as Daniel, who lived amid it all, has written.   It
was so with Persia, as her various records all declare.   It was so with Greece, as her own most
cherished poets sung, her mightiest orators proclaimed, and all her venerated artists and histo-
rians have set forth.   It was so with Rome, as all
her widespread monuments still show, and all the
Christian testimonies, with her own, render clear
and manifest as the sun.   And it will be so with
the last, which is yet to come, as declared in the
apocalyptic foreshowings, and in all the prophecies

in the Book of God upon the subject. It requires but a glance at history to see that spiritual harlotry has ever been the particular pet and delight of all the Beast-powers of time. If ever the worship and requirements of the true God won their respect and patronage, they soon corrupted it to their own selfish and ambitious ends, or never were easy until freed from the felt restraint.

True religion and an uncorrupted Church have never suited the representatives of power, or pleased them long. Dragon agencies are ill at ease without some form of Dragon worship. Only what will dignify, if not deify, lust and selfishness, is in accord with their spirit. They simply favor and honor their own when they favor and cherish the base Woman. Her gaudiness and pomp, her gayety and ready compliances, her ennoblement of " the lust of the flesh, the lust of the eyes, and the pride of life," enamour them, and make them glad to bear her on their shoulders. It is a sad commentary on humanity, but it is the truth, that all the great world-powers, from first to last, are the paramours and props of the Harlot Woman. Government is indeed a thing of God, instituted for human good, necessary to man, and invested with rights from the eternal throne; but Satan has ever known too well how to pervert it to his own base ends. And so the mountains of worldly power have ever served him as grand homes for his adulteress Bride.

What else remains of the story must wait for another occasion. God help us all to keep ourselves from idols!

LECTURE THIRTY-NINTH.

GREAT BABYLON CONTINUED — THE WILDERNESS IN WHICH
SHE APPEARS — HER TWOFOLDNESS, IN MYSTERY AND AS
A CITY — SHALL THE CITY OF BABYLON BE RESTORED —
PROPHECIES OF HER ABSOLUTE OBLITERATION NOT YET
FULFILLED — PROPHECIES WHICH SEEM TO REQUIRE HER
RESTORATION—ZECHARIAH'S EPHAH—HER FEATURES AND
FALL TOUCHING THIS QUESTION—REASONABLENESS OF THE
IDEA.

Rev. 17 : 18. (Revised Text.) And the Woman whom thou sawest, is the great city, which hath rule [kingdom] upon the kings of the earth.

WHEN John was taken to see "the judgment of the Great Harlot," he was borne "into a wilderness." This description of her dwelling-place is very expressive. Where spiritual harlotry occupies the place of the true worship of God, there is desolation. There may be riches and worldly glory, as here. There may be the fulness of power and dominion; there may be purple, and scarlet, and gold, and gems of stone, and pearls, and drink from golden cups; there may be luxuries, sumptuous living, pomp, display, and everything to delight the sensual heart; and yet, where the word, worship, and institutes of God are trampled under foot, it is wilderness. Some set great store on general education, on the achieve-

(133)

ments of science, on the progress of man in his material and social interests, on the success of reforms in government and laws, on the universal spread of liberty, equality, and fraternity, wrought out by the diffusion of intelligence and right reason. Those claiming to be leaders in this line of thought are everywhere full of prognostications of a great and glorious condition of humanity to be achieved by the new ideas over against what they consider the old nonsense, superstition, and ignorance, which, as they say, have too long held dominion. And in proportion to the confidence and zeal in these hopes is the averseness to the Bible and its teachings, or any such way of receiving it as takes it for what it says. Indeed the Church, its doctrines and confessions, are ignored, sneered at, and more and more resisted and set aside, as the particular impediment to the true interests of man, and the worst hindrances to human progress and blessedness. But the Scriptures have anticipated this, and tell us that so things will go on until the world believes itself wiser than its reputed Maker. And when the gospel of the sensual and devilish wisdom has once won its way to victory, as it surely will; when the atheistic materialism to which so many are betaking themselves has attained its bloom; and when the ten thousand goodishnesses for which so large a portion of the professed Church is selling its birthright have brought forth their inevitable fruits, the result will be a universal *wilderness*, with nothing but a monster Beast from the abyss for government, a hell-inspired self-will for law, and the uncleannesses of a gaudy Harlot for paradise. And this is the world in its final outcome, when Antichrist reigns and Great Babylon reaches its full development. The true people of God will then have been removed to the heavenly pavilion, or killed off by the powers of a blaspheming persecution. According to the prophet's figure, they will have become as scarce on earth as the remaining grapes after the vintage has been gathered. The Living Ones will have reached their places in connection with the celestial throne. The Elders will have obtained their crowns and golden seats. The numberless multitude will have taken its stand before the throne of God. The salt of the earth and the light of the world will have been mostly withdrawn. And whatever of accumulated wealth, gorgeousness, luxury, or perfected human civilization may remain, what can this habitation of mortals be but one great moral wilderness and desolation, where the powers are full of blasphemy, and the accredited worship is abomination? Such, at least, is the pictured scene of things to which the Apostolic Seer was carried to see the Great Harlot and the end that awaits her.

When John beheld the Woman, he was much astonished. He tells us himself that he "wondered great wonder." When the Beast first displayed himself all the world wondered after the Beast. (Chap. 13 : 3.) But that was a wonder of admiration; this is a wonder of perplexed horror.

He had had a view of that Beast before. He had
beheld and described his heads and horns. He
had seen the wounding to death and the healing
from the wound, and how men were carried captive by the marvel. But he experienced no such
astonishment as here. But he had seen and described the glorious Woman, whose mystic child
was caught up to God and to His throne. Could
it be that this was the same Woman,—the Bride
of Heaven transformed into such a character, with
such names on her forehead, and thus associated
with the Son of Perdition? God had once exclaimed over the defections of Jerusalem, "How
is the faithful city become an harlot!" (Isa. 1 : 21.)
Was John to understand a similar transformation
here? This was the seat of his amazed horror
and bewilderment. But the angel at once inter-
posed to relieve him. The Beast is the same
which he saw before, but the Woman is not. And
the Beast is here seen in the fulness of his development. No color was noticed on his first rise;
but by this time he has developed his bloody hue
by his slaughter of the saints. Then he had names
of blasphemy on his heads; by this time he is full
of them all over. There his infernal origin did
not so fully appear; by this time he has demon-
strated that he comes up out of the abyss. His
seven heads were there left in mystery; here they
are explained, and his true history and relations
indicated. There his ten horns were noted; but
only here is it told that they are ten contemporaneous kings, who arise contemporaneously with

the Beast, and who colleague with him in one mind and policy, and give their power and authority to him, and join with him and each other in desolating and devouring the Woman whom at first they carried in affection, and finally make war against the Lamb in a contest for the sovereignty of the world. The Woman is a new and different object. The first was the mother of saints; this is the mother of harlots and of the abominations of the earth, first organized in the rebellion of Nimrod, and the gaudy but unclean rider upon all the great mountains of world-power from the beginning, for whose special delectation all the martyr blood that ever flowed has been shed, and who is here shown for the purpose of exhibiting her end.

There is a twofoldness of the judgment upon this great Harlot. Not only is her fall mentioned twice, and each time with a double fall; but two sorts of visitation, and seemingly at different times, are here described. At first the Beast carries the Woman; but the angel says that the ten horns, in connection with him, eventually "hate the Harlot, and make her desolate and naked, and shall eat her flesh, and burn her with fire." In the next chapter, however, there is a different picture, and her final ruin takes the form of a sudden and complete overthrow of a great city, over which these same kings lament and mourn. These two different presentations are owing to the two different aspects in which the Woman is contemplated. In chapter 17 we have the picture of Great Babylon *in mystery* only, in which she has various centres and forms at different times, and presents herself in a variety of ways. The last forms of Babylon *in mystery* are those which the ten kings with the Beast attack and destroy. How this comes about is plain enough. The two great Beasts, as we have seen, set up an entirely new religion upon earth,—a religion which they insist on making as universal as their own dominion, and so must needs make war on all existing religions, true or false. The record is, that they will not permit any one to live under them who will not conform to their new worship, nor allow any one to buy or sell without first accepting their hellish sacrament or mark. Hence every form of existing worship then upon earth, be it Romanism, Mohammedanism, degenerate Protestantism, or any other species of false worship, it will come under the ban of this great infernal confederation. Whatever riches or possessions they may have will be confiscated. Their temples, cathedrals, mosques, institutions, and treasure-depositories, will be rifled, stripped, burned to the ground, and all their owners turned out in perfect nakedness; and any of them daring to resist, or refusing to conform to the new worship of the Beast and his image, will be put to the sword. All this is necessarily implied in what was shown of the doings of the False Prophet, and what occurs under his administrations; but it is here independently stated as part of "the judgment of the Great Harlot." This is the first part of her final calamities.

But Great Babylon in final revelation is also *a*

local city. As a system, its essential principle is alienation of soul from God, and so whatever is developed from the carnal wisdom, either against or in the place of the true worship. But as the sun-clad Woman develops into a heavenly city, the new Jerusalem, embodying all the ultimate glories pertaining to the spiritual wisdom and the true devotion, so the Great Harlot also develops into an earthly city, embodying all the completed temporal results of the sensual wisdom and the ultimate bloom of human apostasy. Hence her final overthrow sums up in the fall and destruction of a great, rich, and powerful city. Hence, also, the angel says: "The Woman whom thou sawest is *the great city* which hath rule upon the kings of the earth." It is the same Woman which, as a system of false worship, rode all the governments and powers of earth, but which makes its final presentation in the form of a literal city.

Some think only an ideal city is meant, but nearly all interpreters, however diverse their ways of looking at these visions, agree that we must here understand a real city. Most of them say it is the city of Rome; some say it is Jerusalem; and a few say it is the island of England, which they take as the great centre of an unclean system of union between Church and State. My own impressions are that a literal city is contemplated in the vision, but that we must look for it in a different region of the world. However much Rome, Jerusalem, or states having national churches may be involved, they do not, and it is hard to see how they possibly can, fill out the picture of this final Babylon. The realization is yet in the future, and we cannot speak with confidence as to how matters will eventuate ; but there seems to be reason for the belief that the literal Babylon will be restored, and that we are to look to the coming up again of that primal city for the fulfilment of what is here foreshown. The mention of such a thing may seem like a wild dream, and appear to clash with some of the prophecies touching the irrecoverable destruction of ancient Babylon. But let us look a little at the subject, and endeavor to construe the Scriptures as they are, and not according to the loose impressions which have found currency as if they were settled truths.

First of all, it seems to be pretty clear that the ancient predictions concerning the utter destruction of Babylon have never yet been entirely fulfilled. Isaiah gives the sentence upon Babylon, in which he says that her destruction shall come suddenly from the hand of the Almighty, that her glory and beauty shall be "as when God overthrew Sodom and Gomorrah," never more to be inhabited, nor dwelt in from generation to generation ; and that the Arabian shall never again pitch tent there, nor shepherds make their fold there. (See Isaiah 13.) So again it was said to Jeremiah, "Babylon shall become heaps, a dwelling-place for dragons, an astonishment, and an hissing, without an inhabitant." At the same time he directed Seraiah to take the manuscript of this prophecy, after reading it, bind a stone to it, cast it into

the midst of Euphrates, and say, " Thus shall
Babylon sink, and shall not rise from the evil that
I will bring upon her." (Jer. 51.) That all this
has been in large measure strikingly fulfilled must
be admitted. It is part of the evidence of the
truth of God's word. And if it all belongs to the
past, it is equally certain that Babylon never can
be restored. Two facts, however, appear, which go
very far to prove that these predictions do not belong exclusively to the past, but await further fulfilment. The one is, that Isaiah locates the destruction of which he speaks in "*the day of the
Lord.*" (Is. 13: 6.) That day, in literal fulness,
has not yet come. The world has witnessed many
earnests and prelibations of it, but that day proper
is still in the future, and only comes when Christ
himself shall come again. And if the utter destruction thus suddenly to come upon Babylon
belongs to " the day of the Lord," she must again
revive in order to become the subject of it. The
other fact is that Babylon, in all the deep calamities and desolations which have come upon her,
never yet experienced all that has been thus
prophesied. When did Babylon ever fall with so
complete a fall, or meet with such an utter obliteration from the earth, "as when God overthrew
Sodom and Gomorrah?" Sodom and Gomorrah
were completely blotted out. But this has never
yet been the case with Babylon. Such was not its
fate when the Medes and Persians seized it from
the hands of the infamous Belshazzar, for they
made it one of their royal cities. In the time of

Alexander it still stood, and was the chosen capital of the Græco-Macedonian empire, the second
city of Alexander's dominions, where he himself
lived and died. It continued to be a populous
place under the Syrian kings, who succeeded Alexander in the rule over it. In the time of the
apostles it was still a populous place, for both Peter
and Bartholomew preached the Gospel there, and
there Peter wrote his first Epistle. As late as
A.D. 250, there was a Christian church there, and
an influential bishopric for many years thereafter.
Five hundred years after Christ there were Jewish
academies there, who issued the celebrated Babylonian Talmud. Here, then, was a lengthening
out of the existence of Babylon as a populated
city for more than a thousand years subsequent
to the taking of it by Cyrus. And even to this
present hour there is a city in the middle of the
area occupied by old Babylon containing 10,000
people, and which pays to its governor a revenue
of 342,000 Turkish piastres, more than $17,000, a
year. Shepherds do make their folds there, as
testified by all modern travellers, and the Arabians
do pitch their tents there. It is not an utter desolation without inhabitant, and never has been since
Nimrod laid its first foundations. The sentence
upon Babylon is therefore not yet fulfilled, and
cannot be unless that city comes up again into
something of its former consequence.

In the next place, there are Scripture prophecies
which I am at a loss to understand except upon the
theory that Babylon will be restored, become a

great commercial centre, and be the last of this world's great centres to go down under the terrific visitations of the day of the Lord.

What is the world's common symbol for commerce, the accepted picture to represent it? I have asked this question, and looked to verify the answer. In general I have found it to be an ornamented coin, weight, measure, or bowl of the scales, bearing a representation of the power that authorizes it, and a figure of a woman on each side,—one surrounded with the implements of navigation looking to the sea, and the other surrounded with the implements of trade, husbandry, and transportation looking toward the land,—the two mutually supporting what is between them, whilst above are the wings of some vigorous bird, to indicate the far-reaching flights of what is thus pictured to the eye and imagination. Nor would it be easy to improve on this. It has been evolved in the course of ages, and the whole modern world, so far as I know, has set the seal of its approval upon it as the accepted emblem of commerce. But it is the same that was shown to the prophet Zechariah 500 years before the commencement of the Christian era. Just at the time when he sees the great flying roll of the curse of God going forth over the face of the whole earth to cut off transgressors, he beholds an *ephah*, the common bushel measure, and *a talent of lead*, the flat rounded weight used in the calculation of tonnage, put upon the mouth or top of the bushel measure, whilst on each side of it was a woman, having

wings " like the wings of a stork," with the winds
in their wings; and they two lifted up the ephah
between earth and heaven to bear it away. Besides, in the midst of the united measure and
weight, was another woman called *Wickedness*, the
Lawless Woman, answering to the Great Harlot
of these chapters. The prophet wondered what it
all meant, and asked the angel in converse with
him what these intended to do with the measure
and weight inclosing the Woman of Wickedness.
The angel said: " *To build it an house in the land
of Shinar ; and it shall be established and set there
upon her own base.*" (Zech. 5 : 1–11.)

Now this joined measure and weight, with the
two winged women bearing them, and the winds
in their wings, is unquestionably a symbol of *commerce ;* not so much as it was then, but as it was
to become in the period verging on the end, and
as it has become in our day. The building of a
house for it, and the establishment and settling of
it upon its own base, can mean nothing less than
the creation for it of a great independent centre,
with its own ruler, king, or government. The
place of this house is specifically stated to be
" *the land of Shinar.*" What that land is we can
have no difficulty in ascertaining. When the
people in Nimrod's time journeyed from the East
they found a plain in the land of *Shinar* and dwelt
there, and there built the city called Babel, or
Babylon. (Gen. 11 : 2–9.) When Nebuchadnezzar,
king of Babylon, invaded Palestine, it is said that
he took Jehoiakim, and part of the vessels of the

house of God, and carried them "*into the land of Shinar,*" that is, Babylon. (Dan. 1 : 1, 2.) "The land of Shinar," then, is Babylon; and in this Shinar the angel said this *commerce,* borne by the favoring winds on mighty wings, was to be established and settled on its own base.

This prophecy was delivered subsequent to the Babylonish captivity, and at least half a lifetime after Babylon had been conquered by the Medes and Persians. It certainly has never yet been fulfilled according to its terms. By the connection in which it is given, its fulfilment belongs to the time when the great curse of God upon the wicked goes forth over all the face of the earth; that is, in the great judgment period. By the indications thus given as to time, and by the whole contents of the foreshowing, its accomplishment belongs to the future, and necessarily includes the revival of old Babylon as a great commercial centre, standing independent of all other powers, and exercising its own peculiar dominion over the governments of the earth. And this is all the more confirmed in that it exhibits the Woman of Wickedness, the Great Harlot, ensconced in it, as the great spirit which pervades the whole.

It is also distinctly prophesied that Babylon shall be the very last of the powers of the earth compelled to drink of the cup of the divine wrath in the great day of the Lord. That cup is to go around to all the nations and potencies of this world, to " all the kings of the north, far and near, one with another, and all the kingdoms of the world which are upon the face of the earth; *and the king of Sheshack shall drink after them.*" (Jer. 25 : 17–26.) All the Jewish interpreters agree that *Sheshack* is only another name for *Babylon*, and so, in another place, Babylon is called "the hindermost of the nations," because thus belated in the judgment which is to make her "a wilderness, a dry land, a desert," so as to be "wholly desolate," and "no more inhabited forever." (Jer. 50 : 12, 13, 35–40.) Thus far Babylon has been *the foremost* of the nations in experience of the judgments of God, and cannot possibly be "*the hindermost,*" as thus described, except as rebuilt and become once more a great centre of independent power existing at the time when the final day of vengeance comes.

Furthermore, it seems to me impossible to do justice to the description which John here gives of the features and fall of the Great City which he was called to contemplate, except on the supposition of such a revival of the old Chaldean metropolis.

The name itself is a tower of strength to the idea. There is no great city, Babylon, now; nor has there been for many ages. Nor is there any other great city on the face of the earth that answers to the picture, or that is at all likely ever to answer to it on any possibilities that can be imagined. And yet the name of this great city is *Babylon*—Babylon living and ruling over the kings and nations of the earth when the day of judgment reaches its consummation. It is not Babylon in mystery, but simply "the great city Babylon, the mighty city;" and there is no intimation whatever that this city of Babylon does not mean the city of Babylon. By what right then are we to think of any other city than that which has been known by this name ever since Nimrod lived?

The city here described is pre-eminently, if not exclusively, a commercial city,—a great commercial city,—a mart of nations. There is nothing military, nothing ecclesiastical, nothing educational, alluded to in the account; everything is *commercial,* or merged into the one idea of exchange, trade, and what relates to mercantile aims and accumulations. Ships, merchants, commodities, are the main subjects of the description. And when this city falls, it is "the merchants of the earth" that "mourn and weep over her," and with them such as are most concerned with commerce,—" every ship-master, and every one who goeth by sea, and sailors, and as many as trade by sea," for "all who had ships in the sea were made rich from her costliness." The lamentation is of the same character as that over the fall of Tyre (Ezek. 26 : 15–18), and we know that Tyre was the great mercantile metropolis of its time; therefore this city must also be a corresponding commercial centre. It cannot, therefore, be Rome, for Rome never was a great centre of commerce. In all the Bible we never read of "a ship of Rome," or of one sailing *from* or *to* Rome. It cannot be Paris for similar reasons. It might be London, New York, or San Francisco, but there is nothing whatever in the account to fix the picture on either of them, whilst none of them could become so independent of all government but its own, as indicated in this case. The land of Shinar is named as the locality in the old prophets, and the particular city of that land, in its own proper name, is given by John as the subject of what he describes. And such is the location of that city politically, geographically, and in all the qualities of accessibility, commercial facilities, remoteness from interferences of Church or state, and yet centralness with regard to the general trade of the whole world, as to point it out above any other known as the elect spot for just what is predicted of this great city.

Even apart from the direct Scriptural prophecies and implications on the subject, the prospect is as they represent. The whole world is rapidly developing a system of things which, in the ordinary working of human affairs, must inevitably result in something of the kind. In what, indeed, does the mightiest and furthest-reaching power on earth now already centre? A power which looms up in all lands, far above all individual or combined powers of Church, or state, or caste, or creed? What is it that to-day monopolizes nearly all legislation, dictates international treaties, governs the conferences of kings for the regulation of the balance of power, builds railways, cuts ship-canals, sends forth steamer-lines to the ends of the earth, unwinds electric wires across continents, under the seas, and around the world, employs thousands of engineers, subsidizes the press, tells the state of the markets of the world yesterday that every one may know how to move to-day, and has her living organizations in every land and city, interlinked with each other, and coming daily into closer and closer combination, so that no great government under the sun can any longer move or act against her will, or without her concurrence and consent? Think for a moment, for there is such a power; a power that is everywhere clamoring for a common code, a common currency, common weights and measures; and which is not likely to be silenced or to stop till it has secured a common centre on its own independent basis, whence to dictate to all countries and to exercise its own peculiar rule on all the kings and nations of the earth. That power is COMMERCE; the power of the ephah and the talent —the power borne by the winged women, the one with her hand on the sea and the other with her hand on the land,—the power which even in its present dismemberment is mightier than any pope, any throne, any government, or any other one human power on the face of the globe. Let it go on as it has been going, and will go, in spite of every-thing that earth can interpose to hinder, dissolving every tie of nationality, every bond of family or kindred, every principle of right and religion which it cannot bend and render subservient to its own ends and interests; and the time must come when it will settle itself down somewhere on its own independent base, and where Judaism and Heathenism, Romanism and Protestantism, Mo-hammedanism and Boodhism, and every distinction of nationality,—English, German, French, Italian, Greek, Turk, Hindoo, Arab, Chinee, Japanee, or what not,—shall be sunk in one great universal fellowship and kingdom of *commerce*.

And when it once comes to that, as there is every prospect that it will, for Providence in judgment for the greed and covetousness of men will prosper it, filling the wings of the women with the winds of heaven, where on earth is the spot so suited to the purpose as that where the first city this side the flood was built? There is the great navigable river, emptying out into the open sea, whose waters lave every country and island most filled with the treasures of the far East.* From thence there are almost level avenues for railway lines to Egypt, Smyrna, and Constantinople, connecting with Vienna, Paris, and London, for some of which the Turkish Sultan, it is said, has granted Firman, and which Western Europe in its own defence will presently be compelled to construct. There could all the great mercantile combinations unite in one common centre, with no other power on earth to interfere with them. All the considerations which bear on the question speak for old Babylon.

And with a world-wide commercial organization

---

* G. Rawlinson, in his notes on *Herodotus*, says, with General Chesney's *Euphrat. Expedition*, that the Euphrates "is navigable without any serious interruption from Samosata to the sea, nearly 1200 miles;" that from Busrah to the sea it is on an average 30 feet deep and 1200 yards wide, and at Babylon it averages 15 feet in depth and 200 yards in width.—Vol. i, pp. 446, 447.

thus established on its own independent base, with
the great mercantile houses of England and her
colonies, of the Americas, of the other countries
lining the Mediterranean, of the maritime and
monetary centres everywhere, represented in corresponding houses there; with the ships, and passengers in ships, congregating in and about the
Euphrates as the central exchange of the world;
and with the gold-kings, money-lords, and merchant princes of the earth, thus combined without
regard to creeds or nationalities in the one great
interest of regulating and managing the commerce
of the globe, it is easy to see how every feature in
the Apocalyptic picture of Babylon would be filled
out. Her merchants would thus be the great men
of the earth. Her chief purchases would necessarily be as here described: (1) the most precious
and valuable metals; (2) the costliest articles of
clothing, ornaments, and display; (3) the most rare
and sumptuous of furniture and materials for it;
(4) precious aromatics, spices, and ointments; (5)
the finest of eatables; (6) the most luxurious of
equipages, chariots, and horses; and (7) slaves and
attendants necessary to the maintenance of the
style and grandeur going along with such wealth,
consequence, and power. The city would thus
literally be " clothed in fine linen, and purple, and
scarlet, and decked with gold, and precious stone,
and pearl," creating a market for the skill and most
excellent products of the whole world, enriching artisans, ship-masters, ship-owners, ship-senders, and
all the traders in these things in all nations. Kings

of the earth would thus naturally find it their interest and their delight to be on good terms and friendliest intimacies with a power so much wider and greater than their own. Governments would have to throw their influence in its favor, legislate out of the way what it wishes away, direct their policies according to its desires, and make war and conclude peace as it dictates, as is even now already largely the case, for commerce is the law-maker of the world. The purse-strings of the nations would thus be in the hands of a universal independent power, whose ban would be worse than the Pope's edicts of excommunication in the Middle Ages; and to make war with it would be to make war against the allied world. All the kings of the earth would thus necessarily become participant in everything belonging to the system, the very organization of which is the utter negation of all distinctive creeds, and the complete abrogation of all religious and moral laws which stand in the way of its purposes.

And thus also the old harlotry would necessarily be the chief spirit of the whole thing. Zealous and earnest worship there would needs be, but a worship concentrated upon the ephah and the talent; a worship which makes temples of banks, and warehouses, and exchanges, and pleasure-parks; a worship not of the sun, or moon, or stars, or emperors, or popes, but of pounds, and francs, and piastres, and dollars; the worship of greed, and epicurean luxury; the worship of Mammon perfected, and overriding and supplanting all other devotions; the perpetuation and crown of the great moral defilement of the ages, only taking to the soul's embrace and into the place of God the meaner object which the divine word stigmatizes as "*filthy lucre.*" Covetousness is idolatry, and a form of it which is the root of all evil; and here will be covetousness, deep-wrapped in the embracing arms of its god, and dazing and defiling the world with the glory and grandeur of its abominations.

Such would Babylon be under the suppositions to which I have alluded, and such is the Great Babylon of these chapters in its final outcome. Is it not reasonable, therefore, to believe that this is the way in which this prophetic description is to be realized?

Besides, it would be a strange thing if Babylon were to be the only exception to the general revival and renewal which is to come to the long desolations of the East in general. Egypt, long the basest of the kingdoms, is rapidly coming up again, and is everywhere presented as prominent in the time when Christ comes to take the sovereignty of the earth. The English occupation of Cyprus must give strong impulse to the rebuilding of the mighty cities which once had place upon and around that island. Tyre and its associated cities, and Antioch, and Damascus, and Tadmor, and Nineveh, and all the ancient localities, are becoming more and more the objects of interest to the Western peoples and powers, and plans for the revival of some of them, including especially old

Babylon, have been put forth with eloquence and received with favor.*

---

* In 1857 a work was published in London, entitled *Memoir of the Euphrates Valley Route to India, with Official Correspondence and Maps*, by W. P. Andrew, F.R.G.S., etc. After a large circulation the same was enlarged, and published in a volume, entitled *The Scinde Railway and its Relations to the Euphrates Valley and other Routes to India*. This enlargement and republication of the work was undertaken, on the considerations stated in the preface, viz., that " it is believed to be *essential*, not only to the vital interests of this country (England) in the East, and the well-being of Turkey, but to the peace and progress of the world, to establish, with as little delay as possible, steam and telegraphic communication, *via* the Euphrates, between England and India;" and "to indicate to statesmen the political power, to the philanthropist the enlightenment, and to the merchant the profit, that would of necessity accrue from re-establishing this highway of forgotten empires and ancient commerce."

The author of this book recounts the many and glowing histories which cluster around the Euphrates and its tributary, the Tigris; points out the extraordinary capabilities of the country, and adds: "Every way, commercially, historically, and politically, the Euphrates Valley route is a grand scheme, and must affect immediately the commerce, and, in some measure, the destinies of our race; and that depends not on a thorough traffic, but holds within its own confines the elements of a great prosperity.

" Why have the governments and peoples of the West combined to uphold the Sultan in the possession of Constantinople? And why has he who thought fit to menace that position met with the armed opposition of Europe? Because the passage from the Mediterranean to the Black Sea is of so much importance that whatever European power might become master of it would domineer over all the rest, and destroy that balance which the whole world is interested in preserving. Establish then, at another and far more extensive point of the Ottoman Empire, a similar and yet more important position; make the Valley of the Euphrates *the highway of the commercial world*, and you would restore millions of unproductive acres to the revenue,

Jerusalem, we know, is to be rebuilt and re-established as a great national and religious centre,

bring thousands of merely vassal tribes within the pale of order and fair tribute, and create in the East another immovable seat of power for the great powers of Europe."

So, also, an article in *Colburn's Monthly*, quoted by this author, says: "England and France, and even other nations, appear now called to great works, which throw into the shade the most striking deeds of history. Among these works of the future it appears that the opening of the Euphrates Valley, and *the restoration of Syria and Mesopotamia, of Assyria and Babylonia*, stands first in rank. Such a proceeding, by multiplying and strengthening the ties by which people of all climates, of all races, of all beliefs, are united to Great Britain and France, would connect forever the general prosperity of nations with the happiness of those countries, their security with their power, and their independence with their liberty."

Mr. Andrew further says: "Amongst the numerous administrations of a wise and merciful design of Providence, it is not unreasonable to believe that the opening of the valleys of the Euphrates and the Tigris, and *the resuscitation of the great nations of antiquity*, are amongst the events designed to minister to the growing wants and improvements of the human race. . . . . It is not too much to say that there is no existing or projected railroads that can for a moment compare, in point of interest and importance, with that of the Euphrates Valley. It brings two quarters of the globe into juxtaposition, and three continents,—Europe, Asia, and Australia,—into co-relation. It binds the vast population of Hindustan by an iron link with the people of Europe; it inevitably entails the colonization and civilization of the great valleys of the Euphrates and Tigris, *the resuscitation in modern shape of Babylon and Nineveh*, and the reawakening of Ctesiphon and Bagdad of old."

In the *Life of Sir C. Napier*, vol. iv, p. 70, there is given an extract from his journal, in which he writes: "Civilization was travelling west in Alexander's time, but now how changed is the drama! More than 2000 years have passed, and civilization arises on the rear of barbarism; we English have seized of a very numerous, rich, and powerful people. And when Israel with its wealth and commercial energy begins to rally again around its old metropolis, the Euphrates will again be needed as much as Germany needs the Danube, Egypt the Nile, or London the Thames; whilst the prodigious fertility of its great alluvial plains, and the unbounded riches of nature which there spring up almost unbidden to the hand that would gather them, and a ready progress of opulence that would realize the wonder-working power of Aladdin's lamp, cannot fail to arrest and command the sharp-sighted covetousness of the human heart. How, then, are we to suppose it possible that Babylon will not also come up again with the rest of these Eastern schemes and renovations? Already a walled town there exists, taking in both sides of the river, as old Babylon did. It is encircled

---

the baggage, are following up our blow, *and in a few years shall be at Babylon, a revived empire!* We shall go slowly, but *one hundred years will see us at Babylon!*" This was written fifty years ago.

A letter written at Mosul (Nineveh), February 26th, 1854, and published in the *New York Tribune*, says: "There is but little soil in the world like that of the valleys of the Tigris and the Euphrates. . . . . It is among the possibilities that a railway will ere long be built from Antioch to Seleucia along the Orontes, across Mesopotamia to Mosul, and thence down to Bagdad and Busrah,—the second short route to India. If this part of Turkey should fall into the hands of England, there is no doubt that such a road would be speedily constructed. *The line has been surveyed.* These barren fields are too rich always to remain idle. ITS TIME HAS NEARLY COME!"

All these statements are quite apart from what many are too prone to call mere prophetic speculations.

with villages, and approached through an out-spread country dotted with beautiful groves of date-trees, forming a broad and verdant colonnade to a growing city. That city, strangely enough, also bears the name of *Rest* (Hillah), as if inviting the wide-wandering tribes of an apostate world to come back to the bosom of the old mother, there to plant and erect the final tower of their finished greatness.

I conclude, then, that such a great commercial city, different from all that now exist, will yet be, and that it will be old Babylon rebuilt. When the New Jerusalem, the Lamb's Wife, comes down out of heaven from God, there is every intimation that it will be stationed over the old Jerusalem. And when the wisdom, progress, and harlotries of this world come to their final culmination and em-bodiment in Great Babylon, there is correspond-ing reason to believe that it will be centralized upon the very spot where it first started, and meet its ultimate doom in the selfsame locality in which it was born.

But the description of that doom, its character, and its results, must be deferred for another occa-sion. I can only ask you now to think over what has been presented, and not to be envious at the prosperity of the wicked. Let the gold, and the silver, and the scarlet, and the purple, and the fine linen, be to those who make them their God. We have quite another Saviour, and quite another calling. They that worship these things shall lose them, and perish with them; but they who, for the kingdom of heaven's sake, deny themselves and refuse to be beguiled and swayed by the deceitful glitter and sumptuous allurements of wealth and fortune, shall live to enjoy a far sublimer estate,—one which shall never fade away. Yet a little while, and they shall come forth in a city whose gates are pearl and its streets gold, themselves as pure as the gates through which they pass, and as excellent and glorious as the streets on which they tread; immortal parts of a new and everlasting system of God, when Babylon has gone down into perdition, as a millstone cast into the midst of the sea.

LECTURE FORTIETH.

Rev. 18 : 1–8. (Revised Text.) After these things I saw another angel coming down out of the heaven, having great authority, and the earth was lighted up from his glory. And he cried with mighty voice, saying, Fallen, fallen Babylon the great, and become a habitation of demons, and a hold of every unclean spirit, and a hold of every unclean and hated bird ; because of the wrath of her fornication all the nations have fallen, and the kings of the earth committed fornication with her, and the merchants of the earth became rich out of the power of her wantonness.

And I heard another voice out of the heaven, saying, Come out of her, my people, that ye may have no fellowship in her sins, and that ye receive not of her plagues ; because her sins have been builded together as far as the heaven, and God hath remembered her iniquities. Reward to her even as she rewarded, and double double according to her works ; in the cup which she mixed, mix for her double ; insomuch as she glorified herself and was wanton, to that proportion give to her torment and grief ; because she saith in her heart, I sit a queen and am not a widow, and shall see no mourning ; therefore in one day shall come her plagues, death, and mourning, and famine, and with fire shall she be burnt, because strong the Lord who hath judged her.

HAVING already consumed two evenings in our endeavors to identify and understand what is meant by Great Babylon, we come now to the consideration of her final fall.

But before proceeding directly to that subject,

it may be well first to relieve a perplexity into which some may have fallen by reason of what I have said concerning the restoration of the literal city of Babylon.

When we speak of the day of the Lord, or the judgment period, many have the notion that it is but one day, or a very brief space of time. They are consequently led to wonder how we can speak of the impending nearness of that day, and yet look for the rebuilding of a great city then to be destroyed. The difficulty, however, does not lie in the nature of the things, but in the popular misapprehensions of what the day of the Lord means, and the length of the period which it covers. The mistake is in taking the day of the Lord, or the coming again of our Saviour, as if one particular moment of time, and one single event or scene were to be understood. What the Scriptures describe as the day of the Lord, and the second coming of Christ, is no more limited to a single event or moment of time than was the day of his first coming, which extended over more than thirty years, and embraced various stages and successive presentations. If we take the prophecies concerning the first advent, we find it impossible to apply them to any one day, year, or scene, in the evangelic history. Micah said that Christ should " *come* " out of Bethlehem (Ephratah), but Hosea said that he would *come* " out of Egypt." Malachi said that he should " suddenly *come* to his temple," and Zechariah that he would *come* to Zion " riding upon an ass, upon a colt the foal

of an ass;" whilst, according to Isaiah, "the land
of Zebulun and the land of Naphtali " were to
see the "great light." All these presentations
were his coming. He did *come* when he was
born at Bethlelem; he did *come* out of Egypt;
he did *come* when he announced himself at Nazareth; he did *come* as a great light among the
people of Northern Galilee; he did *come* riding
into Jerusalem on the ass; he did *come* suddenly
to his temple when he twice drove out the money-
changers; and he *came* when he reappeared after
his resurrection. Each one of these particular
incidents is alike called his *coming;* but they were
only so many separate presentations, at different
dates, extending through a period of thirty-three
years, all of which together are required to make
up the first advent as a whole. And just as it was
then, so it will be again. The second coming, like
the first, is complex and distributive, extending
through a variety of successive and diverse scenes,
stages, events, and manifestations, requiring as
many, if not still more, years. Just what length
of time will intervene between the first and sudden catching away of the watching and ready
saints, and the final overthrow of Babylon and
Antichrist, we may not be able precisely to determine; but I am fully persuaded that it will be a
goodly number of years. Antichrist reigns for a
full week of years,—that is seven years,—three
and a half as the friend and patron of the Israelitish people, and three and a half as the great
Beast. (Dan. 10 : 27; Rev. 11 : 2; 12 : 6.) But the

Antichrist is not revealed until after the Hinderer
is taken away; who is only taken away when the
saints are removed, the removal of whom is the
taking away of the Hinderer. The Antichrist
does not appear at all amid the scenes of the Apocalypse until after the seven seals have been opened,
and six of the succeeding trumpets have been
sounded. How many years those seals and the six
trumpets may consume we are not informed, but
we have every reason to believe that they may be
counted by tens, if not by scores, subsequent to
the opening of the door in the heaven and the
taking up of the saints, which is the first act in
the great drama. The space occupied in narrating
what occurs under the seals and trumpets would
indicate this. The long waiting of the Ten Virgins
for the coming of the Bridegroom, which is subsequent to the first translation, indicates the same
thing. Forty years, at least, perhaps a whole jubilee period of fifty years, or even a full seventy
years, answering to the period during which the
judgment was upon Israel for its sins, are likely
to be embraced in what the Scriptures call the day
of the Lord, and the second coming and revelation
of Jesus Christ.

Supposing, then, that Babylon should not even
begin to be rebuilt until after the day of the Lord
has commenced in the rapture of the eagle-saints
(Luke 17 : 34–37; 1 Thess. 4 : 14–17; Rev. 4 : 1),
there still would be ample time for it to come up
in all the grandeur and force indicated before the
great acts of destruction in which that day reaches

LECTURE XL. CHAP. 18 : 1-8.   163

its consummation. Much can be accomplished in forty, fifty, or seventy years.

A few years ago I was the guest of a man, scarcely older than myself, who was already grown, and secretary of a frontier trading company, before the first dwelling was built of what is now the great and powerful city of Chicago. And if the rich merchants, money-kings, and great mercantile organizations of the world were to unite for the establishment of such a centre of wealth, influence, and trade, as the foreshowings are respecting great Babylon, with the treasures, facilities, and energies that would at once be brought to bear, a much shorter time would be required to realize all that has been foretold, even if nothing special were to occur to hasten the project. But the indications are that there will be special providences in its favor. Zechariah saw the winds of heaven filling the wings and favoring the flight of the two women bearing the ephah to its house in the land of Shinar. It will then be the midst of the judgment time, when great and startling events are to succeed each other in quick succession, when things will move under other and mightier impulses than now, and when God in the administrations of His wrath upon nations and systems will hurry them on to the destructions which await them, or so give them over to the spirits and powers of hell because of their unbelief, that the most wonderful changes and achievements will go forward with a celerity of which we now have no conception. And even if the great day of the Lord should

break in upon the world this night, it would not
at all embarrass the idea, or prevent the possibility
of the restoration of old Babylon in all the magnificence and power ascribed to her in these chapters. The time would stlil be ample for it all.

But it is with the *fall* of Babylon, and not with
the time and incidents of her restoration from
present depression that we are now concerned.
God help us to understand it as we should!

A glorious being from heaven appears. To
John he seems like an angel, but quite "another"
from the one who was showing him these things.
This angel does not speak from heaven, but comes
down out of the heaven. He comes also with
"great authority." There is reason to believe that
it is Christ himself whom we are to see in this
angel ; for the Father "hath given him authority
to execute judgment, because he is the Son of
Man." (Jno. 5 : 27.) When Satan was cast out of
heaven the celestial worshippers celebrated this
εξουσία, authority, dominion, or power, as the particular possession of Christ, who is appointed to
"put down all rule and all authority and power."
(Cor. 15 : 24.) It is said that " *the earth was lighted
up from his glory.*" Such language is nowhere
used concerning created angels, but is quite common to all the prophets with regard to our Divine
King and Saviour. The Psalmist (72 : 18, 19)
blesses the glorious name of the Lord God of Israel, and speaks of a scene in which "the whole
earth is filled with his glory." Isaiah (6 : 1–3), in
his vision of the enthroned Messiah, heard the

seraphim cry, "The whole earth is full of his glory." Ezekiel (43 : 2) beheld the glory of the God of Israel coming from the way of the East, and says: "His voice was like the noise of many waters [answering to the 'mighty voice' here], and the earth shined with his glory." The garment of Jehovah is light, and such intense luminousness everywhere attaches to what is divine; whilst the enlightening of things by the glory of God and the Lamb is specially spoken of in these visions. (Rev. 21 : 23; 22 : 25.) We are not likely to be mistaken, then, in taking this angel for the Lord Jesus himself, and the more so as the remembrance of Great Babylon to give to her the cup of the wine of the fierceness of divine wrath is specially said to be "*in the presence of God*," as if God in Christ were then manifested and personally revealed upon the earth. (Chap. 16 : 19.)

From this glorious being the word goes forth in tremendous power: "*Fallen, Fallen, Babylon the Great.*" It is not simply the word of information as to what has been or what is to be, but the word which effects what it describes,—the word which brings Great Babylon down, and makes it "a habitation of demons, and a hold of every unclean spirit, and a hold of every unclean and hateful bird." The twice-repeated word describes two separate parts or stages of the fall, answering to the two aspects in which Babylon is contemplated, referring first to Babylon in mystery, as *a system* or spirit of false worship, and second to Babylon as *a city*, in which this system or spirit is finally embodied. The thrice-repeated cry of "woe, woe, woe," in chapter 8 : 13, meant three distinct woes, as the subsequent account makes plain; and so here, the twice-repeated "fallen, fallen," means two distinct falls. The first fall, or the fall of Babylon in mystery, is accomplished through the agency of the Beast in confederation with the ten kings (chap. 17 : 16, 17), which occurs soon after the Antichrist is fully revealed; but after the denudation and burning which they inflict, she is represented as still existing as a city, who sits as a boastful queen, promising herself an immortality of worldly glory, and from which certain people are called out that they may not share her doom. Two falls are thus inevitably implied, and the last is more than three years after the first; for the reign of the Beast is three and one-half years, and the setting up of the enforced worship of his image, and hence the first great Babylonian disaster occurs at the beginning of those years, whilst the final catastrophe occurs at the pouring out of the last bowl of wrath, which sweeps the Beast as well as Great Babylon to perdition.

But before the mighty word of this glorious angel goes into full effect upon the final Babylon, a voice from heaven says: "*Come out of her, my people, that ye may have no fellowship in her sins, and that ye receive not of her plagues.*" It seems that there will be children of Abraham among the population of the final Babylon, for wherever there is great trade and banking we may expect to find

Jews, and these are the people to whom this call is made. If the glorious angel is Christ, it is the Father who here speaks, and who now again acknowledges Israel as his earthly people. The New Testament Church is here out of the question. Every divinely acknowledged part of that has been by this time taken, and is with the Lord Jesus in heaven. But the times of the Gentiles being fulfilled, the *Lo Ammi* (not my people) is reversed with regard to Israel, and this is the time when the Spirit comes upon them again, and they are recovered to life and salvation. Jeremiah (50 : 4-9) writes : "In those days, and in that time [the very time of the threatened destruction of Babylon], saith the Lord, *the children of Israel* shall come, *they and the children of Judah together*, going and weeping; they shall go and seek the Lord their God. They shall ask the way to Zion with their faces thitherward, saying, Come, let us join ourselves to the Lord in a perpetual covenant that shall not be forgotten. My people hath been lost sheep; their shepherds have caused them to go astray, they have turned them away on the mountains; they have gone from mountain to hill, they have forgotton their resting-place. All that found them have devoured them; and their adversaries said, We offend not, because they have sinned against the Lord, the habitation of justice, even the Lord, the hope of their fathers." And in immediate connection with this description the command is : " *Remove out of the midst of Babylon, and go forth out of the land of the Chaldeans*, and be as the he goats before the flocks." "*Flee out of the midst of Babylon, and deliver every man his soul; be not cut off in her iniquity;* for this is the time of the Lord's vengeance; he will render unto her a recompense" (51 : 6). "*My people, go ye out of the midst of her,* and deliver ye every man his soul from the fierce anger of the Lord" (verse 45). "*Though Babylon should mount up to heaven, and though she should fortify the height of her strength, yet from me shall the spoiler come unto her, saith the Lord*" (53). "And I will make drunk her princes, and her wise men, her captains, and her rulers, and her mighty men : and they shall sleep a perpetual sleep, and not awake, saith the King whose name is Lord of hosts" (57). Thus beautifully and unmistakably do the records of the ancient prophet explain what the Apocalyptic seer was shown. The merciful providence of God has by this time again taken hold on the long-rejected children of Israel and Judah, and such of them as are in Babylon are divinely warned of what is coming, and brought away from the impending destruction, as Lot was called out of doomed Sodom (Gen. 19 : 15–22), and as the people in Moses' time were called to get them up from the tents of Dathan and Abiram in the day that judgment came upon these rebels (Numb. 16 : 23–26).

The particular calamities which then break forth are described as *death, mourning, famine, and burning with fire.* Both the calling out of those who are not to share Babylon's doom, and the nature of these inflictions immediately following, prove that a literal city is meant. Part of the trouble is also of just such a character as to fall in with the idea, and so to prove that that city is Babylon, and that the drying up of the waters of the Euphrates under the sixth bowl of wrath is a literal occurrence. Terrible mortality and famine would be the natural and inevitable result of the failure of that river to a city built upon it, and so dependent on its waters. All her shipping would thus be disabled. All the fertility of her gardens and surrounding country would be turned to dust and barrenness. The exposed and stagnant filth of so great a river, together with the decaying vegetation for the space of nearly 2000 miles, would be a source of deadly pestilence, which no skill or power of man could abate or stay. With such a plague over all the place all helpers would fear to approach, their markets would be unsupplied, their communication with the rest of the world, already so largely emptied and desolated by the march of the kings with their armies to the scene of battle against the Lamb, would be without avail. And thus black death and helpless want would stalk through every street, and highway, and lane, and alley, of the whole city, and fill all the region round about with unexampled suffering, mourning, and horror.

And amid it all comes the great unprecedented earthquake, by which the cities of the nations are thrown down. Fires break forth, and there is no water to extinguish them, and no hands to apply it if it were to be found. The whole city burns to ashes, and all its population with it, "as when God overthrew Sodom and Gomorrah," making the very land vitreous round about.

Thus would be fulfilled what Isaiah sung: "Come down, and sit in the dust, O virgin daughter of Babylon; sit on the ground; there is no throne, O daughter of the Chaldeans; for thou shalt no more be called tender and delicate. Sit thou silent, and get thee into darkness, O daughter of the Chaldeans; for thou shalt no more be called, the lady of kingdoms. Thou saidst, 'I shall be a lady forever,' so that thou didst not lay these things to thy heart, neither didst remember the latter end of it. Therefore hear now this, thou that art given to pleasures, that dwellest carelessly, that sayest in thine heart, 'I am, and none else beside me; I shall not sit as a widow, neither shall I know the loss of children;' these two things shall come to thee in a moment, in one day, the loss of children and widowhood; they shall come upon thee in their perfection, for the multitudes of thy services, and for the great abundance of thine enchantments. For thou hast trusted in thy wickedness; thou hast said, 'None seeth me.' Thy wisdom and thy knowledge, it has perverted thee; and thou hast said in thine heart, 'I am, and none else beside me.' Therefore shall evil come upon thee; and thou shalt not know from whence it riseth; and mischief shall fall upon thee; thou shalt not be able to put it off; and desolation shall come upon thee suddenly, which thou shalt not know. Stand now with thine enchantments, and with the multitude of thy sorceries, wherein thou hast labored from thy youth; if so be thou shalt be able to profit, if so be thou mayest prevail. Thou art wearied in the multitude of thy counsels. Let now the astrologers, the star-gazers, the monthly prognosticators, stand up, and save thee from these things that shall come upon thee. Behold, they shall be as stubble; the fire shall burn them; they shall not deliver themselves from the power of the flame." (Isa. 47 : 1-15.)

Babylon burned Jerusalem and the temple of God, and her end is a conflagration, which leaves nothing of her. As the Lord said by Jeremiah, so it cometh to pass: "I will render unto Babylon, and to all the inhabitants of Chaldea, all their evil that they have done in Zion." (Jer. 51 : 24.) The voice from the heaven says that her iniquities come into remembrance. So long a time had passed since the early wickednesses of Babylon that it might seem as if Jehovah had forgotten them, or never meant to recall them to mind; but the last Babylon is but the final outgrowth of the same principles and spirit which animated the first, and is so interiorly identified with that same old apostasy that all the old offences come forward again with the new, and help to inflame the final vengeance; just as the full punishment of the sin of Israel respecting the golden calf is not yet over (Ex. 32 : 34), and as all the martyr blood of all the ages still cries to be further avenged.

In connection with these final plagues upon Babylon the voice from heaven says: " *Render to her even as she rewarded, and double [the] double according to her works ; in the cup which she mixed, mix for her double ; insomuch as she glorified herself and was wanton, to that proportion give to her torment and grief."* Some take this as a commission to the returning house of Israel, which is to become a cup of trembling and a burdensome stone to the people round about in connection with these events; but I do not so understand it. Israel will at that time be so inclosed, and under the heel of the great beast, as to be quite disabled from such an office until Christ himself has gone forth to avenge them of their enemies. Besides, the final judgment upon Great Babylon is so miraculous and direct from heaven, that mere earthly agents have but little to do with it, if anything. There is also another and far mightier class of operators in the infliction of these great judgments. Angels are concerned, and the descended Son of God himself. But there are others in addition to these, and taking part with them in these administrations. Among the promises to the overcomers out of the seven churches, was one that they should have authority over the nations, and rule or judge them with a rod of iron, *and break them to shivers as a vessel of pottery is dashed to pieces* (Rev. 2 : 26, 27). Of old it was sung of the saints in glory, that, with the praises of God in their mouth, and a two-edged sword in their hand, they should *execute vengeance upon the nations*, even punishments upon the people, to bind their kings with chains, and their nobles with fetters of iron, *to execute*

upon them the judgment that is written. " This honor
have all the saints." (Ps. 149 : 5-9.) Paul reminded
the Corinthians, as if indignant at their low appreciation of the Christian calling: "*Do ye not
know that the saints shall judge the world?*" (1 Cor.
6 : 2.) Of the mystic man-child caught up to God
and to his throne, the record was that he should
rule or shepherdize all the nations with a rod of
iron. (Rev. 12 : 5.) When the Beast and the False
Prophet, and their allied kings and armies perish
at Harmageddon, the saint-armies of heaven,
robed in fine linen, and riding on white horses,
are those taking part in the terrible vengeance
then to be executed. (Rev. 19 : 11-21.) And it
would be strange, indeed, if in the rendition of
final judgment upon Babylon, which sends a thrill
of joy through all the holy universe, they were to
have neither place nor part. To these, then, and
to all the avenging powers of heaven, are we to
consider this direction and commission to be ad-
dressed.

In the days of mercy and forbearance God is
not strict to mark iniquity, or to punish it at once
according to its deserts. There is much that he
winks at and suffers to pass for the present. But
it is all written in his book, and when the final
recompense comes there is no more sparing. As
the sinner has measured, so it will be measured to
him again. It is an awful thought, but true, that
by the ills and wrongs which people do on earth
they are themselves setting the gauge or measure

by which they are to have judgment dealt to them
at the last.

The language here might seem to imply that
God meant to double up vengeance upon Babylon
without proportion to her deservings; but a more
attentive consideration shows that such is not the
case. God is always just, and the duplication and
intensifying of the torment and grief still has a
righteous rule underlying it. The judgment is to
be double, and double double; but it is to be "*as
she rewarded*,"—"*according to her works*,"—a cup of
mixture such as she herself gave, doubled because
her administration was only half of her iniquity.
There may be great self-sins, over and above the sins
against rights and peace of others. And such are
here charged against Babylon, even blasphemy, self-
honor, self-security, wantonness, and the deification
of wealth and luxury. For these, as well as for the
cup of uncleanness and oppression given by her to
others, the cup is doubled to her. Her real evilness
is double, and she must drink her own cup double.
She is herself double, being both *a system* of abominations, and *a city* of abominations; and what is
visited upon the one is repeated or duplicated on
the other.

The result of all this is that Great Babylon will
be blotted from the earth, "as in the day when
God overthrew Sodom and Gomorrah," and so
fulfil to the letter all that the old prophets have
spoken. The symbolic act which Jeremiah commanded Seraiah to perform at Babylon to signify
the utter extinction that was to come upon her

(Jer. 51 : 63, 64), John beholds repeated in a still more striking form: *"A mighty angel took up a stone, as a great millstone, and cast [it] into the sea, saying, Thus with a bound shall the great city Babylon be cast down, and shall not be found any more."*

When Jesus was upon the earth, he said: " Whoso shall offend one of these little ones which believe in me, it were better for him that a millstone were hanged about his neck, and that he were drowned in the depth of the sea." (Matt. 18 : 6.) But who or what is a greater stumbling-block to the believers in God, and to the faith of Jehovah's humble worshippers, than Great Babylon! In every form in which she has existed, and through all the ages, in all the world, she has been holding up the golden cup of her abominations wherewith she has intoxicated and demented the nations, and filled the whole earth with spiritual madness. Therefore, to her neck the stone is hanged, and into the depths she is cast, descending with still increasing speed towards the seething abyss of everlasting fires.

Babylon is a region full of bitumen. The mortar of its buildings from the beginning was not clay, but bituminous slime. All the earth around it is, therefore, full of inflammable material, as was the vale of Siddim before the conflagration of the cities of the plain, which was " full of slime-pits," so that when the fiery judgment of God descended, and it began to rain " brimstone and fire out of heaven," the thunderbolts ignited the oil-springs, and naphtha, and petroleum, and bituminous wells, till "all the land of the plain glowed and burned as a furnace," sinking as the burning went on, and swallowing up the doomed cities in a literal "lake of fire," which has left nothing but a dead sea and everlasting desolation where they stood. With corresponding conditions of the ground, and the ancient prophets assuring us that "the beauty of the Chaldees' excellency shall be *as when God overthrew Sodom and Gomorrah*" (Is. 13 : 19; Jer. 49 : 18; 50 : 40), we may readily infer something of the nature of the fires amid which Great Babylon is to find her perdition. First is the drying up of her waters, as God said by the mouth of Jeremiah, "I will dry up her sea, and make her springs dry" (Jer. 51 : 36); then the consequent death-plague, mourning, and famine; and then the fires which run over her, and around her, and under her, feeding on the parched and pitchy ground, and sinking the whole region into a charred and igneous desolation, never again to be inhabited. Nimrod called it, "*The Gate of God*," and lo, it proves *the mouth of hell*, where the unclean spirits throng, and the very filth of the universe finds its hold! The world's greatest power was concentrated there, which all the kings of the earth were delighted to court and serve; but "in one hour" all her greatness, might, and majesty, come to nought. She was a mart for the nations, enriching multitudes on land and sea, but in one day the harvest of her soul's desire is gone, and all her bright and dainty things perished, with no one left to buy or enjoy them any more. She

had " great riches," and was " clothed in fine
linen, and purple, and scarlet, and decked with
gold, and precious stone, and pearl," but not a
scrap or fragment of all her costliness and treasure
is left. She was the very paradise of musicians,
harp-singers, and flute-players, and trumpeters;
for these are always a great feature and one of the
chief glories of a rich, gay, luxurious, and worldly
city; but every note is silenced, and no voice of
song, or dance, or opera, is ever heard there again.
The finest artists and artisans of the world, of
every order, had found there a very Golconda, but
in one hour their glorious elysium is gone, and
they and their works with it. It was the centre
of the grandest and most noted of bridals, and the
sublime resort of grand bridal tours, but with one
stroke of heaven's judgment every sound of joy
is hushed, " and the voice of bridegroom and
bride " ceases to be heard there any more.

When the curse upon Jerusalem was spoken, it
was that " the voice of mirth, and the voice of
gladness, the voice of the bridegroom, and the
voice of the bride," should cease from her streets
(Jer. 7 : 34); but it was at the same time added
that God would " restore the captivity of the land,
as at the first," and that, in the place of the
threatened desolation, there should yet again be
" the voice of joy, and the voice of gladness, the
voice of the bridegroom, and the voice of the
bride, the voice of them that shall say, Praise the
Lord of hosts; for the Lord is good; for his mercy
endureth forever." (Jer. 33 : 10, 11.) But in the

case of Great Babylon there is to be no recovery, no restoration. There shall be no remnant left to rebuild it, no workman to lift up tool to reconstruct it, no mills to sound there any more, no light of candle or token of joyous civilization to shine again amid its darkness; but it shall be "a habitation of demons, and a hold of every unclean spirit, and a hold of every unclean and hated bird;" and "it shall be no more inhabited forever, neither shall it be dwelt in from generation to generation." (Jer. 50 : 39, 40.)

So great a judgment argues gigantic crimes. Glance a moment then at these, that we may learn to stand in awe and "have no fellowship in her sins;" for it does not require that we should live in Babylon when she falls in order to be involved in her perdition. Every place is Babylon to them that have her spirit and exhibit her iniquities, and the same judgment awaits them.

To the credit of Babylon's worldly greatness, but also as a marked ingredient of what procures her doom, it is said : " *Thy merchants were the great men of the earth.*" Most people would see no crime in that. What harm is there in buying and selling and getting gain, and in making the weight of fortune felt according to its greatness? Nothing, indeed, if no wrong spirit is under it, and no wrong principles animate the accumulation, or control its management when it is made. But, the son of Sirach hath truly said: "As a nail sticketh fast between the joinings of stones, so doth sin stick close between buying and selling."

(Ecclesiasticus 17 : 2.) And commerce is certainly indicated as the chief vehicle, support, and embodiment of the great defiling wickedness of the last days. In the bushel measure, and under the weighing talent, sits the Woman whom the angel says is *Wickedness*. Nor should it be thought strange that commerce, and the machinery connected therewith, should supply the formative principles of a great and godless apostasy. Is there a prominent country now on earth in which commerce does not rule, or where things are not all being determined by commercial principles, ideas, and interests? "Have we heard nothing respecting the wondrous results expected from commerce in making nations happy, in bringing men together in ties of amity and brotherhood, in developing the resources of the earth, in making nations conscious of their mutual dependence on each other, and so effecting, by the suggestions of self-interest, a result which the Gospel (it is said) has failed to accomplish. These and such like sayings are continually being sounded in our ears. Nor can we say that they are altogether untrue, or that there is no wisdom in them." (B. W. Newton.) But who that looks with an attentive eye but can see in it the coming forth of a wisdom which is not from above, but which savors of him who said to Jesus, "All these things will I give thee, if thou wilt fall down and worship me." Commerce is not necessarily sinful. Exchange on just and right principles may be a thing of beneficence and good, involving nothing against God or his truth.

But the tendency is otherwise. The disposition is to concentration and consolidation on selfish principles for selfish ends. The struggle is continually more and more to monopolize, to crush out rivalry and competition, and to enter into world-wide combinations to seize first one interest and then another, till everything is finally swallowed up in one great centralized aristocracy of unbounded wealth, to which all the kings and governments on the earth must truckle. In our day an association of merchants has commanded the riches of the Indian seas, dragged along with it the armies and legislation of England to effect its ends, and enriched itself at the sacrifice of innocent blood, national treasure, and every honorable principle, whilst the good Queen Victoria, helpless in its hands, must submit in royal gratitude to bear for it the title of the Empress of India! The eloquence of a Burke, in sentences which shall never die, has given a tongue to a few of the abominations which have accompanied those administrations; but not a moiety of them has been told, as they have added stain upon stain to the escutcheon of England, and dishonored the whole Anglo-Saxon race. This is but one instance, and one belonging to the babyhood of these great commercial combinations; what then may we not expect when these privileged associations, which control the local exchanges, money markets, and commercial affairs of the nations, have fully consolidated, and a great, united, money aristocracy, takes command of the commerce of the world? These would indeed be

" the great men of the earth," and their rule would
be the rule of the earth.

But what sort of a rule would it necessarily be?
Would it be God's kingdom come, and God's will
done, on earth as it is in heaven? So the arguments and oratory of the priests of that interest
would seem to say. But, is it so? Can it possibly
be so? Look at the root-principle of these commercial compacts. Co-equality of man with man
is to them the greatest absurdity. What right, or
place, or standing, can a man who has no money
have in them? Wealth is the only ticket of admission, and for that all seats are absolutely reserved. But who would ever think of going
among these money-lords and bourse-kings to
find saints of God! There are some rich men
from whose hearts the Holy Ghost has not been
choked out; but " how hardly shall they that have
riches enter the kingdom of God? It is easier for
a camel to go through the needle's eye, than for a
rich man to enter into the kindom of God."
(Mark 10 : 23-25.) It has become an axiom that
" corporations have no souls," and upon this all
great moneyed corporations act, though the men
who constitute them will find out a different doctrine when they come to the day of judgment.
And when it comes to these great and ever mag-
nifying commercial compacts and interests, there
is not a law of God or man which is not compelled
to yield if found in the way. Protestant and
Papist, Pagan and Jew, Mohammedan and Infidel,
believer and unbeliever, Bible, Talmud, Vedas,

Shasters, Koran, and Book of Mormon, are all alike, and stand in these organizations on one and the same footing, provided only that there is power of wealth to aid and direct the one great scramble for the world's trade and riches. If the question were ever pressed in these circles, *What is truth?* it would be hooted and laughed to scorn. The cry would be, " What have we to do with that? Let every one quietly enjoy his own opinions. Give each a share, not only in the protection of the government, but in its fostering and sustaining care, for the office of government is to minister for the governed, not to concern itself with the laws and revelations of God." Accordingly, also, the greatest mercantile government on earth, England, Protestant England, which claims to maintain the only true church, and hails all her sovereigns as " Defenders of the Faith," at the dictation and demand of secular and commercial interests makes her appropriations to Romish institutions, salaries Roman priests and professors, advances Jews to her highest offices, expends her blood and treasure to sustain the tottering existence of the deadly curse of Mohammedan dominion, pensions Brahmin nobles, and pays and pampers Pagan priests. And such is the tendency and bearing of legislation in general, and from the same causes. Governments are in the hands of commerce and the money-kings; and commerce knows no God but gold, and no law but self-interest and worldly gain. Church is nothing, State is nothing, creed is nothing, Bible is nothing, Sunday is nothing, religious scruples are nothing, conscience is nothing, everything is practically nothing, except as it can be turned or used to the one great end of accumulation and wealth. To make common cause with all classes of men, to honor Mohammedan festivals and Jewish rites alike with those commanded by the one only rightful King of the world, to pay Hindoo and Romish priests, to endow their seminaries, and to give aid and comfort to their idolatries alike with all Christian institutes,— which is now not only being done, but advocated and defended on the ground that this is the only rightful sphere of government, and these the only principles on which the true progress of humanity depends,—is already the incipient dethronement of all positive truth, the turning of it into a lie, or into a mere ideal thing without claims upon the human soul; the systematic inauguration of a latitudinarian infidelity, removing human society into many degrees of greater distance from God than ever it has been in all the ages. And when once the earth has come to acknowledge the representatives and embodiments of such a system of ideas and rule as its true and only "*great men,*" there lies couched in this one simple statement a whole world of iniquitous apostasy, which well deserves the doom which makes an end of Great Babylon. Yes, commerce will yet have an account to settle, at which the world shall shake.

Another ingredient in the cup of Babylon's doom, is her bewitching sorcery, by which she leads all the nations astray. Some understand by this that she is to be the great patron and head centre of spiritism and necromancy. Magicians constituted an integral part of the state officials there in Daniel's time, and it is quite likely that a goodly share of her wisdom, and policy, and influence, will come from familiar intercourse with demons and their unclean teachings. But it does not seem to me that this touches the nerve of what is here called her sorcery. The great preponderating idea which runs through the whole description, is that of *commercial* greatness, success, and power; and the potent and contaminating sorcery must be something which is naturally construable with this,—some bewitching attractiveness going along with a mercantile system, and drawing after it the admiration and sympathy of the world. Meretricious allurement, gathering around it the homage of governments and kings, is the idea. And it is in Great Babylon's management to ennoble her chief aims and spirit that we are to find her witchery.

It is hardly possible to separate traffic, and especially great commercial combinations and schemes, from *covetousness*, which is idolatry. But naked covetousness is not attractive. Even the natural heart is repelled by it, and is ready to condemn and denounce it. When the possession of wealth is made the final end, when it is treasured in the coffer and not expended, or when means disreputable are adopted for its attainment, the pursuit of riches is regarded with disdain. The acquisition, under such circumstances, is connected with what is so repulsive to pride, and taste, and respectabilities which hold in approved society, that it meets only with frowns and disfavor. To array it in honorable garb, to dignify it, to make it appear good and praiseworthy, so that men may love, bless, and follow it as something noble and beneficent,—this is what calls for the magician's wand and the wizard's power. And here it is that Great Babylon's delusive witchery comes in. If a godless and unscrupulous commerce can be made to appear as the great and only availing civilizer, if it can show its end to be, not only the welfare of individuals, but the prosperity of nations and peoples; if its office is the development of the resources of the whole earth, and for that end visits every land and traverses every sea; if it is really the great stimulant to intellectual effort, the helper of science, the procurer and disseminator of all useful wisdom and intelligence, the rewarder of inventive genius and engineering skill, the self-sacrificing handmaid of all social, moral, and legislative improvement; if it is not the mere possession of wealth for its own sake, but to secure the beneficent power, and influence and glory to result from its wise and proper employment that makes up the end and aim of its endeavors, then will the ugliness of avarice be voided, bitter will have been made sweet, and all attendant deflections from right and truth swallowed up in the grandeur, and beauty, and beneficences of its purposes. The demon of covetousness would then have become an angel of light. A halo of glory would encircle its head. Nations would hail its undertakings, admire its enterprise, and praise its wonderful benignity. The arts and the sciences, the museums and the universities, would lay their chaplets at its feet. Kings and governments would cheerfully become its nurses and patrons. Religions would be glad to bestow upon it their prayers and benedictions. The apostles and prophets of this world's progress would clap their hands and shout over its success. And myriads would celebrate its triumph as the ushering in of the long-dreamed millennium.

And here is the sorcery with which Great Babylon leads all the nations astray. Linking the false doctrines of human progress and perfectibility to the worst of passions, she lures the world to her support, and makes mankind the willing slave of her base idolatry. And already, from pulpit and platform, from philosopher and political economist, from orator and poet, are we compelled to hear just these very glorifications of the cupidities of man as the forerunner, if not the instrument, of this world's regeneration. Alas, for such philosophy and such hopes! What estimate God puts upon them may be learned from what he has revealed of the doom of Babylon. It is *sorcery*, the penalty for which is death. (Ex. 22 : 18.)

I can mention now but one more particular in the count of Great Babylon's sins, and that is her presumptuous self-glorification, conceit, and arrogance. She has no rights of kingdom from God or man, and yet she presumes to bear rule over all

the kings of the earth, to dictate their policies, to
fashion their laws, and to be their protector and
redeemer. She acknowledges no God, no Christ,
no Holy Ghost, and yet proposes to do for the
world what she assumes to be beyond the power
of the institutes and administrations of heaven.
She makes no claims to sacred prophecy, acknowledges no sacred books, and glories in being entirely secular in her sphere and aims, and yet presumes to teach the nations the ways and means of
their highest prosperity and redemption, and to
realize for them their sublimest peace and good.
She is but human in her derivation, her principles
and her power, and purely earthly in her dependence, her treasures, and her glory; yet she presumes to think herself invincible, immortal, and
forever sufficient in her own possessions against
all adversity. *"She saith in her heart, I sit a queen,
and am not a widow, and shall see no mourning."* She
thus exalts herself over the Church of God, in
which all that is divine on earth resides, and where
the preaching has ever been about divine sonship,
and kinghood, and a glorious kingdom, but to
which no dominion has ever come. The saints are
to reign; but while the Devil reigns their kingdom
is in abeyance, and Babylon taunts them and con-
gratulates herself with having in reality what they
have only in empty promise. They do not reign;
she sits a queen. While Christ is away the Church
is in widowhood; her husband is absent. All her
hope is in his return. Babylon boasts that she experiences no such privation. She is no widow.

Her lovers are plenteous. Her joy is full. She claims to have in fruition what the Church has in mere expectation. The people of God have perpetual sorrow and trial on earth. Like their Lord, they are poor, despised, persecuted, with scarce a place to lay their heads in peace from their enemies. Great Babylon glories in being far above a condition so mean, or vicissitudes so afflicting. She is rich; she is mighty; she hath all her necessary goods secure; she is not the one to see mourning. Thus she vaunts, professes, and glorifies herself. Though the world from the beginning is crowded with monuments of the wrath of heaven upon every such spirit, and though through all the long gallery of ages the voice comes echoing down, " *They that walk in pride God is able to abase,*" she heeds not the lesson, and defies all judgment. Hence Jehovah writes it once more in larger letters, drawn with the black cinders of her own eternal desolation, that all the universe may read and tremble.

Friends, let *us* learn the lesson. It is to this end that all these things have been written. Participation in Great Babylon's sins must needs bring Great Babylon's doom, be the offender who or where he may. And to but little avail will we have considered this subject if it does not serve to imprint upon our souls at least this one eternal truth of God, that "*whosoever exalteth himself shall be abased; and he that humbleth himself shall be exalted.*" (Luke 14 : 11.)

LECTURE FORTY-FIRST.

Rev. 18 : 9–24. (Revised Text.) And shall wail and mourn over her
the kings of the earth, who committed fornication with her, when they
see the smoke of her burning, standing afar off through the fear of her
torment, saying, Alas, alas (woe, woe), the great city Babylon, the
mighty city! because in one hour came thy judgment.

And the merchants of the earth weep and mourn over her because
no one buyeth their merchandise [or *ship's freight*] any more,—merchandise of gold, and of silver, and of precious stone, and of pearl,
and of fine linen, and of purple, and of silk, and of scarlet, and all
thyne [or *citron*] wood, and every article of ivory, and every article of
most costly wood, and of brass, and of iron, and of marble; and cinnamon, and amomum, and odors, and ointment, and frankincense, and
wine, and oil, and fine meal, and wheat, and cattle, and sheep; and
[merchandise] of horses, and of chariots, and of bodies and souls of
men. And thy harvest of the soul's desire has departed from thee, and
all dainty things and bright things have perished from thee, and they
shall not find them any more. The merchants of these things, who
were made rich from her, shall stand afar off through the fear of her
torment, weeping and mourning, saying, Alas, alas (woe, woe), the
great city which was clothed in fine linen, and purple, and scarlet, and
decked with gold, and precious stone, and pearl, because in one hour
such great riches hath been desolated.

And every shipmaster, and every one who goeth by sea, and sailors,
and as many as trade by sea, stood afar off and cried out when
they saw the smoke of her burning, saying, What is like to the great
city! And they cast heaped-up earth upon their heads, and cried out,

weeping and mourning, saying, Alas, alas (woe, woe), the great city by which all who had ships in the sea were made rich from her costliness [or *treasures*], because in one hour she hath been desolated !

Rejoice over her, O heaven, and saints, and apostles, and prophets, because God hath judged your judgment out of her.

And one, a mighty angel, took up a stone, as a great millstone, and cast [it] into the sea, saying, Thus with a bound shall the great city Babylon be cast down, and shall not be found any more. And the sound of harpers, and musicians, and flute-players, and trumpeters shall not be heard in thee any more, and every artisan of every art shall not be found in thee any more ; and sound of the millstone shall not be heard in thee any more ; and light of a candle shall not shine in thee any more; and the voice of the bridegroom and bride shall not be heard in thee any more ; because thy merchants were the great men of the earth ; because by thy sorcery all the nations were led astray.

And in her was found the blood of prophets, and of saints, and of all that have been slain upon the earth.

Rev. 19 : 1–6. (Revised Text.) After these things I heard as a great voice of much multitude in the heaven, saying, Alleluia, the salvation, and the glory, and the power, of our God, because true and righteous his judgments, because he judged the great harlot that corrupted the earth with her fornication, and avenged the blood of his servants out of her hand. And a second time they say, Alleluia; and her smoke goeth up for the ages of the ages.

And the twenty-four Elders and the four Living Ones fell down and worshipped the God, the sitter upon the throne, saying, Amen, Alleluia.

And a voice came out from the throne, saying, Praise our God all his servants, those that fear him, the small and the great.

And I heard as a voice of much multitude, and as a voice of many waters, and as a voice of mighty thunders, saying, Alleluia, because the Lord God the All-Ruler hath assumed the kingdom.

THE fall of Great Babylon is one of the most marvellous events of time. More is said about it in the Scriptures than perhaps any one great secular occurrence. And when it comes to pass the whole universe is thrilled at the sight. But the emotions are not all of the same kind.

Two worlds are concerned, and in nothing are they more sharply in contrast than in the manner in which they are respectively affected by the dreadful catastrophe. Great Babylon does not mean the world, as some have erroneously supposed; for there is still a world of unsanctified people left to mourn and lament over her after she is no more. And great is the lamentation and terror which her destruction calls forth. Let us look at it for a moment and see to what sudden disappointment and helplessness the schemes of human progress and development are leading. Just when the wisdom, and reforms, and utilitarian philosophies of apostate man have wrought themselves out, and their glorious fruits are being realized, the strong hand of judgment strikes, and all is confounded and blasted in an hour. And the terribleness of the disaster may be read from the lamentation which ensues.

First of all the apostolic Seer hears the wailings of royalty and dominion. "The kings of the earth wail and mourn." They were all in close affinity with Babylon. They had lent themselves to her bewitching schemes and policy. They were enamoured with the enriching and glorifying power of her greatness. They had given their influence and favors to her, and consented to be the willing ministers to her wantonness. She was their particular love, in whom was their chief delight, and on whom they were glad to lavish their treasures. And when she falls, the main artery of earth's glory is cut, and every government feels its life-

blood ebbing away. They contemplate the smoke
of her burning with horror. They stand afar off
in dread of her torment, alarmed and terrified at
the consequences of her ruin. They leaned upon
her mightiness, but the strong staff is now stricken
from their hands. The mightier power of judgment is before them, and they tremble before its
disastrous strokes. They show no penitence, but
Alas, alas,—woe, woe,—is the note of outcry from
every capital when it is seen and known that
Babylon is no more.

Next come "the merchants of the earth," full
of tears and grief over the sudden collapse of
their enriching trade. It was promised that the
wand of the sorceress would give prosperity to
nations, and that as commerce ruled all people
would be blest by its administrations; and a great
tidal wave of mercantile thrift and glory is indicated as having come over the world by this grand
unification. There never was so great a market
or so brisk a trade as that which grows up with the
revival and restoration of Babylon. The whole
world becomes alive with traffic in "merchandise
of gold, and of silver, and of precious stone, and
of pearl, and of fine linen, and of purple, and of
silk, and of scarlet, and all thyne or citron wood,
and every article of ivory, and every article of
most costly wood, and of brass, and of iron, and
of marble; and cinnamon, and amomum [a
precious preparation from an Asiatic shrub], and
odors, and ointment, and frankincense, and wine,
and oil, and fine meal, and wheat, and cattle, and

sheep; and merchandise of horses, and of chariots, and of bodies and souls of men." Never before was there such a demand for these things, and for all things dainty and goodly, as when the house of the Ephah is built in the land of Shinar, and that Ephah is settled there upon its own base. "The merchants of these things" the world over never before experienced so great a harvest, and double up riches on riches with a rapidity which seems like miracle. Everything looks like secure and perfect triumph for earth's wisdom and inventions. But all at once this mighty commerce stops, and all its wheels stand still. The mercantile circles of the whole earth are stricken with consternation. Every counting-room becomes a place of mourning. The great traders all weep and mourn, not so much for Babylon's sufferings, for man's sympathy for man shall then have been eaten away by the common sordidness; nor yet for their great sins, for the day of repentance is then over for them. The centre of their distress is that *their market is gone*, that "no one buyeth their merchandise any more," that "in one hour such great riches hath been desolated," that the scorching of the great city's torment reaches them even at the remotest distances. *Alas, alas,—woe, woe,*—is the cry that comes from all their warehouses and homes.

But there is a third and still larger class of mourners. Great firms have more employés than heads, and very many are dependent on them for occupation and livelihood. Shipmasters, and seagoers, and sailors, and as many as trade by sea, with all their helpers and crews, also have their harvest out of this great and enriching Babylonian traffic. And these still more sorely feel the calamity of its sudden interruption. Therefore, from them also comes the cry of lamentation when they behold the smoke of Babylon's burning. And so bitter is the realization of the calamity to them, that "they cast heaped-up earth upon their heads and cry out, weeping and mourning, saying, *Alas, alas,—woe, woe,*—the great city by which all who had ships in the sea were made rich from her costly treasures!"

Thus, from every throne on earth, and from every power behind the throne, from every seat of trade, and every city,—from every continent, every island, every sea, and every ship that plies upon the sea,— comes forth the voice of woe and irremediable disaster. It is a triple voice, each part of which is double. It is the evil six complete. It is the inconsolable lament of all the potencies and activities of earth, exhibiting another star in the crown of this world's wisdom and progress.

But whilst the chorus of lamentation, disappointment, and terror is upon the earth, a grand jubilation fills the sky. As this world's great ones, and rich ones, and dependent ones cry *Woe, woe,* over Great Babylon's fall, all the peoples on high pour out their mightiest *Halleluias.* No sooner has the harlot city gone down amid her judgment fires, than a voice springs up spontaneous over all the holy universe: "*Rejoice over her, O heaven, and*

*saints, and apostles, and prophets, because God hath
judged your judgment out of her."*

For all the ages had God's messengers and
people been protesting, prophesying, and declaim-
ing against these worldly philosophies, systems,
hopes, and spirit. It lies in the very nature and
essence of the profession of all saints to "re-
nounce the Devil and all his works, the vanities
of the world, and the sinful desires of the flesh."
No one in any age can have place among God's
holy ones without this. As Noah by his faith, so
the children of God in all time, by the very act of
becoming God's children, "condemn the world,"
and give judgment against its wisdom, its principles, its spirit, and its hopes. So, too, all the
teachings of the apostles, all the holy messages of
the prophets, and all the sermons of God's faithful
ministers the world over. What, indeed, has been
the great controversy ever since the race begun,
but that between revelation and the sensual wisdom, between the system of God's salvation and
that which men propose to work out for themselves, between the bringing up of the world on
principles of human progress and the only redemption through faith in Christ Jesus? And between
these two there is an inherent, irreconcilable, and
eternal antagonism. That which makes and marks
the saints, the apostles, and the prophets, is at
perpetual variance with what characterizes and
animates all the rest of the world, condemns
it, and ever pronounces and prophesies against
it. Thus far, however, as respects this world,

the saints, apostles, and prophets have had the worst of it. Always in the minority, the world at large has never listened to them, never agreed with them, never consented to accept their system, never sympathized with their hopes, never respected their profession. They depreciate its interests too much. They are too severe on its principles. They are in the way of its liberties. They would draw a cowl over its joys. They would disable its beneficent progress. They are *pessimists*, who shut off all blessed outcome from its philosophies and efforts touching the amelioration of the condition of the race. In a word, they are intolerable to the world, a poor croaking set, fit only to be killed off by the hand of power where they are too persistent and loud, and unfit at best to receive respectful attention. If the world can find a Balaam, ready to compromise himself for gold, to bless it for a price, and to speak God's benediction on its lusts and passions, him it will honor, and to him will Balak's nobles come; but for the Elijahs, Isaiahs, Jeremiahs, Peters, and Pauls, their fate has ever been to be mocked, scourged, imprisoned, stoned, sawn asunder, slain with the sword, nailed to the cross, thrown to wild beasts, or compelled to seek asylum in deserts, mountains, and dens and caves of the earth, being destitute, tormented, afflicted, because they condemn the godless world, its Ahabs, its Jezebels, its Herods, and its sins. Compared with the great mass of mankind, the true Church has always been a "little flock," toiling with difficulties, opposition, and hatred, and never able to make effective headway against the powers holding sway over the race. Now and then the course of history seemed on the point of justifying her principles and profession, but then came internal defections, setting her back again, and almost extinguishing her being. And so it will be unto the end. So far as this present world is concerned, the general verdict of mankind, sustained by the great current of human history for 6000 years, is against the faith and testimonies of the saints, apostles, and prophets of God. To the general population of the earth their profession stands branded as mere hallucination and lies. But at last their vindication comes. When the vaunted wisdom, and progress, and experiments of unregenerate man are consummated, and there is nothing to show from it but a valley of burning cinders and desolation, with the whole earth from highest kings to meanest subjects howling in helpless lamentations, terror, and despair, history will have added its seal to all that saints, apostles, and prophets have said and maintained. Then will their judgment have been judged out of that world which despised and persecuted them, and spurned their hated *pessimism* for more flattering philosophies. Then will their renunciation of this world and its delusive hopes be justified by the ruin of its most cherished greatness. Then will the false verdict under which they have lain and suffered for sixty centuries be reversed in the living facts, of which they never ceased to tell and prophesy. Now they have sorrow, and can only weep and lament, whilst the world rejoices and sets them at naught; but then the sorrow and joy will exchange places, and the sorrow of the one be turned to joy, and the joy of the other to enduring lamentation.

It is in answer to this call for heaven, saints, apostles, and prophets to rejoice, that the sublime outbursts described in this chapter occur. John listens and looks, and sounds fall on his ears, and sights pass before his eyes, which stir and affect him more deeply than anything he yet had seen or heard since the first vision.

First of all he hears "a great voice of much multitude in heaven, saying, *Alleluia*." Here, for the first time in the New Testament, we come upon one of the most admirable words of praise ever made known on earth. It is the same that occurs so often in the most exultant of the Hebrew Psalms. Anselm, of Canterbury, considers it an angelic word, which cannot be fully reproduced in any language of man, and concurs with Augustine that the feeling and saying of it embodies all the blessedness of heaven. The Apocrypha (Tobit 13 : 21) gives it as among the great glories of the New Jerusalem that all the streets shall say, *Alleluia*. And this word John hears sounding from the sky,

> Loud as from numbers without number,
> Sweet as from blest voices uttering joy.

It is one of the very highest acknowledgments and celebrations of God. Where it is understandingly sung there is at once the profoundest adoration and the most exultant joy. And this is the feeling and experience in the heaven when the proud system of this world's apostate wisdom and glory falls.

We are not told precisely from whom this voice comes. It may be from the souls under the altar who waited so long to be avenged. It may be from that multitude which no man could number who come out of the great tribulation. It may be, but not so likely, from the host of holy angels who had been ministering for all these ages for what is then being realized. It may be from the 144,000 remembering the terribleness of the Antichristian severities they suffered, whose acclaim is elsewhere compared to mighty thunder (chap. 14 : 2). But whoever the particular parties may be, it is the voice of a multitudinous company of people in the heaven, and it is the voice of exultant adoration, celebrating " *the salvation, and the glory, and the power of our God.*" Thus, what the kings, merchants, and shippers on earth mourn and lament as destruction, is celebrated in heaven as divine " salvation." What is considered nothing but woe here is praised as divine glory there. And what is here regarded as the unmaking of all that earth called mighty is sung there as the very triumph of divine goodness. Heaven's estimate of things is widely different from that entertained by this world. The object of earth's fondest love and delight is the object of God's intensest wrath. That which men most work for, and most fondly serve, is that which God most severely judges.

And that which the great ones most deplore is the very thing which evokes the sublimest heavenly Halleluias.

The destruction of Great Babylon is an illustrious exhibition of the truth and righteousness of the divine administrations. Often it would seem as if God had forgotten his word, or quite abandoned the earth, so great is the prosperity of the wicked, the triumph of injustice, the wrongs and afflictions which those who most honor him suffer. But it is not so. He is true. His ways are just. Everything will come out fully equalized at the last. And here is a signal demonstration of the fact. The godless wisdom and pride of men are left to work themselves out to the full, but when the harvest is ripe the sweep of the sharp sickle of judgment comes against it and it suddenly falls, and all its just deservings it gets. The harlot has her day; but then comes her night, with never a star of hope to rise upon her any more. She is permitted to lure, delude, and debauch the world, because men preferred her abominations to the truth and kingdom of God; but only that her judgment may be the more conspicuous, and her destruction the more signal and complete. And the Halleluia of eternity is all the louder and more intense because her judgment comes as it does. Ah, yes, God's ways are right; his judgments are true and righteous. Perplexing and trying as they may be for the time, our Halleluias will be all the deeper and the sweeter by reason of what we may now deplore. Nay, they will be double then, by reason of the darkness now; for "a second time they say, *Alleluia.*"

And what the unnamed heavenly multitude so exultantly express, the twenty-four Elders and the four Living Ones equally feel and indorse. They even prostrate themselves in profoundest adoration, and "worship the God, the sitter upon the throne, saying, *Amen, Alleluia.*"

And here we meet with another of those peculiarly sacred and expressive words, reasonably supposed to have had their origin in heaven. From our first meeting with it in the Scriptures (Numb. 5 : 22) to the concluding word of this Book, we find it used as the special word of holy acquiescence and sacred ratification. It was constantly on the lips of the Saviour in his most solemn enunciations. It is the sealing word to all the Gospels and Epistles. It is not an oath, yet it has much of the solemnity and force of an oath. It contains no adjuration or appeal, yet it authenticates, confirms, binds, seals, and pledges to the truth of that to which it is affixed. It is not an imprecation upon him who utters it, but it is a tying up and giving over of his whole being and life to what he thus acknowledges and confirms. When placed at the end of an utterance or act of devotion, as placed by the Saviour at the end of the prayer he propounded as our model and form, it has the office of an underwriting or subscription, carrying the hearty consent and confidence of the worshipper with what has gone before. It is the word of fervency and soul-earnestness by which every utterance is grasped up again, and renewedly laid before God, as the full and ardent desire of our hearts, and as that which our souls most feel and most sacredly rest in. And so it is in the case now before us. The Elders and the Living Ones hear the triumphant celebration of the salvation, and the glory, and the power of our God, as sounded forth in the great voice of the much multitude, and feel the convictions and emotions of their own souls so completely expressed that they adoringly bow down and sacredly make it their own. All heaven is of one mind and of one soul. Therefore the self-prostrated Elders and Living Ones answer the Halleluias of the unnamed host with a third *Halleluia*, prefaced with the *Amen*, which makes the other two theirs also.

But this triple utterance of exultant praise and celebration of the salvation, glory, and power of our God, is still further urged on by a voice that comes out from the throne itself, saying, "*Praise our God, all his servants, those that fear him, the small and the great.*"

We are not told whose voice this is. Some take it as the voice of Christ, who is elsewhere said to be "in the midst of the throne." (7:17.) If it is his voice, he thus recognizes the Father as his God, as he did in the days of his earthly life, and at the same time owns all the glorified as his associates. But whether it is Christ's voice or not, it is the voice of the throne, a voice having authority to command and lead off in further exultation for the marvellous things then being accomplished.

Nor is it unlikely that the Saviour himself leads in the praise enjoined. So the promise runs in Psalm xxii: "I will declare thy name unto my brethren; in the midst of the congregation *will I praise thee.* Ye that fear the Lord, praise him. *My praise* shall be of thee in the great congregation; *I will pay my vows before them that fear him.*"

The subject of the praise here called for seems to look two ways, embracing the judgment just executed, and new glories about to be realized, of which that judgment is the pledge and inauguration. The voice which gave the first and second *Halleluias* was the voice of a vast heavenly multitude. The *Amen* and third *Halleluia* were from the Elders and the Living Ones. These all centre in the display of divine truth, justice, and almightiness in the judgment of Great Babylon, and the avenging of the blood of the saints out of her hand. If there be any other servants and fearers of God, great or small, they are also called to join in the exulting praises for the same. But as response comes to this admonition from the throne, the songs take in other subjects, and seem to embrace all that is described in the latter part of the chapter. The *Halleluia* which now comes with redoubled power and majesty celebrates the assumption of the kingdom by the Lord God, which would seem to imply that the victory in the battle of the great day is included. The marriage of the Lamb, the readiness and array of the Bride, and the blessedness of those who are called to the marriage banquet are likewise recounted, which can hardly be

taken as coincident with the fall of Babylon. A
point would, therefore, seem to be indicated in
this call, from which the contemplation is both
backward to Babylon's overthrow and forward to
the fall of the Beast, and the contemplation of the
Church's blessedness in her Lord ; the main stress
gravitating now toward what follows the judgment
on Babylon.

No sooner does the voice from the throne give
command for praise than John " heard as a voice
of much multitude, and as a voice of many waters,
and as a voice of mighty thunders, saying, *Alleluia,
because the Lord God the All-Ruler hath assumed the
kingdom.*" This is a mightier *Halleluia* than either
of the preceding. It refers also to an ampler subject. The judgment of Great Babylon demon-
strated, indeed, that God is mighty, and that he is
the All-Ruler. It also showed a potent taking up
and enforcement of his sovereign and righteous
authority. But what was thus shown in one aspect
and relation is at once followed out to a much
wider and more direct assumption of active rule
and sovereignty. When the seventh trumpet was
sounded a great voice anticipatively exclaimed :
" *The kingdom of the world* [not kingdoms, as some
versions and unsupported copies read, but ἡ βασιλεία
τοῦ κοσμου, as all the great manuscripts have it,
rendered by Wickliffe, the Rheims version, the
old Vulgate, and the still older Syriac, *the kingdom
of the world*], *is become our Lord's and his Christ's.*"
The kingdom of the world means the political
sovereignty of the world, the rulership of the
world, the kingly dominion or government of the

world, the same which is now exercised by the potentates and authorities of the earth. And this
kingdom of the world, this sovereignty, this rule,
this power of making and enforcing the laws regulating human society, the great voice said was
then about to pass into the hands of the Lord. It
does not mean the leavening of existing governments with Christian principles, the spiritual conversion of countries and empires, leaving them in
existence, and simply Christianizing them so as to
exhibit something of Christ's spirit in their administrations; but the total displacement of all this
world's sovereigns and governments, the taking
of all dominion and authority out of their hands,
and the putting of it in the hands of Christ, as the
true and only King of the world. And the actual
assumption of this rulership of the earth in the
place and stead of existing governments and lord-
ships is what the song of praise to God here so
mightily celebrates. "As a voice of much multitude, as a voice of many waters, and as a voice of
mighty thunders," comes forth the grand "*Alleluia, because the Lord God, the All-Ruler, hath assumed
the kingdom;*" that is, has himself entered upon
the actual administration of the sovereignty and
government of the world.

The fall of Great Babylon heralds and begins
the political regeneration of the earth.

And well may the tide of holy exultation swell to
its sublimest height over such an actuality. What
is the crown and consummation of that prayer
which the Lord Jesus put upon the lips and into

the hearts of all his followers when he said, pray,
" *Thy kingdom come?*" Does it mean no more than
that our own hearts may be thoroughly subdued
to our Maker, purged of idolatry and lust, purified by the Holy Ghost, and filled with all pureness, heavenly knowledge, devotion, obedience,
and grace? That might be, and yet the earth be
crushed with misrule, tyranny, corruption, and
oppression. Does it mean simply that the Church
may be ever dear and faithful to God, its ministers
multiplied, its membership increased, its Scriptures distributed, its faith kept pure, its sacraments
observed, its defections healed, its weaknesses removed, its success augmented, and all its members
blessed with all spiritual riches in Christ Jesus?
That might all be and the world still be to her a
valley of Baca, a Bochim, a wilderness of sorrow
and hardship. Does it mean only the removal of
what hinders the preaching and belief of the
Gospel, or the progress of faith and piety in the
individual and in the world? That might also be
and still God's kingdom be no nearer than it is at
present. When Isaiah prophesied of Christ, he
said : " *The government* shall be upon his shoulder;
of the increase of his *government and peace* there
shall be no end, *upon the throne of David, and upon
his kingdom*, to order it, and to establish it with
judgment and justice." (Is. 9 : 6, 7.) When the
Holy Ghost explained the meaning of the all-
crushing stone in Nebuchadnezzar's dream, which
broke to atoms the whole statue of worldly power
and dominion, took its place, and filled the whole

earth, the word was, This is the kingdom which
the God of heaven shall set up, which shall break
in pieces and consume all other kingdoms, and it
shall stand forever. (Dan. 3 : 32–45.) When Daniel
was beholding till " the judgment was set and the
books opened," he saw in the night visions, like to
the Son of Man, brought before the Ancient of
days, " and there was given him dominion, and
glory, *and a kingdom*, that all people, nations, and
languages should serve him," even *" the kingdom,
and dominion, and the greatness of the kingdom under
the whole heaven," " an everlasting kingdom."* (Dan. 7.)
When Gabriel announced to Mary the child to be
born of her, he said : " He shall be great, and
shall be called the Son of the Highest, and the
Lord shall give unto him *the throne* of his father
David, and he shall *reign* over the house of Jacob
forever, and of *his kingdom* there shall be no end."
(Luke 1 : 26–33.) When he himself was among
men, because some " thought that the kingdom
of God should immediately appear," he spake a
parable, and said that the matter is as a nobleman
going " into a far country to receive for himself *a
kingdom*, and to return," meanwhile intrusting to
his servants certain possessions with which to trade
and occupy till he should come. (Luke 19 : 11–13.)
And so again he said : " When the Son of Man
shall come in his glory, and all the holy angels
with him, *then shall he sit in the throne of his glory.*"
(Matt. 25 : 31.) All these and many like passages
treat of that very *kingdom*, for the coming of
which all are commanded to pray. Nor can they

be explained according to their plain and pointed terms without taking in the coming again of Christ to reckon with his servants, to take the rule out of the hands of those who have usurped dominion over the earth, to dethrone Satan and all his agents, and to reign from sea to sea, the only rightful *King* of the world. And thus, when Great Babylon falls, it will be God's kingdom come, as it never yet has come, and the burden of the prayer of all these weary ages answered.

This assumption of the rule of the world will likewise bring with it the great desideratum of the race. When Adam was in Eden God was king. In the days of Israel's greatest triumph it was the same. And until the original Theocracy is restored, and the powers of heaven again take the rulership and control of the nations, there is no peace, no right order for man. There is no earthly blessing like that of good, wise, and righteous government; but there is no such government outside of the government of the Father and the Son. Some are better than others, but none are satisfactory. Men have experimented with power for 6000 years, and yet there is no department in which there is more disability, corruption, and unsatisfactoriness than in the administrations of government. There is nothing of which all people so much complain, or have so much cause to complain, as of the manner in which their political affairs are managed and administered. Those who live on government patronage and plunder are enthusiastic enough in

behalf of what they call their country, and consider it piety to eulogize the instrument which
pampers their greed and passions; but the helpless multitude is left to sigh and cry in vain over
the abominations that are done. The best governments man has ever tried have invariably disap-
pointed their founders, and proven themselves too
weak or too strong, too concentrated or too dis-
severed, and in one way or another have turned
into instruments of injustice, ambition, selfishness,
and affliction. The demonstration of the ages is,
that "that which is crooked cannot be made
straight, and that which is wanting cannot be num-
bered." So true is this that one has said, with a
pathos that shows how deep the conviction was,
" I know no safe depositary of power among mortal men for the purposes of government. Tyranny
and oppression, in Church and State, under every
form of government,—social, civil, ecclesiastical,
monarchical, aristocratical, or democratic,—have,
sooner or later, characterized the governments of
the earth, and have done so from the beginning."
Bad government is doubtless better than no government. In the nature of things we must have
government of some sort. Because of the worse
ills of anarchy we take the lesser afflictions of government in such forms as we can get it. But what
right-thinking and right-feeling man is not outraged every day at the injustice, maladministration,
perversion, and abominations that go along with
every government of man? So it ever has been,
and so it ever will be while "man's day" lasts.

" The kingdom is the Lord's," and till he comes and assumes it there will be disappointment, misrule, revolution, and incurable trouble in all human calculations and affairs. Nothing but the sway and reign of heaven can redeem this fallen world out of the pestilential morasses of its incompetent and oppressive governments. But there is an All-Ruler who will yet assume the kingdom, and give the race the reign of blessedness. " He shall come down like rain upon the mown grass, as showers that water the earth. In his days shall the righteous flourish, and abundance of peace so long as the moon endureth. He shall have dominion also from sea to sea, and from the river unto the ends of the earth. They that dwell in the wilderness shall bow before him, and his enemies shall lick the dust. All kings shall fall down before him; all nations shall serve him. For he shall deliver the needy when he crieth, the poor also, and him that hath no helper. He shall redeem their soul from deceit and violence, and precious shall their blood be in his sight. He shall live, and to him shall be given of the gold of Sheba; prayer also shall be made for him continually, and daily shall he be praised. His name shall endure forever, and men shall be blessed in him. All nations shall call him blessed."

Thus flowed the glorious numbers from David's prophetic harp, telling of the All-Ruler's assumption of the kingdom, and exulting in it, until the royal singer's soul fired up into the very *Alleluia* of the text, crying, "*Blessed be his glorious name forever! and let the whole earth be filled with his glory. Amen, and Amen.*" Human utterance could go no higher. The mountain summit of the promised blessedness was reached. And there the prayers of David, the son of Jesse, ended. (Ps. 72.)

We thus begin to see something of the dawn and character of those better times to come when once the mystery of God is finished. Tyrants, despots, and faithless and burdensome governments shall then be no more. Like wild beasts, full of savage instinct for blood and oppression, have the world-powers roamed and ravaged the earth, treading down the nations, their will the only law, the good and happiness of men the furthest from their hearts. But it will be otherwise then. "The Lord shall be king over all the earth," and therein is the signal and pledge of the dominion of right and everlasting peace. Wars shall be no more. Injustice and unequal laws shall be done away. Enemies will be powerless. Men will then have their standing according to their moral worth. The salvation of God will be nigh to them that fear him. Truth shall spring out of the earth, and righteousness shall look down from heaven. And sorrow and sighing shall flee away. Therefore the voice of eternal right is, "*Praise our God, all his servants, those that fear him, the small and the great,*" and from all the holy universe comes the song, in volume like the sea, in

strength like the thunder, " ALLELUIA, BECAUSE
THE LORD GOD THE ALL-RULER HATH ASSUMED THE
KINGDOM."

LECTURE FORTY-SECOND.

Rev. 19 : 7–10. (Revised Text.) Let us rejoice and exult, and we will give the glory to him, because is come the marriage of the Lamb, and his wife [the Woman] prepared herself. And it was given to her that she should clothe herself in fine linen, bright pure ; for the fine linen is the righteousnesses of the saints.

And he saith to me, Write, Blessed they who have been called to the supper of the marriage of the Lamb. And he saith to me, These are the true words of God.

And I fell down before his feet to worship him. And he said, Take heed, no ; I am a fellow-servant of thee and of thy brethren that have the witness of Jesus ; worship God ; for the witness of Jesus is the spirit of the prophecy.

THE fall of Great Babylon lifts a heavy load from the hearts of all the holy universe. The day and reign of apostate man then reach their final close. The hopes and prayers of faith, and all the gracious prophecies and promises of God, then come to the goal of their fulfilment. Earth's true, invincible, and eternal king then takes the sovereignty, never again to pass it into other hands. The heavenly worlds understand it, and pour forth

their mightiest exultations. And thick and throng-
ing are the subjects of joy which now crowd upon
their enraptured attention. Among the rest is one
singled out with special interest and delight.
Whilst the song of *Halleluia* swells to the dimensions of mighty thunders, because the Lord God
the All-Ruler hath assumed the kingdom, a call
goes forth, "*Let us rejoice and exult, and we will
give the glory to him, because is come The Marriage
of the Lamb.*" The Harlot swept away, the faithful Woman comes to her rightful honors. The
betrothed, so long waiting amid privation, persecution, and contempt, now becomes a Bride. The
time of her marriage has at length arrived, and
the grand nuptial banquet begins. And that marriage and that banquet are what we are now to
consider. God help us to understand it, and to rejoice ourselves in the contemplation!

Expositors generally have taken it for granted
that this marriage is so familiar to the readers of
holy Scripture, and so well understood, as to need
no explanation. Perhaps had they attempted to
set forth in definite form what they pass as so plain,
they would have found the task less easy than they
thought. Though the subject is common to both
Testaments, there is not another of equal prominence and worth upon which so little direct attention has been bestowed by modern divines, or upon
which clear ideas are so scarce. In my study of
it, question after question has come up, even with
regard to some of the most essential points, which
I find it very hard to answer satisfactorily. And

if others have found it so plain and easy as to render the explanation of it a work of supererogation, they would have relieved me much, as well as an almost total blank in our theologies with regard to one of the most frequently recurring subjects of Holy Writ, if they had condescended to record the results of their examinations. As it is, we must examine for ourselves.

I. *Who is the Bridegroom?* On this point, fortunately, there is not much room for misunderstanding. It is "The Lamb," the blessed Saviour, who gave himself to death as a sacrifice for our sins, and is alive and living forever. It is the everlasting Son of the Father made incarnate for our salvation, and in his twofold nature exalted, glorified, and enthroned in eternal majesty. And yet it may be a question whether, in his character and marriage as *The Lamb*, everything is to be understood to which the Scriptures refer under the figure of man's marriage to God; whether there is not some particular and special intimacy or relationship meant to be set forth in this case; whether it respects the Jewish people only, or Christian people only, or all saints alike. The Old Testament Church is everywhere represented as betrothed to God as a candidate for a glorious union with him in due time. (Isa. 14 : 1-8; Ezek. 16 : 7 seq.; Hos. 2 : 19 seq.) It is the same with regard to the New Testament Church. Christ represents himself as the Bridegroom. (Matt. 9 : 15.) He speaks of the kingdom of heaven being "like unto a certain king which made a marriage for his son," and those called by the Gospel as "bidden to the marriage." (Matt. 22 : 1–13.) He speaks often of the judgment time as the coming of the Bridegroom for his Bride. (Matt. 25 : 1–10.) John the Baptist spoke of Christ as the Bridegroom, and of himself as "the friend of the Bridegroom, which standeth and heareth him, and rejoiceth greatly because of the Bridegroom's voice." (Jno. 3 : 29.) Paul speaks of those whom he begat in the Gospel as espoused to one husband, whom he desired to present as a chaste virgin to Christ. (2 Cor. 11 : 2.) Earthly marriage is likewise spoken of as a mystery, significant of Christ's relation to his Church. (Eph. 5 : 23–32.) All this proves, as clearly as may be, that in the economy of grace and redemption our blessed Saviour takes the character and relation of a Bridegroom or Husband to his people, of one class or another, and that a great and blessed union between himself and them remains to be celebrated. Whether the marriage in each case is precisely one and the same thing, or respects the same identical parties, it is equally certain that it is *The Lamb*,—the glorified Lord Jesus Christ,— who is here contemplated as the Bridegroom and Husband.

II. *Who is the Bride?* Upon first blush the answer would be, the Lord's true and faithful people, all who by faith and obedience were affianced to him, and continued faithful to the end. In a general way this answer may be accepted as the truth, but in a narrower and closer view of things it cannot be taken as strictly and absolutely correct.

The 45th Psalm unmistakably refers to this subject. The qualities and doings of the King, come forth from the ivory palaces, are there described with great vigor and animation. But there is also the Queen, the King's Bride, standing on his right hand, in gold of Ophir, and all glorious within. It is said of her that "she shall be brought unto the King in raiment of needle-work." But, besides the Queen, the King's Bride, there is another blessed company, who are also to enter with rejoicing into the King's palace, and to share the light of his countenance. They are called "the virgins," the "companions," associates, and bosom friends of the Queen, but plainly distinct from the Queen herself. They do not go with her when she is taken, but "follow her,"—come after her,— and are "brought unto the King" at a subsequent time, and in quite another capacity from that of the Queen and Bride. All of them belong to the general congregation of the saved. All of them are made forever happy in their Lord, the King. But the Queen is one class, and "the virgins her companions that follow her," are another class.

So, too, in the Song of Solomon (6 : 8–9), we read of queens, concubines, and virgins, whom the fathers, for the most part, understood as referring to the various classes which make up the Church as a whole. Theodoret, and some others, have held that these are not to be taken as representing the true people of God; but why then are they called by names so descriptive of the King's most intimate associates and household? Or how could they have that devout and admiring sympathy with the Bride, blessing and praising her as they do, if not of the same general fellowship with her? Some narrow Churchmen see here the various sects which stand opposed to what they consider the Church; but opposition and secession are not significant of admiration and blessing, and if these queens, etc., be of the household of faith in any sense, their relation to the King, in the very nature of the terms, must be true and real. The oldest Christian interpretation, and that which is best sustained, sees in them none but genuine believers, but of different degrees of honor and nearness to their Lord; in which case, again, not all have the Bride's place.

So the parable of the Ten Virgins tells of a coming Bridegroom, and of friends of the Bride going out, as in ancient custom, to meet and welcome him, and to go in with him to the marriage; but where is the Bride? Both the connection and the terms of this parable imply that she is then already within the Father's house, there awaiting the coming of the Bridegroom, whilst these her friends go out to meet him,—not in hope of becoming his Bride, but of having the blessedness of going in with him to the marriage. As a matter of fact, distinctly stated, the day of the Lord has already commenced when the kingdom of heaven assumes the precise shape here indicated. In the verses preceding, the Saviour spoke of the gathering of certain eagle saints to that body on which they live, of the mysterious taking of some, while others are left, and of the sadness of being cut off from the high privileges and honors of that first class; and it is "*then*," he says, only *then*, that matters take the shape described in the parable. Those who are "*taken*" before "then" are people of pre-eminent saintship and watchful preparedness. (Comp. Luke 17 : 33–37; 21 : 34–36.) They correspond to the Bride, whilst the wise virgins come after, not being ready when the Bride was taken. Nay, it is the removal of these waiting and ready ones which awakens the intense adventism of those that are "left," and serves as the means of bringing at least half of them in as guests and witnesses of the marriage. The "left" know now that Christ is presently to come as the Bridegroom, on his way to join his Bride. To be ready for that Bridegroom coming, that they may go in with him to the marriage, is now the one great thought. In all ordinary custom—to which the allusion is—the going in would be the going into the Father's house where the Bride already is, arrayed and ready for her coming Lord.

To say nothing, then, of the place and fate of the five unwise virgins, this parable, taken in its connections, inevitably implies that not all of those who finally get to heaven are of that class which actually constitutes the Bride of Christ, however related to that Bride.

It is also the common doctrine of the Scriptures that there are great diversities in the portions awarded to the saints. There are some greatest and some least in the kingdom of heaven. There are some who shall be first and some who shall be last. There are some who get crowns, and there are some who get none. There are some who are assigned dominion over ten cities, some over five, and some who lose all reward, and are saved only "so as by fire." The four Living Ones, and the four-and twenty Elders, are the representatives of men saved from the earth. They sing the song of redemption by the blood of Christ. But they are in heaven, crowned, glorified, and installed in blessed priesthoods and kinghoods in advance of the vast multitude whose rewards are far inferior. Diversities so great are incompatible with the peculiar honors and regality of the wife of a king.

Besides, princesses and queens, above all on occasions of their marriage, always have their associates, companions, maids of honor, attendants, suites, and friends, who, in a general way, are counted with them as making one and the same company, but who in fact are very distinct in honor and privilege from those on whom they find it their happiness to attend. Just as the Bridegroom comes not alone, but with attendants, companions, and a long train of rejoicing ones who make up his party, the whole of whom together are called the Bridegroom's coming, whilst, strictly speaking, there is a wide difference between him and those with him; so it is on the side of the Bride. She has her companions and attendants too,—"virgins which follow her." They make up her company and train. In coming to wed her the Bridegroom comes also into near and close relation to them. To a blessed degree they share the Bride's honors.

And in general terms we must include them when we speak of the Bride, although, in strict language, they are not all the Bride. The Bride has relations to the Bridegroom which belong to her alone, and it is only because of her and their association and companionship with her, and not because they are the Bride in actual fact, that the whole company of the saved Church of God is contemplated as the Lamb's Wife.

Hence, also, the angel directed John to write, "Blessed they who have been called to the supper of the marriage of the Lamb." It is the wider and the more general blessedness of the occasion that the seer was thus to attest. If all the saved were actually the Bride, it would have been enough, and more to the point, to say, " Blessed they that are called to be the Wife of the Lamb." But there is a blessedness of being called to witness his marriage, and a blessedness of participation with the bridal company in the marriage banquet, as well as a more special blessedness of being the actual Bride of the Lamb. The call is indeed to make up the Bride. It is out of these called ones that the Bride is chosen. But the choosing of the Bride does not, therefore, exclude the rest of the company from the honors and privileges of the marriage supper, or from companionship with the Lamb and his Wife. The blessedness of the marriage supper is much wider than that of becoming the Bride, though the Bride has honor and nearness to the Lord which belong to her only. Hence the writing was to be, not simply " Blessed they that are called to be the Wife of the Lamb," but " blessed they who are called to the supper of the marriage of the Lamb,"—called as in the parable of the marriage of the king's son, which call includes the opportunity to become the Bride as well as happy guests.

In this sense also am I constrained to take the subsequent showing of "the Bride, the Lamb's Wife," "that great city, the holy Jerusalem, descending out of the heaven from God." It is called the Bride, because it embraces the Bride, and because it is the Bride's everlasting home and residence. But for the very reason that it is the home and residence of the Lamb's Wife, it must include her retinue, her companions, and her attendants, who share the glory with her, but who are not strictly the Bride herself. In general terms the whole city, as made up of those who inhabit it, including all the saved up to the time of the resurrection of all saints, is the Bride, the Lamb's Wife, because all that are there pertain to her company, fill out the grandeur and glory of her estate, and share immensely in it; albeit, some are there who, in a narrower and more particular discrimination, are not actually the Bride.

III. *What is the making of Herself ready?* The allusion seems to be to something of the same sort with the putting on of the wedding garment, of which so much is made in the parable of the marriage of the king's son. (Matt. 22 : 1–14.) There one of the guests was found without a wedding garment, and for that deficiency was put away from the happy

company amid shame and sorrow. But in this
case the Bride "prepared herself. And it was
given to her that she should clothe herself in fine
linen,—bright, pure,—for the fine linen is the
righteousnesses of the saints." Thus it is said in
Isaiah (61 : 10), "I will greatly rejoice in the Lord,
my soul shall be joyful in my God; for he hath
clothed me with the garments of salvation, he hath
covered me with the robe of righteousness, as a
bridegroom decketh himself with ornaments, and
as a bride adorneth herself with jewels." Thus,
also, when the seer saw the holy city coming down
from God out of heaven, she was "prepared as a
bride adorned for her husband." (21 : 2.) The excellencies in which the Bride here arrays herself
are described as the finest linen, of the intensest
purity and lustre; but it is at the same time a
spiritual linen, which is "the righteousnesses of
the saints."

Three things appear in the notice of this ready-
making. (1) There is self-activity on the part of
the Bride to prepare herself. (2) There is gratuity
and bestowment, putting what is requisite at her
command. And (3) she is receptive and obedient
in making the intended use of what is given her.
The description evidently takes in the whole previous career of those who make up the Bride.
The preparation refers not only to something that
is done at this time, but also to what has been in
the course of doing all along, and now comes to
its fruit and award. The coming to Christ, the
learning of him, the espousal to him in holy con-

fession, and justification by faith in his blood and merit, are unquestionably included. Paul was aiming at this very preparedness and honor of the Bride of the Lamb, and counted all temporal possessions as nothing, and exerted himself in every way to be fit for it. But that fitness, he tells us, was his being found not having his own righteousness, which is of the law,—a mere show of human works,—but having that righteousness which is through faith of Christ, the righteousness which is of God by faith. (Phil. 3 : 8–14.) But the righteous acts and good works of the justified are also included. The word is in the plural— "the righteousnesses of the saints." Some call it the plurality of dignity, and make nothing special of it. Others say it is the distributive plural, in allusion to the many who have it. But parallel instances are wanting to sustain either of these theories. It distinctly implies that the saints have more than one righteousness, as the Scriptures elsewhere teach.

There is a righteousness of justification, and a righteousness of life and sanctification. There is a righteousness which is the free gift of God in Christ Jesus, and a righteousness of man's own active obedience to God's ordinances and commands. True, saints have both; a righteousness by imputation through faith without works, and a righteousness which is the fruit of faith, consisting of works springing from and wrought in faith. And both enter into that adornment of the Bride wherein she maketh herself ready. She is clothed with the fine and shining linen of " the *righteous-nesses* of the saints," the righteousness of a free justification by faith in her Lord who died for her, and the righteousness of a life of earnest, active, and grateful devotion to make herself meet and worthy for so good and gracious a Husband. (Comp. Luke 20 : 35; 21 : 36; Eph. 4 : 1; Col. 1 : 10; Rev. 3 : 4.)

But it is not certain that the clothing of herself in these righteousnesses is all that is embraced in the Bride's preparation for the wedding. That is the part of her ready-making as respects this life; but who knows what else remains for her to do after this life is over, or what practical activities remain for the saints between the moment of their removal to immortality and the heavenly solemnities which are shadowed to us under the idea of the marriage of the Lamb? Heaven is no more a scene of quiescence than earth. There is history in the career of saints after they leave this world as well as in it, and far greater and sublimer history than pertains to them here. And who knows into what grand activities the people of God are ushered when their mortality is swallowed up of life? or with what preparations they may then be called to busy themselves for the sublime events and ceremonies that lie before them in their instalment into the relations and dignities of their everlasting estate? The celestial population seem to know of ready-making in heaven, which comes after the ready-making on earth, which is to them a subject of glad rejoicing, and

of new and special giving of glory to God. But
just what it is, or exactly to what it relates, we
must content ourselves not to know till the time
for it comes.

IV. *What is the Marriage?* Here again we must
be satisfied with very imperfect information. John
did not see the marriage, neither was it explained
to him. He only heard the heavenly rejoicing
that the time for it had come, that the Bride had
prepared herself, and that he was to declare the
blessedness of those who are called to the banquet
then to be spread. That the marriage and the
supper are not one and the same thing, the nature
of the case, as well as the manner in which they
are referred to, would seem to make evident. The
marriage is accompanied with a becoming feast,
but the feast is one thing and the marriage is
another, though occurring at the same time and
most intimately correlated.

It is curious to observe how various are the notions which interpreters have given of this marriage of the Lamb. Beza, Robertson (of Leu-
chars), Clarke, and others are confident that it
refers to a happy condition of the Church in this
world, when " whole contemporary churches are
in covenant with Christ in a most upright manner." It is supposed by these that when the
Church becomes more pure in her doctrines, more
pious in her experiences, and more righteous in
her conduct than ever she has yet been, this whole
showing will be exhausted. Accordingly, the
Bride of Christ would be nothing but the Chris-

tians of one particular generation, and the Living Ones, and Elders, and the multitude which no man can number, and the 144,000 sealed ones, and other classes which this Book shows to be in heaven before the marriage of the Lamb is announced, have no part nor lot in it. Fuller and William Jones see the whole picture fulfilled in a fancied Millennium on earth, "when Jews and Gentiles from every nation under heaven shall be brought to believe in Jesus, and led to confess him as their true Messiah, Saviour, and King;" which likewise cuts off all those who have lived and faithfully served Christ in all the long ages prior to the thousand years, and equally vacates the whole marriage idea as contrasted with the already existing union between Christ and his people. Hengstenberg thinks that "we are here beyond the thousand years, beyond the last victory over Gog and Magog," though he thus makes the people in heaven say it *is come* a thousand years before it does come. Some refer it to the taking again of the seed of Abraham to be God's peculiar people, after the present church period has reached its termination. This would well accord with a variety of Scripture passages otherwise obscure, but it does not meet some of the main features of the case. If at all in the contemplation, it cannot be more than an earthly and inferior correspondence of the chief thing, which must relate to heaven, for when the Bride was shown to John he beheld her in the form of a glorious city coming down from God out of heaven, proving that her marriage must needs have been in heaven. Vaughan speaks of the marriage as "the ideal concourse and combination of the blessed company of all faithful people on their entrance into their rest." This would seem to accord with the presentations as to time and place, but tells nothing as to what the marriage itself is. Düsterdieck understands it to be "Christ's distribution of the eternal reward of grace to his faithful ones, who then enter with him into the full glory of the heavenly life;" which may be true enough in general, for the marriage is surely the result, award, and consummation of grace toward the Bride; but it still leaves us in the region of mist and darkness as to any difference between the marriage and the judgment. The translator of Lange (*in loc.*) comes closer to the truth when he represents the marriage as "the union of the whole body of the saints with a personally present Christ in glory and government—the establishment of the kingdom." As the writer of *The Apocalypse Expounded* says, "It is a scene taking place in the heaven, after the resurrection of the saints, and ere Jesus and his risen ones are manifested to the earth, as heaven is not opened till the marriage has occurred." The blessedness of it is not inaptly described by Lange to be "the reciprocal operation of a spiritual fellowship of love." It is Christ in the character of the Lamb, the mighty *Goel*, formally acknowledging and taking to himself as copartners of his throne, dominion, and glory, all those chosen ones who have been faithful to their betrothal, and appear at last in the spotless and shining apparel of the right-eousnesses of the saints, thenceforward to be with him, reign with him, and share with him in all his grand inheritance, forever.

Just what the ceremony of this marriage is we are nowhere told. Some have thought that it is the first opening of the city of God, the New Je-rusalem, to the footsteps of the redeemed. Jesus says that he is now preparing a place for us. The ancient saints looked for a city whose maker and builder is God. That city John saw and describes in a subsequent chapter. That city was shown him as the Bride, the Lamb's Wife, so called on ac-count of those who inhabit and dwell in it. The placing of the redeemed with their Redeemer in that sublime and eternal home necessarily involves some befitting formality. Nor is it far-fetched to connect that first formal entrance into that illus-trious heaven-built city with the ceremonial of what is described as the marriage of the Lamb. When the sacred tabernacle was first opened and used it was with great solemnities, which God himself prescribed, and in the observance of which there was also a marked coming together of God and his people. By visible manifestations of Deity a point of union and communion was then and there established between man and Je-hovah, so direct and close that the holy prophet could say of Israel, " Thy Maker is thy Husband." And the fact that God so ordered and honored the occasion is ample warrant for taking it as the type of a corresponding formality in the heavens, answering to the coming together of the Lamb and his affianced people for the first time in that glorious city, which even the great voice from the throne calls "THE TABERNACLE OF GOD." (Chap. 21 : 2, 3.)

V. *What is the Marriage Supper?* Contrary to all congruity, many take it as about one and the same with the marriage itself. Marriage is the establishment of relationship and status; a marriage feast is the refreshment, the eating, and drinking, and general social joy on the part of those attending upon a marriage. First the Bridegroom comes, next the marriage is solemnized, and then the assembled company is invited to the special repast provided for the occasion. And so in this case. The Bridegroom appears, the marriage takes place, and then the grand banquet ensues; so that the supper is a different thing from the marriage, though following immediately upon it.

Everywhere in the Scriptures do we hear of this feast. As in the matter of the marriage, something of it is to be enjoyed already in this life. There is a supper of Gospel blessings of which we may now partake. But as the actual marriage occurs in heaven subsequent to the resurrection, so also the fulness of the Gospel supper is deferred till then. Isaiah (25 : 6–9) sung of a feast of fat things, of wines on the lees, of fat things full of marrow, of wines on the lees well refined, which the Lord of Hosts is to make. The feast of Gospel blessings is doubtless included; but it is a feast whose glorious fulness is beyond the grave. A chief part of its glory is that then " death is swallowed up in victory," tears are all wiped away by Jehovah's hand, the disabilities and hardships of his people are gone, and the shout is, " Lo, this is our God; we have waited for him; we will be glad and rejoice in his salvation." Of that same feast the Saviour spoke when he said to his disciples, " I will not drink henceforth of this fruit of the vine until that day when I drink it new with you in my Father's kingdom." (Matt. 26 : 29.) So, also, when he had finished the paschal supper, and said, " I will not any more eat thereof until it be fulfilled in the kingdom of God." (Luke 22 : 16.) As Melchisedek, king of righteousness, and king of peace, brought forth bread and wine to Abraham returning from the scenes of judgment upon the marauding kings, so will he whom Melchisedek typified spread before his victorious people the precious viands of a heavenly banquet, of which our holy Lord's supper is the constant prophecy and foretaste.

Of what that supper shall consist we cannot yet know. The Scriptures speak of bread of heaven and angel's food, and the Saviour tells of eating and drinking there. He who supplied the wedding at Cana, and fed the thousands in the wilderness, and furnished the little dinner to his worn disciples as they came up from the sea of toil to the shore trodden by his glorified feet, can be at no loss to make good every word, and letter, and allusion which the Scriptures contain with reference to that high festival. The angels know something about it, and the angel told John that it will be a blessed thing to be there. "Write," said the heavenly voice, "write, *Blessed they who have been called to the supper of the marriage of the Lamb.*"

VI. *Who, then, are the Guests?* Chief of all who sit down to the marriage banquets on earth are the bridegroom and the bride. It is in honor of their union that the feast is held, and to them is assigned the most conspicuous place. This is a genuine marriage feast, the antitype of all the marriage feasts of time, and this particular feature cannot be wanting there. In the after chapters we are told that the Lamb is the light of the golden house in which it is held. He, therefore, is there in unveiled glory, the observed, the adored, the sublimest joy of all. And where he is there his bride is also, for they are united now, never to be separated any more. She is there in all her perfected loveliness, "not having spot, or wrinkle, or any such thing," but "all glorious within," and enfolded in her garments of needlework, and gold, and in the faultless and radiant linen of the righteousnesses of the saints. There also are "the virgins, her companions that follow her," and make up her sublime and glorious train. And whosoever, in any age, in any land, of any language, of any tribe, has heard of the promised seed of the woman, and believed in him, and listened to the calls and promises of God, and directed his heart and pilgrim steps for that blest

city, shall likewise be there. Whether as bride
or guest, the whole Church of the first-born, from
Adam down to the last martyr under the Antichrist, shall be there, radiant in that redemption
for which they hoped and suffered. The quaint
old hymn says truly:

> There be prudent Prophets all,
>   The Apostles six and six,
> The glorious Martyrs in a row,
>   And Confessors betwixt.
> There doth the crew of righteous men
>   And nations all consist;
> Young men and maids that here on earth
>   Their pleasures did resist.
>
> The sheep and lambs that hardly 'scaped
>   The snare of death and hell,
> Triumph in joy eternally,
>   Whereof no tongue can tell;
> And though the glory of each one
>   Doth differ in degree,
> Yet is the joy of all alike
>   And common certainly.
>
> There David stands, with harp in hand,
>   As master of the choir;
> A thousand times that man were blessed
>   That might his music hear.
> There Mary sings " Magnificat,"
>   With tunes surpassing sweet;
> And all the virgins bear their part,
>   Singing about her feet.
>
> " Te Deum," doth St. Ambrose sing,
>   St. Austin doth the same;
> Old Simeon and Zacharie
>   Anew their songs inflame.

There Magdalene hath left her moan,
  And cheerfully doth sing,
With all blest saints whose harmony
  Through every street doth ring.

And in that holy company
  May you and I find place,
Through worth of him who died for us,
  And through his glorious grace;
With Cherubim and Seraphim,
  And hosts of ransomed men,
To sing our praises to The Lamb,
  And add our glad *Amen.*

VII. *What authority have we for all this?* There be those who count it all a dream, a pleasant fancy, a sweet hallucination, by which enthusiastic souls impose upon themselves. And if it were, why deny to poor, sorrowing, and afflicted humanity its consoling radiance? Be it a mere conceit, is not the race the happier and the better for believing it? But no, it is not delusion. The very blessedness which it diffuses through the souls that take it to their thoughts is a voucher for its heavenly reality. The holy being who told of it to the seer propounds it as the sum of all sacred revelations, and says, " *These are the true words of God.*"

Ah, yes; there is a Lamb, once slain, now risen and glorified, moving serene and mighty amid the principalities of eternity, himself the highest of them all, to whom all believers stand betrothed and plighted, preparing and waiting for a wedding day to come, when they shall be joined to him in fellowship, glory, and dominion forever. There

is a city of gold, and light, and jewels for God's
people, building for these many ages, and now
near its readiness for their everlasting habitation.
There is in store a banquet when once the honored
Bride sets foot upon its golden streets, the call to
which, if heeded, is man's superlative blessedness.
Room for doubt, is none; for " *these are the true
words of God.*"

The revelation to John was overpowering. It so
thrilled upon his soul, and so stimulated his sense
of grateful wonder and adoration, that he fell down
before the angel's feet to worship him.   It was an
error to offer such honor to a fellow-servant with
himself, and the same was promptly checked; but
it helps to tell the entrancing magnificence of the
final portion of the saints—the overwhelming
majesty of the glory to come when the Bridegroom
comes. It bends the soul in awe even towards the
messengers who tell of it.   It is more than heart
of flesh can well stand up under, even in prospect.
What then will be the actual realization? A
holy apostle falls upon his face in adoration when
he hears of it, and the glorified in heaven cry,
"Let us rejoice and exult, and we will give the
glory to God," when the time for it arrives.

What then, O man, O woman, is the state and
feeling of your heart concerning it?   To you has
come the call to the supper of the marriage of the
Lamb; what is the response you have made to it?
To you is offered the wedding garment to appear
there in honor and glory; have you accepted it,
and put it on, and kept its purity unsoiled?   The

cry has long been ringing in your ears, " Behold, the Bridegroom cometh !" Are your loins girded about, your lights burning, and ye yourselves like unto those who wait for their Lord ? Five virgins once set out to reach that festival, but when they came " *the door was shut.*" They knew what was required; but the Bridegroom came, and this was the consequence of their unreadiness. God forbid that this should be your experience !

> Wake, awake, for night is flying,
> The watchmen on the heights are crying ;
>   Awake, Jerusalem, at last !
> Midnight hears the welcome voices,
> And at the thrilling cry rejoices ;
>   Come forth, ye virgins, night is past !
>   The Bridegroom comes, awake,
>   Your lamps with gladness take ;
>   Halleluia !
> And for His marriage feast prepare,
> For ye must go to meet Him there.

LECTURE FORTY-THIRD.

Rev. 19 : 11–21. (Revised Text.) And I saw the heaven opened, and
behold a white horse, and one seated upon him, Faithful and True,
and in righteousness he judgeth and warreth; his eyes flame of fire,
and on his head many diadems, having a name written which no one
knoweth but himself, and clothed in vesture dipped [or *stained*] with
blood, and his name is called THE WORD OF GOD. And the armies,
the ones in the heaven were following him on white horses, clothed in
fine linen, white, pure. And out of his mouth proceedeth a sharp
sword, that with it he may smite the nations; and HE shall rule [or
shepherdize] them with a rod of iron; and HE treadeth the winepress
of the wine of the anger of the wrath of the God, the All-Ruler. And
he hath upon his vesture, even upon his thigh a name written, KING OF
KINGS AND LORD OF LORDS.

And I saw a certain angel standing in the sun, and he cried with a
great voice, saying to all the fowls that fly in mid-heaven, Hither, be
gathered together to the great supper of God, that ye may eat flesh of
kings, and flesh of captains of thousands, and flesh of mighty men,
and flesh of horses, and of those that sit on them, and flesh of all
[classes], both free and bond, and small and great.

And I saw the beast, and the kings of the earth, and his armies,
gathered together to make the battle with the sitter upon the horse,
and with his army. And the beast was taken, and with him the false
prophet who wrought the miracles in his presence with which he de-

(237)

ceived those who received the mark of the beast and those who worship his image; these two were cast alive into the lake of fire which burneth with brimstone; and the rest were slain with the sword of the sitter on the horse, which (sword) proceedeth out of his mouth; and the fowls were filled from their flesh.

THE marriage of the Lamb, and the grand banquet which attends it, are speedily followed with the closing scene of this present world. It is a scene of war and blood. It is the battle of the great day of God Almighty. It is the coming forth of the powers of eternity to take forcible possession of the earth. It finds all the confederated kingdoms of man mustered in rebellion against the anointed and rightful sovereign of the earth. A collision ensues, which is the most wonderful that ever occurs under heaven. And the result is a victory for the right, which is to be forever. The description is one of the grandest contained in these Revelations. In proceeding to contemplate it four things are to be considered:

    I. THE MIGHTY CONQUEROR.
    II. THE HOSTS WHICH FOLLOW HIM.
    III. THE ARMIES HE ENCOUNTERS.
    IV. THE COMPLETENESS OF HIS TRIUMPH.

God help us to take in these particulars to our edification and spiritual profit.

I.

The sublime Hero of the scene is none other than our ever blessed Lord Jesus. His name is

not given, but the marks and inscriptions which he
bears, and all that is said of him, infallibly identify
him as that same Jesus who went up into heaven
from the summit of Mt. Olivet, and whose holy
feet are to stand again on these self-same heights.

He comes forth out of the heaven. For this purpose John saw it opened. When Jesus came up
from the waters of baptism, "the heavens were
open unto him," and the Spirit descended upon
him, and a voice from the empyrean depths said,
"This is my beloved Son, in whom I am well
pleased." (Matt. 3 : 16.) When Stephen was mar-
tyred he saw "the heavens opened, and the Son
of Man standing on the right hand of God."
(Acts 7 : 55.) When Jesus was on earth he
promised his disciples that they should see the
heaven opened. (Jno. 1 : 51.) At the beginning
of these visions John beheld a door opened in the
heaven, and through that opening he was called
up, while all was closed to the general mass of
men. (Rev. 4 : 1.) But here was quite a different
opening from any that has occurred or will occur
till then. This is that rending of the heaven for
the glorious Epiphany of Christ with his people,
to which the Scriptures refer so much. For, as
we believe that "he ascended into heaven, and
sitteth on the right hand of God the Father Almighty," so we believe that "from thence he shall
come to judge the quick and the dead." So the
Lamb, being married now, leaves the Father
house and comes forth to take possession of what
is peculiarly his own.

He rides upon a white horse. This horse tells of royalty, judgment, and war. His white color tells of righteousness and justice. Light is the robe of divine majesty, and *white* is the color that most attaches to Christ in all these judgment scenes. When the first seal broke he rode a white horse; when the great harvest is reaped he sits upon a white cloud; and at the end of the thousand years he sits upon a white throne; and so here he is seated on the white steed of battle, for "in righteousness doth he make war." In the day of his humiliation he rode but once—when he came to the Jewish nation as its anointed king. But he then rode upon an ass, a colt, the foal of an ass. Then he was the meek and lowly one; but here the little domestic animal is exchanged for the martial charger, for this is another and mightier coming as the King of the World, "just and having salvation." In his majesty he rides prosperously, because of truth, and meekness, and righteousness.

He is Faithful and True. This presents him in sharp contrast with those whom he cometh to judge and destroy. The Dragon is the deceiver; the Beast is the False Christ; his companion is the False Prophet, and the great confederacy is made up of false worshippers. These are to be handled now, and it is the embodiment of all faithfulness and truth that comes to deal with them. There is then no hope for them, for if justice be done them they have no show whatever. The worst thing that can happen to some is to give

them what they deserve.   But greatly do these attributes exalt this Hero.   They lift him far above
the level of humanity.   They bespeak almightiness and essential Godhead. (Comp. chaps. 3 : 7;
6 : 10; 15 : 3; 16 : 7.)   They cannot be predicated
of any mere man.   "Cursed be the man that
trusteth in man."   There is too much deceit and
treachery in human nature for it to be always and
implicitly trusted. (Com. Ps. 72 : 9; 116 : 11; 118 :
8; Jer. 17 : 5.)   But here is one who is absolutely
true and faithful.   It is not in him to be or to
prove unreliable.   Though all men be liars, he is
true, and cannot disappoint.

In righteousness he judgeth and warreth.   In the
letter to the Laodiceans he was "the Faithful and
True *Witness,*" reproving and instructing his
friends; here he is the Faithful and True *Warrior and Judge,* for the punishment of his enemies.
Heaven cannot be at peace with iniquity, and justice cannot be at amity with falsehood and rebellion.   When sin is once incorrigible, and incurable by remedial measures, it must be put down
by force of arms.   Mercy slighted and abused
brings the executioner.   The world banded together in arms against its true Sovereign brings
against it the sword of insulted majesty.   Not as
human kings and nations war,—out of covetousness, pride, and an ambition for selfish greatness
and dominion,—but in absolute justice and right,
and in strictest accord with every holy principle
and every holy interest he now unsheaths and
wields the sword of infinite power.   Dreadful is

the carnage which follows, but no one can ever
say that it is not precisely what was merited and
demanded. The powers of judging and making
war are often separated in earthly sovereignties,
but it is only a conventional separation. They
necessarily go together after all. Wherever there
is war there is first a judgment made or entertained against those upon whom it is made, or in
behalf of those whom it is to benefit. The general in the field is simply the sheriff and hangman
of the court. And Christ is both judge and executioner, all powers in one, and all exercised in
righteousness. To the Church he is the High
Priest, with girdle and ephod, stars and lamps, the
minister of righteousness unto salvation. To the
world in armed rebellion he is the mounted Warrior, the minister of righteousness unto destruction; but in both and always "Jesus Christ The
Righteous."

His eyes flame of fire. To judge rightly he must
see through and through, search all depths, look
beneath all masks, penetrate all darkness, and try
everything to its ultimate residuum. Hence this
flaming vision, which likewise tells of the fierceness of his wrath against his enemies. There is
often something wonderfully luminous, penetra-
ting, overawing, in the human eye. Men have
been killed by the look of kings. It is like the
living intellect made visible, which seems to read
all secrets at a glance, and before which the be-
holder cowers. It is this infinitely intensified,
flashing like a sword of fire from the visual orbs,

that the holy apostle here beheld in this Warrior
Judge. It is an eye-flame of Omniscient percep-
tion and out-breaking indignation and wrath,
which seizes and unmans the foe before he feels
the sword.

On His head many diadems. He is not only
Judge and General, but at the same time the King
himself. When David conquered the Ammon-
ites, he put the crown of the vanquished king on
his own head, in addition to the crown he already
had. (2 Sam. 12 : 30.) When Ptolemy entered Antioch, he set two crowns upon his head, the crown
of Asia and the crown of Egypt. (1 Macc. 11 : 13.)
The Popes wear a triple crown, emblematic of
three sovereignties united in one. The Dragon
has *seven* diadems on his seven heads, as the possessor of the seven great world-powers (chap.
12 : 3). The Beast has *ten* diadems on his ten horns,
as combining ten sovereignties. (chap. 13 : 1.)
In all these cases, the accumulation of crowns expresses accumulated victory and dominion. It is
the same in this case. Christ comes against the
Beast and his confederates as the conqueror on
many fields, the winner of many mighty battles,
the holder of many sovereignties secured by his
prowess and power. He comes as the One anointed
and endowed of heaven with all the sovereignties
of the earth as his rightful due and possession.
When he came as the mighty Angel, with the little book in his hand as his title to the earth, the
rainbow was on his head (chap. 10); but he then
came in mercy and promise to his own. He comes

now as the Warrior, Judge, and King against combined usurpers in arms, against those who dispute his right to the dominion purchased with his blood, and he puts on all his royal rights.

He has an unknowable Name. John saw it written, and was awed with its splendor; but it was too much for him, or any other man, to understand or know. Jesus once said, "No man knoweth the Son but the Father" (Matt. 11 : 27); and here he appears in all those unrevealed and unknowable wonders, which connect him with incomprehensible Godhead. The Beast is full of names, great, high, and awful names; but they are false names— "names of blasphemy." This Warrior, Judge, and King has a name ineffable and unknowable, but it is a true and rightful name,—a name of reality, "which is above every name." We do not yet know all the majesty of attributes or being which belong to our sublime Saviour; and when he comes forth out of heaven for the war upon the Beast, he will come in vast unknowableness of greatness,—in heights of majesty and glory, "which no one knoweth but himself." (Comp. Judges 13 : 18; Rev. 2 : 17.)

Clothed in vesture dipped or stained with blood. Some are embarrassed, that the blood should here appear upon Christ's garments before the engagement begins, and so talk of anticipation. It is a needless perplexity, although these bloodstains are certainly not from his own blood. They have no reference whatever to his having died upon the cross. They are stains from the blood of ene-

mies slain,—enemies previously vanquished,—and
so the marks of a veteran in battle. This conquering Hero is not now for the first time to try
his capacities for war. Who but he was it that
"cut Rahab and wounded the Dragon?" Who
but he was it that fought for Israel "in the days
of Joshua, when opposing kings with kings were
put to the sword and all their armies?" Who but
he was it that "fought from heaven" against the
kings of Canaan in Taanach by the waters of Megiddo, when "the stars in their courses fought
against Sisera?" Who but he was the vanquisher
of the six great blasphemous world-powers already
dead and gone? And as the seventh, and last, and
worst of all is now to be overwhelmed, and the
same almighty Conqueror comes forth to execute
the doom, he properly comes in the same garments worn and stained on so many battlefields,
indicating that he comes in the same capacity, for
the same ends, and with the same invincible power,
as in other judgments upon his enemies. That red
apparel, and those garments like one that treadeth
the vinefat, are at once the memorials of the past,
and the prophecies of what is now to be consummated upon these last confederates against his
kingdom.

His Name is called THE WORD OF GOD. This is
one of the pre-eminent designations of the Son of
God, who became incarnate in Jesus Christ. "By
the Word of the Lord were the heavens made."
(Ps. 33 : 6.) "In the beginning was the Word, and
the Word was with God, and the Word was God.

All things were made by him. And the Word was made flesh, and dwelt among us, and we beheld his glory, the glory as of the only begotten of the Father, full of grace and truth" (Jno. 1:1–14.) He is the Word of God—the Logos—as the true and only expression of the eternal Godhead, as the great subject and substance of the written Word, as the accomplishment and fulfiller of the written Word, and the very expression and revelation of the Father, the same as words express the thoughts of the heart.

Out of his mouth proceedeth a sharp sword, that with it he may smite the nations. Some take this as "the sword of the Spirit, which is the Word of God;" but that is an instrument of mercy and salvation; this is an instrument of wrath and destruction. It is "sharp" like the sickle, and fulfils the same office. It is the word of almighty justice. It proceeds out of his mouth. So Isaiah (11:4) said, "He shall smite the earth with the rod of his mouth, and with the breath of his lips shall he slay the wicked." This shows the ease with which he accomplishes his purposes. He speaks, and it is done. He commands, and it is accomplished. Something of this was preintimated when the armed mob came forth against him in Gethsemane. "When Jesus spake to them, I am he, they went backward, and fell to the ground." (Jno. 18:5.) If so mild an utterance prostrated his enemies then, what will it be when he girds and crowns himself for the "battle of the great day of God Almighty"—when he comes with all the

cavalcade of heaven to tread the winepress of the
fierceness of Jehovah's anger? "The Word of
God is quick, and powerful, and sharper than any
two-edged sword, piercing even to the dividing
asunder of soul and spirit, and of the joints and
marrow " (Heb. 4 : 12); and when that Word goes
forth in execution of Almighty wrath upon those
in arms against his throne, what a flow of blood,
and wilting of life, and tornado of deadly disaster
must it work!

*And he hath upon his vesture, even upon his thigh
a name written,* KING OF KINGS AND LORD OF LORDS.
Thus the Psalmist in anticipation sung, "Gird
thy sword upon thy thigh, O most Mighty." (Ps.
45 : 3.) It is on his thigh that the warrior carries
his sword; but here the sword proceeds from the
mouth, and hence in its place is a name representing it; for the Psalmist defines the sword
in this case as his glory and majesty. The sword
stands for authority and the right to punish rebels
and evildoers. It tells of the majesty and dominion of him who bears it. And the authority, majesty and dominion of Christ is this, that he is
"King of kings and Lord of lords," now no longer
in mere theory or appointment, but in present
assertion, armed to enforce his rights. For ages
the government of the world had been in other
hands. Beasts held the sword and reigned. They
have ever abused it against him and his people.
And now they have confederated with Hell to hold
it even against the forces of Omnipotence. Dreadful miscalculation! The Lion of the tribe of Judah

comes to meet them. He comes in the claim and
majesty of the sharp sword of the King over all
these kings and Lord over all these lordly ones.
On his thigh is the name of his authority—the
sword name of his sovereignty. And woe to the
powers that now think to withstand him. "The
Lord shall swallow them up in His wrath, and the
fire shall devour them." (Ps. 21 : 19.)

Such, then, is the mighty Hero who comes forth
from the opened heavens to fight this "battle of
the great day of God Almighty." Let us look
next at the HOSTS WHICH FOLLOW HIM.

II.

When the Lord Jesus is revealed from heaven,
in flaming fire taking vengeance upon them that
know not God and that obey not the Gospel, he
does not come alone. He is married now, and
his Bride is with him. Even before the flood,
Enoch prophesied of this epiphany of the promised
One, and said, "Behold the Lord cometh with ten
thousand of his saints to execute judgment upon
all." (Jude 14, 15.) They are with him now, therefore they must have been taken before. John saw,
and writes, " *The armies, the ones in the heaven, were
following him.*" Christ is the Head and Leader,
and he goes before; his saints follow in his train.
The promise from the beginning was, that the
seed of the woman should bruise the serpent's
head, and here it is emphasized that " He himself
treadeth the winepress of the wine of the anger of

the wrath of the God, the All-Ruler." He himself
is the Great Hero and Conqueror in this battle.
But he is " Jehovah of hosts." He has many under
his command. The armies of the sky are his, and
he brings them with him, even "the called and
chosen, and faithful" (chap. 17: 14).

On white horses. The great Captain is mounted,
and they are mounted too. He comes as the
Warrior, Judge, and King, and they share with
him in the same character. They are warrior
judges and kings with him. In chapter 9, we
were introduced to cavalry from the under world,
of spirit horses from beneath; why not then celestial horses also? Horses and chariots of fire protected Elisha at Dothan. Horses of fire took up
Elijah into heaven. And heavenly horses bring
the saints from heaven when they come with their
great Leader for the final subjugation of the world
to his authority. It is up to the bridle-bits of
these horses that the blood in that battle is to flow
(chap. 14 : 20). These horses are all white, the same
as the Great Captain rides. Everything is in harmony. The riders all are royal and righteous ones,
and the same is expressed in the color of their
horses.

Whether literal horses are to be understood, it
is not necessary to inquire. Power is an abstract
quality, incapable of being seen with the eye. It
must put on shape in order to become visible. It
is best shown in living forms. So we had to do
with symbolic horses in chapter eleven. But here
the whole character of the showing is different.

This opening of the heaven, the coming forth of Christ with his heavenly armies to the battle which ensues, the destruction which is wrought, the victory which is won, and the kingdom which is set up, is so essentially literal in each particular, that it is hard to find room in the record for any other conclusion than that the horses are as literal as the sitters on them. They are at least the pictures of holy power bearing the King and his hosts to battle and victory over literal armies. There was reality in the powers which carried up Elijah, and there is reality in the powers on which these heavenly armies ride forth to the battle of the great day; and I know not why these powers should not be in the form of real horses, of the character of the world to which they belong. "The four Spirits of the heavens, which go forth from standing before the Lord of all the earth," were shown to Zechariah (6: 8) as horses, drawing four chariots; and I know not why we may not here understand the same or similar "spirits of the heavens," put forth in similar forms. Habakkuk (3: 8), referring to this very scene, addresses the Lord, and says, " *Thou didst ride upon thine horses, thy chariots of salvation.*" There are "chariots of God;" and so there must be horses of God. It is never safe to explain away what may have in it a momentous literal reality, even though it may be very different from anything we know of. At any rate, the armies of heaven, as they here appear, are all cavalry.

" *Clothed in fine linen, white, pure.*" The fine linen

was explained in the verses preceding. It is "the righteousness of the saints." Therefore these armies are saints, and not angels, as some have supposed. Those who share the kingdom with Christ are everywhere called "the righteous," and these have the apparel of the righteous, even that with which it was given the Bride to be clothed. Long ago, referring to this very scene, the Psalmist (58 : 10, 11) sung, "The righteous shall rejoice when he seeth the vengeance: he shall wash his feet in the blood of the wicked; so that a man shall say, verily there is a reward for the righteous: verily He is a God that judgeth in the earth." They reign with the mighty Conqueror after the battle; and so they share in the battle and triumph which bring the Kingdom. "Do ye not know that the saints shall judge the world?" (1 Cor. 6 : 2.)

They wear no armor. They are immortal, and cannot be hurt; and they are not the executors of this vengeance. It is Christ's own personal victory, in accordance with the Apostolic declaration, that "for this purpose the Son of God was manifested, that *he* might destroy the works of the Devil." (1 Jno. 3 : 8.) He bears the only sword, and he alone uses it. He treadeth the wine press *alone*. Those who accompany him in the scene of conflict therefore need no weapons. The sword of the great Captain is enough. Their defence is in him, and their victory is in him. They follow up the achievements of his sword. They ride through the blood it causes to flow.

They "wash their feet in" it, for it is up to the horses' bridles. But it is *David* who slays Goliath, and the hosts of God's Israel have only to follow up the mighty triumph, shouting their songs along the path of the victory. When the wicked are cut off, they shall see it; they shall diligently consider the place of the wicked, and it shall not be; but the meek shall inherit the earth, and delight themselves in the abundance of peace. (Ps. 37: 10, 11, 34.) BUT WHO ARE THE ARMIES ENCOUNTERED?

III.

Here we are left in no doubt. John says, "*I saw the Beast, and the kings of the earth, and his armies, gathered together to make the battle with the Sitter upon the horse, and with his army.*" How they were gathered, we were told in what occurred under the pouring out of the sixth bowl of wrath (chap. 16: 12–16). Devil agents working devil miracles, were brought into requisition. They went forth " unto the kings of the earth, even of the whole world, to gather them to the battle of that great day of God Almighty." It was through these devil oracles that they learned of Christ's coming to unseat and destroy them; and by these devil miracles they were led to believe themselves competent to withstand all the armies of the heaven. Therefore they agreed to try it, and to defeat all these Jehovah purposes of ill to their usurped dominion and blasphemous pretensions. Had they not a supernatural and immortal leader in the Beast, that was not but is again present? Had they not with him a great supernatural and equally immortal Prophet, who knew everything, who had power over the forces of nature, who could even command fire from heaven and give spirit to a metalic image? Would not these additional miracle-working spirits be their efficient helpers? If they made no effort, no resistance, what hope was there for them? Was not the Beast God, "above all that is called God?" Had eternity anything that could harm or vanquish such powers? Had not every soldier in their armies learned how to strengthen and sustain himself by spirit influences far above unaided human ability? Let the Rider on the white horse come;—let him be supported by myriads of his white-robed cavalry on their white horses;—if he did work miracles in his lifetime, neither he nor his followers ever wrought such as those which the potencies now urging them to armed resistance had shown. The struggle might be a hard one, but a combined and energetic effort would surely be successful. So they were taught; so they reasoned; so they believed. "*Strong delusion*" was upon them, "that they should believe a lie, that they all might be damned." (2 Thess. 2 : 9-12.) So they all with one accord, went zealously into a great hell-indited and hell-sealed compact and confederation, to make battle with the Lamb, the Sitter on the horse, and his army.

We may wonder how rational men could be carried with one impulse into an attempt so daring and so absurd; but when people put the truth from

them, and submit themselves to the Devil's lead,
what is there of delusion and absurdity into which
they are not liable to be carried? How many
among us comfort and assure themselves in their
selfishness and sins with the belief that either there
is no God, or that he is too good and merciful to
fulfil his threatenings upon transgressors? To this
there needs to be added only one step more, to
defy his judgments, and with that goes pledge of
battle and declaration of war with his Omnipotence. And the final outcome of this world's
wisdom, unbelief, and repudiation of the rule and
government of Jesus Christ, is the assembly of all
the kings and armies, and captains of thousands,
and mighty men, and men of all ranks and classes,
upon the hills and valleys of Palestine, from Idumea to Esdraelon, equipped, resolved, eager, and
confident of success, to meet the Son of God and
his army in hostile collision, to decide by dreadful
battle whether they or he shall have the sovereignty in the earth. Every one that denies Christ,
is on the way to defy Christ, and to take up arms
for the Usurper to conquer Christ. Every one
who refuses to be baptized into Christ, and objects
to the oath of allegiance to Christ, is a fit subject
for the branding irons and infamous mark of the
Antichrist; and when that is once impressed, there
is no more recession from this gathering together
to fight Christ, and to be dashed to destruction
against his invincible throne. And when Hell's
emissaries come, with all their marvel of word and
deed to encourage the enemies of God to join,

assemble, strike, and have the world forever to themselves, deluded mortals are persuaded, and march their armies to that field of blood from which there is no more return. " The heathen rage, and the people imagine a vain thing. The kings of the earth set themselves, and the rulers take counsel together against the Lord, and against his anointed, saying, Let us break their bands asunder, and cast away their cords from us." (Ps. 2 : 1–3.) Never was there a more wicked or more disastrous madness. But when men cut loose from the bonds of obligation to their Maker, there is no limit to the delusions to which they expose themselves, and no enormity of daring or wickedness into which they are not liable to be betrayed, thinking it the true wisdom. And thus the kings of the earth and their armies gather toward Jerusalem, to conquer the Son of God, and to crush out his rule and Kingdom for ever. WHAT, THEN, IS THE RESULT?

IV.

One of the most awful expressions in the Word of God, is that which the Psalmist utters with regard to these enraged and deluded kings, and this their expedition, where he says, " *He that sitteth in the heavens shall laugh : the Lord shall have them in derision.*" (Ps. 2 : 4.) That laugh of God, who shall fathom it! How shall we even begin to tell its dread significance! From the depths of his eternal being, he so loved the world, as to give his co-eternal and only begotten Son for it. No gift was too precious in his sight, no sacrifice too great, to be made for its redemption. For six thousand years he has been ordering his gracious Providence in heaven and earth for its recovery from sin and death. His prophets and his Son have labored, wept and died, and the ministries of his sublimest servants have been unceasingly employed, to bring it to salvation. But now he *laughs!* What failure of love, what exhaustion of grace, what emptying of the sea of his infinite mercies, what decay and withdrawal of all kindly interest and affection must have occurred that there should be this laugh! The demonstrations of these confederates with the Beast are tremendous. The whole world moves with one heart, one aim, with all its genius and power concentrated on one end, and with all the potencies of Hell to nerve and help and guide it. Never before was there such a combination of forces, natural and supernatural, directed with such skill, or animated with so daring and resolved a spirit. Yet, Jehovah *laughs!* What an infinitude of majesty and sovereign contempt does he thus express? The rebels are confident. They believe their leader invincible. They are sure of powers to handle all nature's forces. They have no question about being able to cope with mortals or immortals, with men or gods. They despise alike the names and the sword of Him who rides the white horse, and all his heavenly cavalry. They deem themselves ready and equal for any emergency of battle even with him who calls himself

Almighty. But God *laughs!* Oh the disappointment and destruction which that laugh portends!

An angel stationed in the sun anticipates the
coming result. With a great voice he cries to all
the birds of prey that fly in mid heaven to come to
a supper on the flesh of kings, captains, mighty
men, horses and their riders, free and bond, small
and great. This tells already an awful story. It
tells of the greatest of men made food for the vul-
tures;—of kings and leaders, strong and confident,
devoured on the field, with no one to bury them;—
of those who thought to conquer Heaven's anointed
King rendered helpless even against the timid
birds;—of vaunting gods of nature turned into its
cast off and most dishonored dregs. And what is
thus foreintimated soon becomes reality. The
Great Conqueror bows the heavens and comes
down. He rides upon the cherub horse, and flies
upon the wings of the wind. Smoke goes up from
his nostrils, and devouring fire out of his mouth.
He moves amid storms and darkness, from which
the lightnings hurl their bolts, and hailstones min-
gle with the fire. He roars out of Zion, and utters
his voice from Jerusalem, till the heavens and the
earth shake. He dashes forth in the fury of his
incensed greatness amid clouds, and fire, and pil-
lars of smoke. The sun frowns. The day is
neither light nor dark. The mountains melt and
cleave asunder at his presence. The hills bound
from their seats and skip like lambs. The waters
are dislodged from their channels. The sea rolls
back with howling trepidation. The sky is rent

and folds upon itself like a collapsed tent. It is the day for executing an armed world,—a world in covenant with Hell to overthrow the authority and throne of God,—and everything in terrified Nature joins to signalize the deserved vengeance. So the Scriptures everywhere represent. John saw it, but does not describe it. He only tells the result he beheld.

And the Beast was taken. The great Judgment strikes the head and leader first. He is not a system; or he would not fall till the myriads of his supporters fall. He is a *person*, as truly as his Captor is a person. He is distinct from his armies, as Christ is distinct from his; or he could not be taken in advance of his armies. He is the living god and confidence of all his hosts, and all this war is for his glory; therefore the assault is first made upon him. He is a supernatural being, a man resurrected from the dead by the Devil's power, and seemingly incapable of corporeal death; for he is not slain. No sword smites him. He does not die. In contradistinction from all save his companion, the False Prophet, it is specifically stated that he is simply "*taken*"—taken "*alive*," and "*cast alive* into the lake of fire." His worshippers held him to be invincible. They asked in the utmost confidence and triumph, Who is like unto the Beast? Who can war with him? But, without the striking of a blow, and with all his worshippers in arms around him, he is "*taken*," captured as a lion seizes his prey, dragged away from the field as a helpless prisoner. With all his

power, greatness, and resurrection-vigor and im-
munity from death, he is "taken." With greater
ease than the Jewish mob took the unresisting
Jesus, the Sitter on the white horse catches him
away from the very centre of his hosts. All the
resistance he makes is the same as if it were not.
He cannot help himself, and all his armies cannot
help him. He must go whither his mighty Captor would take him. Tophet gets its own. And
into the lake of fire he sinks to rise no more.

*And with him the False Prophet who wrought the
miracles in his presence.* This is no warrior; but
still a main author of this culminated wickedness
of the nations. From him, together with the
Dragon and the first Beast, went forth the miracle-
working spirits who wrought this terrible deception, and stirred up the world to this war. By
his instigations were these armies equipped and
gathered to the dread attempt to vanquish the Son
of God. He caused men to adore the Beast, and
he shares the Beast's fate. He is no system, no
abstraction, no succession, no mere ideal figure,
but a person. He is not slain; he does not die;
he seems like the Antichrist incapable of death.
But he is "taken," as the Beast was taken, made
a captive, and hurried away to the same seething
prison. All his miraculous power cannot save
him. All his boasted wisdom cannot help him.
All the armies of the world cannot rescue him
from the grasp of the Sitter on the white horse.

The two great leaders gone, short work is made
with their followers. A few awful words tell the

story. They are mortals all, and there is no salvation for them. In terrible brevity, the Seer records what came to pass. " *And the rest were slain with the sword of the Sitter on the horse, which sword proceeded out of his mouth;* AND THE FOWLS WERE FILLED FROM THEIR FLESH." Such a feast of death was, perhaps, never before seen.

Long ago had the holy prophets sung of this Mighty One, and this his triumph. As the Psalmist foresaw, his arrows are sharp in the heart of the King's enemies, whereby the people fall under him. (Ps. 45 : 5.) He sends out his arrows, and scattereth them; and shoots out lightnings, and discomfits them. (Ps. 18 : 14.) He marches through the land in indignation; he threshes the heathen in anger. (Hab. 3 : 12.) All the strength of the nations is dashed to fragments before him, like pottery struck with an iron rod. (Ps. 2 : 9.) The stone from the eternal mountain falls on the great statue of this world's power, and it is ground to powder, never again to be regathered. (Dan. 2 : 35 ; Matt. 22 : 44.) The victory of the Sitter on the white horse is complete!

And He shall rule or shepherdize them with an iron rod. With many a severe judgment on the survivors of that day, the Conqueror now assumes the dominion. With their heads and armies destroyed in the winepress of the wine of the anger of the wrath of the God the All-Ruler, he now sends forth the new law from Jerusalem. After the sword of destruction, comes the rod of correction and reorganization. The world now gets a new Master, a King whose eternal right it is to reign, and whom they must at once obey or die. The shepherdizing rod of iron, is the administration which follows up the battle, gathers the populations of the earth into their proper flocks, assigns them their laws and rulers, and allows of no more disobedience.

Thus ends this present world. Thus comes in the final reign and kingdom of the Prince of Peace. It only remains to tell the Devil's fate, and then come the glorious pictures of the other side of this "great and terrible day of the Lord."

I only add, that our contemplations to-night will fail of their end, if they do not serve to teach us, and to write it indellibly upon our hearts, that rebellion against God is death;—that no weapon formed against Jehovah can prosper;—that those who will not have Christ to rule over them must perish! Though the wicked should wield the power of archangels, they cannot withstand the punitive majesty of the Warrior Judge and King who rides upon the white horse. His sword is mightier than Satan, mightier than the Beast deemed invincible, mightier than the command of infernal miracle over nature's laws, mightier than all the forces of earth and hell combined. And that sword is pledged to drink the life-blood of all who neglect his mercy, despise his laws, and stand out against his authority. All may seem well and promising now. People may indulge their unbelief and passions during these days of forbearance and grace, and see no disadvantages growing out of it. They may get angry at our earnestness, and account us croakers and fools when we put before them the demands and threatenings of the Almighty. But *"woe to him that striveth with his Maker!"* There is a deluge of bottled fury yet to be poured out on them that refuse to know God, and on the families that call not on his name, from which there is no escape, and from whose burning and tempestuous surges there is no deliverance. God help us to be wise, that we come not into that sea of death!

> Righteous Judge of retribution,
> Grant thy gift of absolution,
> Ere that day's dread execution!

LECTURE FORTY-FOURTH.

THE BINDING OF SATAN—HIS FOUR NAMES—THE ANGEL WHO
APPREHENDS HIM—A LITERAL TRANSACTION—THE ECON-
OMY OF THE UNDERWORLD—THE WORD "HELL," SHEOL,
HADES—CHRIST'S DESCENT INTO HELL—HADES NO LONGER
THE ABODE OF DEPARTED SAINTS—"ABADDON," THE ABYSS
—TARTARUS—GEHENNA—THE BEAST AND FALSE PROPHET
IN GEHENNA—SATAN IMPRISONED IN THE ABYSS—OBJECT OF
HIS IMPRISONMENT—SATAN NOT BOUND AT THE COMMENCE-
MENT OF THE CHRISTIAN ERA, NOR AT THE CONVERSION
OF CONSTANTINE, IS LOOSE NOW.

Rev. 20 : 1–3. (Revised Text.) And I saw an angel coming down
out of the heaven, having the key of the abyss, and a great chain in [or
resting upon] his hand. And he laid hold on the dragon, the old serpent, which is the devil, and satan, and bound him a thousand years,
and cast him into the abyss, and locked and sealed [it] upon him, that
he should not lead astray the nations any more until the thousand
years be accomplished : after these he must be loosed a little time.

THE issue of the battle of the Great Day goes
beyond the disaster to those found in arms
against the Sitter on the white horse. There is
another and still greater power back of those
armies, by whose instigation this war was undertaken, by whose influence these kings and mighty
ones with their troops were deceived into the fatal
idea of conquering the King of kings and Lord of

(263)

lords, and by whose malignant cunning they were marched into the wine-press of the wrath of God. The judgment, therefore, proceeds to deal with this chief culprit.

He is called by four names, the same that were given him in chapter 12 : 9. The Sitter on the white horse also had four names; and as in his case, so here, the names describe the being who wears them. He is called " *the Dragon.*" This is his designation with particular reference to his connection with earthly sovereignties and his administrations through the political world-powers, which, up to this great day, are continually contemplated in the Scriptures as the Dragon powers. But when these kings and their armies fall, the Dragon power ceases. Though the same evil spirit comes up again after the thousand years, he comes with only two of his four names, and not as "the Dragon;" for he never again gets possession of the sovereignty of the earth. Christ and his saints reign on the earth from this time forth forever; so that whoever those may be whom Satan then deceives and brings into rebellion, they are not the governors, kings, and rulers of the earth. They are from its distant corners, not its great central administrations. He is the Dragon now, as he ever has been since the days of Nimrod, and as he ever will be till the confederated kings of the earth meet their final fall at Harmageddon ; and he is " the Dragon " with particular reference to the relation which he holds to this world's political powers.

He is further called " *the Old Serpent ;*"—" *old* " in allusion to the fact that he has been in existence since the beginning of human history ; and " *the Serpent*" in allusion to his subtlety, his crooked and deceiving ways, his subtle poisons, and his deadly malignity. It was as the serpent that he beguiled our first parents and seduced them into sin and death. It is as the serpent that he deceives souls, insinuates false doctrine, unbelief, and presumption into the human heart, corrupts the purity of the Church, and deludes men with a false and perverted wisdom. It refers, particularly, to his subtle temptations of the good. Since the days of Adam's innocence in Eden, and on to the glorious Epiphany of his great Conqueror, he fulfils this particular designation ; but it does not appear that he ever comes up again in that precise capacity. The good are thenceforward beyond the power of temptation, and the deception by which he finally brings Gog and Magog against the citadel of the saints does not seem to be of the sort which he now practices as "the Old Serpent." He is still the same evil spirit as to his individuality, but his particular serpentine manifestation seems to cease with the present order of things, the same as his Draconic manifestation. Only as " *the Devil and Satan* " does he reappear at the end of the thousand years.

The word *Devil* means a slanderer, a calumniator, a malignant liar ; and this has been one of this evil spirit's chief characteristics from the beginning. His first suggestions to Eve were full of base aspersions cast upon God, and burdened with all manner of ruinous falsehood. Hence the Saviour says: "He was a murderer from the beginning, and abode not in the truth; when he speaketh a lie, he speaketh of his own; for he is a liar, and the father of it." (Jno. 8 : 44.) This is his essential character, the same everywhere and always. And as a murderous liar, calumniator, slanderer, and author of malignant untruth, he comes up again subsequent to the thousand years. The lie is his deepest nature, and it is that which makes him in bad pre-eminence "*the Devil*."

Satan means an adversary, an accuser. It is a Hebrew word simply transferred. It is mostly used as a proper name of some great spirit of evil. It is used in this sense about forty times in the Scriptures. It denotes one who lies in wait to entrap, to oppose, to disable, to bring under condemnation or into disaster. And such the evil one has ever shown himself. So he accused and opposed God at the beginning. So he accused Job and sought to destroy his peace. So he assailed Christ, questioning his divine Sonship and power, if not proven to him as he chose to dictate. And so he is the adversary of all the children of God, and still stands as their accuser before God, even when the time comes for their birth to immortal glory. In this character he also reappears after the thousand years, stirs up enmity to God's holy people, and instigates an attack upon their citadel.

It is in all these particular aspects that this great

spirit of evil was concerned in bringing about this war against the Sitter on the white horse and his army. It was first and principally as "the Dragon," operating with and through the political powers; for he gave the Beast his power, throne, and great authority, and sent the lying spirits to influence the kings of the earth in this fatal business. It was next as "the Old Serpent," beguiling, deceiving, and leading into the wickedest unbelief and false faith. It was furthermore as "the Devil," calumniating and blaspheming God and Christ, all true worship, and all rightful divine authority. And it was finally as "Satan," the malignant adversary and opponent of God and all good, disputing his right to reign, and bent on defeating his becoming the King of the earth. And as this great spirit was thus the life and soul of all this tremendous rebellion against the Son of God, the anointed All-Ruler, it was impossible that he should be permitted to escape, or to remain at liberty, when the Warrior King and Judge comes forth to enforce his royal rights.

We accordingly read of an Angel from heaven advancing to dispose of this old, malignant, and subtle Deceiver. Who this Angel is, we are not told. The particulars would seem to indicate, as many able commentators have concluded, that he is the Lord Jesus Christ himself. It was Christ who, in the first vision, claimed to have "the Keys of Hades and of Death," which would most naturally seem to include "the Key of the Abyss," which this Angel possesses. The whole achieve-

ment of this victory is also so emphatically ascribed
to the Saviour himself, that it would seem incon-
gruous, if not conflicting, to make the arrest of the
chief of all this dreadful antagonism the work of a
created Angel. The mere fact of the angelic appearance argues nothing against its being Christ
himself, for we have seen him appearing several
times already in the character of an Angel. (Comp.
chap. 10 : 1–7; 14 : 18, 19; 18 : 1.) When he comes
to vanquish and destroy armies, it is fitting that
he should appear as a mighty Warrior; but when
he appears for the seizure and binding of a fallen
angel, it is equally fitting that he should appear
as an Angel. His appearances continually vary
according to the work to be done, and, all things
considered, we would most naturally expect that
this particular act would be done in the character
of an Angel. The point is of no great consequence
either way; for it is still the act of Christ, and part
of his victory, whether done by himself or by a
created angel. It was Michael the Archangel who
fought Satan in the battle in heaven (chap. 12 : 7),
but that was rather a *forensic* contest. This is a different work, the grasping of the Devil's person, the
chaining of him, and the casting of him into prison.
This Angel possesses the Key of the Abyss, and
carries a great chain. He lays hold on the Dragon,
the Old Serpent, which is the Devil and Satan,
binds him with the chain, casts him into the Abyss,
and locks and seals him in, that he may no more
delude the nations for a thousand years.

Is this a literal transaction? Certainly it is;

The battle is literal; the taking of the Beast and the False Prophet is literal; the slaying of the kings and their armies is literal; Satan is literal; and his binding must be equally literal. It will not resolve itself into anything else, and fit to the connections or the terms. Some have asked, with an air of triumph, How can a chain of iron or brass bind a spirit, and that spirit an archangel? But the record does not say that it is a chain of iron, or brass, or steel, or any other material of earthly chains. It is a chain of divine make, as the sword that proceeds from the mouth of the Son of God. It is a spirit-chain, as the horses of the celestial army are spirit-horses. It is a chain of a character that can bind spirit and fetter angels. Jude tells of such chains, actually holding now (Jude 6), and which not even the angels can break. What they are made of, and how they serve to bind the freedom of spiritual natures, it is not for us to know or show; but they are not therefore any less real and literal chains. Figures, tropes, and shadows cannot bind anybody, unless it be some commentators, who seem to be hopelessly entangled in them. The Abyss is a reality, and the chain is also a reality, or it is not what inspiration says it is. It is called " a *great* chain ; " and " great " it must be to hold and confine the great Red Dragon.* But it is adequate to its purpose. Heaven makes no miscalculations. It is fastened on the limbs of the old monster. He cannot resist it, nor shake it off.

* See vol. ii, pp. 307–311.

Archangel as he is, he is compelled to submit, bound as a helpless prisoner, and violently cast into his dungeon, there to lie in his fetters for a decade of centuries.

The place into which Satan is cast is called ἡ ἄβυσσος, *the Abyss.* This is a different place from that into which the Beast and the False Prophet are cast. They were thrown into " the lake of fire which burneth with brimstone." The Devil, after the thousand years, is also cast into that same burning lake (chap. 19 : 10); but here he is cast into "*the Abyss,*" whence the Beast came (chap. 17 : 8), and also the terrible plague of the spirit-locusts (chap. 9 : 1–3).

The question thus arises, What is the difference between " the Abyss " and " the lake of fire ?" I might answer truly, that " the lake of fire " is the final Hell, the place of the eternal punishment of the damned; whilst " the Abyss " is a sort of fore-hell, a prison in which evil spirits are detained prior to their final judgment. The relation between the two is much like that of the county jail in which accused criminals are detained prior to their sentence, and the state penitentiary to which they are assigned for final punishment. But, as the question calls up the whole economy of the underworld, about which the Scriptures tell us more than is generally suspected or understood, it may be proper and desirable to look a little deeper into the matter.

In general, people have very dim, confused and inadequate ideas with regard to the whole unseen world. This is owing in part to the reserve of the Scriptures on the subject, but more particularly to the obscuration of what is revealed by the faulty manner in which our English translators, though generally so correct, have dealt with the words and phrases of the sacred writers referring to this particular subject, begetting erroneous impressions, which reappear in our theological systems. Thus the word *Hell*, which in the Saxon vocabulary means simply the covered or unseen place, is used as the equivalent of words of very different signification, whilst those for which it is properly the equivalent are frequently rendered by other words which carry the mind quite aside from the real meaning. And so again, in popular language, the word *Hell* is carried away from its etymological signification, and made to stand for the place of final punishment, with which all other terms referring to the hidden abodes of wicked spirits are again confounded, whilst some of the original terms for which it is made to stand do not refer to the place of final punishment at all. The whole matter has thus become most sadly confused, involving in that confusion the article of the Creed respecting Christ's descent into Hell, and urgently needing to be unravelled and set right according to the true ideas of Revelation and of the early Church.

There is a word used sixty-five times in the original Hebrew of the Old Testament, which our English translators in thirty-one instances render *Hell*, in thirty-one instances *Grave*, and in three

instances *the pit*. That word is *Sheol*, uniformly
rendered *Hades* in the Greek of the Old Testament,
and wherever the New Testament quotes the passages in which it occurs. By common consent the
Greek word *Hades* is the exact equivalent of the
Hebrew *Sheol*. It occurs eleven times in the New
Testament, and always in the same sense as the
Old Testament *Sheol*. To all intents and purposes,
therefore, Sheol and Hades denote one and the
same thing. But Sheol or Hades is never used to
denote the *Hell* of final punishment. Neither is it
ever used to denote the mere receptacle of the body
after death, the grave. Nor yet is it ever used to
denote the mere state of being dead as to the body;
and still less to denote *the pit* or *Abyss* as such. A
careful inventory of all the passages conclusively
proves that Sheol or Hades is the name of *a place*
in the unseen world, altogether distinct from the
Hell of final punishment or the Heaven of final
glory. Its true and only meaning is, " *the place of
departed spirits*,"—the receptacle of souls which
have left the body.* To this place all departed

---

* " Translating the word *Hades*, according to its etymology
and its use among the Greeks, it is rendered an invisible place,
which was all that Homer intended when he said the souls of
his brave heroes were hurried, by the Trojan war, into Hades,
where he exhibits them celebrating the Elysian games. The
fathers, therefore, condemn the language of our translation (of
the New Testament), and in the article of what is called the
Apostles' Creed, which says Christ descended into *Hell*, misleading the vulgar by an English word, which *now* conveys an
idea not contained in the original. This is so well known as to
require no argument; but so little regarded as to demand re-

spirits, good and bad, up to the time of the resurrection of Christ, went. In it there was a department for the good, called *Paradise* by the Saviour on the cross, and another department for the bad. Thus both the rich man and Lazarus went to Hades when they died; for the word is, "*in Hades* he lifted up his eyes, and seeth Abraham afar off and Lazarus in his bosom." Lazarus was then in Hades too, as well as Abraham; and the only difference between them and Dives was, that the good were separated from the bad by an impassable gulf, and that Lazarus was comforted and Dives tormented.* So the dying Saviour told the penitent malefactor that they would yet that day be together *in Paradise;* that is, in the more favorable part of Hades. There they were neither in Heaven proper, nor in Hell proper; but simply in *Hades.* To this *Hades* all departed spirits went, the good with the good, and the bad with the bad. There was comfort there for the pious, and privation and torment for the wicked; and they of the one part could

---

peated protest."—*Bennett's Theology of the Early Christian Church,* pp. 323, 324.

"I cannot give a better periphrasis of it (the word *Hades*) than by translating it, *that invisible place where the souls that leave their bodies live*, whether it be a place of bliss or torment. In this sense it is taken in Scripture, the Apocrypha, Fathers, yea, and in heathenish authors too. And as for the Latin *inferi*, it is often taken in the same sense, and mostly used to express *Hades*."—*Beveridge on the XXXIX Arts.*, pp. 115, 116.

* "Lazarus in *Hades* obtained comfort in Abraham's bosom; the rich man, on the other hand, the torment of flame."—*Tertullian, De Idol.* 13.

not pass over to the other part; but still they could see and converse with each other, and none of them were yet in their final happiness or misery. Even at the best, it was not a place to be coveted. With all the blessed release which it brought to pious sufferers, and the good promise it bespoke of something better for them at the resurrection, the Scriptures everywhere describe it as a sombre world,—a place of detention and waiting even for the best. There is nothing ever said about going up to it, or of full compensation there for works of piety and deeds of love. The ancient saints drew satisfaction from the thought of being gathered to their fathers, and of resting there with the holy dead; but never as enjoying there the bright presence of God and the society of angels. All the higher and better recompenses to which they looked, they invariably connected with the resurrection, and located quite beyond the Hadean world. It was to the Paradise side of this Hades that the Saviour and the penitent thief went when they died, as all the pious dead up to that time.

But this going of Christ into the place of departed spirits with the penitent thief was not the descent into Hades of which the Creed speaks. By virtue of having died, Christ thus became an inmate of Hades, just as all other good men who had died before him; whilst the descent into Hades, of which the Creed speaks, was part of his active redemption work, and the beginning of his exaltation as the successful Redeemer, which wrought a great change in Hades itself, and in the whole condition of the pious dead from that time on. His dead body having been requickened and glorified by his divine power, recalling his departed soul to it, even before he reappeared on earth, he went to Hades, not as a subject of death, but as the Conqueror of death, heralding his victory to the spirits therein detained (1 Pet. 3 : 18, 19), and actually bringing out with him all faithful souls, even resurrecting many of them. (Matt. 27 : 52, 53; Ps. 68 : 18.) It is with special reference to this, that he announced himself to John, in the first vision, as having "the Keys of Death and of Hades." Paradise now is no longer in Hades, but above, in the heavens, where its inmates enjoy a far more blessed portion than was ever enjoyed in Hades. Christ "led captivity captive" when he made his triumphant descent into Hades of which the Creed speaks, and no true believer now ever goes to Hades. Christ said of his Church, that the gates of Hades should never prevail against it; that is, it should never close on any true members of his Church. Paul, in triumphant exultation over the portion of believers now, exclaims: "O Death, where is thy sting? *O Hades, where is thy victory?*"

The "grave" holds the victory now just as it ever has done, but Hades does not; and the victory of which the Apostle speaks and gives thanks is a victory over Hades, not over the "*grave*" as our translators have put it. Hence our Confession says, "Christ descended into Hades, *and abolished*

it for all believers." (*Formula of Con.*)* Hades now
is, therefore, the receptacle of only such departed

---

* Speaking of the several opinions concerning the descent of
Christ into Hades, and the efficacy of it, Bishop Pearson makes
this observation : "Of those who did believe the name of *Hades*
to belong to that general place which comprehended all the souls
of men, as well those who died in the favor of God as those who
departed in their sins, some of them thought that Christ descended to that place of *Hades*, where the souls of all the faithful,
from the death of the righteous Abel to the death of Christ, were
detained ; and there dissolving all the power by which they
were detained below, translated them into a far more glorious
place, and estated them in a condition far more happy in the
heavens above." Pearson did not himself accept this view,
which is so evidently that of the Scriptures, still he adds this testimony concerning it : " This is the opinion generally received in
the schools, and delivered as the sense of the Church of God in
all ages; but though it were not so general as the schoolmen
would persuade us, yet it is certain that many of the fathers did
so understand it." He then quotes Eusebius, Cyril, Ambrose,
and Jerome in evidence of this fact.

The same author quotes Justin Martyr, Irenæus, Tertullian,
Hillary, Gregory of Nyssa, and others, as holding and teaching that the souls of believers do not enter heaven immediately
upon their death, but go into the bosom of Abraham, into Paradise, where the patriarchs and prophets are, where they all remain till the time of the resurrection, when first they get their
crowns, and enter upon the fulness of their blessedness. But the
place where departed saints now are, or go at their death, is
plainly no longer in *Hades ;* for when Paul in vision was taken
to behold that place, the action or motion which took him to it
from the earth is described as an *ascent*,—" he was caught *up to
Paradise*" (2 Cor. 12 : 4),—whereas the action or motion describ-
ing the entrance into *Hades*, even for the saints, is everywhere
represented as a *descent*. Not only is it declared that Korah and
his company " *went down* alive into Hades," or Sheol, but Jacob
said, " I will *go down* into Hades unto my son." (Gen. 37 : 35.)
So also Samuel, after his death, and in his rest, said, " Why

spirits as have no share in Christ's redemption,—a mere prison of bad and unbelieving souls, who there pine over their crimes, awaiting the day of judgment, when all in Hades, and Hades itself, shall be cast into the Hell of final punishment (chap. 20 : 14). Sheol or Hades then is not *Hell*, except in the old and now obsolete sense of *the covered place*, the hidden temporary receptacle of departed spirits, into which *all* departed souls formerly went at death, but since Christ's resurrection only the bad and unbelieving go.*

The Old Testament speaks of another place in the underworld, called in Hebrew *Abaddon* (Greek *Apoleia*), which our English Bible renders *destruction*. Thus we read "Hades is naked before him, and *Abaddon* hath no covering." (Job 26 : 6.) "*Abaddon* and death say, We have heard the fame

---

hast thou disquieted me to *bring me up?*" (1 Sam. 28 : 15.) And so of Jesus, when he went to that place, it is said he "*descended into the lower parts of the earth.*" (Eph. 4 : 9.) Paradise then was below in Hades ; now, since the resurrection of Christ, it is above, in the heavenly regions, and no longer in Hades. Thus Basil, Cyprian, and Ambrose speak of Paradise now as a place of rest *in heaven*, in which the pious are, but still not in heaven, in the same way as they shall be after the resurrection.

* From these representations of the economy of the underworld, which are the result of a more matured study of the whole subject, some obvious modifications are required to the statements made in Vol. I, page 99, which were written some fourteen years prior to the writing of this Lecture. I then believed that all departed souls went to Hades, whereas, it is now plain to me that, since the resurrection of Christ, none of the souls of the saints ever go there, as they did previously. When a man has learned better, it is due that he should be allowed to correct himself.

thereof." (Job 28 : 22.) "It is a fire that consumeth to *Abaddon.*" (Job 31 : 12.) "Shall thy loving kindness be declared in the grave, or thy faithfulness in *Abaddon?*" (Ps. 88 : 12.) "Hades and *Abaddon* are ever before the Lord." (Prov. 15 : 11.) "Hades and *Abaddon* are never full." (Prov. 27 : 20.) Abaddon thus connects with Sheol or Hades, but is a deeper, darker, and a more wretched place. "The pit of the Abyss," referred to in chapter 9 : 1–3, and from which came the plague of spirit-locusts, seems to identify with this Hebrew Abaddon; for the Angel of this pit, and the King over these locusts, has a name "which in the Hebrew tongue is *Abaddon*, but in the Greek tongue hath his name Apollyon." Nine times do we read of this *Abyss* in the New Testament. The demons, whom Christ cast out of the wretched man of Gadara, besought the Saviour not to command them into *the Abyss.* (Luke 8 : 26–31.) Paul says that our faith needs not to inquire "Who shall descend into *the Abyss*, that is, to bring Christ up again from among the dead" (Rom. 10 : 7), as if he were only one of the more powerful of these demons. Thus also the great Beast, the Antichrist, cometh up out of *the Abyss* (Rev. 11 : 7; 17 : 8). Abaddon and the Abyss would therefore seem to be the abode of demons, a sort of deeper pit beneath Hades, where the wickeder and baser spirits of dead men, and other foul spirits of the lower orders, are for the most part held as melancholy prisoners till the day of final judgment. It is a place intermediate between Hades and the final Hell, as Paradise is

now a sort of intermediate place between Hades
and the final Heaven. It is a remove below Hades,
as Paradise is now a remove above Hades.

It does not appear that fallen angels now have
their place in Hades. The Lucifer of whom Isaiah
(14:15) speaks as having been "brought down to
Hades" is explained (verse 4) to be the king of
Babylon, and so a bad man, and not an angel.
Fallen angels are never said to be in Hades. The
place of their present detention is described by
quite another name. Thus Peter tells us that
"God spared not the angels that sinned, but cast
them down to *Tartarus*, and delivered them into
chains of darkness to be reserved unto judgment."
(2 Pet. 2:4.) Our translators also call Tartarus
Hell, as if Tartarus, Hades, the Abyss, and the
final lake of fire were all one and the same thing.
The truth is, that they are each distinct and separate, though all departments of the underworld.

The burning lake is the only true *Apoleia*, perdition, destruction, second death, or the final *Hell*.
It too has its own proper name. It is called *Tophet*
in the Old Testament. (Is. 30:33; Jer. 7:31, 32.)
In the New it is twelve times called *Gehenna*, which,
in the Greek, is the same as Tophet in Hebrew.
From denoting a place of horrible burning on
earth, it came to be used to denote the place of
final punishment. Our translators have uniformly
translated Gehenna by the word *Hell*. But Gehenna is altogether a different Hell from Sheol,
Hades, the Abyss, or Tartarus. Thus the Saviour
says, that whosoever indulges malignant and

devilish spite towards his brother "shall be in danger of *Gehenna* fire" (Matt. 5:22); that it is much better to sacrifice a right eye or a right hand in this world than that "the whole body should be cast into *Gehenna*" (Matt. 5:29, 30); that we are not to fear them which kill the body, but rather to fear him "who is able to destroy both soul and body in *Gehenna*" (Matt. 10:28); and that "it is better to enter into life with one eye, than having two eyes to be cast into *Gehenna* fire" (Matt. 18:9). Thus also he denounces the hypocritical Pharisees as the candidates for "the greater damnation," the "children of *Gehenna*" (Matt. 23:14, 15), and asks them, "How can ye escape the damnation of *Gehenna?*" (Matt. 23:33). This Tophet or Gehenna, as will be seen at once, is something different from Hades, Tartarus, or the Abyss. It is manifestly the same which John here calls "*the lake of fire which burneth with brimstone*," and into which the Beast, the False Prophet, Satan, Death, Hades, and whosoever is not found written in the book of life, are finally cast, and swallowed up forever; that is, it is the ultimate Hell of full punishment.

Into this final Hell no one has ever yet entered. It is "prepared for the Devil and his angels;" but none of them is there now. The first persons that ever go into this place are the Beast and the False Prophet, at the time of the battle of the great day of God Almighty (chap. 19:20). The next to get into it is Satan himself, more than a thousand years afterwards (chap. 20:10), where the Beast and the False Prophet are represented as still alive

and suffering at the time when he is cast in with
them. And then follows the casting in of all the
wicked, along with Death and Hades (chap. 20 :
14, 15).

It is not a little surprising that things should
come out so clearly from the original Scriptures, and
that there should be such confusion on the subject
in the popular mind, and even in our theologies.
But in the light of what I have thus briefly indicated, any one can readily see the consistency and
propriety of all these terms and references touching the underworld, and what is meant by the
different places from which or to which these infernal actors either come or go. The Beast is
from the Abyss, the under-pit of Hades, as twice
distinctly stated. The False Prophet, his companion and prime minister, is doubtless from the
same place. Under the fifth Trumpet, "the Key
of the Abyss" was given to the fallen star, which
is none other than Satan, and he unlocks the
Abyss for the bringing up of the spirit-locusts,
and then for the bringing forth in Satanic resurrection from thence these two great instruments
of his malice and deception, the Beast and the
False Prophet. It is not in the Devil's power
thus to resurrect any one from the Abyss now;
but in the ongoing of the judgment, and for
the greater punishment of the unbelieving, the
power is given him to do it, and he does it. He
is allowed to have " the Key," and he uses it, unlocks the Abyss, and brings forth again into the
activities of life the two ablest of his particular

servants. They go through with their blasphemous and dreadful work in judgment upon the world for its unbelief. And when the end comes, they are at once cast into the final Hell, the very first that ever try those awful fires, which they so richly deserve. The kings and armies whom they deceive into this presumptuous war are mortal men, who are simply "slain,"—*killed*,—and so turned into Hades, there, with the wicked dead, to await the judgment at the end of the thousand years, when they all shall be brought forth together, and assigned their place in the same final Hell of the burning lake. The old Serpent, the Devil, who has been at the back of it all, is arrested and imprisoned. But there is still a reason in the divine purposes why he should not yet be finally disposed of; therefore he is not yet cast into the burning lake of ultimate perdition. Nevertheless, he is chained as to his power, and locked and sealed up as to his place, in that under-pit of Hades, where only the foulest and basest of spirits are,—in the Abyss whence he brought up the two Beasts and their demon helpers,—there to writhe in his helplessness till the thousand years are fulfilled.

The particular object of this binding and imprisonment of Satan is not so much for his due punishment, as for the temporary restraint and prevention of his deceptions of men. It is specially stated to be, "*that he should not lead astray the nations any more until the thousand years be accomplished.*" Ruinous deception is the Devil's trade, and all false ones and deceivers are his apprentices and children. The truth is ever against him; therefore falsehood is his particular recourse and instrument. But naked falsehood is only repulsive. What we know to be a lie cannot command our respect. "In vain is the net spread in the sight of any bird." There is in the very framework of the soul an impossibility of feeling toward known falsehood the same as if it were truth. The structure of our being revolts against it. Untruth can only gain credence and acceptance by being so disguised as to appear to be the truth. Falsehood can have no power over us until we are led to believe and conclude that it is the truth. And this deluding of men, getting them to accept and follow lies and false hopes, under the persuasion that they are accepting and following truth, is the great work and business of Satan in every age. From this work and business he never rests so long as he has the liberty to act. In this work and business he has been engaged from the beginning. And in this work and business he is engaged now; for his binding and imprisonment do not occur until after "the Battle of the great Day of God Almighty," and that battle has not yet come off.

Some assume and teach that this binding and imprisonment of Satan occurred at the opening of the Christian dispensation, and point to the miracles wrought by the Apostles and early Christians, the silencing of the Pagan oracles, and the onward march of the Church to political victory over

Paganism, as the evidence of it. But then the inspired Peter was all wrong; for he sent out a general Epistle to all Christians, in which he wrote: "Your adversary the Devil, as a roaring lion, *walketh about*, seeking whom he may devour." (1 Pet. 5 : 8.)

Others assume and teach that this binding and imprisonment of Satan occurred at the conversion of Constantine and the consequent triumph of Christianity over Pagan Rome. But that event was followed by a millennium of corruption and apostasy for the Church, and of darkness and barbarism for the world, far worse than had occurred during the thousand years before; whilst the termination of the thousand years after Constantine brought a period the brightest in evangelic purity and activity, and the most triumphant for truth and constitutional liberty, that has ever been since Constantine occupied the imperial throne.

Still others assume and teach that, to whatever date we are to refer this binding and imprisonment of Satan, he is bound now, because imperialism in government has been wellnigh banished from the earth, and hierarchism in the Church is quite disabled from its old dominion, and general intelligence and freedom are becoming the common possession of the race. I wonder that there should be sane men who can come to such a conclusion. If ever there was a time when the Devil was loose, active and potent in human affairs, *that time is now*, in the days in which we live. The Devil's dominion is the enthronement of error, falsehood, decep-

tion, lies, and moral rottenness; and when was
this dominion ever more patent than in these years
of the existing generation? The Devil bound!
And yet the people who claim to be the most
enlightened, and occupy the very top waves of
modern progress, do not hesitate to give out that
it is with them a matter of serious doubt whether
there is a God, a Providence, a soul to live after
this life, anything eternal but matter, any Lord but
Nature, any retribution but what natural laws
administer in this world, any principles of morality but expediency, and scout all idea of a personal
incarnation of Deity, of atonement by divine sacrifice, of justification by faith in the merits of a substi-
tute, of any coming again of Christ as King to judge
the world and reign in righteousness. We look
abroad upon society in general, and what do we see?
Reverence, that great balance-wheel in the economies of life, scarcely exists any more; oaths are nothing; good faith is scarce as grapes after the vintage;
and all moral bonds are trampled down without
compunction under the heels of greed, and lust, and
deified selfishness. Falsities and treacheries confront us unblushingly at every point. People not
only make falsehoods, speak falsehoods, print falsehoods, and believe falsehoods; but they eat them,
and drink them, and wear them, and act them,
and live them, and make them one of the great
elements of their being. One-half, at least, of all
that the eye can see, or the ear hear, or the hands
touch, or the tongue taste, is bogus, counterfeit,
pinchbeck, shoddy, or some hash or other of un-

truth. A man cannot move, or open his eyes, without encountering falsehood and lies. In business, in politics, in social life, in professions, and even in what passes for religion, such untruthfulness reigns, that he who would be true scarcely knows any more whom to trust, what to believe, how to move, or by what means to keep his footing, amid the ever-increasing flood of unreality and deception. And yet the Devil is bound! Do I color the picture too deeply? Look, consider, and see for yourselves. Is not the world full of people, many of them your neighbors and personal acquaintances, some of them under your own roofs, in your own homes,—people with their apostles, male and female, on the rostrum everywhere with applauding crowds around them,—people to whom the Church is a lie; the ministers of the Gospel, a fraud; the sacraments, absurdity; prayer, a weak delusion; the Bible, a dull record of superannuated beliefs; special providence, an impossibility; a personal God or Devil, a superstitious conceit; moral accountability to a future judgment, a thing to be laughed at; society, marriage, and the body of our laws, mere faulty conventionalities; government a mere device of the ambitious and self-seeking; immortality, a mere fiction; and even life itself, something of an impertinent imposition, or a mere freak of mother Nature! And with such ideas afloat, and swaying the hearts and minds of the multitude as the new Gospel of advanced thought and human progress, *what is truth?* *Where* is it? On what are we to rest?

How find a foundation to build on for anything? To such a philosophy, what is not a lie, a perversion, a delusion, a superstition, a cheat? And, on the other hand, if our Gospel be true; if what the Bible says of God, and Christ, and the nature and destiny of man, is indeed reality; was there ever a more subtle, more specious, more potent, more Satanic deception and misleading of the race, than that which the wiseacres and savants of our time would thus palm upon our world? And yet the Devil is bound! By what eccentricity of the human intellect, or freak of human intelligence, or stultification of man's common-sense, could such all-revolutionizing and infernal falsehood find place on earth, and pass current for the true and higher wisdom, but for the living presence and effective operations of that old Deceiver who cheated our first parents out of Paradise, beguiled the early world to its destruction in Noah's flood, and is now engaged preparing the way for his favorite son to captivate all the great powers of the earth to their inevitable damnation!

No, no, my friends; the Devil, that old Serpent, is not bound. He is loose. He ranges at large, with his ten thousand emissaries, all the more active and earnest in his Satanic schemes as he seeth that his time is short. He has his nests and conventicles in every city, town, and hamlet all over the world, labelled with all sorts of attractive and misleading names. Clubs, institutes, circles, societies, conventions, lyceums, and a thousand private coteries, under show of investigating science, improving knowledge, inquiring into truth, and cultivating the mind, free from the disturbing influences of sect, religion, tradition, and old fogy notions,—these are among the common machinery through which he instils his deceits and subtle poisons. A broader philosophy, a more compliant church, a more active humanity disdaining theological dogmas and positive creeds, a larger liberality to take every one for a child of God who refrains from denouncing the devilish atheisms and heresies of the times,—these are the flags he hangs out for the rallying of his unsuspecting dupes. And see how he induces men and women to usurp ministerial functions without ministerial responsibilities, and gives them power on the plea of breaking down denominationalism and making better saints without any church at all; how he prostitutes the pulpits to entertaining sensationalisms, defying all sense and sacred decency, or narrows them down to sweet platitudes which serve to bury the true Gospel from those whom it was meant to save,—and how he stirs up Christian ministers of place and influence to say and make believe that all this attention to sacred prophecy is nothing but a stupid craze, that the holy writers never meant just what they said, and that all these ill-bodings touching the destiny of this present world are but the croakings of birds that love to fly in storms! And yet he is bound! O, ye people, on your way to the nearing judgment of the great Day, "Be not deceived; God is not mocked." You may be sincere, but that is not

enough. Eve thought she was innocent and safe
when she took the Devil's recommendation of the
forbidden fruit; but her trustful confidence did not
excuse her. No delusion can serve to justify before God. No tricks or disguises can impose on
him. He will be true though that truth should
make every man a liar. His old and everlasting
Word must stand till every jot and tittle of it be
fulfilled. The existence of a Devil is not a myth,
but an awful reality, and to his doings and destiny
we have other relations than that of mere spec-
tators. His dread power over those who will not
have Christ as their Saviour is not a nightmare
fancy, or the dream of a disordered mental digestion, but a thing of living fact. And these solemn
and momentous Revelations are Jehovah's finger-
boards, set up in mercy along the path of human
life, to point out the places of danger and the way
of safety. To despise, neglect, or disregard them
is not a characteristic of wisdom. To refuse to
note and heed them, is to try the insane experiment of seeing how near you can graze the brink
of perdition, and yet win the credit of not tumbling
in. Can you be wiser than God who made you?
Then mark the signals he has given, and follow
them implicitly.

LECTURE FORTY-FIFTH.

Rev. 20 : 4–5, (Revised Text.) And I saw thrones, and they sat
upon them, and judgment [the power of judging] was given to them.

And (I saw) the souls of them who had been beheaded on account of
the testimony of Jesus, and on account of the word of God, and [of
those] who did not worship the beast nor yet his image, and did not
receive the mark on [their] forehead and on their hand; and they lived
(= lived again) and reigned with the Christ a thousand years.

The rest of the dead ones lived not (*again*) until the thousand years
be completed ; this [being] the resurrection the first.

A RICH and magnificent revelation here comes
before us.   Beautiful and blessed contemplations would it also afford were it not for the noise
and dust of controversy which surrounds it.   Unfortunately it has become a battle-ground of opposing schemes, not only of the interpretation of the
Apocalypse, but of the whole outcome of God's
promises and man's redemption.   A war of the
theologians has hung upon it for centuries. Hence
it is seldom treated otherwise than polemically, or

with partisan bias. Nor is it possible to touch it at all without entering in some degree into the deep and far-reaching controversy which here comes to its intensest and final tug. It is a great pity that it is so. The effect is disastrous in many directions. It turns multitudes from looking at the subject. It creates suspicions of any doctrines that seem to depend on the passage in question. It induces numbers to accept the unwarranted conclusion that the whole thing is so mysterious, incomprehensible, and dark, that no light or spiritual edification is to be gained from it. It has led disputants into inventions, assertions, and ways of dealing with the Divine Word, which, if consistently followed out, would undermine every distinctive doctrine of Inspiration. Nor is there, perhaps, another section of holy Scripture the consideration of which so much needs the aid and guidance of the Holy Ghost to keep the inquirer in balance and temper, to look and see with unprejudiced eyes, and to form conclusions with sound and conscientious regard to what has been written for our learning. God help us in our handling of the subject that we may rightly conceive, embrace, and rest on his own everlasting truth!

I.

The first point to which I direct attention, and one too much overlooked, is the connection of these presentations with the scenes and statements of the preceding chapter. We there saw the heaven opened, and the Lord of lords and King of kings, with his risen and glorified saints, coming forth to meet the Beast and his confederated kings and their armies in dreadful battle. The result was the taking and casting of the Beast and the False Prophet alive into the final Hell, the slaying of the rest with the sword, and the chaining and locking up of Satan in the prison of the Abyss. But, in connection with these administrations, it was said of the Sitter on the white horse, as it was said of the Manchild in chap. 12 : 5, *" And he shall rule or shepherdize the nations with a rod of iron "* (chap. 19 : 15). The repetition of this declaration renders it particularly significant, and calls for our special attention. The numerous references to it in the Scriptures assign to it every element of a special dispensation.

That it does not refer only, if at all, to the calamities inflicted on the Beast and his armies is clearly evident from the record. The instrument of that infliction was not *a rod*, but is twice stated to be *the sharp sword*, proceeding from the mouth of the Sitter upon the white horse. The effect in that instance was slaughter and death; but *shepherdizing*, with whatever severity of judgment and invincible force, is not the taking of life. The word ποιμαινω occurs often in the New Testament, but always in the sense of *feeding, tending, directing, and helping*, with a view to preservation, not destruction. Thus Christ was fore-announced by the Father, as "a Governor that *shall shepherdize* (margin, *feed*) my people Israel." (Matt. 2 : 6.) So

Christ speaks of one " having a servant ploughing or *feeding cattle*," literally, *shepherdizing*. (Luke 17 : 17.) So his command to Peter was, " *Feed (shepherdize)* my sheep." (Jno. 21 : 16.) And so Paul said to the elders at Miletum, " *Feed (shepherdize)* the Church of God." (Acts 20 : 28; also 1 Pet. 5 : 2.) In all these instances the word is used to express a gracious and merciful proceeding, the very contrary of slaughter and destruction. And when it is here said of the King of kings that he (ποιμανεῖ) *shall shepherdize* the nations, even though it be " with an iron rod," we would do great violence to the word to interpret it of the slaying of the armies of the Antichrist.

Besides, this *shepherdizing* is a dealing with "*the nations*" as such; whilst the subjects of the destruction at Harmageddon are not " the nations" as such, but " the kings of the earth and their armies." Kings may fall, and armies in the field of battle be destroyed, and the nations, or peoples to which they belong, still continue to exist. The defeat and capture of Napoleon at Sedan did not extinguish the French people, or even the French nationality. Had he and every French soldier perished on that field, France would still have remained; though the conqueror might have followed up the victory, and given to the French quite other laws and institutions, and organized them under a new rule for an entirely new life. In that case he would have done to and for the French something of what is implied in these terms as done to all nations by the Conqueror of

the Beast and his armies. The kings fall, and
their armies are clean swept away, making an
utter end of the Dragon dominion upon the earth;
but then comes the rod of iron in the hands of the
Conqueror, to *shepherdize*, provide for, and put into
new and better order, the home-peoples out from
among whom these armies went into the disastrous field. The battle of the Great Day of God
Almighty is one thing; the shepherdizing with
the rod is another. The two are closely connected.
They are both judgment administrations. The one
is the sequel to the other. But they are wholly
different in their immediate subjects, character,
and results. The one is temporary, the other is
continuous. The sword comes first, and strikes
down the enemy in the field; and then follows
the shepherdizing with the rod of discipline and
new rule over the peoples whose kings and armies
are no more. The two together fulfil what is
stated in Psalm 2 : 5–12, Isaiah 11, and Matt.
25 : 31–46, where the same rod power and shepherdizing are further described.

The Shepherdizer is the same who conquers in
the battle with the Beast and his confederate kings.
He is the All-Ruler, and it is his power and dominion which are thus enforced with justice and
with judgment. But his army of glorified saints
accompanies him. They follow him in his victorious treading down of his armed enemies. They
ride through the blood of his foes up to the horses'
bridles. They pursue the triumph with him.
And particularly in this shepherdizing with the

rod of iron, the Scriptures everywhere assign *to them* a conspicuous share. Hence the Psalmist sung: " Let the saints be joyful in glory; let them sing aloud upon their beds (resting-places). Let the high praises of God be in their mouth, and a two-edged sword in their hand, *to execute vengeance upon the heathen, and punishments upon the people; to bind their kings with chains, and their nobles with fetters of iron; to execute upon them the judgment written:* THIS HONOR HAVE ALL HIS SAINTS." (Ps. 149.)

The same is also very pointedly declared by the Saviour himself. To his twelve Apostles he said, that when he should sit in the throne of his glory, they also should " *sit upon twelve thrones, judging the twelve tribes of Israel.*" (Matt. 19 : 28.) In the address to the Church at Thyatira, he said: " He that overcometh, and he that keepeth my works unto the end, to him will I give *authority over the nations, and he shall shepherdize them with a rod of iron; as a vessel of earthenware shall they be broken to shivers* AS I ALSO RECEIVED OF MY FATHER." (Rev. 2 : 26, 27.) If there were not another passage on the subject, this alone would be decisive of the point, that this shepherdizing of the nations is shared in by the saints in resurrection glory. But there are other passages (see Dan. 7 : 26, 27; 1 Cor. 6 : 2, 3; Rev. 3 : 21). One particularly to the point is that in which it is said of the *Manchild*, born into immortality, and caught away to God and his throne, that he shall " *shepherdize all the nations with a rod of iron.*" (Rev. 12 : 5.) We have seen that this Manchild is a figure or symbol of the

true Church, with Christ at its head, and that the
birth and catching away to God is the resurrection and glorification of the saints with their
Lord.* No other consistent interpretation of that
marvellous " sign" is at all possible. And yet, to
that Manchild, after its removal to glory, is assigned this very shepherdizing of the nations.

It is therefore scripturally certain that this
ruling or shepherdizing with the rod of iron,
which follows up the destruction of the armies of
the Antichrist, is a thing in which the glorified
saints have a very conspicuous part.

Where, then, in the apocalyptic chart do we
find this very particular administration but in the
grand vision now before us? As I have been led
to view things, we have here the picture of the
victorious Christ, with his enthroned and glorified
saints, in the rule or shepherdizing of all the nations with a rod of iron, the same which is celebrated by the Psalmist, promised by Christ, and
so distinctly affirmed in the description of the
Manchild, as well as in the account of the coming
forth of the Sitter on the white horse.

II.

With this view of the connection and *scope* of
this vision, we pass to the more direct consideration of its presentations, every item of which goes
to prove that this is the natural, true, and necessary conception of the whole matter.

---

* See Lectures XXVI and XXVIII in Vol. II of this work.

John saw "*thrones.*" Judicial or regal administrations imply seats of authority. The Sitter on
the white horse came *crowned.* His shepherdizing
of the nations is in his character as conquering
King. It is therefore, in its very nature, an administration of sovereign authority. The saints
share with him in it, as we have seen. Hence the
need for thrones, or royal seats, for these sovereign shepherdizers. Daniel speaks of these same
thrones. He saw them set, and the going forth
of authority from them, which is further described
as the authority of one like a Son of man, to whom
was given " dominion, glory, and a kingdom, that
all people, nations, and languages should serve
him." (Dan. 7 : 9–14.) They are the same of which
the Saviour spoke to his twelve Apostles, and concerning which he has promised, " To him that
overcometh will I give to sit with me on my
throne, as I also overcame and sat down with my
Father on his throne." (Rev. 3 : 21.)

These are not empty seats. John says : " *They
sat upon them.*" Who "*they*" are, seems to have
troubled commentators to determine. Some say
" they" are the martyrs ; some say " they" are the
spirits or disembodied souls of the martyrs ; some
say "they" are the *principles* of the martyrs ; some
say " they " are the men of that generation quick-
ened from the death of sin and raised up to emi-
nent zeal, saintship, and influence while yet living
in mortal flesh ; some say "they" simply represent a more potent dominion of Christianity, the
sway of the Gospel over the nations ; and some

are entirely at a loss to say who "they" are. But there must be something fundamentally wrong in men's theories of the Apocalypse as a whole, or they could not here be in such straits of uncertainty.

Surely the sitters on these thrones are those to whom this implied judicio-regal authority is everywhere promised. Nor are the passages few in which those promises are given. In the text itself it is expressly said that these sitters upon these thrones are "*priests of God and of Christ, and reign with him*,"—"*reign with Christ.*" But what attentive reader of the Bible does not know that God's chosen and anointed kings and priests are none other than his true and faithful people? In the opening of this Book, John spoke of himself and fellow-Christians,—all who are freed from sin by Christ's blood,—as those whom God hath made kings and priests (chap. 1:5, 6). The Living Ones and the Elders gave glory to the Lamb for making them "*kings and priests of God*," destined to "reign on the earth." Who are they but glorified men, redeemed unto God by the blood of the Lamb "out of every tribe, and tongue, and people, and nation?" (Rev. 5:9, 10.) These king-priests must therefore be God's ransomed people; Peter pronounces his fellow-Christians "a chosen generation, a *royal priesthood*," who, "when the *chief Shepherd* shall appear," for this shepherdizing of the nations, "shall receive a glorious crown." (1 Pet. 2:9; 5:4.)

To what did he thus refer but these very dignities,

and to the true people of God as the inheritors of them? Daniel, in vision, saw the judgment sit, and the dominion of the Beast taken away by the mighty power of God, and declares that then "*the Kingdom and dominion, and the greatness of the Kingdom under the whole heaven, shall be given to the people of the saints of the Most High.*" (Dan. 7 : 26, 27.) What did he mean but the very thing here beheld by John, and that the sitters on these thrones are the saints of God? Paul wrote of "*a crown,*" for which he strove, which is to be the possession of all "good soldiers of Jesus Christ," and which the Lord, the righteous judge, would give him "at that day," and "unto *all them that love his appearing.*" (2 Tim. 2 : 3–5 ; 4 : 7, 8.) And so the Saviour himself exhorts his "little flock" not to fear, as it is the Father's good pleasure to give *them* the kingdom (Luke 12 : 32), enjoins upon his disciples to hold fast that no one take *their crown* (Rev. 3 : 11), and promises every faithful and good servant to "make him *ruler over all his goods*" (Matt. 24 : 46, 47). It is also an inevitable principle, that the conquerors take the dominion? The Sitter on the white horse conquers in the Battle of the Great Day, and by virtue of that triumph he becomes the Supreme King. But with him through all the mighty engagement were his glorified saints, in white apparel, on white horses, indicative of their character of associate *governors and judges.* (Judges 5 : 10.) With him in the fight, they are with him in the victory, and share the sovereignty which that victory secures. He conquers, and therefore reigns; *they* conquer with him, and therefore *they* "reign with him." Thus the sitters on these thrones are none other than Christ's saints whom John saw following their Lord when he came forth to make an end of the antichristian domination, and inaugurate his own shepherdizing of the nations.

Their sitting upon these thrones is not an empty show. As Christ's taking of the sovereignty of the earth is a sublime reality, so must that of his victorious peoples' participation in it also be. Nor are we left to gather this by mere inference. John says expressly that *"judgment was given to them,"*— κρῖμα,—*the act or power of judging,* including the forming of sentences and the execution of the same, as in Matt. 7 : 2; 19 : 28; Jno. 9 : 39; Rom. 2 : 2, 3; 1 Cor. 6 : 7. That is, as Alford remarks, "they were constituted judges." The work of shepherdizing the nations with a rod of iron necessarily involves intrustment with discretionary power to act; and this is the office and power here said to be given to these sitters on these thrones.* The "judgment" which they thus receive is otherwise expressed when it is said of them that they *"reign."* The possession of the judging power is most intimately conjoined with sovereignty, or the office of reigning. Thus "David *reigned* over all Israel; and David *executed judgment and justice* unto

---

* "The word κρῖμα in this clause may be interpreted as applying to the supervision or making of statutes, ordinances, arrangements, etc., by those who are in a superior station. This seems to many to be the most easy and natural construction."—Stuart, *in loc.*

all the people." (2 Sam. 8 : 15.)   Thus the Queen
of Sheba said to Solomon : " The Lord made thee
king, to do judgment and justice." (1 Kings 10 : 9.)
They are enthroned kings and priests, and they
are thus endowed with the prerogatives of the regal
office.   They are to reign.   They are to exercise the
royal functions.   Therefore they get the power of
judging and of executing judgment and justice,
which is the very office of the shepherdizing promised to the victorious children of God, and so emphatically set forth in what was said of the particular destiny of the Manchild.   Up to this time
it is a matter of promise and hope, but here it is
made a matter of possession and actual fact,—a
thing finally reached and realized.

Once it was the fate of believers to be judged
by the ungodly world-powers.   Jesus told his followers that they should be brought before councils,
governors, and kings, and that time would come
when men would think it a holy thing to adjudge
them worthy of stripes, imprisonment, and death.
So Paul stood before the courts of earth, saying :
" *I stand and am judged.*"   But man's day has a
limit, and then comes another order, when, as
Mary sung, God " shall put down the mighty from
their seats," and " exalt them of low degree,"—
when the Pauls shall be the royal judges, and the
Felixes, and Festuses, and Agrippas, and Cæsars,
then in place, shall be obliged to accept the sentences of heavenly justice from God's immortal
potentates, who once stood helpless at earth's tri-
bunals; for so it is written, "the saints shall judge

the world" (1 Cor. 6:2), and "shall take the Kingdom, and possess the Kingdom forever, even forever and ever" (Dan. 7:18); and Christ, the victorious All-Ruler, according to his promise, will "give them *authority over the nations*, to shepherdize them with a rod of iron" (Rev. 2:26, 27), invincibly and effectually.

Among those who suffer the greatest penalties and privations for their faith are the holy martyrs and those who hold out faithful under the dreadful Antichrist. When a man lays down his life for his Lord, he surrenders all that he can surrender, and lets go what all the instincts of humanity lead one to cling to to the last. Human law knows no heavier penalty than the taking of a man's life; and when this is accepted, rather than deny the Saviour or his Word, the common world, as well as Christianity, takes it as the sublimest testimony a man can give of his devotion. And when people consent to suffer nakedness, banishment, and death, rather than make themselves guilty of an act of homage to the Antichrist, it is a demonstration of steadfastness as great as it is possible to furnish. Hence there is a somewhat special vision vouchsafed to the Apocalyptic seer to indicate the rewards of such fidelities. Not only does he behold the sitters on the thrones in general, and the giving of judicial and royal authority to the body of the saints as a whole, but he is particularly shown that the martyrs, and those who worship not the Beast, are surely among them. Thus he tells us:

" *And (I saw) the souls of them who had been beheaded on account of the testimony of Jesus, and on account of the word of God, and [of those] who did not worship the beast nor yet his image, and did not receive the mark on [their] forehead and on their hand; and they lived (= lived again) and reigned with the Christ.*"

Whilst the body of the saints in general participate in these rewards, it is thus shown that the martyrs in particular, together with the faithful ones of the last evil time, are specially included. The martyrs and the faithful ones under the Beast are not different parties from the sitters on the thrones, but special classes specifically included. A somewhat parallel presentation occurs in chapter 1 : 7, where it is said of the Saviour at his great Epiphany, that " every eye shall see him, and they which pierced him." The meaning is not that " they which pierced him " form a separate class apart from " every eye," but that even those who slew Christ shall also be among those denoted by " every eye," and that they too shall look upon him. It deserved to be thus noted specially that the murderers of Christ will have to confront him, as well as men in general; and so here it deserved to be noted specially that the holy martyrs, and the faithful ones under the Antichrist, have their part and place with the sitters upon the thrones, and that they particularly are among those who reign with Christ.

Special notice of the martyrs in their disembodied state was taken in chapter 6 : 9. They were not enthroned then, but in depression, anx-

ious for their final vindication. The record says:
" When he opened the fifth seal, I saw beneath
the altar the souls of those that had been slain on
account of the Word of God, and on account of the
testimony which they held fast : and they cried
with a great voice, saying, Until when, thou Master,
the holy and true, dost thou not judge and avenge
our blood from them that dwell on the earth. And
there was given to each of them a white robe, and
it was said to them that they should rest yet a
little time, until their fellow-servants also, and
their brethren, shall have been completed, who
are about to be slain as also they themselves had
been." The very parties there spoken of are here
specified as among the sitters upon the thrones;
to wit, the martyrs then under the altar, their fellow-servants who were subsequently to fall because
of their refusal to worship the Beast. A necessity
was thus begotten for some subsequent notice of
them in connection with the final outcome for
which they were told to wait. That notice we have
in the text, which notice takes its special character
from the previous allusion to these particular parties, and the implied promise given them, not as
over against the sitters on the thrones, or as the
only sitters there, but as specially included among
them. It is a gracious note of testimony from
heaven to the greatest sufferers for Christ that,
when it comes to the inheritance of the Kingdom
and the reigning of the saints with their Lord,
they are to be specially considered. Having laid
down their lives for their faith, or having held out

faithfully against the horrible deceptions and persecutions of the Antichrist, the assurance is, that they particularly shall be among these priests of God and of Christ, to share in his sublime dominion. Though in the ashes before, they are to live again for this very purpose.

Some stumble at the word *souls* ($\psi\upsilon\chi\grave{\alpha}\varsigma$), by which these martyrs are denoted, as if that introduced a peculiarity determinative of the whole character and interpretation of the vision. But it is nothing but a metaphysical quibble, by which to obscure and get rid of a plain doctrine of the Word of God which some do not like. It is a sufficient answer to say, that one of the common uses of this word in the New Testament is to denote individual beings, and persons in the body, rather than spirits of men out of the body. So the converts on the day of Pentecost are called "about three thousand *souls;*" and Jacob and his kindred who went down into Egypt are spoken of as "threescore and fifteen *souls ;*" and those sailing with Paul in the ship were "two hundred threescore and sixteen *souls ;*" and in the ark with Noah " eight *souls* were saved." In such passages disembodied souls are out of the question. Indeed, one of the rarest uses of the word by the sacred writers, if ever so used, is that which confines its meaning to the designation of that part of man capable of existence apart from the body. More commonly, it means corporeal life as distinguished from corporeal death. And as respects principles, or a mere moral influence, there is no instance in all the Word of God of its

use in that sense.   That the word *souls*, in John's
vision of the martyrs beneath the altar, means *per-*
sons dead as to their bodies, is very evident, not,
however, from the meaning of the word, but from
the accompanying statement that the *souls* he saw
were people *slain* on account of their faith.   He
sees the same people, persons, *souls*, here; but this
time ἔζησαν—"*they lived again.*"*   As mere souls
separate from the body, they never were dead.
John saw them, and heard them speaking, and
beheld them invested in white robes, and recognized them as still living and waiting, though dead
as to their bodies.   The *living again* in which he
now sees them, must therefore be a living in that
in which they were dead when he first saw them,
that is, *corporeally dead.*   There is a resurrection of
the bodies of dead men, but there is no such thing
as the resurrection of *the spirits* of dead men.   For
living men there may be a spiritual resurrection
from the death-state of sin, but there is no such
spiritual resurrection for *dead* men.   John had seen
these " souls" under death as to their bodies, but
here as "*living again ;*" of course, living now in that
in which they were dead then ; that is, *in corporeal*

---

* " I argue from the Greek text that the *souls* must in this instance be a synecdoche for *the persons*, and that the *living again*
must signify the union of body and soul.   For first, in the passage ' which, or who, had not worshipped the Beast,' the word
which (οἱτινες) is in the masculine gender, whereas *souls*, which
is the antecedent to it, is feminine.   So, also, ' the rest of the dead,
(οἱ λοιποὶ) is in the masculine, in antithetical opposition to those
that were beheaded, των πεπελεκισμενων."—Dr. N. Holmes's *Res-*
urrection Revealed, p. 58.

resurrection, for as to their spirit life they had not been dead.*

So far, then, from this word *souls* introducing an element requiring the exclusion of any thought of literal corporeal resurrection, it the rather proves that we cannot possibly understand any other sort of resurrection. That of which their martyrdom deprived them, their *living again* restores to them; hence, necessarily, corporeal resurrection, — the

---

* "How can we avoid coming to the conclusion that ἐζησαν here must mean *reviving* or *rising from the dead?* The use of ζάω elsewhere in the Apocalypse shows very plainly that it may mean *revived, lived again,* in reference to the body which had been dead. Thus the Saviour speaks of himself, in Rev. 2 : 8, as being he who had been *dead, καὶ ἔζησε, and had revived, lived again,* after the death of the body. Thus, too, it is said of the Beast (Rev. 13 : 14) which had the deadly wound of the sword, that ἔζησε, *it revived.* Thus also it is said, the rest of the dead οὐκ ἔζησαν, *lived not again.* Surely the writer does not mean that Christians of lower rank, or the wicked, have no existence at all after the death of the body."—Stuart *in loc.*

"It does not mean that they lived *spiritually,* for so they did before. and whilst they bore their testimony to Christ and against Antichrist previous to their death; nor *in their successors,* for it would not be just and reasonable that *they* should be beheaded for their witness of Christ and his word, and *others* should live and reign with Christ in their room and stead. Nor is this to be understood of their living in their souls, for so they live in their separate state; the soul never dies; God is not the God of the dead, but of the living. But the sense is, that they *lived again,* as in verse 5; they lived corporeally; their souls lived in their bodies, their bodies being raised again, and reunited to their souls; their whole persons lived, or the souls of them that were beheaded lived; that is, their bodies lived again, the soul being sometimes put for their body; and this is called the first resurrection in the next verse."—Dr John Gill *in loc.*

only resurrection of which martyrs are capable.
Spiritual resurrection is out of the question, for
they were spiritually resurrected before they became martyrs, and could not be holy martyrs
without it. Mere influential resurrection is equally
out of the question, for their living again is to
possess the rewards of martyrdom, which would
be a mere farce in any case not involving a literal personal resurrection. What reward is it to
a man under the altar who has lost his head
for his fidelity, that somebody else after him
shows the same fidelity! What compensation was
it to Paul for his execution at Rome, that Constantine some centuries after sat on the throne of
the Cæsars, and inscribed the sign of the Cross
upon his banners! Such a result was indeed worth
sacrifice to achieve; but that achievement was
nothing of a personal reward to Paul. The souls
under the altar knew there were men of their own
faith and spirit on the earth, who should be as true to
God as they had been; but that was no compensation to them, and did not keep them from crying
with a great voice: " Until when, thou Master,
the holy and true, dost thou not judge and avenge
our blood!" Besides, the Scriptures everywhere
place the recompenses of the sacrifices and devotions of the saints " *at the resurrection of the just.*"
(Luke 14 : 14.) Neither martyrs nor saints get
their rewards till then. (2 Tim. 4 : 8; 1 Pet. 1 : 7, 8;
5 : 4.) The compensations of the saints must therefore wait till " the resurrection of the just." But
here we have the rewards of God's faithful wit-

nesses; therefore the resurrection spoken of can be none other than a literal and real resurrection, the same which is set forth in all the Scriptures as the great hope of all saints.

So likewise the antithesis between the living again of these "souls" and the non-living again of "the rest of the dead till the thousand years be completed," evidences that the resurrection spoken of is a literal resurrection. The deadness of this "remainder of the dead" certainly is a bodily deadness; otherwise there are to be no conversions on earth for full a thousand years. Their living again at the completion of the thousand years is a bodily resurrection; for they come up out of the sea, out of death, out of Hades, where they could not have been without being corporeally dead. John says expressly that they are "*the dead, the great and the small*," and that they thus live again, in a state of recovery from death and Hades, for the purpose of receiving their final doom. If this does not signify a literal resurrection of them at the end of the thousand years, there is no way of proving that there ever will be a literal resurrection for anybody. But if their living again at the termination of the thousand years is a literal resurrection, then their non-living again during those thousand years must be a state of literal corporeal deadness. And if their non-living again till the thousand years are accomplished is a continuation in a state of corporeal death, then the living again of those to whom they stand correlated as "the remainder of the dead" must be a literal corporeal resur-

rection also.* There is no escape from this argument. As Alford well says, "If in a passage where
two resurrections are mentioned, where certain
'souls' live again at the first, and 'the rest of the
dead' live again only at the end of a specified
period after the first,—if in such a passage the *first
resurrection* may be understood to mean spiritual
rising with Christ, while the *second* means *literal*
rising from the grave; then there is an end of all
significance in language, and Scripture is wiped
out as a definite testimony to anything. If the first
resurrection is spiritual, then so is the second;
but if the second is literal, then so is the first,
which, in common with the whole primitive
Church and many of the best modern expositors,
I do maintain, and receive as an article of faith
and hope." (*Gr. Test.* in loc.)

Furthermore, it is inwoven and implied in every
particular in the presentation concerning these
sitters on these thrones, that the scene to them is
a post-resurrection scene.

In chapter 11 : 18, it was adoringly said by the
holy Elders, that the time of the sounding of the
seventh trumpet is the time or season for judging
the dead, to give reward to the servants of God,

---

* "In the phrases *first* resurrection, and *second*, a discrep-
ancy as to *time* is implied. Any great change from a degraded and wretched condition, temporal or spiritual, may indeed be figuratively called a *resurrection*, a *restoration to life*,
i. e., to happiness; but it would be out of the question to name
it a *first* resurrection. This implies of necessity a comparison
with a *second*, in which the first must be like the second in
kind."—Stuart *in loc.*

the prophets, the saints, and them that fear his name, the small and the great. The description before us belongs to the season of the sounding of the seventh trumpet, which terminates at this point a thousand years before another resurrection of any sort occurs. Either then this sets forth the reward given to the servants, prophets, and saints of God, inclusive of their resurrection, or these holy Elders were altogether mistaken and misinformed, and John was in error in recording what they said as true.

Paul says, that when Christ, who is our life, shall appear, *then* shall his people appear with him in glory. (Col. 3:4.) But here Christ has appeared. The heaven has opened, and he has come forth as triumphant King of kings and Lord of lords, crowned with all his many diadems, consigning the Beast and the False Prophet to final perdition, striking their assembled armies dead, and locking up the Devil in the Abyss. Where, then, are his people who are to be revealed with him in resurrection glory when these things come to pass, if these sitters upon these thrones be not they?

These enthroned ones have had their judgment and obtained reward; otherwise they could not be thus enthroned, for enthronement is reward. But the time of such reward of the saints is the time of their resurrection, and not before; therefore, these enthroned ones must here be in their resurrected and glorified estate.

They occupy thrones, and they reign; therefore, they must have received their crowns; but the saints are not crowned till the chief Shepherd appears, and they have been recalled from their graves (2 Tim. 4 : 8 ; 1 Pet. 5 : 4) ; therefore, again, these crowned ones must here be in their resurrected condition.

They are kings and priests, they reign, they are enthroned as royal judges and potentates, they share with Christ in his judging and shepherdizing of the nations ; but it is only to those who have overcome, and been crowned by the great Judge of all as victors,—to the Manchild born into immortality and caught up to God and his throne,—that this power over the nations thus to rule or shepherdize is given. (Rev. 2 : 26, 27 ; 12 : 5.) How, then, can these enthroned and reigning ones be any other than resurrected saints, in possession of post-resurrection rewards and glory ? I wonder at the strange obtuseness of candid and sensible men, that they should have the slightest question on the subject. Either human theorizings are more authoritative than God's positive revelations, or those are all wrong who refuse to take these sitters on these thrones as the resurrected and glorified saints.

And still the evidence is not exhausted. There is a word in the record which makes the matter doubly sure. This whole presentation concerning the lifting and placing of these enthroned ones in their royal seats to live and reign with Christ for a thousand years, John pronounces " *The Resurrection*"—" *The Resurrection the First.*" The word *Resurrection* (ἀνάστασις) is never once used in the New Testament, except to denote the coming up again of the fallen body from the grave. It occurs more than forty times, and always in this one, uniform, and exclusive sense. Yet the emplacement of these people in these sublime seats is called their ἀνάστασις—their *Resurrection*. Nay, more, the Holy Ghost calls it ἡ ανάστασις, emphatically *the Resurrection*, partly in its relation to a second, and partly with reference to its own transcendent preeminence, as the particular object of our highest Christian hopes. How men, who profess loyalty to the Scriptures, and hold themselves in conscience bound to the Word of God, can get over such facts, and reduce the whole picture of this glorious enthronement of the saints, to what they call "special respect to their principles, their memory, and their character" rendered by mortal men, or to a mere revival of the martyr spirit and faith in times of glory for the Church on earth when there is no more room for martyrs, is utterly beyond my comprehension. It upturns all acknowledged principles of interpretation from their very foundations. It opens the door for the explaining away of every distinctive feature of the Christian faith. And it turns all the great promises of God and hopes of his Church into mist, dimness, and dreamy nothing. If these thrones, this royal judgeship, this reigning with Christ, this thousand years' dominion and rulership, this lifting of the holy martyrs including prophets and apostles into seats of sovereignty and shepherdizing of the nations, do not belong to the awards which only the Resurrection can bring, it is simply impossible to find any solid basis in God's Word for any special doctrine of our faith which we claim to derive from that source.

Look at it, my friends. The Bible tells us unmistakably that the illustrious apostles do not get their thrones till "the regeneration when the Son of man shall sit upon the throne of his glory" (Matt. 19 : 28); and yet men would teach us that some of their disciples in the flesh shall sit on exactly such thrones, and reign with Christ as his kings and priests for a thousand years, "*as if they were apostles raised from the dead,*" whilst yet those apostles themselves are all the while still sleeping unrewarded in their graves! The holy martyrs we know do not get their recompense till "the resurrection of the just;" and yet we are to accept it as the revelation of God, that mortal men, who are not martyrs at all, and have no chance of becoming martyrs, ascend martyr thrones, and sit and reign with Christ as kings for ten centuries, "*as if they were martyrs raised from the dead,*" whilst the martyrs themselves are meanwhile left in the ashes beneath the altar, crying, How long, O Lord, how long! Apart from all the linguistic and exegetical arguments which stand out against such notions, as a continent against the sea, the very absurdity of the implications ought to be enough to satisfy every one that such anomalies certainly cannot belong to the administrations of a just and holy God.

But I cannot go further into the subject tonight. Believing that I have contributed something toward a right understanding of this much-abused passage of the divine revelation, I close with the single remark: How sublime and glorious is the portion which remains for God's true people! Here are thrones to last a thousand years, and forever, and they are to occupy them. Here is sovereignty and judicial rule over the nations, and they are to exercise and wield it along with their victorious Redeemer and King. Here are a thousand years of glorious life over against a thousand years in the sombre abodes of Hades,—a life which they are to possess and enjoy forever free from all fear or power of " the second death." What is beyond will appear as we come to the concluding chapters; but this alone presents a prospect and honor for the saints well worth a life of suffering and trial, and for which life itself is not too dear a price.

LECTURE FORTY-SIXTH.

THE FIRST RESURRECTION—A RESURRECTION OF SAINTS ONLY—
TAKES PLACE IN SUCCESSIVE STAGES—NOT DESCRIBED IN
ANY ONE VISION—INTRODUCES A WONDERFUL CHANGE IN
THE EARTH'S HISTORY — PROMOTES ITS SUBJECTS TO A
TRANSCENDENT DIGNITY AND GLORY.

Rev. 20 : 6. (Revised Text.) Blessed and holy he that hath part in
the resurrection the first ! Over these the second death has no power,
but they shall be priests of the God and of the Christ, and reign with
him a thousand years.

MY conviction is clear and positive that the
resurrection here spoken of is the resurrection of the saints from their graves, in the sense
of the Nicene Creed, where it is confessed : "I look
for the Resurrection of the dead, and the life of the
world to come." With the distinguished Dean of
Canterbury, Dr. Alford, to whose critical labors the
Christian world is much indebted; "I cannot consent to distort words from their plain sense and
chronological place in the prophecy, on account of
any considerations of difficulty, or any rise of
abuses which this doctrine may bring with it."
With Paul, "I can do nothing against the truth,
but for the truth." (2 Cor. 13 : 8.) The word here
rendered *Resurrection* is more than forty times

used in the New Testament and four times in the
Apocrypha, and always in the one only sense of a
rising again of the body after it has fallen under
the power of death. The emphasizing of it as
The Resurrection cannot, with any degree of propriety, be understood of any mere metaphorical
or symbolic rising. The placing of it as *the first*
in a category of two resurrections, the second of
which is specifically stated to be the literal rising
again of such as were not raised in the first, fixes
the sense to be a literal resurrection. What it
describes is located in the time of the judging of
the dead and the giving of reward to the saints,
for which recovery from their graves is a pre-
requisite. It exalts to an office of judging, shepherdizing, and reigning, the same which is elsewhere dependent upon the final victory and the
complete redemption of the whole man. All the
rewards, dignities, and honors promised to saints
at and after the resurrection, are necessarily included in what is assigned to those who share in
this resurrection. All the connections and surroundings, antecedent and consequent, and the
impossibility of consistently adjusting it to the
rest of the Apocalypse or the Scriptures in general
on any other supposition, combine to show that the
reference is and must be to persons in resurrection life and glory. I am also perfectly sure, that
any candid critic, set to work to make out an
honest list of the men of the first three centuries
of the Church who believed in a literal resurrection of saints a thousand years before the resur-

rection of the wicked, would find in this chapter the most ample and cogent reasons for placing the Apostle John among them. I cannot, therefore, but take it as the true meaning and intent of the Holy Ghost, that we should here understand a real and literal resurrection of saints and martyrs from their graves.

Who partake in it? is the question suggested and answered in the text now before us, concerning which I remark:

1. *It is a resurrection of saints only.* They that have part in it are "blessed and holy." Whether the reference be to the qualifications for it, or to what it brings, or to both, the result is the same, that none but true members of Christ are in this resurrection; for none but such are "blessed and holy." Neither in this life, nor in that which is to come, can an unbeliever, a wicked or profane person, be reckoned with the "blessed and holy;" but every one that hath part in this resurrection is "blessed and holy."

Many have the idea that there is but one resurrection for all men, good and bad alike. It is also true that "as in Adam all die, even so in Christ shall all be made alive." (1 Cor. 15 : 22.) But it is immediately added, "*every man in his own order.*" It is not a summary thing, all at once, and the same in all cases. The resurrection of the wicked is in no respect identical with that of the saints, except that it will be a recall to some sort of corporeal life. There is a "resurrection of life," and there is a "resurrection of damnation" (Jno. 5 : 29);

and it is impossible that these should be one and the same. There is a " resurrection of the just,"— " a better resurrection,"—a resurrection out from among the dead (εξαναστασις εκ νεκρων), for which great zeal and devotion are requisite (Luke 14 : 14; Heb. 11 : 35 ; Phil. 3 : 10, 11), — which is everywhere emphasized and distinguished from another, more general, and less desirable. As it is " the resurrection of the just," the unjust have no share in it. As it is a resurrection from among the dead ones, it is necessarily *eclectic*, raising some, and leaving others, and so interposing a difference as to *time*, which distinguishes the resurrection of some as in advance of the resurrection of the rest. Hence the Scriptures continually draw a line of distinction between the resurrection of the good and the resurrection of the bad; and when the two are mentioned together, the resurrection of the good is always mentioned first. Hence, in the celebration of the standing up again of the congregation of the righteous, the Psalmist is particular to say that sinners shall *not stand up* with them. (Ps. 1 : 5.) Thus Paul also assured the Thessalonians that " *the dead in Christ shall rise first.*" (1 Thess. 4 : 16.) If we understand this " first" as over against the translation of living saints, as some take it, or as over against the resurrection of the dead *not in Christ*, as Professor Stuart claims the meaning to be, it is all the same. The declaration is that only " *the dead in Christ*" are partakers of this resurrection; and if there is this difference in time between " the resurrection of the dead in Christ" and the translation of the living " in Christ," all the more surely will there be a still wider difference in time between the rising of " the dead in Christ " and the rising of the dead *not* in Christ, who are altogether excluded from those who are said to rise *first*. It is not true, therefore, that we go contrary to the analogy of Scripture when we construe " the first resurrection," in which only the blessed and holy have part, as a literal resurrection of the saints, occurring long before and apart from the resurrection of the non-blessed.*

---

* " There is a general impression that the belief in the First Resurrection at a different time from that of the general resurrection rests solely on this passage. (Rev. 20 : 6.) But this is a great mistake. Omitting the passages from the Old Testament Scriptures, sustained by the promises of which the ancient worthies suffered and served God in hope of 'a better resurrection ' (Heb. 11 : 35), our Lord makes a distinction between the resurrection which some shall be accounted worthy to obtain, and some not. (Luke 20 : 3, 5.) St. Paul says there is a resurrection ' *out from among the dead* ' (ἐξανάστασις), to attain which he strove with all his might as the prize to be gained. (Phil. 3 : 11.) He also expressly tells us, that while as in Adam all die, so in Christ shall all be made alive ; yet it shall not be all at once. (1 Cor. 15 : 22–24.) It is to be remarked, that wherever the resurrection of Christ, or his people, is spoken of in Scripture, it is a ' resurrection *from*, or *from among*, the dead ; ' and wherever the general resurrection is spoken of, it is the ' resurrection *of* the dead.' This distinction, though preserved in many instances in the English translation, is too frequently omitted ; but in the Greek the one is always coupled with the preposition ἐκ, *out of* or *from among*, and the other is without the preposition ; and in the Vulgate it is rendered by *à mortuis*, or *ex mortuis*, as distinct from *resurrectio mortuorum*. In Rom. 8 : 11, ' the spirit of him that raised up Jesus from the dead,'

2. *It is a resurrection which takes place in different stages*, and not all at one and the same time. Paul tells us expressly that there is an "*order*" in it, which brings up some at one time, and others at other times. It starts with "Christ the first fruits;" *afterwards* they that are Christ's at his coming; *then* (still later) the end, "completion, or last." (1 Cor. 15 : 23, 24.) Christ's resurrection was also attended with the resurrection of others. The Gospel says: "The graves were opened, and many bodies of the saints which slept arose, and came out of the graves after his resurrection, and went into the holy city." (Matt. 27 : 52, 53.) This, Selnecker, one of the authors of the *Formula Concordiæ*, says, "places and parcels out the resurrection of those who are raised to eternal life before the general resurrection at the last day; and the meaning properly is, that not only those of whom the Evangelist is writing become alive again, but also others, as Luther and Ambrose have written, and that such resurrections occur at various times throughout the whole

---

it is ἐκ νεκρῶν, *à mortuis.* So in Rom. 10: 7; Eph. 1 : 20; Heb. 3 : 20; 1 Pet. 1 : 3, 21. So Lazarus was raised ἐκ νεκρῶν. (Jno. 12 : 1, 9.) Our Lord, in his reply to the Sadducees, made the distinction between the general resurrection of the dead and the resurrection which some should be accounted worthy to obtain. (Luke 20: 34, 35.) St. Paul, when he spoke of a resurrection to which he strove and agonized to attain (Phil. 3 : 8, 11), as if one preposition was not enough to indicate or emphasize his meaning, uses it doubled, τὴν ἐξαναστασις τὴν ἐκ νεκρῶν, *ad resurrectionem, quæ est ex mortuis*—the special or eclectic resurrection, *that one from among the dead.*"—Consult M. Staart on the Apocalypse, vol. ii, pp. 474–490.

period or dispensation of the New Testament, even up to the final day." These various particular resurrections he also calls "The First Resurrection, to which," he says, "belongs everything raised up again to eternal life before the final day."*

This statement agrees also with what we have found in the course of our exposition of this Book. In chapter 4, immediately following the sentences to the Churches, John saw a door open in the heaven, through which he was called to come up. That door and ascension indicate a resurrection and rapture of saints (answering to 1 Thess. 5 : 16, 17); for John immediately beheld Living Ones and Elders in glory. They were saints from earth, for they sing of being redeemed by Christ's blood "out of every kindred, and tongue, and tribe, and people." They are in resurrection life, for they are enthroned and crowned; and no saints are crowned till "the resurrection of the just." They correspond to "the Eagles" gathered together where the body they live on is, who are thus sheltered in the heavenly pavilion from the sorrows of the great tribulation. (Matt. 24 : 27, 28; Luke 17 : 34–37; 21 : 34–36; Rev. 3 : 10.) They are already in heaven, before ever a seal is broken, a trumpet sounded, or a bowl of wrath emptied.

Further on, in chapter 7, under the sixth seal, a great multitude was seen, also in heaven, clothed

---

* *Exp. of Rev. and Daniel*, Gena, 1567. See also Danhauer. Kromayer's *Elenchticus in Aug. Conf.*, 501–2, and Lange's *Ap. Licht, u. Recht*, 179.

with white robes, and bearing palms of victory. John beheld them with the Living Ones and Elders, but distinct from them, and then just arrived. Whence they came, is asked and explained. They come "out of the great tribulation,"—a tribulation from which the Elders or seniors in heaven were saved altogether, being "accounted worthy to escape all these things." They answer to the wise virgins, who were not ready when the watchful and far-sighted Eagles were "taken," but who, in sorrow and mortification, had now repented out of their misbeliefs, taken up the lamps of a better confession, and gone out in true advent faith to meet the Bridegroom, thus washing their robes and making them white in the blood of the Lamb, securing a heavenly portion indeed, but with certain losses, and at a period subsequent to the taking up of the Elders and Living Ones.

So at a still later period, even after the revelation of the blasphemous Beast, two great Witnesses appear, whom he finally slays. Three days and a half their bodies lie unburied. But, at the end of that time they come to life again, stand on their feet, and ascend to heaven in sight of their enemies. Whether any of their disciples are taken up with them, as might reasonably be inferred, or whether they alone are raised at this time, here is certainly another special or particular resurrection which goes to make up the company of the "blessed and holy."

Yet further on, in chapter 14, still another special company appears, quite distinct from any thus far named, consisting of 144,000, "redeemed from the earth" and "from among men," singing a new song of their own, and joined with the Lamb to follow him whithersoever he goeth. They certainly belong to "the children of the resurrection," to the congregation of God's glorified saints; but the season of their inbringing is not the same as that of the others referred to.

So, in connection with the gathering of the kings and their armies at Harmageddon, there is a note of indication that other saints were then on the eve of being taken (chap. 16 : 15); whilst here in the vision of the whole body finally made up, some are described as having lived in the very last days of the Antichrist, yet did not worship him or receive his mark; indicating that the first resurrection is not finally complete until the very last period of the Man of sin.

It is thus clear and manifest, even to the extent of demonstration itself, that the First Resurrection is not one summary event, but is made up of various resurrections and translations at different times, beginning with the resurrection of Christ, who is the head and front of "the resurrection of the just," and receiving its last additions somewhere about the final overthrow of the Beast and his armies.

3. *It is a Resurrection which as a whole is nowhere pictorially described*. As it does not occur all at once, it is not fully given in any one vision, as in the case of "the rest of the dead." The nearest to such a scenic presentation is that given

in chapter 12, in the picture of the birth of the Manchild, which is immediately caught up to God and to his throne. That birth and ascension is the pictorial "sign" of the bringing forth of all "the Church of the first-born" into eternal life and resurrection glory, which began in the resurrection and ascension of Christ himself, and which reaches its completion when the last martyr under the Beast attains his final blessedness. But even there, no circumstantial details appear, except the malignant and murderous attempt of the Dragon to prevent it. It is quite too varied and diverse in its several sections, and in the different parts which the blessed and holy have in it, for any one picture adequately to represent it. Hence there is no such picture. What John here sees and describes is not so much the scene of its occurrence as the body of its subjects, the estate to which it brings them, the blessedness and honor with which it clothes and endows them. He beholds who and what they are that have part in it; but when, how, or in connection with what times, formalities, and surroundings they are made to live again, he does not here see or state, as in the case of those who live not again till the thousand years are ended. The reason is, that the subject is not capable of it, because so parcelled out in various particular scenes, relating to different classes and times, and with very diverse circumstances and attendant facts.

It is not so with " the rest of the dead." As none of them share in the First Resurrection, so none of them belong to "the blessed and holy." They are all of the one general class of the non-saved. The reading in the Codex Sinaiticus is, that they are all κατεκρίθησαν—*condemned.*

The book of life is opened and searched from end to end, but there is no account of any name of any one of them being found there. Leaving out the Beast and the False Prophet, who are then already in the lake of fire, they are all resurrected together. They all have their judgment at one and the same time, and all meet the same fate. One picture can readily give the whole scene, with all the circumstances and particulars. And so it is given, in connection with the great white throne. But, in the nature of the case, thus it could not be with "the resurrection of the just." Nor does Christ ever mount a throne of judgment toward his Church and people. They are his familiar servants, friends, and brethren. Leaving the world, he leaves them to occupy for him, and in his name. The Kingdom he gets is not against them, but for them, that they may share it with him. They are of the King's party and household. When he comes, he comes, according to the Parables, first to one, and then to another, and so in succession, advancing each band of faithful and good servants to their reward one after another, "every man in his own order." He meets and rewards the best first, and so descends from class to class, as from time to time, till the whole body of his redeemed ones is made up in all its variety of orders and degrees, according to fidelity to his word and service.

4. *The completion of this Resurrection introduces a wonderful change in the earth's history.* It is the breaking through of an immortal power;—a power which sweeps away, as chaff before the wind, the whole economy of mortal and Dragon rule, and thrusts to death and Hades every one found rising up or stiffening himself against it;— a power which shears the Old Serpent of his strength, binds him with a great chain, locks and seals him up in the Abyss, pulls down all his works, tears off and clears away all his hoary false-hoods, which have been oppressing, deceiving, misleading, and swaying the world to its destruc-tion for so many ages;—a power which gives to the nations new, just, and righteous laws, in the administration of immortal rulers, whose good and holy commands men must obey or die;—a power which cuts at once the cords of life for every dissembling Ananias and Sapphira, blasts every Nadab and Abihu that ventures to offer strange fire before the Lord, consigns to death and burning every Achan that covets the Baby-lonish garment or wedge of gold which God hath pronounced accursed, and causeth the earth to open her mouth and swallow up on the spot every Korah, Dathan, and Abiram that dares to open his mouth against the authority of the holy princes whom Jehovah hath ordained;—a power which grasps hold of the plethoric fortunes accumulated in meanness and oppression and held in greedy avarice for the pampering of lust and pride, hew-ing them down in righteousness and scattering

them in restitutions to those out of whom they have been so uncharitably and dishonestly ground and wrung;—a power which goes forth in vindication of the worthy poor, the oppressed, the weak, the friendless, and the downtrodden, the righting of their cause, the maintenance of their just claims, and the enforcement of truth and brotherhood between man and man;—a power which lifts the mask from deceit, pretence, and false show, puts each one in his true place according to what he really is, gives credit only where credit is due, stamps an effectual condemnation on all false weights and measures, and tries everything and everybody in the balances of a strict and invincible justice. I think of the coming in of that power,—of the havoc it must needs make in the whole order of things,—of the confusion it will cause in the depraved cabinets, and courts, and legislatures of the world,—of the revolution it must work in business customs, in corporation managements, in political manipulations, in mercantile and manufacturing frauds, in the lies and hollownesses which pervade social life,—of the changes it must bring into churches, into pulpits, into pews, into worship, into schools, into the newspapers, into book-making and book-reading, into thinking and philosophy, and into all the schemes, enterprises, judgments, pursuits, and doings of men,—of how it will affect literature, art, science, architecture, eating, drinking, sleeping, working, recreating,—of what it must do concerning playhouses, and rumshops, and gambling hells, and the unhallowed gains by which great masses of people have their living and keep themselves up in the world. And as I thus begin to realize in imagination what the irresistible enforcement of a true and righteous administration in all these directions and relations necessarily implies, I can see why the Book of God describes it as a shepherdizing *with a rod of iron*, and calls it a breaking like the dashing to pieces of an article of pottery. Think of the sudden collapse of all the haunts of sin, the rooting out of the nests and nurseries of iniquity, the clearing away of the marshes and bogs of crime, where every style of damning pestilence is bred, and the changes that must hence come;—think of the summary abolition of all infamous cliques, combinations, and rings,—political rings, whiskey rings, municipal rings, state rings, railroad rings, mercantile rings, communistic rings, oath-bound society rings, and a thousand kinds of other rings,—all the children of wickedness, hindering just law, suppressing moral right, crippling honest industry, subsidizing legislation, corrupting the press, robbing the public treasuries, eating up the gains of honorable occupation, perverting public sentiment, spotting and exorcising men who cannot be made the tools of party, transmuting selfish greed and expediency into principle, razeeing the dominion of virtue and intelligence, subordinating the common weal to individual aggrandizement, and setting all righteous administration at defiance;—think of the universal and invincible dragging forth to divine justice of every blatant infidel, perjurer, liar, profane swearer, drunkard, drunkard-maker, whoremonger, hypocrite, slanderer, trickster, cheat, thief, murderer, trader in uncleanness, truce-breaker, traitor, miser, oppressor of the poor, bribe-taking legislator, time-serving preacher, mal-practitioner, babe-destroyer, friend-robber, office-usurper, peace-disturber, and life-embitterer;—think of the instantaneous going forth into all the world of a divine and unerring force, which cannot be turned or avoided, but which hews down every fruitless tree, purges away all chaff from every floor, negatives all unrighteous laws, overwhelms all unrighteous traffic, destroys all unrighteous coalitions, burns up every nest of infamy and sin, ferrets out all concealed wickedness, exposes and punishes all empty pretence, makes an end of all unholy business, and puts an effectual stop to all base fashions, all silly conceits, all questionable customs, and all the hollow shams and corrupt show and fastidiousness of what calls itself society, transferring the dominion of the almighty dollar to Almighty Right, and reducing everything in human life, pursuits, manners, and professions to the standard of rigid truth and justice;—think of the tremendous revolution, in all that the eye can see, the ear hear, the hand touch, the heart feel, or earthly being realize, that must needs attend the putting into living practical force of such an administration,—the high it must make low, the famous it must make infamous, the rich it must make poor, the mighty it must make power-

less, the loud it must sink to oblivion, the admired
and worshipped it must turn to disgrace and abhorrence, and the despised and contemned poor
it must lift into place and respectability,—the different impulse under which every wheel must then
turn, every shuttle move, every hammer strike,
every foot step, every mind calculate, and every
heart beat;—the change that must come over the
houses we enter, over the streets we walk, over
the people we meet, over the words we pronounce,
over the food we eat, over the air we breathe,
over the sunlight of the day, over the repose of
night, over the spirit of our waking hours and the
very dreams of our slumbers, and over all the elements, relations, activities, and experiences which
go to make up what we call *life;*—think, I say, of
all this tremendous revolution, and conceive it
going into invincible effect, unchangeably, without
compromise, at once, and forever; and you may
begin to have some idea of the alteration which
The First Resurrection is to introduce into the history of our earth. For this, and nothing less than
this, is the meaning of this sitting upon thrones,
receiving power of judgment, shepherdizing the
nations, and reigning on the earth, on the part of
these blessed and holy immortals.

And a good thing it will be for the nations when
that day comes. There can be nothing better than
God's law. There can be nothing more just, more
reasonable, more thoroughly or wisely adapted to all
the well-being of man and the highest wholesome-
ness of human society. All the blessedness in the

universe is built upon it. All that is needed for the establishment of a holy and happy order is for men to obey that law, for it to be put in living force, for it to be incarnated in the feelings, actions and lives of men. And this is what is to be effected when " the children of the resurrection" get their crowns, and go into power, with Christ the All-Ruler at their head. They are to shepherdize, and deal with the nations, and with all that make up the nations, as unerring and immortal kings and priests, to direct, instruct, and feed them with all the loving care of angels, but with "a rod of iron" in their hands to enforce docility, obedience, and unreserved surrender to all the laws and requirements of the Lord God Almighty. And under this reign shall be fulfilled what the prophets have prophesied, and sung in golden numbers, about the peace and blessedness which is in reserve for this sin-hurt and long downtrodden inheritance of man. You may call it Judaism, if you like ; you may sneer at it as fantastical conceit; you may denounce it as a carnal dream; you may brand it as heresy; but it is nevertheless the truth of God, to which you, and I, and all men, are inexorably bound; and which has every prospect of becoming experimental fact before the century approaching has passed away. I hail its coming, and I bid it welcome, as the great hope and regeneration of our depraved and misgoverned world.

5. *The completion of this Resurrection promotes the subjects of it to a transcendent glory.* Saintship means

honor. It is not so in this present world. The greatest of the Apostles, with all his great achievements and sublime experiences, was compelled to say, "If in this life only we have hope in Christ, we are of all men the most miserable." (1 Cor. 15:19.) The great Master of all told his disciples from the beginning, "If ye were of the world, the world would love his own; but because ye are not of the world, but I have chosen you out of the world, therefore the world hateth you." (Jno. 15:19.) The unregenerate heart does not like the Gospel philosophy and the Gospel requirements; and whilst it continues unregenerate, it has no favors for those who defend and live it, and insist on its acceptance as the only hope for man. Hence the history of the Church, wherever it has been truest, purest, and most itself, is a *Book of Martyrs*. But "the resurrection of the just" brings the people of God their compensation. "*Blessed and holy is he that hath part in the Resurrection the First! Over these the Second Death has no power, but they shall be priests of the God and of the Christ, and reign with him a thousand years.*" Analyze a little the exultant statement.

First of all, they are partakers of *resurrection*, the first resurrection, the blessed resurrection. Not all of them actually suffer death. Such of them as are alive, and remaining, and ready, when the time comes, are "caught up," translated, carried off into the resurrection life, without dying at all. But the translation in those instances is the equivalent of the resurrection. It is the same change to incorruption and immortality, not from the grave indeed, but from mortal life, and so is included in the one term, which means, that, to all of them alike, a power is vouchsafed which strikes from every one of them forever every vestige of the old slavery to corruption, death, or mortal disability. Mere living again, great and wonderful as that is, is the smallest part of the matter. By the prophets, by Christ, and by the apostles, some were recalled to life, resuscitated, made to live again after they were dead, and yet died again as men ordinarily die, the same as if they had never been recalled from death. The living again in this case involves a far " better resurrection," even the renewal of the whole corporeal being, refashioned to a heavenly model, with heavenly qualities, and to a vastly sublimer life than ever was enjoyed before;—a *resurrection,* in which corruption puts on incorruption, dishonor puts on glory, weakness puts on power, and the earthy body becomes a spirit body, lifted quite out of the sphere of the earthly life, and over which neither the first death nor the second has any further power. Having been " accounted worthy to attain that world," they " neither marry nor are given in marriage; neither can they die any more ; for they are *equal unto the angels ;* and are the children of God, being the children of the resurrection." (Luke 20 : 35, 36.)

They are *holy.* They were holy in their lives and aims while they lived in the flesh. They had " the testimony of Jesus " and " the word of God," and confessed it over against a gainsaying world, and held it fast against persecution and death, and willingly suffered the loss of all things, counting them but refuse and offal, rather than let go their confession and hope in Christ Jesus. They were the salt of the earth and the light of the world, the golden candlesticks of eternal truth in the realm of abounding sin and darkness, yet never content with that to which they had attained, but ever reaching forth unto still higher and better things, and, like the Olympian racers, pressed toward the mark for the prize of the high calling of God. Reviled, persecuted, evil spoken of, and accounted the very offscourings of the world, because of their faith, devotion, and self-sacrifice for their Saviour and his cause, they resented not, but counted it all joy, and were exceeding glad, sure that it was working for them a far more exceeding and an eternal weight of glory. Many of them were tortured, not accepting deliverance, that they might obtain the better resurrection; and others had trial of cruel mockings and scourgings, of bonds and imprisonments, were stoned, sawn asunder, tempted, slain with the sword, wandered about in sheepskins and goatskins, being destitute, afflicted, tormented, of whom the world was not worthy. But consecrated and set apart to God as his servants and lightbearers in their earthly lifetime, they are a hundredfold holier now. Released forever from the deathworking law in their fleshly members, their whole being has come under the power of a complete and untemptable sanctification, which sets them apart and conse-

crates them to a sublime and unapproachable
holiness, to which dwellers in the flesh must stand
in greater awe than ever was called for in the
sublimest of earthly kings or the most sacred of
Jewish high-priests;—a holiness which inspires
while it awes, which attracts while it reproves and
condemns, and which lifts and assures those whom
it strikes with humiliation and dread. When Isaiah
saw the Lord sitting upon his Almighty throne,
and the seraphim with covered faces round about
him saying, Holy, Holy, Holy, is the Lord God of
Sabaoth, he fell down and cried, " Woe is me! for
I am undone; because I am a man of unclean lips,
and dwell among a people of unclean lips." (Is.
6 : 1–5.) And something of this same awful holiness is then to appear in the immortal king-priests
of this resurrection, before which men and angels
will veil their eyes in reverence; for in them and
through them God will set his glory among the
nations, and all the earth shall be filled with it.
(Ezek. 29 : 21; Is. 6 : 3.) There is a great and
awful majesty of consecration in a true child of
God even while living and walking here in the
flesh. To the outward eye and carnal view there
is but little that is special. The thoughtful brow,
the sober mien, the dignified behavior, the reserved
and careful utterance, the keeping aloof from the
world's wild pleasures and gayeties, and the solemn
regard for holy names and holy things, along with
a calm and firm confession of the truth as it is in
Jesus, is about all that can be externally noticed.
But his name is in the books of heaven. He is

there enrolled as a celestial citizen and prince.
The angels are ministers and servants to him. He
is allied by regeneration to the blood-royal of eternity. He is marked with the name and sacrament
of the King eternal, immortal, and invisible. He has
upon him an unction from the Holy One, consecrating him for transfiguration to supernal prin-
cipality. He is brother and joint-heir with Him
who sits enthroned at the right hand of eternal
Majesty, and who is presently to be revealed as the
King of kings and Lord of lords. The very ground
on which he treads takes on sacredness from his
presence. The Holy Ghost dwells in his body,
breathes in his breath, walks in his steps, and
speaks in his words. Through that Saviour in
whom he trusts, he is already in a measure a divine man, partaker of the divine nature. All of
which shall be made complete, manifest, and visible when he comes forth in the sublime sanctity
of the First Resurrection; for " *blessed and holy is
he that hath part in the Resurrection the First.*"

Further, *they have very exalted place and occupation.* John saw them seated on thrones. He beheld them endowed with judgeship. He pronounces
them kings and priests. They share in the administrations of government. They reign with Christ.
Their business is to shepherdize nations. These
things all tell of official relations and prerogatives.
They are not mere names and empty titles. The
saints know no sinecures. No meaningless ceremonials or hollow designations find place in
heaven. Nothing is there but substantial realities.

The children of the resurrection are no sham kings, and no mock judges, but everything which these high titles and offices imply. They are not co-regents and co-shepherdizers with Christ, without being and doing what such words import and express. The dignity is transcendently exalted, but it is all real; and the reality of the offices necessitates the reality of the activities which pertain to them. I said that saintship means honor; but saint honor means *duty*, *activity*, *work*, not idleness, not quiescence. There is no heaven for laziness; much less is heaven made up of it. Not for parade badges, but for corresponding services, do the children of this resurrection get their dignities. As kings, they are to fill the places and do the work of kings. As judges, they are to judge and administer justice. As priest-regents, they are charged with the cares and duties of royal priesthood. They not only have the name and place of sovereigns, but they *reign*, as truly and really as ever Saul, or David, or Solomon *reigned*. The end of their salvation is not to sit on clouds and sing psalms, or to luxuriate in the idle bliss of an eternal languor or ecstasy. They are redeemed and glorified for sublime offices and the work pertaining to those offices. The life of Christ in heaven is an intensely busy life. He is administering the Kingdom of the universe. When the present dispensation ends he will deliver up that Kingdom to the Father, and enter upon a new and particular administration of his own, in which the children of the resurrection are to be joined with him, as angels are now associated with him in the adminis-

tration of the Kingdom of the Father, yea, in a
still closer union. The work to be done is the
shepherdizing of the nations with a rod of iron,—
the following up of the victory of the great day of
God Almighty, putting in force the rule of eternal right and justice where the blasting rule of the
Dragon has so perverted things and held disastrous
sway for so many ages. For this they have their
thrones. For this judgment is put into their
hands. For this they are lifted high above all
the infirmities of mortal life. For this they are
perfected in holiness and invested with such divine and awful consecration. And in this they
have their honor and their blessedness. Through
their completed redemption in Christ Jesus they
come into such full harmony with the mind and
will of God, and into such living consociation
with their Redeemer, as to know no higher dignity or joy than to fill out the great administration of reducing the mortal survivors of the
awful day to divine order, and to employ their
immortal energies in tutoring the race from which
they have sprung, till returned to that Paradise
from which it has been in exile for 6000 years.

These are quite different ideas from those usu-
ally entertained about heaven. People spiritualize and explain away the great things of God's
Revelation until the whole matter evaporates in
their hands, and the true Christian hope vanishes
into insipidity and nothingness. They make ado
about getting to heaven, but have lost all understanding of what it means. All the singing, and
longing, and fond anticipation on the subject

really amounts to very little more than a going to
see Jesus, to meet some departed friends, and to
make the acquaintance of some distinguished people who once lived. Crowns are sometimes alluded
to, but they are only fancy crowns, glittering
shadows, empty dreams, badges without corresponding dignities, administrations without subjects, thrones to which nobody is amenable. They
talk of rest; but rest is not heaven, any more than
sleep is life. And the impossibility of finding realities with which to fill up the scriptural images
and descriptions of the final portion of the redeemed, on the part of those who spiritualize the
First Resurrection, is ample evidence of their
tremendous mistake. They, in effect, abolish everything that makes heaven heaven, and all their pictures of futurity are simply the taking of God's
ransomed kings into a world of shadows, to find
their eternal bliss and ever-growing greatness in
the languor of songs, or the dreamy joys of an endless spiritual intoxication, all as impossible as it is
uninviting to rational natures, or to beings invested
with immortal powers. No, the joys and honors
of the children of the resurrection are, that they
are made kings and priests unto God and Christ,
installed and endowed as immortal benefactors of
the nations upon the earth, the unerring lords,
rulers, and invincible shepherds, of a renewing
and renewed world, the everlasting guides, judges,
and potentates of a redeemed race. So the word
before us is; and to this outcome all the promises
in the Book of God are fitted.

LECTURE FORTY-SEVENTH.

Rev. 20 : 7-15. (Revised Text.) And when the thousand years are completed, Satan shall be loosed out of his prison, and shall go out to lead astray the nations which are in the four corners of the earth, Gog and Magog, to gather them together into war, of whom the number (of them) as the sand of the sea.

And they went up on the breadth of the earth [or *land*], and encompassed the citadel of the saints and the beloved city. And there came down fire out of the heaven, and devoured them. And the Devil, who leadeth them astray, was cast into the lake of fire and brimstone, where also the Beast and the False Prophet [are], and shall be tormented day and night to the ages of the ages.

And I saw a great white throne, and the one sitting upon it, from the face of whom fled the earth and the heaven, and place was not found for them.

And I saw the dead ones the great and the small standing in the presence of the throne, and books [or *rolls*] were opened, and another book [or *roll*] which is [that] of the life ; and the dead ones were judged out of the things written in the books according to the works of them.

And the sea gave the dead ones in it, and Death and Hades gave the dead ones in them, and they were judged [Codex Sin. *were condemned*] every one according to their works.

And Death and Hades were cast into the lake of fire.   This is the death the second, the lake of fire.

And if any one was not found written in the book [or *roll*] of the life, he was cast into the lake of fire.

THE reign of Christ and his glorified saints is a reign on or over the earth.   It is a shepherdizing of "the nations," and "nations" belong to the race of man in the flesh.   The Living Ones and Elders sung of being made kings and priests unto God, and proclaimed themselves thus ordained to "*reign on the earth.*" (Chap. 5 : 10.)

This reign is to last a thousand years, a millennium, a chiliad.   Any thousand years is a millennium; but because of the peculiarities and preeminence of this particular thousand years, it has come to be called *The Millennium*, about which there is much unfounded oratory and empty song.

The prevailing modern doctrine is, that the world is to progress, and is progressing, towards a golden age of wisdom, righteousness, liberty, and peace, when error, false worship, vice, wickedness, oppression, and all anti-christianism, will be effectually eradicated, and all nations and peoples brought under the sway of a purified and all-governing Christianity; that this is to be accomplished by the gradual advancement of civilization, science, reforms, political revolutions, the spread of liberality, beneficence, and Christian principles, and the revival of the churches in devotion and missionary zeal, helped by increased measures of the Spirit of God and such providential directions of human affairs as may augment the efficiency of the appliances we now have; and that this is the consummation for which all Christians are to look, labor, and pray, as the glorious outcome of this world's history. This men call *The Millennium*, and about this they dream, and sing, and preach. You will find it in nearly all the popular teachings of our times, just as I have stated it. That it involves some dim elements of truth, may be admitted; but they are so sadly disfigured and overlaid as to make out of them a system of very faulty philosophy, manipulated into an article of faith, wholly unknown to the Church in the first thousand years of its existence, and as much an invention of man as the Romish dogmas of the immaculate conception and the Pope's infallibility. It is certainly not taught in any respectable creed in Christendom. It is not to be found in any of the Church's books of devotion, liturgies, hymnals, or accepted songs, for the first fifteen centuries, including the period of its greatest purity and faithfulness. All the great confessions, either by implication or direct specification, are adverse to it, and unconstruable with it. The old theologians, such as Luther, Melanchthon, Calvin, Knox, Hutter, Hunnins, Quenstedt, and even the Wesleys, are against it. Daniel Whitby, who died in 1726, by whom mainly it was brought into vogue, offered it to the consideration of the learned as only a *hypothesis*, which he considered *new* in his day. And the Scriptures everywhere, on every principle of just interpretation, negative and contradict it. The Church, in its very name and divine designation, is an *Ecclesia*, a body called out from the rest of mankind, with the majority ever outside of itself. By every saying and fore-showing of the Saviour, it lies under the cross for the whole period of its earthly career, and from that state is never lifted this side of the resurrection. The tares and the wheat occupy the same field, and both grow together till the harvest, which is the end of the age, the termination of the present dispensation. Everywhere the last days are painted as the worst days, and men as waxing worse and worse till the end comes. And all the precepts and admonitions divinely given to the Church with reference to the coming again of the Lord Jesus, are such as to render it impossible for them to be kept by any people of any generation believing that a thousand years would have to pass before that coming could take place. I therefore arraign all such teaching as full of chiliastic error, and as one of those subtle, plausible, but delusive insinuations of the great deceiver, by which God's people are beguiled from the truth to his ruinous lies.

I. Notice then the Scriptural teachings with regard to what is called the Millennium.

1. It is a period of "a thousand years," dating from the overthrow of the Beast and his confederates, in the battle of the great day of God Almighty, the casting of him and the False Prophet into the lake of fire, and the binding and locking up of Satan in the Abyss. I understand these to be literal years, the same as all other dates given

in this Book. The year-day interpreters, to be
consistent with themselves, must needs lengthen
out this period to at least three hundred and sixty
thousand years, which is a most astonishing elon-
gation of the "*little while*" and the "*quickly*" in
which Christ promised that he would come again.

2. These thousand years begin only after this
present world, αιων, *age*, or dispensation is closed.
The intent of the Church period is stated to be the
gathering together of an elect, the taking out of a
people for the name of the Lord, the development
and qualification of a particular number of the
human family to be Christ's immortal king-priests.
That object being attained, all the present arrangements terminate. There is not a command to
preach, make disciples, baptize, observe the Eu-
charistic supper, or anything else peculiar to the
Church, which is not limited in its own specific
terms to the coming again of Christ to avenge
his people, and judge his enemies. Such a coming
was shown us before the introduction of these
thousand years; but no such coming is shown us
at their termination. A fiery judgment is there,
and a great white throne of terrific adjudication
upon the unholy dead, but not a word about any
coming of Christ either for or with his people, any
gathering together of his elect, any taking of the
eagle watchers to where he is, any coming as he
was seen going up from Mount Olivet, or any
coming whatever. The fact that the saints appear
on thrones, in the blessedness and holiness of
resurrection life and glory, at the beginning of

this period, and that they reign through it, demon-strates that Christ's coming to raise his saints to glory, give them their rewards, and thus end this dispensation, has then already taken place. This Millennium, therefore, lies altogether on the further side of that occurrence; and the present Church, so far from finding an earthly blooming time in it, does not get into it at all, except in the immortal kinghoods and priesthoods of the children of the resurrection.

3. The so-called Millennium brings with it an altogether different dispensation from that under which we now live. During the whole course of the present order of things, Satan is loose and ac-tive in his work of leading astray; but he is bound, locked up in the Abyss, and not allowed to enter the world at all, either personally, or with any of his agents, for all this thousand years. The great work and office of the Church now is to preach the Gospel to every creature, and to wit-ness for Christ to an adverse and gainsaying world; but there is not one word said about any such office in mortal hands during all that long period. In its stead, however, there is to be a shepherd-izing of the nations with a rod of iron, an authori-tative and invincible administration of right and justice on the part of immortal king-priests, and a potent disciplining of men and nations far beyond anything which the mere preaching of the Gospel ever has wrought or ever was intended to do for earthly society. Now the sovereignty of the earth is in the hands of the Dragon, moulded by his in-

fluence, and not at all under the command of
saints; but then it is to be exclusively in the hands
of the Lord of lords and his immortal king-priests.
Now we can only beseech men in Christ's stead to
be reconciled to God; then they will be compelled
to take the instructions given them, to serve with
fear and rejoice with trembling, to kiss, give
the required adoration to the Son, or perish from
the way. (Ps. 2 : 10–12.) Now it is left to men's
option to serve God or not, with nothing to interfere with their choice but the judgment to come;
then they will be obliged to accept and obey his
laws, or be smitten and blasted on the spot.

The present is the period of God's mercy and
long-suffering; that will be the period of prompt
and rigid administration, when sentence against
an evil work will be executed speedily. Now the
dutiful and obedient are obliged to suffer, to endure manifold wrongs, and to wait for their reward
till the resurrection of the just; but "then shall
the righteous flourish" in proportion to their
righteousness, and they "shall go forth and grow
up as calves of the stall," "and the work of righteousness shall be peace, and the effect of righteousness quietness and assurance for ever." (Is. 32 : 17.)
Now it is a hard and self-sacrificing thing to be a
saint, justly made hard because of the transcendent
dignity and glory to be gained; but then the difficulty and hardship will be on the other side, so
that people can scarcely help being what they
ought to be, and sin will be embarrassed with
greater disadvantages than a life of faith has ever

been.   Thus, in every particular, the dispensation
of things will then be wholly changed from what
it is now.

4. The general condition of the earth, and man
upon it, will then also be vastly improved.   We
cannot speak with definiteness; but all the inti-
mations show that this whole terrestrial economy
will then be far on in the process of that "regeneration" and renewal of which the Saviour speaks
(Matt. 19 : 28), and in which "the creation"—"the
whole creation"—"shall be delivered from the
bondage of corruption into the glorious liberty
of the children of God." (Rom. 8 : 21, 22.)   Great
and mighty changes in the configuration of the
earth were shown in the visions of the judgment-
time preceding this thousand years,—changes in
the relations of sea and land,—changes in the
mountains, hills, and islands,—changes in the atmospheric heavens,—changes in the sun, moon,
and stars,—changes which must needs alter the
whole climate, fruitfulness, and habitability of the
earth.   As it is the time when "God shall judge
the people righteously and govern [shepherdize]
the nations upon earth," so it is the time when
"the earth shall yield her increase," and when the
nations shall "be glad and sing for joy." (Ps. 77.)
As it is the time when "the Lord bindeth up the
breach of his people," so it is the time when
"rivers and streams of waters shall be upon every
high mountain and every hill," and "the increase
of the earth shall be fat and plenteous," and "the
light of the moon shall be as the light of the sun,

and the light of the sun shall be sevenfold, as the
light of seven days." (Isaiah 30 : 18–26.) The
physical condition of man will be greatly amelior-
ated. " The inhabitant shall not say, I am sick."
(Is. 33 : 24.) Life will be wonderfully prolonged.
" There shall be no more thence an infant of days,
nor an old man that hath not filled his days."
One dying at the age of a hundred years will die
so young only as a judgment for sin, and will be
accounted as having died a child at that great age.
The days of a man are to be as the days of a tree,
as in the antediluvian world. (See Isaiah 65 : 20–23.)
Indeed we read of no deaths during this thousand years, except those which occur by reason of
transgression and disobedience. The population
of the world will have been greatly thinned down
by the various judgments, removals, and plagues
which precede this Millennium ; but " instead of
the fathers shall be the children, who may be
made princes in all the earth" (Ps. 45: 16) ; and a
blessed and happy fruitfulness shall be upon the
race of humanity, as well as in the whole system
of nature, so that by the end of the thousand
years, even the remote corners of the world will be
able to muster people as multitudinous as the sands
of the sea. It will not yet be the eternal state,
called " the new earth," in which there is no more
sin, nor death, nor curse, nor tears ; but it will be
a mighty stride toward it, and the stage next to it.
The mental, moral, social, and political condition
of the people who then live will necessarily be like
heaven itself, compared with the order of things

which now prevails; for they shall be shepherded
by Jesus and his immortal co-regents, and "the
deaf shall hear the words of the book, and the eyes
of the blind shall see out of obscurity and darkness; the meek also shall increase their joy in the
Lord, and the poor among men shall rejoice in the
Holy One of Israel" (Is. 29 : 18, 19); "and wisdom
and knowledge shall be the stability of the times
and the strength of salvations." (Is. 33 : 6.)

5. The ending of this period will not be the ending of the blessedness which it introduces. The
years terminate, but what it begins to realize of
the new heavens and earth abides. What marks
the end of the thousand years, and distinguishes
it from the years that succeed, is not a cessation
of the heavenly order that has been established.
Christ and his saints do not then cease to reign
over the nations. Men do not cease to live in the
flesh. The kingdom come does not then recede,
or cease to be the same enduring and everlasting
kingdom. The earth is not disturbed in that
wherein it has advanced toward its complete "regeneration." But that which marks the end of
the thousand years, and divides it off from the
eternal state which follows, is the letting of Satan
loose again for a little time, the testing of the
loyalty and devotion of the nations which have
experienced these high favors, the rebellion of
Gog and Magog, the destruction of the rebels by
fire from heaven, the casting of Satan into the
final hell, the calling up of all the wicked dead to
judgment and final doom, and the putting forth of

what further touches are requisite to complete "the restitution of all things."

II. Notice then more particularly what immediately follows this thousand years.

1. *The Devil is let loose.* He who lets him loose is, of course, the same who bound him, and sealed him in the prison of the Abyss. God uses even the wickedest of beings, and overrules the worst depravity, to his own good and gracious ends. He allows Satan liberty, and denies him liberty, and gives him liberty again, not because the Devil or the Devil's malice is necessary to him, but to show his power to bring good out of evil, to make even the worst of creatures praise him, and to turn their very wickedness to the furtherance of the purposes they would fain defeat.

It seems like a great pity, after the world has rested for a thousand years, that this arch-enemy of its peace should again be let loose upon it. But there seems to be some sort of necessity for it. The statement to John was, that "he *must* be loosed a little time" (v. 3). Some interest of righteousness and moral government renders it proper that he should be allowed this last limited freedom. If for nothing else, it is not unimportant that he should have this opportunity to prove how little an imprisonment of a thousand years had served to change him, or reform his malignity. Even the Devil is granted a final trial to make a better record to himself, if so minded. But neither judgment nor mercy has the least effect. He is, and remains to the last, the same depraved and wicked being, and employs even the little time of freedom before he is cast into perdition in tempting, seducing, and deceiving the happy and peaceful world. Perhaps, too, it was necessary for the millennial nations to be taught that, even after having been so far redeemed as to live a thousand years of holy obedience, they still are unable to stand without the special help and grace of Almighty God. At any rate, this brief period of Satan's last freedom proves, that he is still Satan, and that man is still man, after a thousand years of bonds and imprisonment for the one, and a thousand years' experience of next thing to Paradise for the other; the Devil being just as eager to tempt and deceive, and man liable to be tempted and deceived. Nor can it be of small account to the after ages, or for the generations to whom it is foretold, that the full demonstration of these facts should be made before things are finally settled into the eternal state. Hence Satan is let loose for a little time.

2. *He seduces Gog and Magog into rebellion.* He does not send forth this time to " the kings of the earth," for there are then no mortal kings to be led astray, but he goes direct to the people, insinuates his malice against the rule under which the King of kings has placed the nations, and seeks to persuade them into an attempt to overthrow it. To those who dwell in the outskirts and darker places of the earth, he wends his sullen way. He made his first attempt in Eden by assailing the

weaker and more compliant vessel; and this is his method in his last.

Just who Gog and Magog are we may not be able to tell. A thousand years of uninterrupted peace and prosperity are likely to make great changes in the distribution and locations of peoples. But the allusion to the "corners of the earth" as the regions whence these rebels come, sufficiently indicates that they are among the hindermost of peoples and the least advanced and cultured among the millennial nations. It has taken more than a thousand years to develop the civilization which marks the better portions of the present population of the globe; and a thousand years, even of millennial tutelage, would not avail to bring up the darker and more degraded sections to a very exalted height. And among these ruder peoples Satan finds the pliant materials for a new and last revolt. Jerome and Theodoret identify Gog and Magog with "the Scythian nations, fierce and innumerable, who live beyond the Caucasus and the lake Mæotis, and near the Caspian Sea, and spread out even onward to India." The Koran does the same, and represents them as barbarians of the North, who are somehow restrained until the last period of the world, when they are to swarm forth toward the South in some great predatory irruption, only to be hurled into Gehenna fire. It is doubtful whether we can get beyond this by any ethnic or geographic inquiries in the present state of human knowledge. It is also questionable whether this post-millennial Gog and Magog are the same described by Ezekiel. (37 : 1–14.) They may be the same, or the one may be the type of the other; but in either case the reference is to peoples lying outside of the more civilized world, among whom the old Devil influence lingers longest, and hence the most susceptible to these new instigations. At least Satan succeeds in rendering them dissatisfied with the holy rule of God's glorified saints, and induces them to believe that they can successfully throw it off and crush it out, as the deluded kings under the Antichrist were persuaded a thousand years before. How he does this we are not told; but under him they come forth in swarming myriads, enter the same holy land, and compass about the citadel of the saints and the beloved city, in the vain hope of wresting the dominion from its immortal possessors.

3. *A terrible disaster ensues.* A madder thing than Gog and Magog's attempt was never undertaken upon earth. It is simply a march into the jaws of death, for no rebellion against the kings who then hold the reins of government can be tolerated. The insane war is quickly terminated. One brief sentence tells the fearful story: " *There came down fire out of the heaven and devoured them.*" When Israel was encamped in the wilderness, a guard of Levites was set about the tabernacle, and the command to them was : " *The stranger that cometh nigh shall be put to death.*" (Numb. 1 : 51.) So a guard of immortal king-priests keep the ways to the throne and temple of Jehovah in that day, and the presumptuous dupes of Satan's last decep\

tion who dare to approach with hostile intent, are instantly hurled to a fiery destruction. Not a man of them escapes.

4. *Satan meets his final perdition.* He was imprisoned in the Abyss before; but he is now "cast into the lake of fire and brimstone, where also the Beast and the False Prophet [are]." When the Saviour was on earth, he discoursed to his disciples about an " everlasting fire, prepared for the Devil and his angels." (Matt. 25:41.) This is it; and this is the time when he for whom it is prepared first feels those terrific flames.

Thus ends the last rebellion ever seen upon this planet,—the last sin, and the last deaths, that ever occur in this dwelling-place of man.

III. Notice now what happens to "the rest of the dead," who did not have part in the first resurrection.

1. *A great white throne appears.* A similar throne was beheld by John at the commencement of the great judgments which precede the Millennium. (Rev. 4:2-6.) That was set in the heaven; where this is set we are not told. That had a rainbow over it, to indicate fulfilment of covenant promises; this is naked, for it has no hopes to offer, no covenant of good to fulfil. Out of that proceeded lightnings, thunders, and voices, indicative of revolutionary judgments upon the living world; to this nothing is ascribed but *greatness* and *whiteness,* indicative of immeasurable power, and of pure, complete, unmingled, and invincible justice.

There is no more probation on the part of those against whom its adjudications issue, and hence no further threatenings of coming judgment, as in lightnings and thunder. Around that first throne were sub-thrones, occupied by associate judges, and with it were conjoined Living Ones, taking part in the administrations, for they are varied and mingled, both as to kinds and subjects, and many find occupation in them; here the throne is one only, for the administration is of but one kind, summary, direct, and having respect to but one class. Seven burning torches, representing the seven Spirits of God, were with that throne, because its adjudications were to be partly gracious and remedial, as well as retributive, toward those with whom it dealt; this is accompanied with nothing gracious, for its dispensations are purely retributive, and only damning to what they strike. That throne had before it a glassy sea, pure and crystalline, like a grand celestial pavement, indicative of a place of blessed heavenly refuge, for it was about to exalt many to glory; here there is no celestial landing-place, no platform of heavenly peace, for it has no salvations to dispense. In connection with the first throne there was singing, joyful exultation, the giving of mighty praises to God and the Lamb, for it was the setting in of an administration which was to bring saints to their consummated redemption and rewards; here there is not a song, not a voice of gladness, not a note of exultation, for it is simply and only the administration of retributive justice, which consigns the unsanctified to their final perdition, and which has nothing whatever of gladness about it.

The presentations in both instances correspond to the proceedings issuing from them, and the one helps to explain the other. Indeed they are counterparts of one another,—the right hand administrations and the left hand administrations, the morning and the evening, of the great Day of Judgment viewed as a whole.

2. *This throne has an awful Occupant.* Of course it is the same beheld in the first instance. There is no name, no figure, no shape, in either case; but only an awful, mysterious, and composed presence, which can be nothing less than the One, unnamable, indescribable, eternal Godhead. If it were the Lord Jesus Christ, simply as the God-man, he would appear in some definite form, as in every other instance. He is indeed the Judge, to whom all judgment is committed, and he does the judging in this instance; but he does it under and in the presence of the enthroned Godhead of the Father, the Son, and the Holy Ghost, and not as the absolute and eternal King over all things. In the first instance, the Sitter on the throne had a particular appearance,—an appearance like to a jasper and a sardine stone, a reddish, crystalline brilliancy, like pure and smokeless flames, attractive even in its awfulness; here there is nothing but the naked presence of almightiness, so dreadful that the very earth and heavens seem to flee into nothingness before it. The earth and heaven do not literally fly away and disappear.

Similar language was used in chapter 6:14; but the earth still continued afterwards. And here, in the subsequent verses, the sea is still in its place; and in the next chapters nations are still found inhabiting the earth. (21:24; 22:2.) It is simply the intensification of the description of the awfulness and majesty of the Sitter upon the throne that is thus expressed, signifying that almightiness by which all the creations and changes in the universe are effected, and who here assumes his eternal power to dispose of his enemies forever, and to put the last finishing touches upon the great *re-genesis* of things. And this infinite, repellent awfulness is a further indication that there is absolutely nothing of hope for those objects on which the adjudications now fall.

3. *A resurrection occurs.* No trumpet is sounded; for the sounding of the trumpet is for those in covenant with the King, as his armies and friends; but these are not his people nor his friends. There is simply the going forth of eternal power, into the sea, into the graves, into Hades, into all the depositories of the souls and bodies of the unholy dead, and all the vast multitudes in them suddenly stand in the presence of the throne. Not one of them that ever lived and died, from the beginning of the world till then, save and except the Beast and the False Prophet, but is in that unblest congregation. "The great and the small," the big sinners and the little sinners, rulers and subjects, nobles and plebeians, the learned and the ignorant, the refined and the vulgar,

the civilized and the barbarous, emperors and beggars, all alike are there. We read of no white robes, no spotless linen, no palms, nothing but naked sinners, before the naked majesty of enthroned Almightiness, awaiting their eternal doom.

4. *Books are opened.* Heaven keeps record of all the deeds of men, and of all the thoughts and feelings under which they act. Myriads of human beings have lived and died of whom the world knows nothing; but the lives they lived, the deeds they wrought, the thoughts and tempers they indulged, still stand written where the memory of them cannot perish. Not a human being has ever breathed earth's atmosphere whose career is not traced at full length in the books of eternity. Yes, O man! O woman! whoever you may be, your biography is written. An unerring hand has recorded every item, with every secret thing. There is not an ill thought, a mean act, a scene of wrong in all your history, a dirty transaction, a filthiness of speech, or a base feeling that ever found entertainment in your heart, but is there described in bold hand, by its true name, and set down to your account, to be then brought forth for final settlement, if not clean blotted out through faith in Christ's blood before this present life of yours is ended. And if no other books are to be thought of, the book of your own conscience, and the book of God's remembrance, will then and there attest your every misdeed and ill-desert. Think, ye that fear not God, and make nothing

of trampling his laws, how your case will stand when those books are opened!

But there is " *another book, which is that of the life,*"—the roll-book of the regenerate in Christ Jesus,—the register of the washed and sanctified through faith in his redeeming blood. This must needs be opened too; for many there be whose lives are fair and honest, who spend their days in conscientious purity, who live and die in the persuasion that they have fulfilled all the requirements of virtue, but who have never experienced the regenerating power of the new creation, who have never felt the need of atonement by the propitiation of a crucified Saviour, and who have disdained to build on the merit and righteousness of the one only Mediator as the sole hope of diseased and guilty humanity. Exalted as they may have been in their own goodness and morality, they have not believed on the only begotten Son of God, and therefore have not life, and so are not written in the book of life. The records of their own deeds is therefore not enough for the determination of their proper place and standing. Men may appear well in these, and still not be prepared to pass the final inquisition. There is another and still mightier question in the case, and that is whether they have come to a regenerate and spiritual life through faith in Christ Jesus. Therefore the book of life must be opened too, and its testimony brought into the decision. If the name of any one is not on that roll, no matter how virtuously and honestly he may have lived, there is no help for him; for only " he that believeth on the Son hath everlasting life." (Jno. 3 : 36.)

5. But *judgment is given as the works have been.* There is just gradation in the sorrows of the lost, as well as in the rewards of the righteous. If there is anything in any case to modify the guilt of sinners, or in any measure to paliate their deficiencies and crimes, the plain intimation is that every just allowance shall be made. Though all the finally condemned go into one place, they do not all alike feel the same pains, or sink to the same depths in those dreadful flames. But the mildest hell is nevertheless *hell*, and quite too intolerable for any sane being to be content to make experiment of it.

The judgment of these people according to these books is, in each instance, a judgment of condemnation, whether to the lesser or the greater damnation. There is no account of the name of any one of them being found in the book of life; " and if any one was not found written in the book of the life, he was cast into the lake of fire." Not one of them is adjudged place with the " blessed and holy," or his resurrection would not have been deferred till now. And the Codex Sinaiticus, one of the very oldest and best of the ancient manuscripts of the New Testament, here reads: " The sea gave the dead ones in it, and Death and Hades gave the dead ones in them, and THEY WERE CONDEMNED, EVERY ONE, *according to their deeds.*"

6. And *sentence is followed with immediate execution.* When the Beast and the False Prophet were taken,

they "were cast alive into the lake of fire which burneth with brimstone." (Chap. 19: 20.) A thousand years afterward, when Satan proved himself the same deceiver he always was, he "was cast into the lake of fire and brimstone." And into that same "lake of fire" all the condemned ones in this judgment are hurled. What that "lake of fire" is I cannot tell, I do not know, and I pray God that I may never find out. That it is a *place*, everything said about it proves. People in corporeal life, as these condemned ones are, must needs have locality. That it is a place of woe, pain, and dreadful torment, is specifically stated, and is the chief idea in every image of the description. What God adjudges a just punishment for the wickedness of the great head of all evil, for having ruined many of the sublimest creatures in heaven, and for the mischiefs, impieties, and desolations wrought in our world by more than six thousand years' unremitted exertions against the peace of man and the gracious purposes of God, certainly must involve a length, and breadth, and depth, and height of misery at which the universe may well stand aghast. He who understands it best, calls it "a lake of fire and brimstone," and I do not know what mortal man can tell us better. If perchance it be not material fire, or the brimstone which feeds it be not the article which commerce handles, it still is fire of some sort, fed with its proper fuel,—*fire* which can take hold on body and spirit,—*fire* which preys on the whole being, whether clothed with corporeity or not,—*fire* kindled and kept alive by almighty justice, and a great lake of it, commensurate with the infinite holiness of an infinite law. It is called " *The Second Death*." Hence some think it means extinction of existence, annihilation, a cremation of body and spirit, which leaves no ashes after it. But the Beast and the False Prophet were in that death for more than a thousand years, and at the end of that time the implication seems to be that they are still alive. Concerning those who are compelled to make proof of that death, the specific statement is, " *they shall be tormented day and night, to the ages of the ages*." This does not look like either annihilation or final restoration. Nor is Death an extinction of all existence. The first death is a killing of the body, a mutilation of the being, but not an extinction of it. If death is the equivalent of annihilation, then these resurrected ones are condemned and punished for the crimes and defects of some other beings than themselves, and are not the people who did what is written in these books. The first death is a terrible mutilation and degradation, especially to a wicked man ; though not a blotting out of his being and identity. "The Second Death" must needs be still more terrible and disastrous, for it is a more inward fret ; but not therefore a reduction to absolute nothingness. Angels are regarded in all theology as immortal by inherent constitution ; yet wicked angels are under the horrors of this Second Death. The children of the better resurrection are " *as the angels of God ;*" so these partakers of the " resurrec-

tion of damnation" are *as the Devil and his angels.*
If " the lake of fire" is not annihilation to one, so
neither is it to the other. But it is Death, and it
is torment; and there is every reason to believe
that it is eternal. It is " to the ages of the ages."
Confirmed depravity cannot be cured where no
means of grace are; neither can those cease to sin
whose whole nature has been turned to sin. And
if there can be no end of the sinning, how can
there be an end of the suffering? Remorse cannot
die out of a spirit ever conscious of its self-imposed
damnation! Therefore, " *their worm dieth not, and
the fire is not quenched.*" (Mark 9 : 44, 48.)

And Death and Hades, here viewed as if they
were personal beings, share the same fate. They,
of course, cease to be. There is nothing more of
temporal death or of the place of departed spirits
after this. They are not personal beings, hence
their casting into "the lake or fire" is the end of
them; but, conceived of as persons, they are con-
signed to exactly the same eternal punishment
with the other wicked. They are the products of
sin, and they share the doom of what produced
them. And thus, in an ever-burning Hell, from
which there is no more deliverance, all the enemies of God and his Christ find themselves at
last.

And now, in the presence of these awful verities,
what shall I say to those who know it all, yet go
deliberately on in ways which can have no outcome
but this Second Death? I look at them, and think;
and the terribleness of their hallucination paralyzes

my utterance. I would fain arouse them to their better senses; but when I speak my intensest words seem but ashes in my mouth in comparison with the alarum for which their situation calls.

Ho, ye unbelieving men,—ye dishonest men,— ye profane men,—ye lewd men and women,—ye slaves of lust and appetite,—ye scoffers at the truth of God,—" *How can ye escape the damnation of hell ?*" (Matt. 23 : 33.) Ye men of business,—ye whose souls are absorbed with the pursuit of gain,—ye people of wealth without riches toward God,—ye passengers on the voyage of life, without prayer, without Church relations, without concern for your immortal good, your God, or the eternity before you,—hear : " *Hell hath enlarged herself, and opened her mouth without measure, and your glory, and your multitude, and your pomp, and your rejoicing, shall descend into it !*" (Is. 5 : 14.) Ye almost Christians, lingering these many years on the margin of the Kingdom, looking in through the gates, but never quite ready to enter them, intending but never performing, often wishing but still postponing, hoping but without right to hope,—the appeal is to you : " *How shall ye escape if ye neglect so great salvation ?* " (Heb. 2 : 2–4.) And ye who call yourselves Christians but have forgotten your covenant promises,—ye Terahs and Lot's wives, who have started out of the place of sin and death but hesitate half way, and stay to look back,—ye baptized Elymases, and Judases, and Balaams, who, through covetousness and feigned words make merchandise of the grace of God,—see ye not that

" *your judgment now of a long time lingereth not, and your damnation slumbereth not !*" (2 Pet. 2 : 3.) And if there be any one oblivious or indifferent toward these great matters,—asleep amidst the dashing waves of coming retribution,—the message is to you : " *What meanest thou, O sleeper? Arise, call upon thy God, if so be that God shall think upon thee, that thou perish not !*" (Jon. 1: 6.) For if any one be not found written in the Book of Life, he must be swallowed up by the Lake of Fire.

LECTURE FORTY-EIGHTH.

Rev. 21 : 1-8. (Revised Text.) And I saw heaven new and earth new : for the first heaven and the first earth are gone, and the sea no longer is.

And I saw the city, the holy, new Jerusalem coming down out of the heaven from God, prepared as a bride adorned for her husband.

And I heard a great voice out of the throne, saying, Behold, the Tabernacle of God, with the men [or *mankind*], and he shall tabernacle with them, and they shall be his people, and he, the God with them, shall be their God.

And God shall wipe away every tear from their eyes ; and death shall no longer be, neither sorrow, neither crying, neither pain, shall any longer be ; because the first things are gone.

And the Sitter upon the throne said, Behold, new I make everything. And he saith, Write, because these words are faithful and true.

And he said to me, They are accomplished. I am the Alpha and Omega, the Beginning and the End. I to him that thirsteth will give out of the fountain of the water of the life freely. He that over-cometh shall inherit these things ; and I will be God to him, and he shall be son to me ; but the cowardly, and unbelieving, and polluted, and murderous, and fornicators, and sorcerers, and idolaters, and all the false, their part [shall inherit] in the lake burning with fire and brimstone, which is the death the second.

HUMANITY was created and constituted a self-multiplying order of existence,—*a race*,—to which this earth was given as its theatre, posses-sion, and happy home. God created man in his own image ; male and female created he them,

and said to them, Be fruitful, and multiply, and
replenish the earth, and subdue it, and have dominion over it. When sin first touched man, it
found him thus constituted and domiciled. Had
the spoliations of sin never disturbed him, humanity, as a race, must needs have run on forever,
and been the happy possessor of the earth forever.
Anything else would be a contravention and
nullification of the beneficent Creator's intent
and constitution with regard to his creature man.
Meanwhile came the fall, through the Serpent's
malignity; and then a promise of redemption by
the Seed of the woman. If the nature of the fall
was to destroy the existence of man as a race, and
to dispossess him of his habitation and mastery of
the earth, the nature and effect of the redemption
must necessarily involve the restitution and perpetuation of the race, as such, and its rehabili-
tation as the happy possessor of the earth; for if
the redemption does not go as far as the consequences of sin, it is a misnomer, and fails to be redemption. The salvation of any number of individuals, if the race is stopped and disinherited, is
not the redemption of what fell, but only the gathering up of a few splinters, whilst the primordial
jewel is shattered and destroyed, and Satan's mischief goes further than Christ's restoration.

I therefore hold it to be a necessary and integral
part of the Scriptural doctrine of human redemption, that our race, as a self-multiplying order of
beings, will never cease either to exist or to possess the earth.

There is a notion, bred from the morbid imagination of the Middle Ages, which has given birth to many a wild poetic dream, which has much influenced the translators of our English Bible, which has unduly tainted religious oratory, song, and even sober theology, and which still lingers in the popular mind as if it were an article of the settled Christian creed, that the time is coming when everything that is, except spiritual natures, shall utterly cease to be, the earth consume and disappear, the whole solar and sidereal system collapse, and the entire physical universe vanish into nothingness. How this can be, how it is to be harmonized with the promises and revealed purposes of God, wherein it exalts the perfections of the Deity, there is not the least effort to show. The thing is magniloquently asserted, and that is quite enough for some people's faith, though sense, reason, and Revelation be alike outraged.

There is indeed to be an "*end of the world.*" The Bible often refers to it. But men mistake when they suppose *the world* spoken of in such passages to be the earth as a planet. Three different words have our translators rendered "*world :*" γη, which means the earth proper, the ground, this material orb which we inhabit; κοσμος, which means what constitutes the inhabitableness, the ornamentation, beauty, cultivation, external order, *fashion* of the world, but not the substance of the earth as a terraqueous globe; and αιων, which is used more than one hundred times in the New Testament, but always with reference to *time*, duration, eras, dispensations,—a stage or state marking any particular period, long or short, past, present, or future,—the course of things in any given instance, rather than the earth or any theatre on which it is realized. It may be earth or heaven, time or eternity, a material or an immaterial world, it is all the same as to the meaning of the word αιων, which denotes simply the time-measure and characteristics of that particular period or state to which it is applied.* And this is the word used in all those passages which speak of " the end of *the world.*"

---

* " The word αιων appears originally to have denoted *the life which hastes away in the breathing of our breath, life as transitory,* then the *course of life,* in general, *life in its temporal form—an age* or generation—*a space of time, course of time, time as moving,* —time so far as history is accomplished in it. It always includes a reference to the *life, filling time,* or a space of time, as *sœculum* denotes the time in which life passes."—Cremer's *Biblico-Theological Lexicon of New Testament.*

" Κοσμος is the world, *mundus,* in its wide extension; αιων, the age, *sœculum,* the present world, in its distinguishing character, its course, and the estimate to be formed of it."—James Bryce in Bengel's *Gnomon,* Eph. 2: 2.

" Αιων in its primary sense signifies *time,* short or long, in unbroken duration ; essentially time as the condition under which things exist, and the measure of their existence. All that floating mass of thoughts, opinions, maxims, speculations, hopes, impulses, aims, at any time current in the world, which it is impossible to seize and accurately define, but which constitute a most real and effective power, being the moral or immoral atmosphere which at every moment of our lives we inhale, again inevitably to exhale,—all this is included in the αιων."— Trench's *Synonyms of New Testament,* second series, pp. 38–40. It therefore refers to something altogether different from the substance of the earth as a planet.

It is not the end of *the earth*, but the end of a particular time, age, condition, or order of things, with the underlying thought of other orders of things, and perpetual continuity in other forms and ages. *Æons* end, times change, the fashion of the world passeth away,—but there is no instance in all the Book of God which assigns an absolute termination to the existence of the earth as one of the planets, or any other of the great sisterhood of material orbs.

So in those passages which speak of the *passing away* of the earth and heavens (see Matt. 5:18, 24, 34, 35; Mark 13:30, 31; Luke 16:17, 21, 33; 2 Pet. 3:10; Rev. 21:1), the original word is never one which signifies termination of existence, but παρερχομαι, which is a verb of very wide and general meaning, such as *to go* or *come* to a person, place, or point; *to pass*, as a man through a bath, or a ship through the sea; to pass from one place or condition to another, to arrive at, to go through; to go into, to come forward as if to speak or serve. As to time, it means going into the past, as events or a state of things once present giving place to other events and another state of things. That it implies great changes when applied to the earth and heavens is very evident; but that it ever means annihilation, or the passing of things *out of being*, there is no clear instance either in the Scriptures or in classic Greek to prove. The main idea is *transition* not extinction.

Some texts, particularly as they appear in our English Bible, express this change very strongly,

as where the earth and heavens are spoken of as
perishing, being *dissolved*, *flying away* (Is. 34:4;
54:10; Rev. 6:14; 20:10); but the connections
show that the meaning is not cessation of being,
but simply the termination or dissolution of the
present condition of them to give place to a new
and better condition. At least one such *perishing*
of the earth has already occurred. Peter, speaking of the earth and heavens of Noah's time, says:
" *The world that then was being overflowed with water*,
PERISHED." (2 Pet. 3:5, 6.) But what was it that
perished ? Not the earth as a planet, certainly;
but simply the mass of the people, and the condition of things which then existed, whilst the
earth and race continued, and have continued till
now. Equally strong expressions are used with
regard to the destruction or passing away of the
old in the case of one born again to newness of life
in Christ Jesus; but no one therefore supposes
that the bringing of a man from Satan to God is
the annihilation of him. It is simply the change of
his condition and relations. And so in the case
of the earth and heavens; for the same word which
describes the change in the individual man is used
to describe the change to be wrought in the material
world. It is *regeneration*—παλιγγενεσια—in both instances (Matt. 29:28; Tit. 3:5), and therefore not
the putting out of existence in either case. The
dissolving of which Peter is made to speak, is really
a deliverance rather than a destruction. The word
he uses is the same which the Saviour employs where
he says of the colt, " *Loose* him ;" and of Lazarus

when he came forth with his death-wrappings, " *Loose* him, and let him go;" and of the four angels bound at the Euphrates, " *Loose* them;" and of the Devil, " He must be *loosed* a little season." It is the same word which John the Baptist used when he spoke of his unworthiness to *unloose* the Saviour's shoestrings, and which Paul used when he spoke of being " *loosed* from a wife." It is simply absurd to attempt to build a doctrine of annihilation on a word which admits of such applications. The teaching of the Scriptures is, that the creation is at present in a state of captivity, tied down, bound, "not willingly, but by reason of him who hath subjected the same in hope;" and the *dissolving* of all these things, of which Peter speaks, is not the destruction of them, but the breaking of their bonds, *the loosing of them*, the setting of them free again to become what they were originally meant to be, their deliverance. (Compare Romans 8 : 19–23.) And as to the *flying* or *passing away*, of which John speaks, a total disappearance of all the material worlds from the universe is not at all the idea; for he tells us that he afterwards saw " *the sea* " giving up its dead, the New Jerusalem coming down " *out of the heaven*," the Tabernacle of God established among men, and " nations " still living and being healed by the leaves of the Tree of Life.

Great changes in the whole physical condition of the earth and its surrounding heaven are everywhere indicated; but the idea of the extinction of the material universe amid " the wreck of matter and the crush of worlds," is nothing but a vulgar conceit, without a particle of foundation in nature, reason, or Scripture.* Things have no more tendency to annihilation than nothing has a tendency to creation. There is no evidence that a single atom of matter has ever been annihilated, whence analogy would infer that such a thing is not at all in the will or purpose of God. On the contrary, the teaching of Revelation is, that " one generation passeth away, and another generation cometh; but *The Earth abideth forever.*" (Ecc. 1:4; Ps. 15:5; 119:90.) Whatever new cataclysms or disasters are yet to befall this planet, we are assured that they will not be as destructive even as Noah's flood; for God covenanted then, and said: " *I will*

---

* The subject of the perpetuity of the earth was under consideration in a clerical association some years ago, when one of the members pronounced all such ideas wholly *unscriptural*, and said the word of God is full of passages which prove that the earth is to be utterly destroyed, so that it will no more be. He was pressed to point out even one. He then referred to Psalm 46:2: " Therefore will we not fear, *though the earth be removed.*" This, he said, proved conclusively that the earth is to pass away altogether. He was asked to read a little further, when he gave the parallelism, " *and though the mountains be carried into the midst of the sea.*" To which the remark was somewhat facetiously, but very effectively, made, " Brother, that don't appear to be anything more than *a large landslide.*" The positive objector had no more passages to produce.

Dr. J. Pye Smith, in his *Geology and Revelation* (p. 161), says: "I cannot but feel astonished that any serious and intelligent man should have his mind fettered with the common—I might call it the vulgar—notion of a proper destruction of the earth. I confess myself unable to find any evidence for it in nature, reason, or Scripture."

*not again curse the ground any more for man's sake,
neither will I again smite any more every living thing,
as I have done."* (Gen. 8:21, 22.) It is specifically
promised that "the meek shall inherit the earth,"
and that "the righteous shall dwell in it forever."
(Matt. 5:5; Ps. 37:9, 11, 29; Is. 60:21; Rom.
4:13.) And if the righteous are to inhabit it forever, it must exist forever. The kingdom of which
Daniel prophesied is to be an everlasting kingdom,
which shall stand forever. That kingdom is located "under the whole heaven," and takes in
among its subjects "peoples, nations, and languages," and has its seat upon the earth. (Dan.
2:44; 7:14, 27.) But if the earth is to have an
indestructible kingdom, it must itself be indestructible. John describes the sovereignty of this
world as finally assumed by the Lord, even Christ,
who is to hold and exercise it to the ages of the
ages. (Rev. 11:15.) But how can Christ reign forever in a world which is presently to cease to be?
God has specifically and repeatedly covenanted
and promised a certain portion of the earth to a
certain people for "an everlasting possession"
(Gen. 48), in which they are to "dwell, even they,
and their children, and their children's children,
forever" (Ezek. 37:25), and not cease from being
a nation before him forever (Jer. 31:36). How
can this be fulfilled if the earth is to be annihilated?

There is also a peculiar consecration upon the
earth which makes it revolting to think of its
being handed over to oblivion. The footsteps of

the Son of God upon its soil, the breathing of its atmosphere by his lungs, the saturation of its mould with his sweat, and tears, and blood, the wearing of its dust upon his sacred person, the warming of its fluids in his arteries, ought to be enough to satisfy us that neither the Devil nor destruction shall ever possess it. It is the place where God's only begotten Son was born and reared, and where he taught, and slept, and suffered, and died. It is the territory on which Divine Love and Mercy have poured out the costliest sacrifice the universe has ever known. It is the chosen theatre of the most momentous deeds that ever attracted the adoring interest of angels. It has furnished the death-place, the grave, the scene of the bruising and the triumph of Jesus Christ. And how can it ever be delivered over to everlasting nothingness? Perish what may, a world so consecrated can never be blotted out, or cease to be one of the most cherished orbs in God's great creation.

And with the continuity and redemption of the earth, goes the perpetuation and redemption of *the race*. For why is the one continued if not for the other? As surely as "the earth abideth forever," so surely shall there be eternal generations upon it. Paul speaks with all boldness of "*the generations of the age of the ages.*" (Eph. 3 : 21.) After the termination of the present Æon, he contemplates many more Æons, even an Æon of Æons; and those interminable years he fills up with generations and generations. The covenant which God made with Noah, and all living things, the sign and seal of which still appears in almost every summer shower, is, by its own terms, unending in duration; but that duration is at the same time described as filled in with *unceasing genera- tions.* (Gen. 8 : 22, 23; 9 : 8–16.) Joel tells of gen- erations and generations for Jerusalem through all that "*forever*" in which cleansed and ransomed Judah is to dwell in the covenanted land. (Joel 3 : 20, 21; Ezek. 37 : 25, 26.) Eternal generations were certainly provided for when humanity was originally constituted and made the possessor and lord of earth; eternal generations certainly would have been the effect of God's constitution and com- mands had sin not come in to interfere with the wonderful creation; and as surely as Christ's re- demption-work is commensurate with the ruinous effects of the fall, *eternal generations* must necessarily be. Earth and multiplying man upon it surely would never have passed from living fact into mere legend had sin never come in. Much less, then, can they now pass into mere legend, since the new and more costly expenditures of redeeming love have been superadded to the original gifts of cre- ative wisdom and beneficence.

We thus reach the underlying foundations and background of the sublime presentations of the text. The Apostle here beholds the final redemp- tion of our earth and race, the restitution of all things accomplished, the damages, disorders and spoliations of sin repaired, the glorious picture of The Redeemed World.

I. Observe the Scene of that World.

"*Heaven new;*"—not blotted out; not swept into
nothingness; but retouched, changed, renovated,
cleansed, and brightened up from all its old disorders and imperfections. The heaven over us now is
very charming and beneficent. How beautiful and
blessed the never-ceasing procession of sun, and
moon, and stars, and clouds, and seasons, and
days, and nights, and showers, intermingled as
they are with heat and cold, storm and calm,
gloom and brightness! This old garment of
things is still full of rejoicing, and glory, and
scenes and themes to touch, inspire, and lift, and
discipline, and make glad the heart. What, then,
will that new investment be, to which it is to give
place! We cannot describe the meteorology of
that new heaven; but it will be a heaven which
no more robes itself in angry tempests and men-
acing blackness; nor ever flashes with the thunderbolts of wrath; nor casts forth plagues of hail;
nor rains down fiery judgment; nor gives lurking-
place to the Devil and his angels; nor is disfigured
with dread portents; nor is subject to commotions
breeding terror and disaster to the dwellers under
them. We often look at the blue sky that arches
over us, at the rosy morning's welcome to the king
of day, at the high noon's flood of brightness, at
the mellow glories of the setting sun, at the solemn midnight lit all over with its twinkling star-
gems, and we are thrilled with the perfection and

beauty of Jehovah's works. What, then, shall it be when the great Architect, set to do honor to the love and faithfulness of his only begotten Son, shall put forth his hand upon it the second time, to renew it in a fresh and eternal splendor!

" *And Earth new.*" The earth now is full of ailments and disorders, and in deep captivity to corruption, yet it has much attractiveness. Most men would prefer to stay in it forever, if they could. Ah, this homestead of our fathers for so many generations, carpeted with green and flowers, waving with pleasant harvests and shady trees, girded with glorious mountains, gushing with water-springs, gladdened with laughing brooks, ribboned with rivers that wind in beauty about the rocky promontories, varied with endless hills and valleys, and girthed about with the crystal girdle of the ruffled seas,—these numerous zones, and continents, and islands,—these youthful springtimes bursting out with myriad life under all their dewy steps,—these blazing summer glories,—these gorgeous mellow autumns,—these winters, with their snowy vestments, and glazed streams, and glowing firesides,—and living Nature in its ten thousand forms, singing, and dancing, and shouting, and frisking, and rejoicing all around us,—what pictures, and memories, and histories, and legends, and experiences have we here, to warm our hearts, and stir our souls, and wake our tongues, and put fire and enthusiasm into our thoughts, and words, and deeds! But this is only the old earth in its soiled and work-day garb, where the miseries of a deep, dark, and universal apostasy from God holds sway. Think, then, what its regeneration must bring!—an earth which no longer smarts and smokes under the curse of sin,—an earth which needs no more to be torn with hooks and irons to make it yield its fruits,—an earth where thorns and thistles no longer infest the ground, nor serpents hiss among the flowers, nor savage beasts lay in ambush to devour,—an earth whose sod is never cut with graves, whose soil is never moistened with tears or saturated with human blood, whose fields are never blasted with unpropitious seasons, whose atmosphere never gives wings to the seeds of plague and death, whose ways are never lined with funeral processions, or blocked up with armed men on their way to war, —an earth whose hills ever flow with salvation, and whose valleys know only the sweetness of Jehovah's smiles,—an earth from end to end, and from centre to utmost verge, clothed with the eternal blessedness of Paradise Restored!

And the Sea new, for I take the specification of it here the same as in the third commandment, where it is said, "In six days the Lord made heaven and earth, *the sea,* and all that in them is." (Ex. 20:11; also Rev. 10:6.) It is not mentioned to indicate for it a different fate from that of heaven and earth, but because it is so conspicuous and peculiar a part of them. The sea is not heaven, neither is it earth; hence in God's enumeration of the first creation-work he mentions heaven, earth, *and sea;* and so in the new creation-

work, we have again heaven, earth, *and sea*. It is
the literal sea, just as the heaven and the earth
are literal; but the non-existence affirmed of it is
the same that is affirmed of the first heaven and
the first earth. In other words, it undergoes the
same *Palingenesia* which they undergo, and comes
forth *a new sea*, the same as the old heaven and
earth come forth a new heaven and earth. There
is renewal, but no annihilation.

Some say there was no sea in the pristine condition of the world, and hence none will be in the
finally redeemed world. But they are mistaken
in both instances. The first chapter of Genesis
tells of the formation of *the seas* contemporaneously
with the formation of *the dry land*. (Gen. 1 : 9, 10.)
When the flood came we are told that " all the
fountains of *the great deep* were broken up," and
that " *the sea* broke forth." (Gen. 7 : 11; Job 38 : 8.)
There must then have been a sea from the beginning. It existed when Adam was in Paradise, as
well as since Noah came out of the ark. And so
there will be a sea in the new world, the same as
a new heaven and a new earth. If not, this is the
only passage in all the word of God that tells us
anything to the contrary. We read of a river in
the new earth, as of rivers in the original Paradise;
and where there are rivers there are seas. When
Christ as the cloud-robed Angel (chap. 10) set his
feet on the earth in the solemn act of claiming and
appropriating it as his own, " He set his right foot
upon the sea," and thus claimed and appropriated
it the same as he claimed and appropriated the

ground.* Many passages also which refer to
Israel and the kingdom of God in the blessed
times to come, distinctly speak of *the sea* as being
turned in their favor, and as taking part in the
general acclaim over the ultimate accomplishment
of the mystery of God. (See Is. 42:10; 60:5, 9;
Ps. 24:2; 96:11; 98:6, 7; 2 Chron. 16:32; Rev.
5:13.) When the time to which the text refers
arrives the present sea "*no longer is*," just as the
first heaven and the first earth "*are gone.*" There
is no more left of the one than of the other, but
likewise no less. Just as much of the sea as of the
earth abideth forever. The *Re-Genesis* touches
both alike, just as the first Genesis. As there is a
renewed eternal heaven and earth, so there is a
renewed eternal sea also, for one is a part of the
other. Then, however, it will be no longer a thing
of danger and dread, but only of beauty, joy, and
blessing. Some of the old Rabbins taught that,
in the new world of Messiah, men shall be able to
walk the surface of the sea with equal ease that
they now walk the earth. Nor is this unlikely;
for the Saviour, as a man, walked on the sea, and
did not sink; and so did Peter also, until his faith
and courage failed him. The regeneration is the
making of Christ's miracles universal. The miracles of Christ were the preintimations and beginning of the great Regeneration to come, and the
new creation is simply those miracles carried out
into universal effect. Why not then also this
with regard to the sea? At any rate it will be

---

* See Vol. II, p. 128.

subdued and rebegotten to Him who maketh *all
things new*, and become a joy and service without
being as now an unmanageable and dangerous
hindrance and barrier.   People only misread the
text, and load themselves with endless perplexities,
when they interpret it to mean the total abolition
of all seas.   As the *old sea* it is abolished, just as
the old heavens and earth; but, as in their case,
it is an abolition which eventuates in a more con-
genial sea, even a *new sea*.

A new City.   Occasion will offer to consider this
when we come to the special vision of it in the
after portions of the chapter; but it here presents
itself as the crown of the regenerated world.   It
is called by the old Hebrew name of *Jerusalem*
(Ἱερουσαλήμ), and not by the Grecised name of the
earthly city (Ἱεροσύλυμα).   If the heaven, the earth,
and the sea be literal, then certainly must this also
be a literal city.   The harlot Woman was finally
developed and embodied in a literal city, and it is
the same with the true Woman.   It is the Bride,
the Lamb's Wife, who appears in this new city for
eternal blessedness, as the old Adultress appeared
in the new Babylon for everlasting destruction.
That was man's glory proudly lifting itself in defiance of heaven; this is the Lamb's glory, graciously descending in benediction to the earth.
That was the consummation of this world's progress, and its end; this is the consummation of the
achievements of divine grace, and its memorial
forever.

It is a *new* city, one which never appeared before,

one of which all other cities are but the poor pre-intimations, and one as compared with which all present cities will sink out of mind and memory. It is new in its materials, in its size, in its location, in its style, in its permanence, in its moral purity, and in everything characteristic of it. It is heaven-built; jewelled in its foundations, walls, and streets; perfected in everything that is charming and beautiful, "as a bride adorned for her husband;" lighting the nations with its brilliancy, itself ever luminous with the glory of God and the Lamb; the true "Eternal City;"—the imperishable palace of the immortal kings of the ages.

II. OBSERVE THE BLESSEDNESS OF THAT WORLD.

There is a long list of negations, telling the ills from which it brings relief.

Every tear is wiped away. He who dries them off is God himself. Human hands are poor at drying tears. If they succeed in removing one set, others come which they cannot wipe away. Earthly power, however good and kind, cannot go far in the binding up of broken hearts. Only the hand that made the spirit can reach the deep sources of its sorrows, or dry up the streams that issue from them. The springs of grief yield to no other potency. But then his loving Almightiness shall wipe every tear. " As one whom his mother comforteth, so will I comfort you, and ye shall be comforted," saith the Lord. " *Every tear,*" for they be many;—tears of misfortune and poverty, such as Job and Lazarus wept;—tears of bereaved affection, such as Mary, and Martha, and the widow of Nain shed;—tears of sympathy and mercy, such as Jeremiah and Jesus wept over the sins and calamities of Jerusalem;—tears of persecuted innocence, tears of contrition and penitence for faults and crimes against the goodness and majesty of heaven;—tears of disappointment and neglect;—tears of yearning for what cannot now be ours;—these, and whatever others ever course the cheeks of mortals, shall then be dried forever.

Death no longer exists. O the reign of death! Whom has it not touched! What circle has it not invaded! What home has it never entered!

> There is no flock, however watched and tended,
> But one dead lamb is there!
> There is no fireside howsoe'er defended,
> But hath one vacant chair.

Around our churches lie our graveyards, and all the highways are lined with cemeteries and depositories of the dead. We can scarcely open our eyes without seeing the gloomy hearse, the funeral procession, the undertaker's warehouse, the shop full of mourning goods, or the stonecutter chiselling epitaphs. Every newspaper we pick up has its obituary lists, and every week brings forth its bills of mortality. On the right hand, on the left hand, before us, behind us, around us, beneath us, in all seasons, in all climes, everywhere, is death. We ourselves are only waiting, not knowing what day or hour we shall fall beneath its stroke.

Physicians are sent forth by hundreds and thousands every year from our colleges and universities, and myriads of hands are ever busy collecting and preparing medicines for the sick; and yet there is no check, no restraint, to the career and reign of death! But, at length, an end to his fell dominion comes. The time will be when death itself shall die; not by the power of man, not by mortal skill or earthly medicines, but by the great redemption of God. When the sunlight of the new Genesis dawns upon this stricken world, the grand thanksgiving shall ring out over every zone, from the equator to the poles, that "*Death is swallowed up in victory.*" Never another dying-bed shall then be seen again. Never another grave shall then be dug. For "*death shall no longer be.*"

Sorrow then ceases. Thousandfold are the heartaches and the griefs which now beset and torment the children of men. Choose what path of life we will, we cannot escape them. They follow us like our shadow. Bright as the lives of some may seem, each heart knoweth its own bitterness. Martyrs suffer where no fagots or flames are visible. But there is a boundary line over which no sorrows ever pass,—the line which divides between the new earth and this. There hearts no longer bleed in secret; there the cold shadows never again fall on sensitive souls; there the killing frosts no more settle on the springing plants or blooming flowers of human peace. Christ drank the cup of sorrow for our world, and it will be found empty then.

III. Observe the Occupants and Possessors of that World.

Not the "*cowardly*" who shrink from the conflict with sin, ashamed or afraid to avow and maintain their faith in God and his Christ;—not the "*unbelieving*," who set at nought the testimonies of their Maker, scorn to trust for salvation in the merits of a crucified Saviour, and will not have Christ to rule over them;—not the "*polluted*," who basely degrade themselves with their uncleanness, bestiality, and abominations;—not the "*murderers*," whether such by outward act or inward malice;—not "*fornicators*," whether of the body or the cherished lust of the soul;—not "*sorcerers*," practitioners in the black arts, conjurers, necromancers, and seekers and exercisers of powers such as God has forbidden;—not "*idolaters*," whether in the form of pagan worship, or the giving of the heart to covetousness, selfishness, Mammon, or what is not God;—nor any *false ones*, who make, or love, or act lies;—for " *the cowardly, and unbelieving, and polluted, and murderers, and fornicators, and sorcerers, and idolaters, and all the false, their part [shall inherit] in the lake burning with fire and brimstone, which is the second death*." Not one of all such characters ever comes into the new heaven and earth.

But all the Saints are there—the Church of the first-born—the holy people of God from Abel to the last martyr under the Antichrist. Jehovah has had a people in every age,—a people called out from the world, marked with holy signs, pervaded with a holy spirit,—a people signalized as pilgrims and strangers on the earth ever seeking for a firmly founded and continuing city whose maker and builder is God. Such were the patriarchs of the early ages, who saw the promises, and embraced them, and lived on earth as citizens of another and heavenly country. Such were the prophets, who prophesied beforehand of the sufferings of Christ and the glory that should follow, and searched and inquired into those blessed things which the angels also desired to look into. Such were those in the first centuries of the Church who held fast the name of Jesus, and denied not their faith in him even amid the roaring flames, and when the blood of his confessors flowed like water. Such were those who sighed and cried through the gloom of the Middle Ages, like souls under the altar, and those who afterwards shook the torch of Jehovah's truth afresh to light the modern nations into life. And such are those in every land, of every tongue, of every age, who show by their lives and testimony that they seek a city yet to come. All these are there, not in flesh and blood, not returned to an earthy corporeal life, but in resurrection transfiguration, made like to the angels, like to their Redeemer now in glory, and having their home-place and palace in the Golden City for which they looked, and wrought, and waited, and suffered when on earth. These are there, as occupants of the new heavens, the dwellers in the new city, the sublime and heavenly kings and priests of the eternal nations and generations.

And the still ongoing race redeemed is there. Many can think of none but glorified saints in this grand picture ; but the terms of the record will not construe with that idea. The glorified saints all belong to the celestial city, and have their home and residence in it. That city is the Tabernacle of God which comes down out of the heaven. Yet when it comes, a great voice out of the throne says : " Behold, The Tabernacle of God [is] *with the men,* [*with mankind*], and he shall tabernacle *with them, and they shall be his people, and he, the God with them, shall be their God."* Who then are these to whom the Tabernacle of God comes, and with whom it dwells? Who are these people distinct from it, and whom it is to enlighten and bless ? Who can they be, if not the nations of the ongoing race, dwelling in the new earth in the flesh? They are redeemed now, holy, innocent, undying, and the Lord's people forever ; but only the Church of the after-born, and not of the first-born. Jesus, in Matthew 25, describes a judgment of *"the nations,"* when, as a shepherd, he shall divide the sheep from the goats, and when the sheep " nations" shall be set on his right hand, and " go into life everlasting," whilst the goat " nations " go " into everlasting fire prepared for the devil and his angels." So, in the next chapter, we read of these same sheep " nations " walking by means of the light and aid of this celestial city (chap. 21 : 24), but quite distinct from the royal Church of the first-born, which is the New Jerusalem, the Lamb's Wife. Likewise the whole analogy of the Scriptures, from first to last, bears along with it this implication. There is not a word which asserts any purpose of God to terminate the perpetuity of humanity as an ever-expanding race. It was constituted and given command for unending perpetuity before sin touched it. If it fails to go on forever, it can only be in consequence of the introduction of sin. But there has been promised and constituted a Redeemer to ransom it from all captivity to sin and corruption. And if his redemption does not go far enough to exempt the ongoing race from being finally extinguished, then it is not redemption, and the Destroyer beats out the Almighty Redeemer. There is no escape from this alternative if we do not allow that the race of man as a race continues in the new earth, and there realizes its complete and final recovery from all the effects and ill consequences of the fall. Ransomed nations in the flesh are therefore among the occupants of the new earth, and the blessed and happy dwellers in it, as Adam and Eve dwelt in Paradise. The Sitter on the throne saith, "Behold, new I make everything." That everything includes heaven, earth, and sea, and by necessary implication, had we no other proofs, the race of humanity is also included as a subject of the great Re-Genesis. Hence said the Almighty to Isaiah, "Behold, I create new heavens and a new earth. Be ye glad and rejoice forever in that which I create. And they shall build houses and inhabit them; and they shall plant vineyards and eat the fruit of them. They shall not labor in vain, nor bring forth for trouble; for they are the seed of the blessed of the Lord, and their offspring with them." (Is. 65: 17-25.)

Men may think we dream when we thus propose to read God's word as it is written; but he has anticipated all their rationalizing and skepticism. The Sitter upon the throne saith, " WRITE, BECAUSE THESE WORDS ARE FAITHFUL AND TRUE." There can be no mistake about it. God knew how to say what he meant, and he knew the meaning of what he did say. And to that which he has said, he affixes his own infallible seal, that the words are "faithful and true." Here, then, let us rest till their fulfilment comes.

LECTURE FORTY-NINTH.

Rev. 21 : 9–27. (Revised Text.) And there came one of the seven
angels which had the seven bowls full of the seven last plagues, and he
talked with me, saying, Hither, I will show thee the Bride, the Wife
of the Lamb.

And he carried me away in the spirit on to a mountain great and
high, and showed me the holy city Jerusalem coming down out of the
heaven from God, having the glory of God; her brightness like a stone
most precious, as a jasper stone, crystal-clear; having a wall great and
high, having twelve gates, and at the gates twelve angels, and names
written thereon, which are the names of the twelve tribes of the sons
of Israel; from the east three gates, and from the north three gates,
and from the south three gates, and from the west three gates. And
the wall of the city having twelve foundation-stones, and on them twelve
names of the twelve apostles of the Lamb.

And he that spoke with me had a measure, a golden reed, that he
might measure the city, and her gates, and her walls.

And the city lieth four-square, and her length is as great as her
breadth.

And he measured the city with the reed to the extent of twelve thousand stadia. The length, and the breadth, and the height of it are
equal.

And he measured her wall [height] of a hundred forty-four cubits,
measure of a man, which is of an angel.

And the construction of her wall jasper, and the city pure gold, like
to clear glass.

The foundation-stones of the wall of the city adorned with every precious stone.   The first foundation-stone, jasper, the second, sapphire ; the third, chalcedony ; the fourth, emerald ; the fifth, sardonyx ; the sixth, sardius, the seventh, chrysolyte; the eighth, beryl ; the ninth, topaz ; the tenth, chrisoprasus ; the eleventh, jacinth ; the twelfth, amethyst.

And the twelve gates twelve pearls, each one of the gates separately was out of one pearl.

And the street of the city pure gold as transparent glass.

And a temple I saw not in it, for the Lord God the All-Ruler and the Lamb is its temple.

And the city hath not need of the sun, nor of the moon, that they should illumine it; for the glory of God lighted it, and the Lamb the lamp of it, and the nations shall walk by means of the light of it. And the kings of the earth bring their glory to [or *into*] it. And its gates shall not be shut by day, for night shall not be there. And they shall bring the glory and the reverence of the nations to [or *into*] it.

And there shall not enter into it anything common [or *unclean*], nor he that doeth abomination and falsehood, but only they that are written in the book [or *roll*] of the life of the Lamb.

ONE of the most remarkable paradoxes of the Church of our times is its abhorrence of materiality in connection with the Kingdom of Christ and the eternal future, whilst practically up to its ears in materialism and earthiness.   Were one of the old Christians of the Apostolic age to revisit the world to take a look at our modern Christianity, I think he would be greatly puzzled to understand how, under the guise of spirituality, the whole Church is permeated and loaded down with carnal philosophies, hopes, and aims.   Remembering the sublime simplicity of the ancient times, when the Church was set, like a golden circlet, on the head of the King of Glory, in contact everywhere with Divinity, he would be amazed to see how that circlet has been divorced from its original setting, stained with the flesh, and pushed into the morasses and bogs of this world, whilst earthly glories—crowns, mitres, tiaras, wealth, and secular consequence—are looked to and worshipped everywhere as the insignia of what in sad mockery is called a "spiritual" kingdom! Would he not wonder to find Christians locating their most orthodox rejoicing in monarchs, in popes, patriarchs, bishops, sect leaders, numbers, luxurious arts, boastful speeches, worldly orators, secular education, march of intellect, and a fancied progress toward a "spiritual" millennium of mere secularism, to merge at last into an empty and impossible heaven! And venturing to inquire of some of our popular preachers, whether this is thought to be the proper waiting for the Lord from heaven,—the way to pray "Thy kingdom come,"—the method by which to realize the blessed consummation when it shall be "on earth as it is in heaven,"—the holding fast of the characteristic and animating patriarchal hope of a celestial city which Christ has gone to build and to bring down out of the heaven as the eternal residence of his enthroned saints,—what would be his surprise to get for answer : " Sir, you are laboring under a delusion,—the kingdom was set up 1800 years ago,—the speedy coming again of Christ in person to reign on earth is a carnal idea, long since exploded, and held only by a few eccentric people who cannot rise to a conception of the true spirituality of the Bible;—and as to the heavenly Jerusalem, why that is only a gorgeous Oriental symbol

of the beautiful church state which you see all
around you.   The glory of Christianity is to keep
abreast with the times, to press popular education,
to create machinery to reach and elevate the
masses, to follow up the conquests of arms with
Bibles and missionaries, schools and civilization,
to purify and influence legislation, to improve society by gradual reforms and general enlightenment, to win for the Church the patronage of the
rich and great, and so to progress till the whole
earth shall rest in the embrace of a worldwide
'spiritual' kingdom (located here in Satan's lap!)
to last for indefinite ages!"   With a groan over his
inability to rise to such a philosophy, I can fancy
the ancient saint gladly returning to his grave, to
sleep in honest earth till that resurrection on which
his hopes were fixed, rather than hear any further
about a "spirituality" so carnal, and a Christianity
so doubtful and earthy.

A spiritualized earthiness is simply a white-
washed sepulchre; and an incorporeal and immaterial eternity for man, is equally aside from the
teachings of God's Word.   No wonder that professed believers of our day are anxious to put off
getting into the heaven they believe in as long as
the doctor's skill can keep them out of it, and
finally agree to go only as a last despairing resort.
It has no substance, no reality, for the soul to take
hold on.   It is nothing but a world of shadows,
of mist, of dim visions of blessedness, with which
it is impossible for a being who is not mere spirit,
and never will be mere spirit, who knows only to

live in a body and shall live forever in a body, to feel any fellowship or sympathy.

But such are not the ideas of our futurity which the Bible holds out to our faith and hope. Did men but learn to know the difference between a Paradise of sense and a Paradise of sensuality, the truth of God would not suffer in men's hands as it does, and their souls would not suffer as they do for something solid to anchor to amid the anxious perturbations of life and death. Did men but rid themselves of the old heresy that matter means sin, and learn to know and feel that there was a material universe before sin was, and that a material universe will live on when sin shall have been clean washed away from the entire face of it, they would be in better position both to understand and to enjoy the fore-announcements of the futurity of the saints which God has given for their consolation amid these earthly vicissitudes and falsities. Says one of the greatest of Scottish preachers: "There is much of the innocent, and much of the inspiring, and much to affect and elevate the heart in the scenes and contemplations of materiality,—and we do hail the information, that, after the loosening of the present framework, it will again be varied and decked out anew in all the graces of its unfading verdure, and of its unbounded variety,—that in addition to our direct personal view of the Deity, when he comes down to tabernacle with men, we shall also have the reflection of him in a lovely mirror of his own workmanship,—and that instead of being transported to some abode of dimness and mystery, so remote from human experience as to be beyond all comprehension, we shall walk forever in a land replenished with those sensible delights, and those sensible glories, which, we doubt not, will lie most profusely scattered over the 'new heavens and new earth.' We are now walking on a terrestrial surface, not more compact, perhaps, than the one we shall hereafter walk upon; and are now wearing terrestrial bodies, not firmer and more solid, perhaps, than those we shall hereafter wear. It is not by working any change upon them that we could realize, to any extent, our future heaven. The spirituality of our future state lies not in the kind of substance which is to compose its framework, but in the character of those who people it. There will be a firm earth, as we have at present, and a heaven stretched over it, as we have at present; and it is not by the absence of these, but by the absence of sin, that the abodes of immortality will be characterized." (Chalmers.)

The New Jerusalem, which we now come to consider, is in the line of these ideas. It stands in antithesis to the final Babylon. John is called by one of the same particular angels, in precisely the same way, to be shown it as he was called to be shown the great Harlot. (See chap. 17.) The world and all its activities and achievements is made up of two opposing sides,—the side of the heavenly, the good, the blessed, and the side of the earthy, sensual, and devilish,—the true and the false,—the things which gravitate toward eternal life, and the things which gravitate toward destruction and the second death,—the kingdom of heaven, and the kingdom of the devil. These two are at present intermingled, and are differently situated toward each other at different periods, the one often hard to be distinguished from the other. But everything on either side has an affinity for its own, and is true to its own; so that, in the progress of time, each side becomes more and more itself, developed and consolidated, until the two antagonistic influences, tendencies, and parties crystallize to their true spirit, and finally come out in two opposite cities; the one of the earth and from the earth, and the other of heaven and from the heaven; the one for everlasting extinguishment under the wrath of God, and the other for eternal illumination with his unveiled presence and glory. Whatever, therefore, may be the run of our ideas of the one, the same must hold good of the other also; for what Great Babylon is on the side of the bad, this New Jerusalem is on the side of the good; for they are counterparts of each other, and each is the ultimate consummation of that to which it relates.

The Apostle had already seen this city "coming down out of the heaven from God;" but he saw it only at a distance, and without that particular spiritual transport which was necessary to enable him to see it so as to describe it. God meant that we should have as clear and thorough an outlook upon the ultimate crown on the side of grace and salvation, as he has given us of the ultimate crown and end of the sensual wisdom and the man-wrought progress; and hence this angel comes to show John the Bride, the Lamb's Wife, in her final condition and domicil, and in all the magnificence of her eternal glory. And whatever tabernacle of God, or congregating of true worshippers, or seat or character of Divine economies, constitutions, or manifestations, have been graciously vouchsafed to men, as individuals, nationalities, or churches, from the foundation of the world to this time, is here shown in its final consummation, completeness, and eternal reality.

That a real City as well as a perfected moral system is here to be understood, I see not how we can otherwise conclude. Great Babylon, to which it stands as the exact antithesis, came out finally in a real and universally potent city; so, therefore, must this. All the elements of a city are indicated. It has specific dimensions. It has foundations, walls, gates, and streets. It has guards outside and inhabitants within, both distinct from what characterizes it as a real construction. It is called a city—" *The Holy City.*" It is named as a city, " *The Holy Jerusalem.*" It is called " The *New* Jerusalem,*" as over against an *old* Jerusalem, which was a material city. Among the highest promises to the saints of all ages was the promise of a special place and economy answering to a heavenly city, and which is continually referred to as an enduring and God-built city. Abraham " looked for *a city* which hath foundations, whose maker and builder is God." (Heb. 11 : 10.) Of all the ancient saints it

is written, that "God hath prepared for them *a
city*." (Heb. 11 : 16.) Jesus assured the disciples
from whom he was about to be separated, "I go
to prepare *a place* for you. And if I go and prepare *a place* for you, I will come again, and receive
you unto myself; that where I am there ye may
be also." (Jno. 14 : 2, 3.) Hence the Apostle, in
the name of all Christians of his day, said, "Here
we have no *continuing city*, but we seek *one to come*."
(Heb. 13 : 14.) Hence also it is given as one of the
great exaltations of true believers, even here on
earth, that they "are come unto *the city* of the
living God, the heavenly Jerusalem" (Heb. 12 : 22);
not indeed as to actual possession as yet, but as
having attained to title to it and to citizenship in
it by faith, hope, and sure anticipation. And
whatever difficulty we may have in taking it in,
or in reconciling it to our prepossessions, I do not
see how we can be just and fair to God's Word,
and the faith of the saints of former ages, and not
see and admit that we here have to do, not with a
mere ideal and fantastic city, but with a true, real,
God-built city, substantial and eternal; albeit there
has never been another like it.

The angel calls it "*the Bride, the Lamb's Wife*."
The heavenly city is Christ's Bride, not on account
of what makes it a city, but on account of the
sanctified and glorified ones who inhabit it. Without the saints, whose home and residence it is, it
would not be the Lamb's Wife; and yet it is the
Lamb's Wife in a sense which does not exclude
the foundations, walls, gates, streets and construc-

tions which contribute to make it a city. Mere edifices and avenues do not make a city; neither does a mere congregation or multitude of people make a city. You cannot have a living city without people to inhabit it; and you cannot have a city without the edifices and avenues arranged in some fixed shape for the accommodation of those who make up its population. It is the two together, and the order in which the parts are severally disposed, the animate with the inanimate, which constitute a city. And whilst this holy Jerusalem is the Bride and Wife of Christ with reference to its holy occupants, it is still those occupants as disposed and arranged in that city. So that the city as a city, as well as its people as a people, even the whole taken together, is embraced in what the angel calls "the Bride, the Lamb's Wife," as she finally appears in her eternal form and completeness.

The description which the Apostle gives us of this city, though very brief, is very magnificent, and presents a picture which almost blinds us with its brightness. It is not necessary that I should enter upon a discussion of the numerous details. They can be found more or less accurately given in almost any respectable commentary on the Apocalypse. Only to a few of its broader and more important features do I invite attention at present, with a few brief remarks on each.

1. *Its Derivation.*—John sees it "coming down out of heaven from God." It is of celestial origin. It is the direct product of Almighty power and wisdom. He who made the worlds is the Maker

of this illustrious city. No mortal hand is ever employed upon its construction. The saints are all God's workmanship. They are all begotten of his Spirit, and shaped and fashioned into living stones from the dark quarries of a fallen world, and transfigured from glory to glory by the gracious operations of his hand. They reach their heavenly character and places through his own direct agency and influence. And he who makes, prepares, and places them, makes, prepares, and places their sublime habitation also. It is elsewhere said, in so many words, that the maker and builder of this city is God. (Heb. 11: 10.) It has no architect, no workmen, but himself. He who by his Spirit garnished the heavens, erects and fashions the New Jerusalem.

2. *Its Location.*—This is not specifically told, but the record is not without some hints. John sees it coming down out of heaven. The idea is that it comes close to the earth, and is intended to have a near relation to the earth; but it is nowhere said that it ever alights on the earth, or ever becomes part of its material fabric. Though coming into the vicinity of the earth, it is always spoken of as the "Jerusalem which is *above.*" (Gal. 4: 26.) The nations on the earth "walk by means of its light," which implies that it is *over* them. John could only get a near view of it by being spiritually transported to the top of "a mountain great and high," like the greatest altitudes of the Alps or the Himalayas. The prophecies also speak of a future Jerusalem as set at the tops of the moun-

tains, and exalted over the hills. (Is. 2 : 2.) If a final exaltation of the earthly Jerusalem is contemplated in such passages, the language still is borrowed from something higher, in which alone its literal import can be realized, and hence includes more especially the "Jerusalem which is above," of which the earthly Jerusalem is the type. The probabilities are that it will stand high over Palestine, and perhaps stationary, as the earth revolves under it, not so high as not to be in ample view of all the dwellers of the earth, and not so low as not to throw its illumination upon all nations and countries, and upon at least half the earth at a time. Something like what the pillar of cloud and fire were to the tribes of Israel when they came up out of Egypt, shall the relation and location of this glorious city be, with reference to the generations of men in the new earth.

3. *Its Splendor.*—Here the specifications are numerous and transcendant, as we would expect in a city erected and ornamented by Jehovah, and coming forth direct from the heavens. Everything built by God's direction is the very best and most splendid of its kind. So was the ship in which Noah was saved; so was the Great Pyramid, of which there is reason to believe that it was built by divine direction;* and so were the Jewish Tabernacle and Temple. Much rather then would it be so in a "Great City," built with his own hands, and intended as the sublime crown of the

---

* See my volume, *A Miracle in Stone.*

most marvellous of all his glorious works. And as we would expect, so the description is.

Earthly cities are often very magnificent and charming; but if we take our stand on some high point from which to look down upon them, we can see nothing but irregular heaps of human habitations and buildings, mostly involved in a mist of fumes and smoke, having but a dim light of their own; dusty, dingy, and by no means the most beautiful objects on which the eye can rest. It is very different with this heavenly city. It is as clean, and pure, and bright as a transparent icicle in the sunshine. John describes it as "having the glory of God." *Glory* is brightness, lustre, splendor. The glory of God, or that in which God is arrayed, that which most bespeaks and characterizes Deity, is *Light;* for "God is light," and in him is no darkness at all. And this city has, and is invested with, the glory, light, brightness, and radiating splendor of God. That brightness as it flashed on Saul of Tarsus on the road to Damascus, surpassed the radiance of the noonday sun of Syria. The very intensity of its brilliancy struck him blind. And this brightness the New Jerusalem has, only with its sharpness when manifested against sin and sinners softened, for there are no more sinners, and no wrath. Hence the brightness is like a most precious *jasper stone.* A jasper stone is wavy with the various colors of the rainbow; but it is opaque. This city has this jasper appearance, but without the opacity. It is "like a most precious jasper stone *crystal-clear,*"

perfectly transparent, like a diamond or rock-
crystal. So pure, so bright, so soft, is the luminous and divine splendor in which this whole city
is arrayed.

It has " a wall great and high," which is not
only like jasper, but which is built of jasper itself.
And that wall stands on twelve foundation-stones,
and each of those twelve immense stones is a separate and distinct jewel in itself.   There are certain
substances in nature, found in very small fragments, which are so scarce, rare, beautiful, and
enduring that they are called gems, or precious
stones; so precious that the prices of them are
almost fabulous, and hence they are used almost
exclusively for rich and costly ornament.   Twelve
kinds of these, each a vast, apportioned, and solid
mass, make up the foundations on which the jasper
walls of this city are built.   Through these walls
are twelve openings or gateways, with twelve
gates; and each of these twelve gates is made of
one solid pearl.

From these gates inward there are as many
main streetways, and all the streetway is gold,—
gold in perfect purity, such as cannot be reached
by any earthly refinement,—gold with a peculiar
heavenly quality beyond what is ever seen in our
gold,—*transparent gold* like the most perfect glass.
Men have built some very grand cities, the houses
of which they have constructed of all manner of
costly stones, granite, marble, and other solid pro-
ductions of the earth, dressed, and polished, and
ornamented to degrees of great excellence.   But

there is one part of every such city which they are satisfied to have of inferior material, only so that it is even and smooth; namely, the part which is trodden under every one's feet. It therefore gives a very high touch to the splendor of this celestial city that its very streets are pure transparent gold.

And the city itself is of the same material,— nothing but "*pure gold like to clear glass.*" It is a true *crystal palace*, made of nothing but transparent gold. An object is thus presented, the splendor of which far outshines the most sublime creations of which the human imagination ever dreamed.

4. *Its Amplitude.*—There is no stint or meanness in God's creations. When he set himself to the making of worlds, he filled up an immeasurable space with them. He brought them forth in numbers without number, of grades upon grades, from the moons which play around the planets to luminous masses beyond any power of man to commensurate their enormous magnitude. When he created angels he added myriads on myriads, and orders on orders, till all earthly arithmetic is lost in the counting of them. When he started the human race it was on a career of multiplication to which we can set no limit. When he began the glorious work of redemption, and commenced the taking out and fashioning of a people to become the companions of his only begotten Son and co-regents with their Redeemer, these pictures of the final outcome tell of great multitudinous hosts, in

numbers like the sands of the seashore. And the city he builds for them is of corresponding dimensions.

Starting from the centre of our own city, though perhaps the largest in extent on this continent, we can travel but a few miles till we get beyond its built-up limits; and its breadth is but slight compared with its length. But the golden city for which the Church of the first-born is taught to look as its eternal home, is 1500 *miles square ;* for 12,000 *stadia* make 1500 miles. John saw it measured, and this was the measure of it, just as wide as it is long, and just as high as it is wide; for the "length and the breadth and the height of it are equal." Here would be streets over streets, and stories over stories, up, up, up, to the height of 1500 miles, and each street 1500 miles long. Thus this city is a solid cube of golden constructions, 1500 miles every way. The base of it would stretch from furthest Maine to furthest Florida, and from the shore of the Atlantic to Colorado. It would cover all Britain, Ireland, France, Spain, Italy, Germany, Austria, Prussia, European Turkey, and half of European Russia, taken together! Great was the City of Nineveh, so great that Jonah had only *begun* to enter it after a day's journey. How long then would it take a man to explore this city of gold, whose every street is one-fifth the length of the diameter of the earth, and the number of whose main avenues, though a mile above each other, and a mile apart, would not be less than eight millions! "Stupendous magnitude! Alex-

andria is said by Josephus to have had a length of
30 stadia, and a width of not less than 10 stadia.
According to the same, the circuit of Jerusalem is
defined by 33 stadia; that of Thebes, according to
Dicæarchus, by 43 stadia; that of Nineveh, according to Diodorus Siculus, by 400 stadia. Herodotus,
in his first book, says that Babylon had 120 stadia
in each side, and 480 stadia in each circuit, and
that its wall was 50 cubits thick and 200 cubits
high. This is 12,000 stadia every way. All the
cities in the world are mere villages in comparison
with the New Jerusalem." (Bengel, *in loc.*) Even
the jasper wall which surrounds it is higher than
the highest of our church spires. Earth has no
foundations on which such a city could be set, to
say nothing of the materials of which it is built;
therefore it comes forth out of the heaven from
God, and has its place above the tops of the
mountains.

It has ever been an anxious question to believing souls, what proportion of the people who have
lived, or now live, are likely to reach this blessed
city. Men came to the Saviour when on earth,
inquiring, "Lord, are there few that be saved?"
It is a complex question which could not be made
profitably clear to those who put it, and it has nowhere been directly answered. It is better that
we should be about making our own salvation
sure, than speculating about the number who
finally get to heaven. But the picture here placed
before us casts a light upon the inquiry, as exalt-
ing to the grace of God as it is encouraging to

those who really wish to be saved. This golden
city has not been built in all this amplitude and
magnificence of proportions for mere empty show.
God did not create the earth in vain ; " he formed
it to be inhabited." (Is. 45 : 18.) Much rather,
then, would he not lavish all this glory and splendor upon the Eternal City, without knowing that
enough out of the family of man would embrace
his salvation to fill and people it. And the population to fill and occupy a city 1500 miles long,
and broad, and high, allowing the amplest room
and space for each individual, family, tribe, and
tongue, and nation, would necessarily mount up to
myriads on myriads, who sing the songs and taste
the joys of the redemption that is in Christ Jesus.
Amplitude—amplitude of numbers, as well as
glorious accommodations—is unmistakably signified, in whatever way we contemplate the astonishing picture.

5. *Its System of Illumination.*—What is a city
without light ! And what is more difficult of
management in utilizing city spaces than the
arrangements for light ! Fortunately no gas
trusts are needed in the New Jerusalem, nor
light of the sun, nor light of the moon. It is itself
a grand prism of inherent light, the Light of God
and the Lamb, which illuminates at once the eyes
of the body and of the soul, and shines not only
on the objects without but on the understandings
within, making everything light in the Lord. The
glory of God's brightness envelops it like an un-
clouded halo, permeates it, and radiates through it

and from it so that there is not a dark or obscure place about it. It shines like a new sun, inside and out, sending abroad its rays over all the earth, and into the depths of space, making our planet seem to distant worlds as if suddenly transformed into a brilliant luminary, whose brightness never wanes. And that shining is not from any material combustion,—not from any consumption of fuel that needs to be replaced as one supply burns out; for it is the uncreated light of Him who is light, dispensed by and through the Lamb as the everlasting Lamp, to the home, and hearts, and understandings, of his glorified saints. When Paul and Silas lay wounded and bound in the inner dungeon of the prison of Philippi, they still had sacred light which enabled them to beguile the night-watches with happy songs. When Paul was on his way to Damascus, a light brighter than the sun at noon shone round about him, irradiating his whole being with new sights and understanding, and making his soul and body ever afterwards light in the Lord. When Moses came down from the mount of his communion with God, his face was so luminous that his brethren could not endure to look upon it. He was in such close fellowship with light that he became informed with light, and came to the camp as a very lamp of God, glowing with the glory of God. On the Mount of Transfiguration that same light streamed forth from all the body and raiment of the blessed Jesus. And with reference to the very time when this city comes into being and place,

Isaiah says, " the moon shall be ashamed and the
sun confounded,"—ashamed because of the out-
beaming glory which then shall appear in the
New Jerusalem, leaving no more need for them
to shine in it, since the glory of God lights it, and
the Lamb is the light thereof.

6. *Its Lack of a Temple.*—" A Temple," says the
seer, " I saw not in it." What a vacuum it would
create in every earthly city if its temples were
taken away! What would ancient Jerusalem have
been without its Temple? How much does the
fame and glory of the most renowned of cities,
ancient and modern, rest on their Temples!
Strip them of these and what would be their
nakedness! But it is no privation to the New
Jerusalem that there is no Temple in it. Nay, it
is one of its sublimest peculiarities. Not that
worship is then to cease. Not that communion
with the eternal Spirit and Source of all things is
no longer to exist. While God and holy beings
live, their loving adoration of him cannot cease,
nor acts of worship be discontinued. But then
and there the worship and communion will no
longer be through symbols, veils, and intermediate ceremonials, which now are needed to help
the soul to divine fellowship. Deity will then
have come forth from behind all veils, all medi-
ating sacraments, all previous barriers and hidings
because of the infirmities of the flesh or the weaknesses of undeveloped spirituality. Himself will
be the Temple thereof. The glorious worshippers
there hold direct communion with his manifested

glory, which encompasses them and all their city alike. As consecrated high priests they will then have come into the holiest of all, into the very cloud of God's overshadowing glory, which is at once their covering, their Temple, their God.

When Jesus walked with his disciples on earth, wherever he was they had a Temple. In the mountains and wildernesses of retirement, in the midst of the street concourse, on the heights where he was transfigured, in the upper room where they ate with him the paschal supper, along the way to Emmaus, on the shores of Galilee, on the Mount of Ascension, wherever his divine presence, power, and goodness spoke its " Peace be unto you," was a Temple to them. What an incumbrance and detraction would have been Aaron's garments, and Aaron's breastplate, and Aaron's ceremonials of inquiry and worship, when they had with them " God manifest in the flesh," on whose bosom they could lay their heads, whose cheeks they could kiss, whose feet they could bathe with their tears, whose words they could hear, and whose gracious services and benedictions they could at all times command! What need of Solomon's Temple had they, when the embodied Shechinah himself, in ever-approachable form, was with them by day and by night, their brother, their master, their everlasting friend! And when the saints in immortal glory dwell within the inclosing light of the unveiled presence of God and the Lamb, as his Bride and Wife, what more need have they of Temple, or outward ceremonial, to commune with

Deity, or to have fellowship with the Father and the Son! God and the Lamb are then themselves the Temple, and the intervention of any other Temple would be a disability, a clog, and a going back from the sublime exaltation which the saints there reach and enjoy. Hence John saw no Temple in that city, "for the Lord God, the All-Ruler, and the Lamb is its Temple." The worship there is immediate and direct.

7. *Its Relation to the World at Large.*—Of old, the song of the Psalmist was: "Beautiful for situation, the joy of the whole earth, is Mount Zion, the City of the Great King." (Ps. 48 : 2.) In every land into which the Jewish people wandered, there was a glad thrill upon their souls when they remembered Jerusalem. Night and morning they knelt down with their faces thitherward to chant the praises of Him who there dwelt between the Cherubim; and year by year the pilgrim bands went up from all lands, with gladness of heart, and lute, and song, unto the mountain of the Lord, to the Mighty One of Israel. Thither came the tribes of the Lord, unto the Testimony of Israel, to give thanks unto the Name of the Lord; for there were set the thrones of judgment, the thrones of the house of David. (Ps. 122.) Out of Zion went the law, and the Word of the Lord from Jerusalem. We cannot look back upon those times, even now, without a degree of fascination which draws like a magnet upon every feeling of the heart. And what was then realized on a small and feeble scale, in the case of one people, is to be

the universal experience with regard
blessed city. It is to be the centre and ill
of the world.

"*The nations shall walk by means of*
of it." Spiritual illumination for the sou
as glorious light for the eyes,—the
truth and righteousness, and the light of
all wants, personal, social, and national,
deemed family of man,—shall go forth
sublime city; and "the nations" shall
that light. Their polity, their religion
that goes to make up for them an ec
Edenic blessedness, shall come forth fr
sublime metropolis. Their kings, thei
their priests, their loving guides, their
their only Lord God, are there, visible
eyes, and ever present to their hearts a
What never yet has been upon this eart
holy nation, will then be found where
found, and all people shall be the peo
Lord. Men talk of *Christian nations ;*
this dwelling-place of man, from the
until now, there is nothing of the sort
to the phrase. There is no such thing,
never will be, till the New Earth appear
New Jerusalem comes into the view of
then, all nations, as nations, shall be
and holy; for they shall walk in the li
Eternal City of the Eternal King. T
raised aloft, and filled with the Spirit an
God and the Lamb, will be the illumin
the great glory of the world, the centre o

est interest,—the joy of the waking thoughts and the sleeping dreams of all the children of men.

"*And the kings of the earth bring their glory and honor to* (*or into*) *it.*" The Kings will then be Christ and his glorified saints. These will reside in this city, and whatever pertains to them as kings will have its centre and seat there. Their glory as kings, their authority and their thrones, will all go to honor, dignify, and distinguish this city. And if by "kings *of the earth*" we are to understand sub-kings belonging to unglorified humanity, the statement implies that the omage and gratitude of earthly royalty will then devote everything of greatness and glory that it possesses to the service and honor of that city.

"*And they shall bring the glory and reverence of the nations to* (*or into*) *it.*" All the honor the world can give will be given to that city. All nations, as one man, shall then be happy worshippers, and all devotion shall concentre in the New Jerusalem. All eyes, all ears, shall be turned to it. And all the honor that men can render, and all the delight the human heart can feel, will flow forever to that high tabernacle, whose gates are never shut, and where no night is ever known.

8. *Its Superlative Holiness.*—"Holy, Holy, Holy, is the Lord God of hosts," cried the six-winged Seraphim; and where that God is, only what is holy can find place. This is " the mountain of his Holiness," the city where his glory dwells; there-fore no common or unclean thing can ever enter it, nor any one that doeth abomination, or worketh

what is false. *"Holy things for holy people,"* was
the announcement given out by the Church for
many ages whenever about to present the mystery
of the holy Supper; and a similar word forever
flames around those gates of pearl. The city is
ample; it is magnificent; and there is place
within it for every one ready and willing to become its denizen; but it is *"holy,"* and no one
can ever set foot upon its golden streets who is
not enrolled in the book of life of the Lamb.
Sinners may come there, yes; for sinners it was
made; but only for such as are cleansed in the
proffered bath of regeneration, by the washing
of water and the word. No place is there for them
that believe not in Jesus, and submit not themselves to his saving righteousness. No place is
there for them that say, "Lord, Lord," but do not
the things which he has commanded. And if any
love their sins better than God's salvation, the
New Jerusalem is not for them. It is for those
only whose names, through faith and sanctification of the Spirit, have been written in the Lamb's
book of life.

Such, then, in brief, is that holy City which has
been glittering in the imaginations and the songs
of God's people, in every age and under all dispensation. Its foundations by their colors speak
of grace, mercy, and God's sure covenant earthward. Its gates of pearl speak of righteousness,
obedience, and the heart set on the precious things
of the divine kingdom, as the medium of transit
from earth to glory. Its cubic form, and its

streets and constructions of purest gold, proclaim
it the embodiment of all perfection, the supremest seat of the supremest saintship. And
within those immortal gates, in the very presence
and company of God and the Lamb, surrounded
with light, riches, and splendors beyond all that
human thought can estimate, amid the liberties,
securities, and perfections of the highest of all the
material creations of gracious Omnipotence, as the
jewelled link between the Eternal Father and his
redeemed earthly family, and with a strength that
walks unshaken under all the exceeding and eternal weight of glory, the Church of the first-born,
the Bride and Wife of Christ, shall live and reign
with him, day without end, for the ages of the
ages.

> Exult, O dust and ashes,
>   Thy God shall be thy part !
> His only, His forever,
>   Thou shalt be and thou art !

LECTURE FIFTIETH.

THE NEW JERUSALEM CONTINUED—A MORE INWARD VIEW—
THE WONDERFUL RIVER—THE TREE OF LIFE—THE CURSE
REPEALED—THE EVERLASTING THRONE—THE ETERNAL
BLESSEDNESS.

Rev. 22 : 1–5. 'Revised Text.) And he showed me a river of water
of life clear as crystal, coming forth out of the throne of God and the
Lamb. In the midst of the street of it [the city] and on either side of
the river, tree of life producing twelve fruits [or *kinds of fruit*], according to each month yielding its fruit, and the leaves of the tree
unto healing of the nations. And every curse [or *accursed thing*],
shall not be any more ; and the Throne of God and of the Lamb shall
be in it, and his servants shall serve him, and they shall see his face, and
the name of him [shall be] upon their foreheads ; and night shall not
be any more, and they shall not have need of lamp and light, because
the Lord God shall shine upon them, and they shall reign to the ages
of the ages.

THE Apostle here continues his description of
the New Jerusalem, and for this reason these
verses should not have been separated from the
section which precedes them. They relate to the
same subject, and have nothing to mark them from
what has gone before, except that they refer more
to the interior of the heavenly city. The description throughout is rather external than internal.
John saw from the outside, and from a distance ;
and his account is necessarily more occupied with
what the city is to those who contemplate it from

without, than with what it is in itself or to those
who have their homes in its "many mansions."
The reason may be that it is not possible for us to
form right conceptions of things so much above
and beyond all present experiences. When Paul
recovered from his trance-vision of Paradise, and
the third heaven, he said that it was not permitted
him to tell the transcendent things which he
saw and heard. And so John is not brought to
such a view of the sublime palace of the saints
as to tell us all about its internal economy. Yet,
what was shown him, as narrated in these verses,
relates more to the inside, than what we had before us a week ago. To these more inner particulars, then, let us direct our thoughts, humbly
looking to God to aid us to form right impressions
of his glorious revelations.

It is due to remark that we here have the final
touches in the picture of the eternal future. These
verses give us the furthest and fullest outlook into
the everlasting economies. Precious, therefore,
should it be to us. With what deep and anxious attention should we dwell on every intimation, and
cherish every image ! Even when about to leave
off contemplating some noted earthly picture, we
always turn to take a last impression to carry with
us as we depart. How much rather, then, should
we incline our energies to get a clear idea of these
richest and fullest delineations of that ultimate
home to which we aspire, beyond which there is
no further knowledge to be had till we come to
take up our everlasting residence there !

Very noteworthy also is it that these last glimpses of a finished Redemption end up with the same images with which the first chapter of human history begun. All worlds move in circles; and the grand march of God's providence with man moves in one immense round. It starts with Paradise, and thence moves out through strange and untried paths, until it has fulfilled its grand revolution by coming back to the point from which it started; not indeed to repeat itself, but thenceforward to rest forever in the results of that wonderful experiment. Genesis is the Book of beginnings; the Revelation is the Book of the endings of what was then begun; and the last laps back again upon the first, and welds the two ends of the history into the golden ring of eternity. There was a time of innocence, and then came a long and dreary time of the absence of innocence; and here we are shown the time of innocence returned, to depart no more. Nor is it without the most cheering significance, that in the account of the final consummation we again come upon a group of objects answering to the most conspicuous and fondly remembered in all the bright story of the original opening of the world.

I. The Apostle begins by telling us of a wonderful River.

One of the gladdest things on earth is water. There is nothing in all the world so precious to the eye and imagination of the inhabitant of the dry, burning and thirsty East, as a plen-

tiful supply of bright, pure, and living water.
Paradise itself was not complete without it.
Hence "a river went out of Eden to water the
garden; and from thence it was parted and became into four heads," rolling their bright cur-
rents over golden sands and sparkling gems
(Gen. 2 : 10–12), as if meant to water and gladden
all the earth. "A city without water would be a
most disconsolate and unpleasant thing; therefore we see cities at the greatest pains to provide
themselves with water, and those are reckoned
the best which are the most happily watered. It
is one of the great excellencies of Ezekiel's city,
that it has a river ever deepening as it flows."
(Ezek. 47:3.) And so the New Jerusalem is not
without its plentiful supply of living waters. Of
the angel who came to show him this great metropolis of the saints, John says: "*And he showed
me a river of water of life, bright as crystal, coming
forth out of the throne of God and of the Lamb.*"

With whatever tenacity the interpreters of this
Book cling to the notion that waters, in prophetic
language, always mean peoples, they give it up
when it comes to this River. Peoples do not issue
from the throne of God. But what to make of
this water they hardly know. Some make it
Baptism. Some make it saving knowledge, flowing out from God over all the habitable world.
Some make it the grace of God through the
preaching of Christ crucified. Some make it the
giving of peace to the perturbed nations. Some
make it " the renewing and sanctifying influences

by which the nations are to be imbued with spiritual life." Some make it a mere Oriental image of abounding happiness and plenty. And many who even see in the description a picture of Paradise regained, are still so fettered down to the present world, that they cannot get on with it above or beyond what is purely earthy. Why cannot men see and read that it does not belong to the earth at all, nor to any earthly people, or any earthly good. There is not a word said to show that these waters in this particular form ever touch the earth, or any dwellers on the earth. The river is a heavenly river, and belongs to a heavenly city, and is for the use and joy of a heavenly people. Its waters are literal waters, of a nature and quality answering to that of the golden city to which they belong. Man on earth never knew such waters, as men on earth never knew such a city; but the city is a sublime reality,—the home and residence of the Lamb and his glorious Bride,— and these waters are a corresponding reality. Of old, the Psalmist sung, "There is a river, the streams whereof shall make glad the city of God, the holy place of the tabernacles of the Most High" (Ps. 46 : 4), "the river of God's pleasures," where they that put their trust under the shadow of his wings shall be abundantly satisfied with the fatness of his dwelling-place, even at the head-spring of life, amid visions of light in the pavilion of his glory. (Ps. 36 : 7–9.) Heaven is not a place of dust and drought. It has its glad water-spring and ever-flowing river, issuing direct from the eternal throne, whose crystal clearness cannot be defiled. There flow the immortal waters, for the joy of glorified natures, bright with the light of God, and filling all with life-cheer as immortal as themselves.

These waters are called "water of life coming forth out of the throne." They are the issuing life of the throne, as the city itself is the embodiment of God's glory. The throne is the throne of the Lamb, in whom is the eternal Godhead. The Father reigns in and through the Son, and this is the reviving and all-animating life and spirit of all this embodiment of Deity in that sublime city. It is the Holy Ghost for that celestial Tabernacle, as God and the Lamb are the Temple of it. It is the divine emanation from the Father and the Son which fills and cheers and forever rejoices the dwellers in that place. These waters also come to the inhabitants of the earth, and refresh and bless them too, as these celestial king-priests have to do with the people of the earth; but they reach the earthly population in other forms, and not in the form of this voluminous river. In this form they belong to the Holy City alone. Only these saints in glory come to the throne, and share its life and administration ; and for them alone is the crystal river which issues from it. It is the Spirit of glory which they drink and embody ; and it is for their pleasure and blessedness, as to no other class of the human family. Yet we are not without something of those waters in the saving administrations of the Holy Ghost, even

now, and the dwellers in the New Earth shall
have more of them than we have; but neither now
nor then can those living in the flesh have them in
anything of the unmingled purity, heavenliness,
and glorious fulness with which they flow forever
in the New Jerusalem. In the first Eden, "there
went up a mist from the earth, and watered the
whole face of the ground." (Gen. 2 : 6.) There
was a watering through an earthly medium. And
in some such mediate way these waters come to
the Church now, and will come still more plente-
ously to the nations when this Great City comes
to its place. But in the Holy City they roll as a
river, through no secondary medium, and give
forth their exhaustless blessedness direct from the
throne of God and the Lamb.

The Jordan is often spoken of as a sacred river,
and many sacred memories connect with it.
Palestine's penitent thousands there flocked to
the wild Baptizer, and sought in that stream to
wash away their sins. Thither the Saviour himself came, to receive upon his spotless person those
same consecrating waters. But Jordan is the symbol of earthly, not heavenly life. Bright and
beautiful in its cradle, it laughs away its merry
morning amid the flowery fields of Hulêh; then
plunges with the recklessness of youth into the
tangled brakes and muddy marshes of Merom; and
thence it issues full-grown, like earnest manhood
with its noisy bustle, dashing along till it quiets
into a picture of life's sober midday in the placid
Lake of Genesareth. Thence its course is down,

down, like the declivities of age, sinking lower
and lower amid doublings and windings innumerable, until it finally reaches the sea of death,
where there is no remedy but to breathe itself out
upon the thin air, and vanish in the clouds. Like
human life, it is mostly a turbid and clouded
stream. This, however, is a different river, and
betokens a very different life. It rises from no
dark caves of earth. It does not grow from additions from without. It has no windings, no stag-
nations, no obstructions, no clouds, no muddiness,
no rising and falling, no sea of death, no precipi-
tations of earthiness, no evaporations to deadly
asphalt and salt. The life it symbolizes, and is,
and gives, is divine life, the life of the throne of
God and of the Lamb, the life that rolls forth in
highest fulness from its living source, pellucid as
the city which it supplies, and as unfailing and
all-gladdening as the Spirit of holiness itself. O
the blessedness of the eyes that see and the people
who enjoy this river of God—these crystal waters
of eternal life.

II. In the next place the Apostle tells us of a
wonderful Tree.

What is more beautiful than trees? What a
charm they add to our world! What a joy they
are to the monotony of a city! How did the fancy
of the Greek poets revel in the hanging gardens
and artificial forest scenery with which the king
of Babylon adorned his imperial city to gratify
his Median queen! There trees twelve feet in

circumference, fifty feet in height, grew on mounds of masonry, nodding like woods on their mountains, and still defying the wastes of time in the days of Quintus Curtius. The first Eden had its glad and glorious trees, "the tree of life also in the midst of the garden." (Gen. 2:9.) It was not one individual tree, but a particular tree as to its kind, as we speak of "the apple" or "the oak," denoting a species of which there are many specimens. It has the name of the Tree of Life, because man in innocence was to keep and preserve his life by eating of its fruits. It was the symbol and support of eternal life, both for body and for soul. And it is one of the special joys and provisions of the New Jerusalem that it is supplied with this same tree, in the same multitudinous sense, fulfilling something of the same offices. "*In the midst of the street of the city, and on either side of the river,*" John saw "*the Tree of Life* [in numerous specimens] *producing twelve fruits* [or kinds of fruit], *according to each month yielding its fruit; and the leaves of the tree unto the healing of the nations.*"

In Ezekiel's visions of the renewed earthly Jerusalem, a similar presentation is made. There a river issues from the sanctuary and runs down into the sea, of which the angel said, "By the river, upon the bank thereof, on this side and on that side, shall grow all trees for meat, whose leaf shall not fade, neither shall the fruit thereof be consumed: it shall bring forth new fruit according to his months; because their waters issue out of the sanctuary; and the fruit thereof shall be for meat,

and the leaf thereof for medicine." (Ezek. 47:12.)
But that relates to an order of things on earth,
which comes into being during the thousand years.
What John describes is the order of things in the
heavenly Jerusalem, which comes into existence
only after the thousand years have passed away.
But the one has its model in the other, the earthly
is a picture of the heavenly. The trees in both
cases line the river; but in the earthly order they
are outside of the city; and though bread trees,
they are not the Tree of Life. The heavenly
River issues not from the sanctuary but from the
throne. It does not flow to the sea, but through
the avenues and streetway of the city. From the
grand centre of the whole establishment it seems
to flow through the midst of all the streetway in
the city; that is through every street. And both
sides of it are lined with the Tree of Life; so that
all the myriad mansions of the New Jerusalem
thus open upon the Tree and the River of Life.

These trees, like the River whose sides they
line, are first of all for the joy and blessedness of
the dwellers in the Holy City, to beautify their
eternal home, and to minister to their happiness.
They are fruit-bearing trees, yielding their products every month, and each month a new variety.

It is sometimes asked whether the glorified saints
are to eat in heaven? We may safely answer that
they can eat, although under no need to eat; just as
we can enjoy a rose, and yet not suffer from its absence. The Saviour after his glorious resurrection

did eat, even of the coarse food of mortals. The angels did eat of Sarah's cakes and of Abraham's dressed calf. (Gen. 18 : 6–8.) There is also much that is moral and spiritual in eating. It was by eating that the fall and all its consequences came into the world. All the holy appointments of God in the old economy had eating connected with them. The highest impartation of Christ and his salvation to his people on earth is done in connection with a sacred eating and drinking. The Saviour several times refers to eating and drinking in the kingdom of glory. He again and again likens the whole provision of grace to a banquet, a feast. One of the most emphasized scenes of the future, to which this Apocalypse refers, is *a supper*, even the supper of the marriage of the Lamb. And so the implication here is that there will be eating in this Eternal City, the eating of fruits, the eating of the monthly products of the Tree of Life. The inhabitants there drink Lifewater, and they eat Life-fruits.

The eating of the fruit of the Tree of Life in the first Paradise was the sacrament of fellowship with life, a commemoration, pledge, support, and participation of life eternal, for soul and body. Hence sin cut off man from it; and all the ordinances and ministries of grace since that time are meant for his recovery and readmission to that Tree. Hence also the promise was given to the Church of Ephesus, "To him that overcometh will I give to eat of the Tree of Life, which is in the Paradise of my God." (Rev. 2 : 7.) And so again,

"Blessed they who wash their robes, that they may have right to the Tree of Life." (Rev. 22 : 14.) Like the golden table of shewbread which ever stood in the ancient Tabernacle and Temple for the priests to eat, so the Tree of Life stands in all the golden streetway of the New Jerusalem, with its monthly fruit for the immortal king-priests of heaven. And whether they need it for the support of their undecaying immortality or not, it is everywhere presented as one of the most precious privileges of God's glorified saints. We cannot suppose that they ever hunger or thirst in that high realm, or that there is ever any waste in their immortal energies needing recuperation from physical digestion; but still the participation of these Life-fruits bespeaks a communion with Life, the joy of which exceeds all present comprehension.

But these trees are for a still further purpose. The leaves of them are for the healing of the nations. As the fruits add to the joys of heaven, the leaves add to the joys of earth. Who gathers them, and how they are applied, and what the healing is which they are to work, is not told us, and it is vain to attempt to be wise above what is written. But "nations" are then to be who eat not of these fruits, though benefited by the leaves in connection with which the fruits are produced. Two classes of people are thus distinctly recognized in the new heaven and earth;—a class in glory who get the fruits of the Tree of Life, and a class in the estate of "nations" who get the leaves; but, whether fruits or leaves, a great and glorious blessing. As there will always be need for the ministrations of these celestial king-priests to those dwelling on the earth, so will those ministrations also bring them the healing leaves from the Tree of Life. As the Life-waters are not wholly shut up in the city, but descend in a form to men on the earth; so the Life-tree, in a form, yields its benefits to them too. The meaning is not that the nations are full of sicknesses and ailments; for these remains of the curse are gone then, though it may be from the virtue of these leaves. The meaning rather is the preservation of health and comfort, and not that maladies then exist to be removed. The Life-leaves are for the conservation and augmentation of Life-blessedness of men on earth, as the Life-fruits are for the joy of the saints in heaven.

III. The Apostle further informs us that there all sin and its ill consequences will no more be.

The first Paradise was glorious; but with all its blessedness, sin entered it, and the curse came, under which earth and man have been laboring and sighing for six thousand years. Hence, with all the transcendent glory described by the Apostle, the question might still be open as to its permanence,—whether sin might not again insinuate itself, with its ever-attending spoliations. Man once had a happy and unabridged right to the Tree of Life, but lost it; and that Tree, and all the Garden in which it grew, evanished from him, and left the world smoking under the tokens of Jehovah's anger. The curse came. It came upon man himself and all his seed. It came upon innocent nature with which he stood connected. It came upon the very ground on his account. Might not the same happen again, even to Paradise regained? Therefore the special assurance is here inserted, that *" every curse, or accursed thing, shall not be any more."* The relief from it is to be an eternal relief. Its disappearance from all this scene of things is to be an everlasting disappearance. The glory and blessedness will never again give place to darkness, sin, and death.

I do not fancy that the freedom of man redeemed will be any more constrained than it was when man first sinned; but the victory having been fairly achieved, under far mightier trials, by the second Adam, the Tempter will be restrained, a training and experience will then be upon the redeemed which will stand like a wall between them and danger, and the love and appreciation of what has been so dearly purchased will be so intense and high after all these ages of the reign of sin and death that they will never consent for anything to let it go. Holy angels stand fast in their blessedness forever, not because they are less free to sin than were those who kept not their first estate; but because, having stood the test, the whole momentum of their moral being moves only towards what is true and good, and so they never fall. And such shall be the security of man redeemed. Stationed on the high vantage-ground of a victory won through pain and suffering, and made strong in the unfailing helps and mercies of his God, there will be no more fuel left in him for sin to kindle, and no more curse or danger to him forever.

Being innocent, man ate of the tree of knowledge of good and evil, and learned to know *evil*. For all these weary ages he has been tasting and experiencing the bitterness of evil. Through the redemption that is in Christ Jesus, they that believe in him come to know *good;* and knowing good, there will be no more turning of their hearts from it, and hence no more sinning and no more curse. And man being finally and permanently redeemed, everything that has been disordered, disabled, or cursed for man's sake, shall also be permanently delivered. (Rom. 8 : 9–23.)

When God pronounced judgment upon the sins committed in the first Paradise, " Unto the woman he said, I will greatly multiply thy sorrow and thy conception; in sorrow shalt thou bring forth children ; and thy desire shall be to thy husband, and he shall rule over thee." (Gen. 3 : 15.) All this was imposed as penalty and curse, peculiar to her who "was first in transgression." But here the assurance is that it will be completely lifted off, and be no more. (Com. 1 Tim. 2 : 15.) " And unto Adam he said, Because thou hast hearkened to the voice of thy wife, and hast eaten of the tree, of which I commanded thee, saying, Thou shalt not eat of it; cursed is the ground for thy sake; in sorrow shalt thou eat of it all the days of thy

life; thorns also and thistles shall it bring forth
to thee; and thou shalt eat the herb of the field;
in the sweat of thy face shalt thou eat bread, till
thou return unto the ground; for out of it wast
thou taken : for dust thou art, and unto dust shalt
thou return." (Gen. 3 : 17–19.)   Here was penalty
and curse, whose potent condemnation has been
binding and afflicting earth and man from that
day to this.   It affects all the elements man
touches, and the whole order of things amid which
he lives.   It affects what he eats and what he
drinks, the air he breathes and the ground on
which he walks.   It affects all the growths of nature in all its sublunary kingdoms, and conditions
the seasons and the sea.   It has opened the avenues of disease, calamity, and death, till the earth
is no longer habitable for man, except for a few
brief years.   Everywhere, on everything, we read
and have it flashed upon us, that man is a sinner;
that a fearful condemnation hangs over him; that
a curse for his sin is festering in all that pertains
to him and his dwelling-place.   But it is not incurable.   The remedy may be long in taking
effect, but it is provided,—provided in Jesus
Christ, his achievements as the second Adam, and
his sovereign power and purpose to destroy all the
works of the devil, and to subdue all things to
himself.   The first note that John heard coming
forth from the Throne when the final judgment
was over, was, "BEHOLD, NEW I MAKE EVERYTHING."
(Rev. 21: 5.)   And the effect of that renewal is
further stated in the text to be, that every curse

shall cease to exist. Not of the holy city alone can this be said; for there the curse never was. It is a word which applies above all to the place where the curse has been. It was upon woman, and man, and earth, and the economy of things on the earth, that the sentence was put; and from them therefore must be its cessation. Nor do we go beyond the necessary implications of this divine assurance when we read from its massive terms that this whole scene of earthly life, where sin and death have reigned so long, will yet come up out of all its desolations; that the very blessedness of Paradise shall revisit all its hills and vales; and that throughout this nether world, disordered, cut with graves, and full of miseries, that goal of the prayer our Lord has taught us shall be realized, when it shall be " *on earth as it is in heaven.*"

IV. The Apostle tells us also of a glorious throne.

There is a central throne of the universe where Christ now sits and reigns with the Eternal Father. The dominion which he there holds as " head over all things for the Church," he is to deliver up when the time for the great consummation arrives. He is now with the Father on his throne, but there is another throne peculiarly his own, which he will then take, and on which his glorified people shall reign with him, as he now reigns with the Father. (Compare 1 Cor. 15:24–28, and Rev. 3:21.) This throne is in the New Jerusalem. It is " the throne of God," as Christ is God; and it is " the throne of the Lamb," in that it is held and occupied as the result of Christ's achievement as a sacrifice for sin, and in his particular character as the world's Saviour and Redeemer. It is the throne of God as the Lamb, the All-Ruler, who once was slain, but lives again, and here is to reign with his glorified saints to the ages of the ages.

There is something peculiar about these thrones. In the first three chapters of this Book, Christ appears in the sanctuary, walking amid the golden lamp-stands, noting and pronouncing upon his Churches. There no throne is visible, for the Church is only the kingdom in process of formation, answering to the period of Israel's pilgrimage in the wilderness. In the succeeding chapters a throne appears; but with surroundings indicative of a special dispensation with regard to the old earth, partly retributive and partly remedial. It is the throne of the judgment period which holds only during " the day of the Lord," in which Christ is engaged in enforcing the principles of his Kingdom and his claims by visitations of successive judgments upon the world; answering to the reign of the Judges, when the Ark and its accompaniments were yet in the movable and temporary tabernacle, and the kingdom was not yet established. With the Halleluias over the fall of Babylon, this particular throne disappears, and we see only the thrones of the Shepherdizers, who for a time rule the nations with a rod of iron; answering to the warlike reign of David, when the preparations for the Temple were making. The last rebellion, typified by that enacted by Absalom against his father, having been put down, the "Great White Throne" appears, the final judgment throne, with no signs of blessing, consigning all the unholy dead to their final doom. And then comes the Holy City and the full establishment of the Kingdom of peace, answering to the illustrious reign of the wise and peaceful Solomon, when the Temple took its place on Mount Moriah, and there "was neither adversary nor evil." In the Holy City the throne then takes its position, as the final throne of God and the Lamb with reference to the earth and man. It is a single throne, the seat and centre of all the authority and power ever thenceforward put forth for the regulation and government of human affairs. And its occupants, and the only administrants of its dominion, are God, the Lamb, and his glorified saints. " *And they shall reign to the ages of the ages.*" No more faulty politics, no more false religion, no more rabble rule or oppressive tyranny, shall then be any more. For the reign of righteousness has come, and it will fail no more forever.

V. Finally, the Apostle tells us of the condition of things under this administration.

He has already given us something on this point. He has told us of the directness of communion with God in that Blessed City,—of the centre of light, interest, attraction, and holy reverence which

it will be to the whole earth,—of the joyful obedience with which the nations will walk in its light,—
of the health which is to go forth from its immortal
trees,—of the endless and unintermitting light of
God and the Lamb which shall be in it;—but he
adds still other items as instructed by the angel.

"*His servants shall serve him.*" In general the
servants of a king are his subjects. So taken,
there is in this affirmation a picture of universal
obedience and loving devotion;—no more sin, no
more rebellion, no more forgetfulness or neglect
of the claims or word of the Eternal King. All
life is to be permeated and transfigured with the
most complete and happy accord with the divine
will, which then is done "on earth as it is in
heaven." The prophecies are everywhere full of
the most glowing pictures on this point. Even
the bells or bridles of the horses shall be Holiness
unto the Lord, and the commonest utensils in the
houses and kitchens of mankind shall take on a
sacredness like that of the consecrated vessels of
the temple itself. (Zech. 14: 20, 21.) For the glory
of the Lord shall cover the earth as the waters
cover the sea. It will be the abounding element
in which everything is bathed.

But the servants of a king, in a more particular
sense, are his immediate attendants, those who are
in waiting upon the throne, and who act as its
agents and representatives. Hence, when the
Queen of Sheba saw "the sitting of Solomon's
servants, and the attendance of his ministers and
their apparel, and his cup-bearers," she said:

"Happy are thy men, happy are *these thy servants which stand continually before thee.*" (1 Kings 10: 5, 8.) So Solomon made hewers of wood and drawers of water of some of his subjects, but others he made "men of war, and *his servants,* and his princes, and his captains, and rulers of his chariots and his horsemen." (1 Kings 9: 22.) So the priests, the prophets, the ministers of the Word, and such as hold official rank and place in the divine economies, are more especially called *the servants* of God. Such are all the members of the Church of the first-born, the elect, the citizens of the heavenly Jerusalem, the sharers in the administration of that holy kingdom. And of these especially is this word spoken. It tells of the very highest honor and dignity, of the closest intimacy with eternal power and authority, of the most inward nearness and participation in the administration of divine government. But it tells also of mighty activities and responsible duties. It shows us most clearly that the heaven of the glorified saints is not one of idleness. They have something more to do than to sing, and worship, and enjoy. Indeed the perfection of worship is service, activity for God, the doing of the will of God. And this is to be one of the highest characteristics of the heaven of the saints. They are to do work, heavenly work, the highest kind of work, the execution and administration of the will and bidding of the throne of eternity, the work of the high officials who stand nearest to the throne, and through whom the throne expresses itself. Like "the seven *princes* of Persia and Media which *saw the king's face*, and which *sat first in the kingdom* " (Esth. 1 : 14), so these " *servants* shall serve him, and *they shall see his face, and the name of him shall be upon their foreheads.*"

The Jewish high priest, when fully arrayed as the officer and agent of Jehovah, in addition to his mitre, had a plate of burnished gold upon his brow, on which was engraved the great Name of that almighty Being for whom he served. These dwellers in the New Jerusalem are all priests then, as well as kings, and so they have the tokens of their sublime office and consecration on their foreheads. The name of their King and God is there, to tell of their dignity, their office, and the transcendent authority and glory of him for whom they officiate. In the courts of kings, the most honored servants and favorites wear badges and marks in token of the king's confidence, favor, and affection. The noble knights have their ribbons; and those whom the king delighteth to honor have their chains of gold about their necks, their rosettes, their indications of standing with their sovereign. So these all have the Name of the All-Ruling Lamb upon their foreheads, showing exaltation, honor, and blessedness of the very highest degree. They are the enthroned princes of the eternal realm, the servants of the Supreme God, the very organs and expressions of the everlasting Throne.

Again it is said that " night shall not be any more." The repetition of this particular, emphasizes it as a very special and a very glorious blessing. The light of God and the Lamb shall be so full, glorious, and abiding, that night no longer can exist in that city. Its inhabitants need no shutting off of day to give them sleep. They are independent of all material orbs or their revolutions. Of course, this statement does not apply to "the nations" on the earth. The succession of day and night existed before Adam fell, and he needed the repose of night even in his innocence. He lived in an earthly body, and that body needed sleep. We also have the positive statement that he did sleep, even before he sinned. Likewise those who then live in the flesh, will need sleep, and their seasons of repose. Hence, the covenant with Noah was, that, "while the earth remaineth, day and night shall not cease." (Gen. 8 : 22.) But in the home of the glorified saints there will be no more night. Darkness of all orders, physical, mental, and moral, shall have no place there. As the glory of the Shekinah ever glowed in the Holy of Holies, so shall the Jehovah brightness ever illuminate the heavenly Jerusalem, and all its inhabitants shall themselves be light; for they "shall shine as the brightness of the firmament, and as the stars forever and ever." (Dan. 12 : 3.)

"*And they shall reign to the ages of the ages.*" Not for the thousand years only, but forever shall their glory and dominion last. This tells at once their eternal dignity, and the eternal perpetuity of men in the flesh. If they are to be kings forever, they must have subjects forever; and their subjects,

whom they shepherdize, over whom they rule, and
for whom they hold the dominion, are everywhere
described as "*the nations*"—"all people, languages,
and nations under the whole heaven." (Rev. 2 :
26; 12 : 5; 22 : 1; 24 : 26; Dan. 7 : 14, 27; Matt.
19 : 28, 29 ; 1 Cor. 6 : 2.) Either, then, their kingdom must come to an end for want of subjects, or
nations, peoples, and men on the earth must continue in the flesh, as Adam and Eve before the
fall. But these glorified ones are to "reign to the
ages of the ages," and their "kingdom is an everlasting kingdom;" and as they cannot reign without subjects, so nations on earth must last coequally
with their regency. Both their office, and the
activities in which their sublimest happiness is located, must fail them, if the nations over whom
their rule is, ever cease to be. They neither
marry, nor are given in marriage; for they are as
the angels of God; but their subjects are of a different order, and their dominion and glory shall
grow forever, by the ceaseless augmentation of
the number of their subjects throughout unending
generations.

Such is the final picture set before us in these
wonderful prophecies and foreshowings of the purposes of our God. Such are the fore-intimations
of that new heavens and earth wherein eternal
righteousness dwells. And such are the glimpses
which our gracious Saviour has given us of the
dignities and blessedness to which we are called
by his Gospel.

See, then, my friends, how very high our calling

is. And shall we not value, cherish, and improve it? Shall we throw away our chance for such an eternal home? Shall we slight the offers and opportunities of blessedness like this? Let fortunes pass; let friendships be forfeited; let earthly comforts go unenjoyed; cast honors, titles, crowns, empires to the wolves and bats; but let not the privilege go by of becoming an immortal king and co-regent with the Lamb in the Golden City of the New Jerusalem.

Rise, my soul, and stretch thy wings,
  Thy better portion trace;
Rise from transitory things
  Toward heaven, thy native place.

Sun, and moon, and stars decay,
  Time shall soon this earth remove;
Rise, my soul, and haste away
  To seats prepared above!

LECTURE FIFTY-FIRST.

LAST SECTION OF THE BOOK—CERTAINTY OF THESE REVELA-
TIONS—THE REPEATED BENEDICTION UPON THOSE WHO
TREASURE THEM—EFFECT OF THEM ON THE APOSTLE—THE
DIRECTION TO HIM WHAT TO DO WITH THEM—AN ARGU-
MENT FOR THE SAME—THE CONDITION ON WHICH THE
BEATITUDES OF THIS BOOK ARE TO BE ENJOYED—A PAR-
TICULAR WASHING OF ROBES.

REV. 22 : 6–15. (Revised Text.) And he said to me, These words
[are] faithful and true, and the Lord the God of the spirits of the
prophets sent his angel to show to his servants what things must come
to pass shortly.

And behold, I come quickly : blessed he that keepeth the words of
the prophecy of this book.

And I, John, [was] hearing and seeing these things. And when
I had heard and seen, I fell down to worship before the feet of the
angel who showed me these things. And he saith to me, See, no ; I
am fellow-servant of thee and of thy brethren the prophets, and of those
who keep the words of this book : worship God.

And he saith to me, Seal not up the words of the prophecy of this
book ; the time is near. Let the unjust one do injustice more and
more, and the filthy [or *polluted*] one defile [or *do pollution*] more and
more, and the righteous one do righteousness more and more, and the
holy one sanctify more and more.

Behold, I come quickly, and my reward with me, to give to each as
his work is, I the Alpha and the Omega, First and Last, the Beginning
and the End. Blessed they that wash their robes that they may [in
that they shall] have the power over the tree of life, and enter by the
gates into the city. Excluded [or *outside are*] the dogs, and the sorcerers, and the fornicators, and the murderers, and the idolaters, and
every one loving or making a lie [or, *what is false*].

WE come now to the last section of this wonderful Book—the Epilogue—the closing remarks. The Grand Panorama of an ending and renewing world has reached the point where everything enters upon the eternal state, and we are now to take leave of the wonderful exhibit. We have seen the Church in its universality and varied historic continuity from the days of the Apostle down to the time when Christ shall come for his people, and how he will end its career by taking one here and another there, and leaving the rest, because of their unreadiness to taste the sorrows of the great Tribulation. With the judgment thus begun at the house of God, we have seen it roll along through the breaking of seals, the sounding of trumpets, and the pouring out of bowls of wrath, in ever-varying scenes of miracle and wonder, towards saints and sinners, the living and the dead. We have seen the Antichrist coming up from his abyss, captivating the world, running his course of unexampled blasphemy, and sinking forever in his deserved perdition. We have seen the final doings of Satan, in heaven and earth, his arrest and imprisonment, his short loosing, and his final consignment, with all his, to the lake of fire. We have seen the thrones of the shepherdizers of the nations, the breaking down of all rebellion, and the coming forth into the living world of the eternal principles of righteousness. We have seen the shaking of the old heavens and earth, and the same passed through the throes of the long-expected Regeneration. We

have seen the crowned princes of the first resurrection wedded to the All-Ruling Lamb, and led
into the golden city of their hopes. We have
seen the New Jerusalem come down out of heaven
from God ; Sin, Death, Hades, and the curse swept
into Gehenna; the Tabernacle of God taking its
place among men; redemption complete; Paradise
regained; and the nations of the earth in Edenic
peace and glory setting out under their immortal
kings for an eternity of uninterrupted blessedness.
And it only remains now to give a few closing
particulars with reference to these momentous
Revelations, that men may attend to them with
tha reverence and faith which of right belongs to
the n. May God help us to hear, learn, and in-
wardly digest them to our abiding consolation !

I. The first thing we are called on to note is,
their absolute truth and certainty. There is nothing
in which the difference of the Scriptures from all
other teachings is more manifest than in the posi-
tiveness and authority with which they deliver
themselves on all subjects, even where reason can
tell us nothing, and where the presentations are
so marvellous as to stagger belief. When the
Saviour was on earth, he spake with such clearness and simplicity, and with such knowing majesty and commanding mastery of all wisdom that
men who heard him were amazed, forgot all other
authorities, and hasted away in awe, saying, " *Never
man spake like this man.*" And so it is in all the
word of inspiration. Even where angels would
scarce dare to tread, it enters with perfect free-

dom, as upon its own home domain, and declares itself with all that assured certainty which belongs only to Omniscience. Even with regard to all the astounding and seemingly impossible wonders of this Book, the absolute truth of every jot and tittle is guaranteed with the abounding fulness of the completest knowledge of everything involved. In case of some of the most wonderful of these presentations, the word to John was, " *Write, because these words are faithful and true.*" And so here, with regard to all the contents of the Book, it was said to the Seer, " *These words [are] faithful and true.*"

Thrice is it repeated, that these presentations are faithful and true (19 : 9; 21 : 5; 22 : 6); and twice is it affirmed that these showings are all from God. In the opening of the Book it is said, that he "sent his angel to his servant John" for the purpose of making these revelations, and here at the conclusion, we have it repeated, that " *the Lord the God of the spirits of the prophets sent his angel to show to his servants what things* MUST *come to pass.*" Nay more, Christ himself adds special personal testimony to the fact: "I, JESUS, *sent my angel to testify to you these things.*" Thus the very God of all inspiration, and of all inspired men, reiterates and affirms the highest authority for all that is herein written.

Either, then, this Book is nothing but a base and blasphemous forgery, unworthy of the slightest respect of men, and specially unworthy of a place in the Sacred Canon; or it is one of the most directly inspired and authoritative writings ever given. But a forgery it cannot be. All the Churches named in its first chapters, from the earliest periods succeeding the time of its writing, with one accord, accepted and honored it as from their beloved Apostolic ·Father. Papias, Bishop of Hieropolis, a disciple of St. John, a colleague of the Seven Angels of these Churches, and who gave much attention to the collection of all the memorable sayings and works of the Apostles, accepted and honored this Book as the genuine production of this venerable Apostle. Nor is there another Book in the New Testament whose genuineness and inspiration were more clearly and strongly attested on its first appearance, and for the three half centuries next following. Augustine and the Latin Council unquestionably had good and sufficient reason for classing it with the most sacred apostolic records, and the Church in general for regarding it as a Book of prophecy " from Christ's own divine, omniscient, and eternal Spirit."* And if it really is the Lord Jesus who speaks to us in this Book, there is nothing in all the Canon of Scripture which he more pointedly attests, more solemnly guards, or more urgently presses upon the study and devout regard of all who would be his disciples. People may account us crazy for giving so much attention to it, and laugh at our credulity for daring to believe that it means what it says; but better be accounted possessed, as

* See Vol. I, pp. 26–31.

Christ himself was considered, and be pronounced beside ourselves and mad, after the manner of Paul, than to take our lot with Pharisees, and Festuses, and Agrippas, and Galios. If we err in this, we err with the goodly fellowship of the saints, with the noble army of the martyrs, in the society of many great and good and wise in many ages and nations. And if it should finally turn out that we have been beguiling ourselves with dreams, they still give us the most consistent philosophy of Providence, and the most comforting solutions of life's mysteries, whilst our pretensionless submission to what seems most surely to be our Creator's word and will may serve us best when we come to answer at his judgment-seat. We believe that it is God who tells us, "*these words are faithful and true;*" therefore we so take them, and build our faith upon them, and testify them to all the world.

II. A second particular to be noted in this Epilogue is the repetition of the benediction upon those who treasure what is written in this Book. In the opening verses the inspired writer said: "Blessed he who readeth, and those who hear the words of the prophecy, and observe the things which are written in it." But here the Saviour himself, even he whose nearing Apocalypse these records were given to describe, says, in a voice uttered from his glorious throne in heaven, "*Blessed he that keepeth the words of the prophecy of this Book.*" All this is additional to the seven

times repeated admonition, " *He that hath an ear,
let him hear what the Spirit saith unto the Churches.*"
Is there another Book in the holy Canon so intense, so emphatic, so constant, so full from end
to end, in its expressions of the good to be gained
and the ill to be avoided by the hearing and learning of its own particular presentations? It is precisely as if the Saviour knew and foresaw, as he
certainly did, what neglect, prejudice, and mis-
treatment this Book would encounter in the later
ages of the Church, and how it and the students
of it, and especially the believers in its wonderful
descriptions, would be ridiculed, avoided, and put
aside, as not in the line of proper and wholesome
edification. And how will some of these pious
scorners, whom Christ has set and ordained to feed
his sheep and give them meat in due season, feel
and fare, when from the judgment-seat he shall
say: " Sirs, I gave you the complete chart of my
promised Apocalypse; I caused it to be made as
plain as words and visions can make anything of
the sort; I told you over and over of the momentous importance of studying, treasuring, and
making known to the Churches what I thus sent
my angel and my beloved disciple to show you;
and yet you have held it to be a crazy Book, one
which either finds or leaves crazy those who study
it, and have not believed my word, nor taught it
to my people, nor allowed it to speak in the appointed Lectionaries, and have only sought to explain away its momentous import into a little dim
foreshowing of a few ages of ordinary earthly his-

tory! Was this the way for good servants of their
Lord to act? Was this being faithful stewards of
the mysteries of God? Was this the way to treat
what I have been at such pains to give, and pointed
you to with so much solemnity, and promised to
reward your study of it with such special benedictions?" Alas, alas, what answer will they make?
Will they say that it was too difficult a Book for
them to understand? This would only be adding
insult to their unfaithfulness. Dare we suppose
that the merciful Jesus would hang his benedictions so high as to be beyond the reach of those
to whom they are so graciously proposed? Would
he mock us by suspending his offered blessings
on terms beyond our power? Yet this is the
charge men bring against their Redeemer when
they think to plead the incomprehensibility of this
Book for their neglect and practical rejection of
it. The very propounding of these blessings and
rewards is God's own seal to the possibility of
understanding this Book equally with any other
part of Scripture. Would he, the God of truth,
lie to us? Would he, the God of mercy, mock
us? Would he who gave his life for us, and ever
lives and ministers in heaven and earth for our
enlightenment and salvation, give us a Book to
tell us of the outcome of all his gracious operations, command us to note its words, to believe
and treasure its contents, and promise us a special
blessedness in so doing, if what he has thus put
into our hands is not at all within the limits of
our comprehension and successful mastery? Does

not everything that we know of the dear God above us rise up to condemn all such thoughts as slanderous of heaven, and blasphemy against our precious Saviour's goodness? Therefore these very benedictions pronounce against the common notion that this Book is too difficult for ordinary Christians, and rebuke all who despise and avoid it. If it is anything, these proffered blessings are more than a divine justification for all the time and pains which we have been bestowing upon it, and for accepting, believing, holding, and testifying as the very truth of God all that we have found herein written. Let men estimate us and our work as they please, we have here the unmistakable authority of heaven for it, that this Apocalypse is capable of being understood; that its presentations are among the most momentous in all the Word of God; and that the highest blessedness of believers is wrapped up with the learning and keeping of what is pictured to us in it. And if Christians would rise to the true comfort of their faith,—if they would possess themselves of a right philosophy of God's purposes and providence,—if they would be guarded against the greatest dangers and most subtle deceptions of the Old Serpent,—if they would really know what Redemption means, and what the height and glory of their calling is,—let them not despise or neglect this crowning Book of the New Testament, but study its pages, take its statements as they read, get its stupendous visions into their understandings, treasure its words in their hearts, and believe and know that it is comprehensible for all who are really willing to be instructed in these mighty things. If we wait till they are fulfilled, it will then be too late to get the blessing which the reading, hearing, and keeping of what is said concerning them is to bestow. It is in our understanding of them before they come to pass that the blessedness lies; for when once Christ comes in the scenes of his Apocalypse, the time to begin to put ourselves in readiness for it will be past. We must understand beforehand, as this record was meant to advise us beforehand, or it will be useless to think of getting ourselves in position when once these momentous scenes become accomplished realities. By all that is sacred, therefore, let us beware how we treat this Book, and the showings which it contains, remembering this word of the Lord Jesus, spoken to us from heaven: " *Blessed he that keepeth the words of the prophecy of this Book.*"*

III. Another particular to be noticed is, the effect which these showings had upon the Apostle

---

* Old James Robertson, in issuing his book on the Revelation in 1730, made this remark: "Some are not ashamed directly to flout at, and spit contempt upon these that meddle with the exposition of this Prophecy; which is an indirect battering of a great part of God's word. Thus Dr. South, in one of his sermons, affirms, that none but a madman will meddle with the Revelation; or, if he has wits at the beginning, before he has done they will be cracked. And Davies, a Welsh bombastic barrister, has the impudence to insult a learned and reverend prelate, yet alive, because he consumed two full years and more on this Prophecy." But we can afford to let men sneer when we have the sure benediction of God.

at the time. So wonderful were the revelations, and so wonderful was the knowledge and understanding of the angel which communicated these things, that John was filled with the profoundest adoration. Twice he fell down before the feet of the angel to worship him. He meant no idolatry; but so wonderful in wisdom and intelligence was his heavenly guide, and so transcendent were the things shown, that he could not but think that it was God himself. The presentations all along were such as to make it hard to distinguish whether it was God himself speaking, or whether it was through a created messenger that he spoke. And in this instance particularly, it certainly was the Lord Jesus whom he heard say, "Behold I come quickly;" and not distinguishing between him who spoke, and the messenger through whom he spoke, John "fell down before the feet of the angel." This clearly shows that the holy Apostles held Christ to be a worshipful being, and that he was none other than true God as well as true man. John knew that it was and must be Christ who spoke, and his instant adoration was meant for Christ, therefore he held Christ to be adorable God. The only mistake was that he did not at the moment perceive that it was a created angel speaking for Christ, and not Christ himself in the form of an angel. Even the best and holiest of men may make mistakes from their human impulses, as Moses when he broke the tables of the Law, and Peter when he avoided the Gentile Christians at Antioch. But innocent mistakes, and those which result from the truest and devoutest intentions, may be very injurious, and need to be promptly corrected. There was danger here of a double sin, one on the part of John in giving worship to the angel instead of Christ, and one on the part of the angel in accepting worship which belongs only to Deity. But John was in doubt, which the angel had not, and therefore it belonged to the angel in truth and fidelity to John, as well as to God and himself, to correct John's mistake on the spot. The Devil solicits adoration, but holy angels repel it as a detraction from Jehovah. Hence, when John fell down to worship before this holy angel's feet, promptly came the word, "*Take heed, no; I am fellow-servant of thee and of thy brethren the prophets, and of those who keep the words of this Book: worship God.*" The misapprehension being dispelled, the Apostle of course desisted. The incident shows that no saint or angel worship can have the approval of heaven. If it was wrong to worship this glorious heavenly messenger, in and through whom came forth the very voice of Jesus, how can it be right to worship and pray to the Virgin Mary, to whom is assigned no such dignity or office? The impulse and intention may be devout and good; but it is a great mistake, and we take the side of heaven and holy angels when we say to those who do it: "See, no, no; you do greatly err; you are taking Christ's honor from him and bestowing it upon his human mother or friends; worship God, for it is written, 'Him only shalt thou serve.'"

But whilst this incident brings out the fact that the best of men may mistake, even out of the holiest motives, it also brings out the more important facts, that John fully believed all these revelations, that he was most profoundly convinced that they were from God, that angels also treasure them as the great divine lights touching what is to be, and that John is recognized in heaven as a genuine prophet. The angel calls him a fellow-servant with himself, the same as the whole brotherhood of sacred prophets. Mistaken as he was for the moment in not distinguishing his heavenly guide from his Lord, he yet was duly illuminated as a prophet, and still had the office and inspiration of God for the understanding of these mysteries, and the making of them known to the Churches. Angels have often been commissioned to disclose to men important sacred truths. It was an angel who was thus employed in acquainting Ezekiel and Daniel with many of the most important features of their wonderful prophecies; and so it was in the giving of these particulars of the Apocalypse to John. In this respect angels are prophets too, and prophetically minister to the heirs of salvation. Not only as servants of God are they the fellow-servants of the prophets; but they also become fellow-prophets when engaged in communicating a knowledge of the divine mind and purposes to men. And in this fellowship of servants of the same Lord, and of service in making known divine things, John is here acknowledged as a co-partner with the angel himself. What he writes us, therefore, is true prophecy, and demands to be received as such.

IV. A further particular here to be noted is the direction to John what to do with these revelations. Whether from Christ direct, or through the angel whom Christ sent to show him these things, command was given him: "*Seal not up the words of the prophecy of this Book.*" Some take this as antithetical to the command given Daniel with regard to his prophecies. (Dan. 8 : 26; 12 : 4, 9.) But that is plainly a mistake. There is no reference whatever to Daniel. Besides, the direction given to Daniel was the very reverse of what is thus assumed.* The true antithesis is the command with regard to what the seven thunders uttered, as referred to in chapter 10 : 4. From the beginning of these marvellous experiences John was directed to write what he saw and heard, and to make the same known to the Churches. So, " when the seven thunders spoke," he " was about to write;" but a voice from heaven said, "*Seal up those things which the seven thunders spoke, and write them not.*" The *sealing* enjoined stands over against writing and making known, and hence is quite a different sealing from that which was commanded Daniel. John was to bury up the thing in his own breast, not to write it, not to make it known at all. But what he was not to do respecting the utterances of the seven thunders, he was to do with reference

---

* See my *Voices from Babylon*, pp. 304–306.

to all other " words of the prophecy of this Book."
He was not to seal them up; that is, not to conceal
them, but to record them, to make them known,
to publish them to the Churches.

Not from any self-will on his part, therefore,
have these Apocalyptic records been put before
us; but by direct command of our God and Saviour. They constitute his last and crowning
legacy to his Church and people. They are written by his appointment and command. They are
put into our hands by the specific direction of
eternal power and Godhead. They are therefore
God's word to us.   And if he commanded the
writing of them, I cannot see how men are to excuse themselves from the reading and study of
them; or how any Christian can think lightly of
them, or put them from him as of no practical
worth, and yet retain his holy faithfulness to the
plain will and inculcations of our blessed Lord and
Judge. O, my friends, let us beware how we neglect or despise a Book upon which God Almighty
has laid so much stress, urgency, and importance.
If John had sealed it up, or failed to lay it before
us as it is, he would have forfeited his place and
standing as an apostle of Christ; how, then, can
we think our duty discharged, or the provisions
for our highest blessedness duly accepted and
used, if we pass it by as a dead letter, or make it
to us as if it had never been?

V. Again, there is added here a very singular
argument. It is not easy to give the exact literal

sense of the peculiarly constructed phraseology; but taking the whole connection and bearing of the passage, it may perhaps be best rendered, "*Let the unjust one do injustice more and more, and the filthy one defile more and more, and the righteous one do righteousness more and more, and the holy one sanctify more and more.*" Many take the statement as referring to the eternal fixedness of character, both for the bad and good, when once these Apocalyptic scenes have been fulfilled. It is indeed a great truth, that a time comes to every one when the seal of permanence is set upon the spiritual condition, rendering the unjust one unjust forever, and the righteous one righteous forever. The same is also involved in this statement. But it is hardly to be taken as the main thought. The meaning has immediate reference to the non-sealing, that is, the writing and publication of "the words of the prophecy of this Book," and the nearness of the time of their fulfilment. The direct bearing of the statement is that of an argument for the writing and publishing of these revelations, and the holding of them up to the view of all men, over against the non-effect or ill effect they may have upon the wicked and unbelieving, or upon the Antichrist and his adherents, who is emphatically the unjust and unclean one. Though "wicked men and seducers shall wax worse and worse," and even wrest what is herein predicted of them as if it were a license for their wickedness or a fixing of it by an irresistible necessity, and so are only the more encouraged and urged on in their injustice and abominations; still, this is not to prevent the freest and fullest proclamation of the whole truth. Let the unjust one be the more confirmed in his unbelief and wickedness;—let the filthy one go on in his idolatries and moral defilement with all the greater hardihood and blasphemy;—that is not to restrain the making known of what shall come to pass. If it accelerates the antichristian development, and the wicked are only the more indurated in their wickedness, let it so be. Though the sun breed pestilence and death in the morasses, and only hasten putrefaction in what is lifeless and rotten, it must not therefore be blotted from the heavens, or hindered from shining into our world. There is another side to the question. If it is an ill thing to what is ill, the life of what is living requires it. Believers must be forewarned and forearmed, or they too will be deceived and perish. And if the wicked are made the wickeder, the righteous and holy will be the holier, and without it cannot be defended and kept as they need to be. Therefore, let not this holy book be sealed up, nor its grand prophecies shut off from the fullest record and the most unreserved proclamation. There is always a twofold effect from the preaching of the divine word. It is quick and powerful, and never leaves men where it finds them. It either makes them better, or it makes them worse. If it does not absolve, it the more condemns. If it does not soften to penitence, it hardens in iniquity. If it is not a savor of life unto life, it is a savor of death unto death.

And, unfortunately for the great masses of its hearers, it is an instrument of damnation rather than of salvation. Particularly is this true with regard to the foreshowings of prophecy as set forth in this Book. For the most gracious purposes have these revelations been given. They come to us freighted with spiritual blessing, light, and confirmation. They are the very things, in God's estimate, for the setting of believers right in their conceptions, lives, hopes, and aims, and for shielding them against perils from which it is next thing to impossible otherwise to escape. And yet there is the strangest unwillingness to believe or receive them as they stand written. Even good men are offended at them, denounce them, ridicule them, explain them away, do anything with them but admit them into their belief and expectations of the future. I doubt not, that this Apocalypse has been and will be the rock on which many a one's salvation is wrecked by reason of the offence taken at its presentations. To the savants and scientists of this world, there is no part of all the Scriptures which seems so absurd and impossible. They can get on with everything else a thousandfold better than with the outlines of the future which this Book gives. To their philosophy it is the very consummation of nonsense. And if this is the scheme and outcome of the Gospel system, they will have none of it. They know better. They have got beyond all such puerilities. They would not swallow such things for their lives, and scorn to take for divine what embraces them as the con-

summation of this world. Their sneers, contempt,
and blasphemy nowhere rise to such a pitch as
when they are asked to accept and believe that
this Book is of God, and means what it says. And
all the more so shall the temper be as the sensual
and devilish wisdom matures, develops, and exhibits its proud knowledge and mastery of the
material elements. But the truth of God must be
spoken nevertheless. Let the unjust one do injustice all the more; let the filthy one defile himself all the more; let the offence, and the stum-
bling, and the skepticism, and the scorning, and
the blasphemy, and the condemnation be aggra-
vated by it as they may, "the words of the prophecy of this Book" must not be sealed up. There
are some elect ones whom it will benefit, enlighten,
and save from the toils of the Old Deceiver. There
are righteous ones whom it will establish and secure in their righteousness. And there are some
consecrated ones whom it will the more set apart
for God and the more intensify in their devotion
and their ready-making to join their Lord and
Master in the Golden City of the New Jerusalem.
Though the wicked shall do wickedly, and none
of the wicked shall understand, yet the wise shall
understand, and for them the Book is necessary.

VI. One particular more in this Epilogue is all
that I can notice to-night. It is a particular which
the oldest and best manuscripts and all the most
competent critics agree in giving in a different
form from that in which it stands in our English

Bibles. It relates to the conditions and qualifications upon which the beatitudes of this Book are suspended. Our English version reads, "Blessed are they that do his commandments, that they may have right to the tree of life, and may enter in through the gates into the city." The now better-established reading, to which all consent, literally rendered, is : "*Blessed they that wash their robes, that they may* [*in that day shall*] *have the power over the tree of life, and enter by the gates into the city.*"* The meaning is not essentially different; but the true reading cuts out the possibility of a legalistic interpretation, gives to the passage its genuine evangelic flavor, and conforms its imagery to what was previously said in this Book with reference to what brought the great multitude out of the great tribulation. (Chap. 7 : 14.)

Washing, or cleansing, is the great qualification for heaven,—" the washing of water by the word " (Eph. 5 : 26),—"the washing of regeneration " (Tit. 3 : 5),—cleansing by the blood of Jesus Christ (1 John 1 : 7). There is no doing or keeping of commandments that can save us without this. (Eph. 2 : 8, 9.) Hence Paul speaks of the Corinthian Christians as " washed, sanctified, justified in the name of the Lord Jesus, and by the Spirit of our God " (1 Cor. 6 : 11); and John ascribes glory and dominion to the Lord Jesus for having washed

---

* See the Codex Sinaiticus, Codex Alexandrinus, the Vulgate, the Ethiopic, and some Armenian copies, Lachmann, Buttmann, Ewald, Thiele, Tregelles, Alford, Wordsworth, and all the great authorities.

[freed] us from our sins in His own blood (Rev.
1 : 5); and the writer of the Epistle to the Hebrews
speaks of our drawing near to the holiest of all,
" having our hearts sprinkled from an evil conscience, and our bodies washed with pure water"
as the high priest of old (Heb. 10 : 22). Nor can
we ever hope to enter the Holy City, or eat of its
fruits, or taste of its blessedness, without this spiritual washing from all the filthinesses of the flesh
and of the spirit. " The dogs, or unclean ones,
and the sorcerers, and the fornicators, and the
murderers, and the idolaters, and every one loving
and making a lie [or what is false]," are all excluded from that pure and holy habitation. And
whoever hath good hope of seeing and being with
Christ in heaven, " purifieth himself even as he is
pure." (1 John 3 : 2, 3.)

But the washing of which the text speaks, whilst
presupposing and including this general cleansing,
is something more special. It is a washing of *garments* or *robes*. It has reference to habit in particular, in addition to the nature in general. One's
clothes are reckoned with himself. They are an
outside part of him, but that which marks the
form, order, or habit in which he bears himself.
There is something moral and spiritual in clothes.
They express much of the inward taste and character. They come between us and society, to a
large extent represent us to society, and react
again on our inner consciousness, moral sense, and
state of mind and heart. We cannot always judge
one from the clothes he wears, but we cannot help

the effect which clothes have upon our judgment of people. They tell a story of the wearers of them. And if any one is habitually filthy, slovenly, unclean, and untidy in his garments, it is a blur upon him, a repugnance, a thing to make his presence unwelcome and undesirable in respectable company. When it comes to agreeable social recognition and intercourse, clean clothes are associated with a right heart, a right mind, and a right feeling. Anything short of this is an offence and a disqualification. Hence the Scriptural figure of keeping one's garments and washing one's robes, as a spiritual requirement for the society of heaven. He that hath not on "a wedding garment" is cast out, and not permitted to have place at the supper-table of the king. We must therefore distinguish this washing of robes and cleanness of apparel from the spiritual and more inward washing of the man in general.

What, then, is this particular washing of garments? This question I have nowhere seen answered; and yet it needs to be answered, and can be answered. Nor need we be surprised if it should turn out to have direct reference to the main subject of this Apocalypse. The chief honors of the kingdom at Christ's coming are everywhere connected with a looking and waiting for that coming, and the earnest and loving direction of our hearts and hopes to it as the great goal of our faith. Thus we read, " Unto *them that look for him* shall he appear the second time without sin unto salvation." (Heb. 9 : 28.) " The grace of God that bringeth salvation hath appeared, teaching us that denying ungodliness and fleshly lusts, we should live soberly, righteously, and godly in this present world, *looking for that blessed hope, even the glorious appearing of the great God and our Saviour Jesus Christ.*" (Tit. 2 : 11–13.)   " There is laid up for me a crown of righteousness, which the Lord the righteous Judge shall give me at that day; and not to me only, but unto *all them also that love His appearing.*" (2 Tim. 4 : 8.)   " Ye turned to God from idols to serve the living and true God, *and to wait for his Son from heaven.*" (1 Thess. 1 : 9, 10.) It appears from this, and such like passages, that the attitude of looking, waiting, watching, and constant stretching forth of the heart, for the coming again of the Lord Jesus in his great Apocalypse, is the proper Christian habit, and that we put our prospects in peril where this habit is not cherished and kept as the very spirit and life of our faith.   And the putting of ourselves in this attitude, and the cultivation of this habit, is what I take to be the particular washing and keeping of our garments to which the Scriptures so frequently refer.   It is the general washing in the blood of Christ carried out into the habit of the soul toward his promised return.

An example of this particular washing and whitening of the Christian's robes is given us in the case of the great multitude which comes out of the great Tribulation. (Rev. 7 : 9–14.)   What was the particular defect and trouble which brought them into that tribulation ?   Why were

they not in the company of those who were kept
from that "hour of trial" and already crowned in
heaven before the great tribulation set in? The
Saviour himself, in Matthew 24 : 42–51, and elsewhere, gives the explanation. They would not
believe that Christ could come in their lifetime.
They did not watch and keep themselves in readiness for his return. They said, "My Lord de-
layeth his coming;" and began to smite their
fellow-servants, to run with the common world
around them, to eat and drink with the drunken,
and did not keep themselves girded as servants
that wait for their Lord. Hence they were not
ready when their Lord came, and for that reason
were cut off from the exalted favors of the waiting
and ready ones, and compelled to feel the weight
of the afflictions which then fall in judgment upon
the godless world. And this was the having of
soiled garments, unwashed robes, which had to be
made white to fit them for place in the society of
heaven. A great multitude of them get to heaven
afterwards, because they wash their robes and
make them clean in the blood of the Lamb. And
that washing, as we learn from the Parable of the
Ten Virgins, is the bringing of themselves to a
true advent faith and habit.

So again, in Rev. 16 : 15, this same keeping of
garments is specifically connected with a state or
habit of watching and being in readiness for the
impending advent of the Lord Jesus Christ. "Behold, I come as a thief; blessed is he that watcheth and *keepeth his garments.*"

It is therefore clear to me that this washing of robes and keeping of garments relates to the attitude and habit of looking for the coming of Christ, and keeping in constant expectation and readiness for it as an impending event. And the blessedness of access to and power over the Tree of Life, and of entrance by the gates of pearl into the Golden City, is here made to depend on this very washing of our robes and keeping of our garments. What a lesson for those who despise the advent teachings and make light of the doctrine of the certain and speedy coming of the Lord! Brethren, as you hope to walk those golden streets, and eat of those immortal fruits, see to it that you have your garments clean and " your loins girded about like unto men waiting for their Lord."

Watch ! 'tis your Lord's command ;
  And while we speak, He's near.
Mark the first signal of His Hand,
  And ready all appear.

O happy servant he,
  In such a pasture found !
He shall his Lord with rapture see,
  And be with honor crowned.

LECTURE FIFTY-SECOND.

END OF THE BOOK—CHARACTER AND MAJESTY OF CHRIST—
TIME FOR FULFILLING THESE WONDERS—HOW WE ARE TO
BE AFFECTED TOWARDS THEM—GUARDS ABOUT WHAT IS
WRITTEN—CHRIST'S OWN SUMMATION OF THE CONTENTS
OF THE BOOK—THE ATTITUDE OF THE CHURCH—CONCLU-
SION.

Rev. 22 : 16–21. (Revised Text.) I Jesus sent my angel to testify
to you these things upon [or, *over*] the churches. I am the Root and
the race [or, *Offspring*] of David, the bright, the morning star.

And the Spirit and the Bride say, Come. And let him who heareth
say, Come. And let him who is athirst come. He who willeth let him
take water of life freely [or, *as a gift*].

I testify to every one who heareth the words of the prophecy of this
book, If any one add [or, *shall have added*] to [or, *upon*] them, God
shall add to [or, *upon*] him the plagues which are written in this book;
and if any one shall take away from the words of the book of this prophecy, God shall take away his part from the tree of life and the holy
City which are written in this book.

He who testifieth these things saith, Yea, I come quickly.

Amen, Come, Lord Jesus.

The grace of the Lord Jesus [be] with all the saints.

EVERY attentive reader will observe how much
the conclusion of this Book is like its beginning. Its derivation from God, the signifying of
it by the angel, the seeing, hearing, and writing
of it by John, the blessing upon those who give
due attention to it, the nearness of the time for
the fulfilment of what is described, the solemn

(470)

authentication from Christ, the titles by which he
describes himself, and even the personal expressions of John, recur in the Epilogue, almost the
same as in the Prologue. Much, therefore, which
would here be in place has already been anticipated in the opening Lectures in this course. And
after what was said a week ago, there remain but
a few points more upon which to remark in bringing this exposition to a close.

I. The first of these points relates to the character and majesty of Christ.

Before he was born, the angel said to Joseph,
" Call his name JESUS, for he shall save his people
from their sins." (Matt. 1 : 21.) This name was
given him; and this name he still owns in heaven.
He says: " *I, Jesus*, sent my angel to testify to you
these things." It is as our Saviour that he has
given these revelations, and it is as our Saviour
that he will fulfil them. It is part of his salvation work—the great superstructure of which his
first coming was the foundation—the bloom and
fruitage of what was then planted. As Jesus,
Saviour, he was spoken of by the ancient prophets; as Jesus, *Saviour*, he was born into our
world; as Jesus, *Saviour*, he died, rose again, and
ascended into heaven; as Jesus, *Saviour*, he sent
the Holy Ghost, and ever liveth to intercede for
us; and as Jesus, *Saviour*, he sent his angel to
signify these things, and will come again to fulfil
them.

But, in claiming that *he* sent this angel, he at
the same time claims to be the sovereign of all

sacred wisdom and truth.   In verse 6 it was said
that "the Lord, the God of the spirits of the
prophets," sent this angel; and here he says, " I,
JESUS," sent him—sent him as " *my angel.*"   He
thus identifies himself with the eternal source of
all inspiration—with the very Lord God Almighty.
He is not only a *Saviour*, but " a great one."   What
he thus does, and proposes to do, and tells the
churches that he will do, he does, not as a mere
man, not as a mere prophet and high priest, but
as the possessor of all prerogatives and powers of
Godhead—as the Lord God of angels, and the
Lord God of the spirits of all prophets.   There
is no place for the Arian heresy in this Book.
Whilst he is ever JESUS, born of the Virgin Mary,
and the Lamb that was slain, he is nevertheless
the ever-living JEHOVAH, true God as well as true
man, whom all the principalities of heaven worship even as the Lamb, to whom "the blessing,
and the honor, and the glory, and the dominion,
for the ages of the ages," is to be ascribed.

Nor are these the only titles under which he
here presents himself.   He who says " Behold, I
come quickly, and my reward with me to give to
each as his work is," further adds, " *I, the Alpha
and the Omega, First and Last, the Beginning and the
End.*"   Three times does he take to himself this
designation. (Chap. 1 : 8 ; 21 : 6 ; 22 : 13.)   Of these
three expressions, the first is symbolic, signifying
the same relation to the universe which the first
and last letters of the alphabet bear to the whole
series of letters ; the second is the same in signifi-

cation, and is the Old Testament designation of God, even that by which he encourages confidence in the promises and predictions given through the prophets (Is. 41:4; 44:6; 48:12); and the third emphasizes the same thought only in a more philosophic style. The three together are among the most profound and intense denotations of the eternity, the immutability, the almightiness, the omniscience, and the faithfulness of Deity. In thus appropriating them to himself, the Lord Jesus claims to be the eternal One, from whom all being proceeds, and to whom all being tends and returns,—the source and the end of all history,—he who called the world into existence, presides over all its changes, and brings it to its consummation according to his own will. He thus sets himself before our faith as he who originated all things, who knows equally all that has happened and that will happen, and who is the ever-living and unchanging Administrator of all that is or can be, so that what he makes known as yet to take place may be accepted and relied on with perfect confidence, as rooted and grounded in the eternal Wisdom and Almightiness. He must therefore be very God of very God, the co-equal and co-eternal Son of the Father. And in this character he makes and engages to perform whatever is predicted in the prophecies of this Book.

And still further does he describe himself in relation to these revelations. Sending his angel to testify these things for the churches, he declares, "*I am the Root and the offspring of David, the bright,*

the morning Star." The duality of his nature, as at
once both God and man, is here affirmed. As
God, he is the Root or origination of David,—he
who gave David being and place, and out of whom
David was raised up, even David's Lord; and as
man, he is the offspring of David, David's son, one
born of the house and lineage of David. (Matt. 22:
43.) He is the Kernel in the Kernel of the ancient
Theocracy, at once the source and blossom of it,—
the Jehovah which induced it, at length revealed
as its product, — the object of Old Testament
adoration incarnated as the great promised One
of the seed of Abraham, of the house of David.
Hence the additional statement, that he is "*the
bright and morning Star.*" The covetous prophet,
Balaam, impelled by the Spirit contrary to his
wishes, prophesied of a star to come out of Jacob,
and a sceptre to rise out of Israel, with which
should be the dominion. (Numb. 24: 17–19.)
That star, now come to its full brightness, and
ushering in the morning of the eternal blessedness, Christ here claims to be. And as the God-
man, risen out of Jacob, and possessed of all
authority and dominion, he gives forth these revelations, and pledges to fulfil them. He thus teaches
us what a sublime Lord and Saviour we have, and
what is the foundation on which we may count
that he will fulfil all the wonders of this Apocalypse.

II. A second of these remaining points relates
to the time when these things shall come to pass.

One cannot but be impressed with the constantly repeated expressions touching the nearness of these occurrences. In the very opening verses the note was sounded, " *The time is near.*" The same is heard throughout all that followed. And here, in the conclusion of all, the same is reiterated, over and over, that these things "*must come to pass shortly.*" Three times the Saviour says, " *Behold, I come quickly.*" And the voice which commanded the seer not to seal up what he heard and saw, also adds, " *The time is near.*" Nor is it here alone, but throughout the New Testament in general, that such expressions are used. Everywhere is the promised Apocalypse of the Lord Jesus represented as close at hand, liable to occur at any time. The impression thus made upon the early Christians was, that Christ might come at any day or hour, even in their own lifetime. Exactly when he would come, was nowhere told them. According to the Saviour's word, it was not for them to know the times or the seasons, which the Father hath put in his own power. (Acts 1 : 6, 7.) Nay, from that time to the present, and for all time till the promise itself comes to be fulfilled, the saying of Christ has held, and must hold, " Of that day and hour knoweth no man, no, not the angels of heaven, but my Father only." (Matt. 24 : 36.) It was useless, therefore, for them, and will continue to be useless for any one, to attempt to ascertain or determine, how long it will be till Christ shall come again, or how soon all these things shall be accomplished. When once they begin to come to pass, men will be able to tell where they are, and to know that the time has arrived; but, till then, they must needs remain in ignorance. All the instruction which we have upon the subject is, that what is foreshown will certainly come to pass; and that, from the beginning until the fulfilment commences, we are to be in constant expectation of it any year, any day, any hour; to which the ever-present and ever-intensifying signs, together with the multiplied precepts of the holy Scriptures, continually admonish us. Well has Archer Butler said, " To seek to penetrate more closely into these awful secrets is vain. A sacred obscurity envelops them. The cloud that shrouded the actual presence of God on the mercy-seat, shrouds still his expected presence on the throne of judgment. It is a purposed obscurity, and most salutary and useful obscurity, a wise and merciful denial of knowledge. In this matter it is his gracious will to be the perpetual subject of watchfulness, expectation, conjecture, fear, desire,—but no more. To cherish anticipation, he has permitted gleams of light to cross the darkness; to baffle presumption, he has made them *only* gleams. He has harmonized with consummate skill, every part of his revelation to produce this general result;— now speaking as if a few seasons more were to herald the new heaven and the new earth, now as if his days were thousands of years; at one moment whispering into the ear of his disciple, as if ready to be revealed, at another retreating into the depth of infinite ages. It is his purpose thus to live in our faith and hope, remote yet near, pledged to no moment, possible at any; worshipped not with the consternation of a near, or the indifference of a distant certainty, but with the anxious vigilance that awaits a contingency ever at hand. This, the deep devotion of watchfulness, humility, and awe, he who knows us best knows to be the fittest posture for our spirits; therefore does he preserve the salutary suspense that insures it, and therefore will he determine his advent to no definite day in the calendar of eternity."

But the much-emphasized fact, put forth with all these promises and predictions of his return, that the interval between us and their accomplishment dare never be extended in our estimate, and is always represented as brief,—so brief that we never know but that another year, or month, or week, or day may reveal to us our coming Lord,— ought not to be without the most quickening effect upon our hearts and devotions. Certainly, what we are so solemnly told is "near," and "must shortly come to pass," we are at no liberty to postpone, or to think yet far away. And especially now, that eighteen hundred years of that "shortly" have passed, and that every symptom of the close proximity of the end is so manifest, should we beware of thinking that years and ages are yet to intervene before our Lord's coming can occur. Ever, as the Church moves on through time, and above all in the days in which we live, the next thing for every Christian to be looking for in this world is the coming of Christ to fulfil what is written in this Book. The Bible tells of nothing between us and that Day.

III. A third of these remaining points relates to the proper spiritual affection toward the speedy accomplishment of these holy predictions.

The Apocalypse of Christ is the coming or revelation of Christ in the scenes and achievements which are here described. But it is not made known to us as a thing of cold and barren speculation. It is the living outcome of all our faith and hope as Christians. It is a thing to which every proper Christian impulse necessarily goes out. There can be no genuine Christianity, no true and living sympathy with what we profess to believe, if there be no going forth of the soul to what is thus set before us. This is here expressed with a depth and intensity which should not fail to impress every serious heart.

First of all, the Holy Ghost himself calls for the Apocalypse of Christ. "The Spirit says, *Come;*" that is, *Come thou;* as an answer made to the announcement of the preceding verse. So the Syriac version, and all sound interpreters. When the promise of the Paraclete, the Spirit of truth, was given, Christ said: "He will guide you into all truth: and *he will show you things to come.*" (John 16:13.) Descending upon the Church always to abide with it, that Spirit has ever been active and operative in and through the Church. And in all these gracious operations there is a direct and constant reference to these things to come, to make

them known, to awaken and nurture faith in them,
and to prepare men to become partakers in their
blessedness. In all these operations there is therefore a constant looking and yearning for the fulfilment of what is thus to come, and hence an
unceasing calling of the Holy Ghost to the bright
and morning star to come, as promised and foreshown,—to consummate the great work by that
Apocalypse to which all prophecy, all faith, all
hope, and all the operative graces of the Spirit
have reference. In other words, it is the very
spirit, soul, and aim of divine grace to bring the
great consummation, which comes alone through
the coming of Christ. In the inspiration of prophets and apostles, in the regeneration and sanctification of men, and in all the appointments, en-
dowments, and labors of the Church, in so far as
the Holy Ghost is potent and active in them, there
is one unceasing call and pleading for that return
of the Godman, by whose coming again all things
are to be completed and the whole work finished
up. Two things, therefore, are thus certified to
us; first, that there is no true and saving religion
—no piety originating from and resting in the
Spirit of God—which does not anxiously move
toward and centre on Christ and his promised
Apocalypse; and second, that the fulfilment of
these predictions is absolutely certain, in that
the operations of the Holy Ghost in the Church
are all conditioned to and ever calling for the
bright and morning star to come.

And what the Spirit looks to and calls for is repeated in the spiritual consciousness of the Bride. The Bride is not the Church outwardly taken; for not all who have connection with the Church as a visible body shall be everlastingly joined with the Lamb. None are the Bride but those who in living inward fact are joined to Christ as the branches are joined to the vine. Only those who are spiritually in Christ, "members of his body, of his flesh, and of his bones" (Eph. 5 : 30), are his Bride. And it is here given as a characteristic of the Bride, that she re-echoes and embodies the call of the Spirit, even the call for the bright and morning star to come. When men forget to think of the coming again of the Lord Jesus in his great Apocalypse,—when they cease to look and long for that as the crown and goal of their faith and hope,— when they make light of it, and treat it as a fable, and regard all concern about it as fanaticism,— they show and prove that they do not belong to that elect body of God's saints which constitutes the Bride of the Lamb; for the deepest heart-voice of the Bride, with that of the Spirit itself, is, "Come, Lord Jesus; come as thou hast promised and fore-shown; come quickly." Taking all the precepts and inculcations of the sacred Scriptures with regard to Christ's return, it becomes a plain and evident impossibility for people to be true and obedient followers of the Gospel, and not to look, and watch, and long, and pray, and make it a great point in all their religious activity and devotion to be ready for the glorious coming of the great God and our Saviour Jesus Christ. The Apostles and

early Christians were all alive to this subject beyond everything else in Christianity. It was their
life, their inspiration, the pole-star of their faith
and hope. It was the thing which most marked
them, set them apart from the world, and was
their great distinguishing spirit, as compared with
other people. And if it is not so with Christians
now, it is because they have sunk away from the
original life of their religion, and lost their proper
fellowship with the true and only Bride of the
Lamb; for the voice of the Bride to her Lord continually is, " *Come.*" Nor can she be in the spirit
and life of a true Bride without having this feeling
ever living in her soul, and permeating her whole
being. Destined for Christ, and having her chief
joy and salvation in him and what he is ordained to
accomplish for his people, she cannot but go out
with all zeal and fervency for his revelation, or she
ceases in soul from her character as his Bride.

And what the Spirit and the Bride say, every
one that heareth is to say, and must learn to say,
if ever he is to become partaker in these glorious
things. The hearer is he who is made acquainted
with these great purposes of God, and is informed
of what is in reserve for God's true people. But
his hearing will profit him nothing if it does not
awaken his soul, kindle his desires, and draw him
to devout longing and endeavor to possess and
realize these things for himself. Nor is he rightly
awake and appreciative to what he hears, so long
as he does not care whether Christ is to come
again or not, or does not centre his soul upon what

can only come with Christ's glorious Apocalypse. Therefore the word here is, " *Let him who heareth say, Come.*" Redemption lies in that coming; and if men do not learn to desire it, they do not yet desire the redemption that is in Christ Jesus, and are not yet true and believing hearers. For all effectual hearing of the Gospel must come to fervent and loving desire and prayer for Christ to fulfil all his plan and purposes of grace.

And from this emphatic and all-pervading looking and yearning of everything Christian for the Apocalypse of Christ, the call for it widens and deepens into an invitation and incentive to all who desire eternal blessedness, and to all who have any mind or appetite for the waters of life. " *And let him who is athirst come. He who willeth let him take the water of life freely.*" The meaning is, that the waters of life, as they flow in the New Jerusalem, which comes not till Christ comes, are to be had without money and without price; but that those who thirst for those waters are to join with the company and call of those who thus yearn for the blessed consummation. If any one is athirst for these waters, or has a mind and appetite for them, the word is, " *Let him come.*" Come *whither*, come *to what?* Come into fellowship with the Spirit, the Bride, and every believing hearer of their testimony, in yearning, and looking, and praying for the coming of the Lord to fulfil what he has promised, and this Book describes. Everything in grace is moving and looking to that; and if any are athirst for God's living waters, or if any have a

will to partake of them, this is the way to get
them. No price is set upon them. They are free
as the air to every one who would have them.
But the free partaking of them is by faith in
Christ, by seizing hold upon his promises to his
Church, and by joining the cry of the Spirit, the
yearning of the Bride, and the soul of all right
hope, in "looking for and hasting unto the coming of the day of God," even the glorious Apocalypse of the blessed Christ.

IV. Accordingly there is presented still another
point with reference to the preservation of what is
set forth in this Book. It is the Book of the out-
comes of all the operations of God in our world.
It is the great Redeemer's own foreshowing to his
people how and wherein all their faith in him and
all their expectations as true believers are to reach
their final goal. There is therefore no more
important sacred Book, none more necessary to
regulate the beliefs and anticipations of Christian
people with regard to the future. To tamper with
it, is to tamper with the divinely given chart of
the most momentous things in the destiny of
Christ and his Church and people. And hence,
with a solemnity that we nowhere else encounter, and with a stringency the most intense in all
the word of God, the Saviour himself, from his
throne in heaven, says : " *I testify to every one who
heareth the words of the prophecy of this Book, If any
one add* [or *shall have added*] *to or upon them, God
shall add to or upon him the plagues which are written*

in this Book; and if any one shall take away from the words of the Book of this prophecy, God shall take away his part from the tree of life and the holy City which are written in this Book."

As if this Book were itself the Tree of Life which it describes, here are the Cherubim with flaming sword turning every way to guard and protect it. To Israel, in the days of Moses, God said, "Ye shall not add unto the word that I command you, neither shall ye diminish from it." (Deut. 4 : 2.) At a later period the wise man said, "Every word of God is pure. Add thou not unto his words lest he reprove thee, and thou be found a liar." (Prov. 30 : 5, 6.) But here the warning and prohibitions are far more intense, and the penalties terrible in the extreme. To mutilate this Book, to take from or to add to what it describes as the course and outcome of the divine purposes, is simply to forfeit salvation itself. Could this be if we did not here have the very kernel and consummation of all that prophets have written, and in which grace and salvation have their chief significance and crown? Would God affix the profoundest sanctions of eternity to a dim outline of a little mixed history of this world, which three-fourths of its readers never knew or could understand, and which might never have been revealed at all without any appreciable damage to the piety or to the hopes of God's people in any age? The very absurdity of the thought is demonstration that this Book is something infinitely higher, more solemn, and more essential than the

vast mass of modern exposition makes it. No
man can be lost or saved simply on account of his
receiving or rejecting what the historical interpreters set forth as the chief meaning of the
Apocalypse. On their theory, the whole Book
might be sunk in eternal oblivion, and still no serious damage result to the faith of the Church, or
men's calculations for the future. But in the
estimate of God, he who adds to or takes from
what it presents, disables all right conception of
the system of redemption, and inflicts an injury so
great that he who does it need never hope for salvation. How important, therefore, how precious
in the eye of heaven, how necessary to the right
instruction of God's people, how vital to the proper
Christian faith and hope are the unmutilated and
unchanged foreshowings which this Book was
given to set forth!

The penalty upon every corrupter of these records also helps to fix and establish the right interpretation of them. "Plagues" constitute one of
the prominent subjects; and those "plagues" are
to be laid upon each hearer who involves himself
in the guilt of adding to or diminishing the contents of this Book. They must therefore be literal
"plagues," such as can be laid upon separate individuals, and not mere symbols of disturbances of
nations, shakings of empires, calamities to systems,
and revolutions in governments. Such "plagues"
are incapable of being imposed upon individual
men, and individual men are contemplated in this
anathema. Except, therefore, where otherwise

indicated, "the plagues which are written in this Book" are contemplated by Christ himself as literal "plagues;" and we have simply followed his mind in so explaining them. Just what particular plagues are covered by the threat, we may not be able to determine; but what the wicked suffer, the same is to be the portion of him who dares to abridge or augment the contents of these records. And when we consider how unbelief despises this Book and its philosophy of things,—how a self-wise and rationalistic latitudinarianism neglects it, ridicules all serious attention to it, and empties it of all respectable meaning and worth,—how a presumptuous criticism disables it with wild and stilted theories of poetry and symbolization,—and how even Christian men fight against the admission of its clear teachings when allowed to speak for themselves,—what are we to conclude, but that in these very things we have the sowing for the whole harvest of plagues written in this Book?

O, my friends, it is a fearful thing to suppress or stultify the word of God, and above all "the words of the prophecy of this Book." To put forth for truth what is not the truth,—to denounce as error, condemn, repudiate, or emasculate what God himself hath set his seal to as his mind and purpose, is one of those high crimes, not only against God, but against the souls of men, which cannot go unpunished. With an honest and ever-prayerful heart, and with these solemn and awful warnings ever before my eyes, I have endeavored to ascertain and indicate in these Lectures what

our gracious Lord and Master has been so particular to make known and defend. If I have read
into this Book anything which he has not put
there, or read out of it anything which he has put
there, with the profoundest sorrow would I recant,
and willingly burn up the books in which such
mischievous wickedness is contained. If I have
in anything gone beyond the limits of due subjec-
tion to what is written, or curtailed in any way
the depth and measure of what Jesus by his angel
has signified for the learning of the Churches, I
need not the condemnation of men to heap upon
me the burden of censure which I deserve. If
feebleness, or rashness, or overweening confidence
in my own understanding has distorted anything,
I can only deplore the fault, and pray God to send
a man more competent to unfold to us the mighty
truths which here stand written. According to
the grace and light given me, have I spoken. And
before God, angels, and men, I am compelled to
protest, especially, against all that modern interpretation which dwarfs this Book into an over-
wrought and indeterminate showing of a few
meagre chapters of the Church's history this side
the day of judgment. If I err, God forgive me!
If I am right, God bless my feeble testimony! In
either case, God speed his everlasting truth!

V. Yet one other point remains to be noticed.
It is Christ's own final summation of the contents
of this Book. From the beginning we were told
that it was given to show the Apocalypse of Jesus
Christ. The whole series of visions fit together

as so many successive acts and administrations in the closing up of this present world, and the introduction of the eternal order, according to God's eternal purpose. And so here, in the last words of the Book, the Saviour himself sums up the all-comprehending substance of the whole in this one brief sentence: *"He who testifieth these things saith*, YEA, I COME QUICKLY."

Who that has ever looked carefully into the subject, but has been struck with the towering prominence which the Scriptures everywhere assign to the coming again of the Lord Jesus? The New Testament has more references to this particular topic than it has pages. Of all the seven or eight thousand verses of which it is composed, one out of every twenty-five points forward with eager gesture to the appearing again of the Lord Jesus. Again and again it is set forth as the great hope of the Church. There is not a Christian grace or virtue for the enforcement of which appeal is not made to it. Nor is there another subject upon which more stress is laid in all the Word of God. To many, indeed, it is anything but welcome. There be even professing Christians who would rather not hear about it, and who, if they could have their way, would erase it from the Creed, and silence all preaching concerning it. But the religion of such is much aside from the Scriptures, and occasion is urgent for them to bestir themselves to re-examine and relay their foundations. *Christian faith and hope have no outcome but in the glorious Apocalypse of Jesus.* And only when we come to understand that the coming again of Christ is the fulfilment of the things described in this Book, can we appreciate why so much is referred to that coming, and why the venerable Apostle should here, at the end of his Book, bow his hoary head, and say, and write, his solemn "*Amen. Even so come, Lord Jesus.*"

The truth is, my friends, that there is no greater or gladder promise in all the Book of God, than this last word of Jesus to his people, "*Yea, I come quickly.*" It is the promise of promises—the crown and consummation of all promise—the coronation of all evangelic hopes—the sum of all prophecy and prayer. Nature and grace alike proclaim a glorified Messiah, come again from heaven in his almightiness, as indispensable to complete their appointed course. Nature calls for him thus to come, to rectify her unwilling disorders, to repair her shattered structures, to restore her oppressed energies, to vindicate her voice of conscience long despised, her sublime testimony to the Creator so long questioned and overlooked. But grace sends forth a still mightier call. If the whole creation groans and travails together in pain for the manifestation of the sons of God, how much more those sons of God themselves!

And why should not this be our spirit? Compare the sordidness of this world with the crystal purity and splendor of the New Jerusalem. Think of the dust, and dearth, and soil and toil of earth, in comparison with that River and Tree of Life which refresh, and adorn, and satisfy the dwellers in those eternal mansions. Consider the ill mixtures, defects, wearinesses, vexations, darkness, and disabilities of life here, alongside of the perfections and sublimities which mark the society and estate of those who walk those streets of gold. Why should we wish to suffer, and toil, and sigh amid the miseries of a scene like this, when such a city of unchanging blessedness throws open its gates of pearl for our admission? Are we so in love with aches, and ills, and wrongs, and disappointments, and treacheries, and diseases, and death-beds, and graves, and torments and temptations of Satan, as not to be willing to be done with them forever? With what ardor, then, and delight, and enthusiastic joy, should we embrace this word of our Saviour, *"Yea, I come quickly!"* Have we no mind for the realization of that precious "liberty of the children of God,"—no wish to behold our lowliness glorified in the glory of the Man of Nazareth,—no longing to have our humble labors recognized and approved by our enthroned Redeemer,—no appreciation of the vindication of our persevering faith, of the consummation of our hopes and prayers, of the brightening of our love and charity into rewards eternal and infinite? Ah, yes; everything in and about us, in the weakness of man and in the working of God, yearns and calls and prophesies for the coming again of Jesus,—everything but the cold, unfeeling, unsanctified heart of man! But there, alas, no voice is heard going forth to bid the Lord of salvation welcome! People's hearts are inured

to the world's corruptions, and how can they hail
an immortality of meekness, simplicity, and love?
Men's spirits are habituated to seek unholy ends
by means still more unholy, and how can they endure the bringing in of everlasting righteousness?
Their calculations, hopes, and aims are bounded
to things of time and sense, and how can they regard otherwise than with terror so complete a
change as that when he who now rules behind a
mass of permitted evils visibly assumes the reins
of universal dominion? Of course all such are ill
at ease with our doctrines, and well may tremble,
and call to rocks and mountains to cover and hide
them from the discomfiture and sorrow which
Christ's Apocalypse must bring to souls so earthy.
But let all God's saints hold fast the blessed hope,
and lift up their heads as they see the time approaching. What is there to command our fondest joy, our gladdest anticipation, if not this coming day of our completed happiness and finished
redemption?

Fiction has painted the picture of a maiden
whose lover left her for a voyage to the Holy
Land, promising on his return to make her his
beloved bride. Many told her that she would
never see him again. But she believed his word,
and evening by evening she went down to the
lonely shore, and kindled there a beacon-light in
sight of the roaring waves, to hail and welcome
the returning ship which was to bring again her
betrothed. And by that watchfire she took her
stand each night, praying to the winds to hasten
on the sluggish sails, that he who was everything

to her might come. Even so that blessed Lord, who has loved us unto death, has gone away to the mysterious Holy Land of heaven, promising on his return to make us his happy and eternal Bride. Some say that he has gone forever, and that here we shall never see him more. But his last word was, " *Yea, I come quickly.*" And on the dark and misty beach sloping out into the eternal sea, each true believer stands by the love-lit fire, looking, and waiting, and praying and hoping for the fulfilment of his word, in nothing gladder than in his pledge and promise, and calling ever from the soul of sacred love, "EVEN SO COME, LORD JESUS." And some of these nights, while the world is busy with its gay frivolities, and laughing at the maiden on the shore, a form shall rise over the surging waves, as once on Galilee, to vindicate forever all this watching and devotion, and bring to the faithful and constant heart a joy, and glory, and triumph which never more shall end.

To bring listless and uninstructed souls believingly and intelligently to the position and attitude of that maiden, is the intent of this Book, and of these Lectures upon it. And if by these long studies any hearers are brought to such love-waiting and watching on these dark shores of time, with thanks and praises to Him from whom has come the grace, and with heart and soul set in confident expectation of the speedy fulfilment of the wonders we have been contemplating, I am content to take my leave of these labors.

" *The grace of the Lord Jesus be with all the saints.*"
AMEN.

INDEX.

The lettering, i, ii, iii, *denotes the volumes ; the figures refer to the* pages, *and the letter* n *to the footnotes.*

A.

Abaddon, king of the locusts, ii, 82; as a place, iii, 277, 278.

Abyss, the, opened by Satan, ii, 80–94 ; place of, ii, 93, n ; differs from " lake of fire," iii, 270

Adam of St. Victor, quoted, i, 255, n

Advent, Second, of Christ, i, 53–60, 167–169 ; brings honors to the redeemed, i, 169, 170 ; near at hand, i, 230–232 ; iii, 475–477; gradual, ii, 155 ; extending through a variety of scenes, iii, 161 ; how we are to await the, iii, 478–482; attitude of the church toward, iii, 489–492 ; signs accompanying, i, 57 ; delay of, ii, 143–146 ; certainty of, ii, 146–148 ; invisible stage of, iii, Pref. iv ; visible, i, 56, 57 ; iii, 239–247

Air, convulsions in, during the seventh plague, iii, 96

Alford, quoted ; on Elijah, ii, 189, n ; on the locusts, ii, 88 ; on first Resurrection, iii, 310, 316

Alleluia, iii, 198, 201, 203

Amen, iii, 201

Andreas, quoted, i, 176, n

Angel, the one sent to John, i, 26 ; the mighty, of the sixth trumpet, ii, 124–127 ; act of, ii, 128, 129 ; book in hand of, ii, 133–140 ; proclamation of, ii, 141–144; the Euphratean, ii, 113, 114

Angels, the seven, of God's presence, ii, 19–21 ; prepare to sound the trumpets, ii, 39–42 ; the first

sounds, ii, 42–49 ; the second, ii, 49–53 ; the third, ii, 54–58 ; the fourth, ii, 58–64 ; the fifth, ii, 75–95 ; the sixth, ii, 96–122 ; the seventh, with the golden bowls of wrath, iii, 67–80 , 84–100

Angels, orders of, ii, 19–21 ; ministrations of, ii, 41, 42 ; evil, ii, 77 ; iii, 279 ; direct executors of the woes at sounding of sixth trumpet, ii, 111–114

Angels, of the churches, i, 108–111

Angel-messages of Rev. 14 : 1–13, iii, 28 ; the first, iii, 29, 30 ; the second, iii, 31 ; the third, iii, 32, the fourth, iii, 33, 34

Antichrist, the, ii. 388–390 ; the beast from the sea, ii, 390 ; the embodiment of political sovereignty, ii, 391, 392 ; one particular man, ii, 393, 396, n., 397, n. ; reigns 42 months, ii, 394 ; iii, 76, 161 ; the "man of sin," ii, 395 ; the same as the wilful king of Daniel, ii, 395 ; a supernatural personage, ii, 397 ; his attractiveness and greatness, ii, 401–404; the antagonist of everything divine, ii, 405, 406 ; the consummate persecutor, ii, 407 ; the great blasphemer, ii, 407 ; the importance of the doctrine concerning, ii, 408–412 ; not alone, ii, 413, 414 ; assisted by the second beast, ii, 415, 428, 431 ; image of, set up, ii, 450 ; caused to speak, ii, 452–454 ; worshipped, 450–454; all branded with the mark of, ii, 456, 457 ; number of, ii, 459, 460 ; plagues

(493)

Noel E. Mills